CW00706325

Hobson Library

428065

FIGHTING WORLD WAR THREE FROM THE MIDDLE EAST

Works by the same author

Truman and Israel (1990)

Palestine to Israel: From Mandate to Independence (1988)

The Origins and Evolution of the Arab–Zionist Conflict (1987)

Churchill and the Jews (1985)

Palestine and the Great Powers, 1945–1948 (1982)

Palestine: Retreat from the Mandate, 1936–1945 (1978)

As editor

The Demise of Empire: Britain's Responses to National Movements in the Middle East, 1943-1955 (in press) (with Martin Kolinsky)

Britain and the Middle East in the 1930s (1992) (with Martin Kolinsky)

Bar-Ilan Studies in Modern History, III (1991)

As editor of documentary series

The History of the Foundation of Israel. Part 3: *The Struggle for the State of Israel, 1939–1948* 12 vols (1987)

The Letters and Papers of Chaim Weizmann, 2 vols: 1940–1943; 1943–1945 (1979)

FIGHTING
WORLD WAR THREE
FROM THE MIDDLE EAST

Allied Contingency Plans,
1945–1954

MICHAEL J. COHEN

FRANK CASS
LONDON • PORTLAND, OR.

First published in 1997 in Great Britain by
FRANK CASS & CO. LTD.
Newbury House, 900 Eastern Avenue,
London IG2 7HH

and in the United States of America by
FRANK CASS
c/o ISBS, 5804 N.E. Hassalo Street,
Portland, Oregon 97213-3644

British Library Cataloguing in Publication data

Cohen, Michael J. (Michael Joseph), 1940–
    Fighting World War Three from the Middle East : allied
    contingency plans, 1945–1954
    1. Military planning – Middle East   2. Middle East – Strategic
    aspects   3. Great Britain – History, Military – 20th century
    I. Title
    355.4'756

    ISBN 0-7146-4720-9 (cloth)
    ISBN 0-7146-4269-X (paper)

Library of Congress Cataloging-in-Publication data

Cohen, Michael Joseph, 1940–
    Fighting World War Three from the Middle East : Allied contingency
    plans, 1945–1954 / Michael J. Cohen.
        p.   cm.
    Includes bibliographical references and index.
    ISBN 0-7146-4720-9 (cloth). — ISBN 0-7146-4269-X (pbk.)
    1. Military planning—United States—History—20th century.
    2. Military planning—Great Britain—History—20th century.
    3. Middle East—Strategic aspects.   4. Cold War.
    U153.C65   1996
    355'.033056—dc20   96-44697
                                                            CIP

Typeset by Regent Typesetting, London
Printed in Great Britain by
Bookcraft (Bath) Ltd, Midsomer Norton, Avon

Contents

List of Maps

For Ilan and Natalie

Acknowledgements

I should like to thank the Harry S. Truman Library Institute for a grant which facilitated a research visit to that archive.

In the various archives I have visited, or had correspondence with, I have benefited greatly from the help of the following: Mr Mungo Chapman and Mr. N. B. Travers, of the Royal Air Force Museum, London; Monica Ruscil of the Seeley G. Mudd Manuscript Library, Princeton; Dennis Bilger, Raymond H. Geselbracht, Samuel Rushay, Liz Saffly, Randy Sowell, and Benedict K. Zobrist, all of the Harry S. Truman Library; Thomas W. Branigar of the Dwight D. Eisenhower Library; Yehoshua Freundlich, Israel State archives, Jerusalem; Dr Tuvia Frieling, of the Ben Gurion archives, Sde Boker; and finally to Col.(Res.) Uri Algom, of the Israeli Army archives, Tel Aviv, who was also kind enough to read and make useful comments on the chapters on Israel.

The following friends and colleagues have also given unstintingly of their advice and help; Dr James Cockburn, The University of Maryland, USA; Dr Michael Dockrill, King's College, The University of London; Dr Peter L. Hahn, Ohio State University, USA; Dr Martin Kolinsky, The University of Birmingham, England; Dr Eduard Mark, Historian of the US Air Force, Washington DC; Dr Joel J. Sokolsky, The Royal Military College of Canada, Kingston, Ontario; and Dr Jon Sumida, The University of Maryland, USA.

Special thanks are due to my friend and colleague, Professor Stuart Cohen, of Bar Ilan University, for giving the manuscript the meticulous reading that I knew he would.

And lastly, a very special word of appreciation is due to Dr Steven T. Ross, of the Naval War College, Newport, Rhode Island. Dr Ross provided me with invaluable material on American contingency plans and took the trouble to read the manuscript in draft form. His comments and suggestions were of great value.

Needless to say, none of the above is to be held responsible for any errors or judgements in what follows.

All unpublished Crown copyright material from the Public Record Office appears by permission of the Controller of HM Stationery Office.

Abbreviations

ABC	American–British–Canadian Planners
BMEO	British Middle East Office, Cairo
CIA	Central Intelligence Agency (American)
CIGS	Chief of the Imperial General Staff (British)
C. in C.	Commander in Chief
CINCEAST	Commander in Chief NATO, East Mediterranean (Aegean)
CINCELM	Commander in Chief, US Naval Forces, East Atlantic and Mediterranean (American)
CINCSOUTH	Commander in Chief NATO, Southern Europe (American)
CNO	Chief of Naval Operations (American)
COS	Chief(s) of Staff
DCC	Defence Coordination Committee (British)
DMO	Director of Military Operations (British)
IAF	Israeli Air Force
IDF	Israeli Defence Forces
JIC	Joint Intelligence Committee (American and British)
JCS	Joint Chiefs of Staff (American)
JPS	Joint Planning Staff (American and British)
JSPC	Joint Strategic Plans Committee (American)
JSSC	Joint Strategic Survey Committee (American)
JWPC	Joint War Plans Committee (American)
L. of C.	Lines of Communication
MEAF	Middle East Air Force (British)
MEC	Middle East Command
MEDO	Middle East Defence Organization.
MELF	Middle East Land Forces (British)
NATO	North Atlantic Treaty Organization
NEA	Division of Near Eastern and African Affairs (US State Department)
NSC	National Security Council (American)
P & O	Plans and Operations Branch (American)
PPS	Policy Planning Staff (US State Department)

RAF	Royal Air Force (British)
RCAF	Royal Canadian Air Force
SAC	Strategic Air Command (American)
SACEUR	Supreme Allied Commander, Europe (American)
SACLANT	Supreme Allied Commander, North Atlantic (American)
SACME	Supreme Allied Commander, Middle East
SHAPE	Supreme Headquarters, Allied Powers, Europe
SPG	Strategic Plans Group (American)
UNSCOP	United Nations Special Committee on Palestine
USAF	United States Air Force.

Glossary

Partial list of American and British Strategic Studies and short- and long-term contingency plans

AMERICAN

Pincher: March 1946. Worldwide strategic studies series.

Griddle: Aug. 1946. Pincher area study:Turkey.

Broadview: Aug. 1946. Pincher area study:Continental United States and US overseas bases.

Makefast: Sept. 1946. USAF plan for global Air Offensive.

Caldron: Nov. 1946. Pincher area study:European Alps and Himalayas.

Cockspur: Dec. 1946. Pincher area study: Italy.

Earshot: March 1947. Revision of *Makefast*.

Drumbeat: Aug. 1947. Pincher area study: Spain and Portugal.

Moonrise: Aug. 1947. Pincher area study: Far East.

Deerland: Sept. 1947. Pincher area study: North America.

Broiler: Nov. 1947. Short-term worldwide emergency plan.

Charioteer: Dec. 1947. Long-term plan for war with Soviets in 1955.

Frolic: March 1948. Revision of *Broiler*.

Grabber: March 1948. Revision of *Frolic*.

Bushwhacker: March 1948. Worldwide plan for war by Jan. 1952.

Crankshaft: May 1948. Long-term worldwide emergency plan.

Halfmoon: May 1948. Worldwide emergency, short-term plan based on *Broiler*. First plan approved by JCS (and by ABC Planners – Oct. 1948).

Fleetwood: Oct. 1948. New code-name given to *Halfmoon*.

Trojan: January 1949. Revision of *Fleetwood*, with atomic offensive annex.

Dropshot: Jan. 1949. Long-term worldwide emergency plan, for war in 1957.

Offtackle: Nov. 1949. Long-term worldwide emergency plan.

Reaper: Nov. 1950. Worldwide emergency plan for war in 1954 (revised later to *Groundwork* and then *Headstone*).

BRITISH

Intermezzo: March 1948. War game conducted by GHQ, ME, for defence of Middle East.

Sandown: July 1948. Plan for defence of the Middle East.

Doublequick: Oct. 1948. British codename for American *Halfmoon*.

Speedway: Oct. 1948. New British code-name for *Doublequick*. *Speedway* became the general basis for plans for each individual theatre.

Clatter: Dec. 1948. Plan for operations in Sinai desert in support of Egyptian army.

Barter: Jan. 1949. Plan to aid Jordan, in event of Israeli invasion of Palestine's West Bank.

Binnacle: 1949. Short-term plan for war until July 1951.

Galloper: Dec. 1949. New short-term plan for worldwide emergency, approved by ABC Planners.

Celery: June 1950. Revise of Sandown, following receipt of Galloper.

Cinderella: Nov. 1951. Revise of *Celery*.

Rodeo: Oct. 1951. Plan for military occupation of Egypt, to safeguard British lives and property.

Xenophon: April 1952. Inter-Service plan for movement of forces, for global war in 1953.

Sycamore: June 1952. Short-term plan for deployment of UK forces in global war, until Dec. 1952.

Fairfax: Dec. 1952. Revise of *Sycamore*, for global war until June, 1953.

Introduction

The longest war of the twentieth century was one that was in fact never fought – the so-called 'Cold War'. It lasted from at least as early as 1944, until 1989. Although that war is now a matter of history, it should be remembered that, for some 45 years, the world lived constantly under the shadow of a 'hot war', which very soon assumed the nightmare form of a nuclear holocaust.

After World War Two there could be no graver problem confronting Western leaders than the possibility of a Third World War, this time against the Soviet Union and her newly-annexed satellites. However unlikely or remote that prospect may have been, it was none the less an option taken in all seriousness, if only due to the possibility that war might come through miscalculation or accident. The drafting of contingency plans well in advance to meet that possibility was a mission of the highest priority – one that consumed the energies of the military staffs and planners (and statesmen) on both sides of the Atlantic and, it is to be presumed, in Moscow.

As we now know, fortunately, none of these contingency plans ever needed to be implemented. However, there can be no doubt that the heads of the administration on both sides of the Atlantic took them in all seriousness. They were only too familiar with them, and could not afford to formulate their foreign policies without taking them into account. Most of the post-war leaders, on both sides of the Atlantic, had held senior government and/or military positions during the Second World War.

This book is an attempt to shed some light on one limited theatre of operations that concerned the military planners – the Middle East. Although secondary to the European theatre, the Middle East was thought to constitute a major goal of any Soviet offensive against the West. Until the very close of the period under discussion here, this theatre remained a British responsibility. Although the Americans initially allocated a substantial force to help the British defend the Middle East, in 1949, following the formal establishment of NATO, their planners 'withdrew' this force to North-West Africa.

This book also relates the progress of the Anglo-American debate and search for a realistic, effective Middle East strategy. On the one hand, the British posited that their Base complex in Egypt should be the axis around which all planning should revolve. On the other, the Americans, less fixated on Egypt, and more sensitive than their British ally to burgeoning Egyptian nationalist sentiment, looked from the outset more to the Northern Tier. In the 1940s, their attentions focused on Turkey. But in the early 1950s, especially with the inauguration of the Eisenhower–Dulles administration, the move away from Egypt was finalised, and a full-blown Northern Tier strategy was adumbrated. Turkey, Pakistan, and Iraq were gradually induced to join American-initiated and sponsored defence pacts.

At the same time, in the early 1950s, the British, by now disabused of their early post-war dreams of retaining Great Power status, impecunious and weak, and literally at war with the Egyptians, had little option but to follow suit. It is one of the ironies of history that although the Americans initiated the Baghdad Pact, they refused to join it officially, due to their perennial fear of being tarred with Britain's 'colonialist brush'. And thus, for a further brief period, it was left to Britain to display the allied flag in the Middle East.

The diplomatic historian will rarely, if ever, discover any of these contingency plans in the foreign policy files of the various national or private archives. Most were returned to the Ministry of Defence by the departments concerned (whether Prime Minister or President, Foreign Office or State Department, and Treasury). Indeed, in 1947, when Prime Minister Attlee finally approved the Military's contingency plans for the Middle East, and fearing that they might provoke the Soviets into a pre-emptive attack if the plans were leaked, he issued stern instructions that the plans should *not* mention the Soviets by name, and should have a strictly limited distribution.

With the official opening of the documents after 30 years, most of these highly classified documents, still remaining in departments other than 'military' departments, were 'weeded' out ('withheld by department', in 'archivese') by those (usually ex-Foreign Office officials) who decide which documents the public shall be allowed to read. Thus many diplomatic historians, often working in a single-dimension milieu, have failed to appreciate the role played by vital strategic interests (as perceived at the time) in determining the highest policy.

It will be maintained in the following pages that without understanding those military and strategic considerations that were continually present in the considerations of Western statesmen it is impossible to comprehend fully the diplomatic tensions and upheavals that characterised this area's history during the decade following the end of World War Two.

And finally, I hope that this work will make it apparent to a public beyond the military and military historians, that, at any given moment in today's world, each and every nation with an army of any significant size is, and unfortunately *must* be engaged in contingency planning for a possible conflict with any number of potential enemies.

There is something intoxicating about military planning,
especially when it is imbibed with strong doses of patriotism.

> Wm Roger Louis, *The British Empire in the*
> *Middle East, 1945–1951*, p. 674.

Britannia did rule the waves three to four hundred years
before 1942 – and did so, incidentally, to the great benefit
of the United States.

> Air Marshal Sir John Slessor (Chief of the Air Staff),
> to Gen Dwight D. Eisenhower, head of SHAPE,
> 9 March, 1951.

The strategic emphasis has in fact shifted since 1936, and
our primary strategic requirement is now not so much the
defence of the Suez Canal itself, as the maintenance of a base
in Egypt capable of rapid expansion on the outbreak of war . . .

> Memorandum to the Cabinet by the Foreign Secretary,
> Ernest Bevin, 27 November 1950.

1 American global strategy

In July 1945, at the first post-war peace conference in the Berlin suburb of Potsdam, it soon became apparent that the Soviets were not going to honour the Yalta agreements to permit free elections in those states of Eastern Europe that had been occupied by the Germans and liberated by the Red Army.

The 'Cold War' had in fact begun well before World War Two had been won by the Allies. Stalin had given clear indications of his intentions back in August 1944. At that time, with his own armies approaching Warsaw, he had encouraged the pro-Western Polish Home Army to rebel against the Germans. Cynically, Stalin halted the advance of the Red Army, thereby allowing the Germans to decimate the Polish rebels.[1] This paved the way for the appointment by the Soviets of a pro-communist puppet régime. After the war, in a series of rigged 'elections' and stage-managed coups, communist regimes were installed in Eastern Europe, and an 'Iron Curtain' separated East from West.

At the same time, the Soviets exerted pressure in the Balkans and along the Northern Tier – against Greece, Turkey, and in northern Iran. Soviet support for the Tudeh Party in Iran revived painful memories of Hitler's incitement of local Nazi parties in Austria and Czechoslovakia prior to World War Two. Western leaders prided themselves on having 'learned the lessons' of Chamberlain's now-discredited pre-war appeasement policy.

The years 1946–48 witnessed a series of international crises – in Eastern Europe and across the Northern Tier, culminating with the Communist coup in Czechoslovakia in March 1948, and the Berlin crisis during the summer of that same year. They appeared to many in the American administration to portend a Soviet expansionist trend, a search for buffer zones, or spheres of influence between themselves and Western Europe. But Soviet actions might easily lead, if only by

---

[1] Cf. Michael J. Cohen, *Churchill and the Jews*, London: Frank Cass, 1985, pp.301–2, p.369, n. 149; and David Wyman, 'Why Auschwitz was Never Bombed', *Commentary*, Vol. 65/5, May 1978.

accident, to another global conflict, this time between the Western (capitalist) and the Soviet (communist) blocs.

In March 1946, the American Joint War Plans Committee (JWPC), attached to the Joint Chiefs of Staff (JCS), warned that Soviet pressure against Turkey and Iran might well ignite the spark that would start World War Three. Any Soviet success in Turkey would create pressure on vital British interests in the Middle East (oil and the Suez Canal), and might well force the UK to fight.[2]

After the war, there were two different interpretations of Soviet behaviour. One suggested that Soviet expansionism was motivated by the legitimate needs of self-defence (the erection of a Soviet-controlled barrier of satellites, to prevent another invasion from the West). The other believed the Soviets were embarked on an ideological, anti-capitalist crusade for world domination. The latter school of thought, fathered by George Kennan, was pre-eminent in American military circles.

On 9 February 1946, following a UN Security Council demand that the Soviets withdraw from Iran, Josef Stalin made a speech condemning capitalist designs of encircling the 'peoples' democracies', and stressed the incompatibility of capitalism and communism. Stalin implied that future wars between the two systems were inevitable, until communism replaced capitalism as a world system. The State Department requested an estimate of Soviet intentions from its Moscow embassy. This elicited the highly-influential, so-called 'long telegram' from George Kennan, then a second-rank official at the embassy. Kennan's paper explained the ideological determinants of Soviet expansionist foreign policy, which no American actions could assuage. Kennan endowed the Truman administration with a new policy, the doctrine of contain-ment.[3]

In November 1946, a JWPC strategic study made the following assessment of Soviet intentions:

> . . . Soviet political policy is directed toward the expansion of their totalitarian state. Under the thesis that the world is divided into two irreconcilably hostile camps – Soviet and non-Soviet – Soviet expansionist aims must be considered as unlimited and not confined to areas which are at present of immediate and obvious concern to the Soviet Union. The proximate objective of Soviet foreign

[2] James F. Schnabel, *The History of the Joint Chiefs of Staff*, Vol. 1, 1945–1947, Wilmington: Michael Glazier Inc., 1979, pp.150–51.
[3] John Lewis Gaddis, *Strategies of Containment: A Critical Appraisal of Postwar American National Security Policy*, New York/Oxford: Oxford University Press, 1982; and idem, *The United States and the Origins of the Cold War, 1941–1947*, New York: Columbia University Press, 1972.

policy appears to be the establishment of Soviet domination over the Eurasian continent and control of the strategic approaches thereto.[4]

But the true motives laying behind Soviet strategy were almost irrelevant to Western strategic planners. Soviet actions, even through miscalculation, might lead to World War Three. The mission of the Chiefs of Staff, and their planning staffs, on both sides of the Atlantic, was to recommend measures whereby their countries might best ready themselves to prevail over the Soviet Union and its satellites, in the event of a new global conflict.

A. THE DIMENSION OF THE SOVIET THREAT AND INITIAL STRATEGIC STUDIES

Notwithstanding the strategists' anxieties, the Soviets' expansionist stratagems after World War Two found the United States 'unprepared militarily, politically, and psychologically.'[5] American contingency planning for the eventuality of World War Three was inefficient, *ad hoc*, and beset by civilian-military, and inter-service rivalries. In the initial postwar years, the JCS was able to agree on war plans only for short-term or emergency contingencies, on the basis of forces that would hopefully be available some time in the future. Each of the four strategic plans approved before 1950 was later declared to be infeasible, on the basis of its logistic and force requirements.

Strategic blueprints for war were based on incomplete intelligence estimates, and on unrealistic assessments of the military potential of her new allies in the North Atlantic Treaty Organisation (NATO, established in April 1949). At times, the JCS harboured inflated expectations about the areas the United States would be able to defend. At other times, planning forecasts reflected exaggerated fears about the extent of the territories the Soviets would be able to overrun in their opening ground offensive.

Frequently, planners failed to keep up with the pace of events. The majority of staff plans and studies generated by the various sub-committees of the JCS addressed current problems that, for better or worse, had usually faded from view before the studies had reached their final draft. Had war with the Soviets actually broken out at any time between 1945 to 1950, the Americans would have been forced to

---

[4] *Strategic Study of the Area between the Alps and the Himalayas, short title: 'Caldron'*, JWPC 475/1, 2 Nov. 1946, National Archives (NA). (declassified, 8 Nov. 1976).

[5] Cf., T.H. Etzold, and J.L. Gaddis, eds, *Containment: Documents on American Policy and Strategy, 1945-1950*, New York: Columbia University Press, 1978, pp.21–23.

improvise in the field. They were unable to anticipate, or to plan ahead, and were therefore ill-prepared for a global conflict with the Soviets.

After World War Two, the United States, as leader of the 'free world', assumed prime responsibility for providing a military answer to the Soviet Union's overwhelming conventional military superiority on the ground. This superiority became the more pronounced, as domestic pressures inside the United States led to the rapid, accelerated demobilisation of American armed forces after the war. One week after the dropping of the atomic bomb on Hiroshima (6 August 1945), President Truman promised to release five-and-a-half million men and women from the armed forces within 12 to 18 months. He was better than his word. Within just eight months, nearly seven million members of the armed forces had been demobilised. By June 1946, American armed forces had been reduced from their wartime level of over ten million, to approximately three million. By June 1947, that number had been reduced to just over one and a half million.[6]

In 1946, the Soviet Union was estimated to have a total of four-and-a-half million men under arms. These were distributed among some 208 ground divisions, of which 93 were deployed facing allied forces in Europe. They were also estimated to have some 15,500 combat aircraft (including 11 bomber regiments, comprising 1696 aircraft), of which 7200 aircraft were deployed against Europe. To these, there had to be added some 100 ground divisions and 3,300 aircraft belonging to the Soviet satellites in Eastern Europe. American intelligence believed that, in the event of war, the Soviets would be able to mobilise up to ten-and-a-half million men within 30 days, and to reach a peak of fifteen million in 150 days.[7]

Opinion polls revealed that a majority of the American public believed that a major war with the Soviets was inevitable. On 17 March

[6] Schnabel, *The History of the JCS. . .*, Vol. 1, p.237; and Gregg Herken, *The Winning Weapon: The Atomic Bomb in the Cold War, 1945–1950*, Princeton: Princeton University Press, 1981, p.215.

Schnabel (p.238) gives the following table for the reduction of the American armed forces:

	30 Jun. 1945:	*30 Jun. 1946:*	*30 Jun. 1947:*
Army (less AAF)	5,984,114	1,434,175	683,837
AAF:	2,282,259	455,515	305,827
Navy:	3,377,840	951,930	477,384
Marines:	476,709	155,592	92,222
Total:	12,120,922	2,997,212	1,559,270

[7] Study *Griddle*, JWPC 467/1, 15 Aug. 1946, 381 Turkey, (15 Aug. 46) (new case), National Archives (NA); and Paper delivered by Air Force Major General Lauris Norstad to President Truman, 29 Oct. 1946, in Norstad Speeches, 1946 (2), Norstad papers, box 26, Eisenhower Library (EL).

1948, Truman called for the return of the military draft. It is not to be wondered then that American post-war military thinking was dominated by 'the realization that the United States was unprepared to counter Soviet conventional forces'. However, this situation of potential vulnerability was not accompanied by any immediate, direct threat to American interests.[8]

All contingency planning posited that the Soviets' primary goal in a war would be the conquest of Western Europe. But officials of the Truman administration, both civil and military, did not believe that the threat of a Soviet military attack in that theatre was imminent. They were convinced that the Soviet Union would need several more years to make good the damage its economy had suffered during the war, and to modernise its armed forces. The Soviet potential for war was considered to be low, and Western planners concurred that the Soviets would need considerably more time in which to assimilate their satellites, and to develop a strategic air force or an effective air defence system.[9]

The American military establishment was confident also that its strategic air offensive, partly nuclear, offered sufficient deterrence for the near future. It was hoped that, in the event of war, the Soviets' conventional superiority in Europe would not be given enough time to determine the outcome of the conflict. It was hoped that an opening strategic air offensive would cripple and destroy the operational potential of the Soviet war machine.

The first massive use of air power had been demonstrated in World War Two, culminating in August 1945, with the dropping of the atomic bombs on Hiroshima and Nagasaki. General Henry ('Hap') H. Arnold (commanding general, US Army Air Forces, February 1942–February 1946) played a central part in advocating the key strategic role of the Air Force. In 1949, he published a book (evidently completed before the Soviets exploded their first atomic device), which set the Air Force case very clearly:

> Russia has no fear of an army; she thinks hers is as good as, and bigger than, any in the world; she has no fear of a navy, since she cannot see how it can be deployed against her; but she does fear our long-range Strategic Air Force, which she cannot as yet match, or as yet understand. In the Strategic Air Force, coupled with our atomic bomb, at this writing we hold the balance of power in the world.[10]

[8] Cf. Bruce J. Evenson, *Truman, Palestine, and the Press: Shaping Conventional Wisdom at the beginning of the Cold War*, Westport, Conn: Greenwood Press, 1992, p.179; and David Alan Rosenberg, 'American Atomic Strategy and the Hydrogen Bomb Decision', *Journal of American History*, 66/1, June 1979, p.64.

[9] Norstad paper to Truman, 29 Oct. 1946, supra.

[10] Henry. H. Arnold, *Global Mission*, New York: Harper & Bros., 1949, p.615; Gen. Arnold had set forth the same thesis in his letter to Secretary of the Air Force Stuart Symington, 2 Dec. 1948, in Symington papers, correspondence file, box 1, Harry S. Truman Library (HST).

However, the air offensive, at least for the early Cold War period, would not be primarily a nuclear campaign. The army's Special Planning Division based its assumptions for fighting a future war on the experience of previous ones. The atomic bomb was given a minor role in grand strategy, even when American planners assumed that their nuclear stockpile contained many more atomic bombs than was actually the case.

In March 1946, the JCS initiated a succession of strategic studies of specific military problems in specific areas. The first Joint Basic Outline War Plan, in a sequence that became known collectively as the *Pincher* series, was submitted to the Joint Planning Staff (JPS) on 27 April 1946. The studies were to determine American strategy in the event of war with the Soviet Union within the next three years. By June 1946, the JWPC had drafted an interim plan for overcoming the discrepancies between American and Soviet military capabilities. The plan was the first blueprint for a war between the West and the Soviet Union, projected for some time between the summers of 1946 and 1947.[11]

Despite mounting friction with the Soviets over the next two years, it was not until spring 1948 that the United States had a war plan (*Halfmoon*) approved at the highest level, by the JCS. However, the *Pincher* studies did provide an analytical framework upon which the final American war plan could be based.[12] The *Pincher* studies presumed that the Soviets would swiftly overrun most of Europe west of the Rhine (excluding the British Isles), and seize the Channel ports of Belgium and Holland during their first drive. It was estimated that the attacking Soviet forces would outnumber the defending French, British and American forces by at least three to one. Initial *Pincher* studies planned for an allied withdrawal to Great Britain, to British-held islands in the Mediterranean, and to the Suez Canal and Bahrain in the Middle East. They relied on the eastern Mediterranean as a 'major theatre of concentration and naval operations at the start of any general war'.[13]

In the Middle East theatre, allied forces were expected to slow down a Soviet advance toward the Suez Canal. The American answer

[11] Herken, *The Winning Weapon*, p.219.

[12] Kenneth W. Condit, *The History of the Joint Chiefs of Staff*, Vol II. The Joint Chiefs of Staff and National Policy, 1947–1949. Wilmington: Michael Glazier, Inc., 1979, p.283.

For details of the various studies completed under the *Pincher* series, between April, 1946 to July, 1947, cf. Schnabel, *The History of the JCS* . . ., Vol. 1, pp.159–60.

[13] Schnabel, ibid., p.152; and Eric Grove and Geoffrey Till, 'Anglo-American Maritime Strategy in the Era of Massive Retaliation, 1945–60', in John B. Hattendorf, Robert S. Jordan, eds, *Maritime Strategy and the Balance of Power: Britain and America in the Twentieth Century*, London: Macmillan, 1989, p.275.

to the Soviet conventional offensive, the strategic air strike, was to be launched from bases in Britain, Okinawa and the Suez–Cairo area.[14]

By July 1947, American planners concluded that the *Pincher* studies had progressed far enough to warrant the preparation of a short-term emergency war plan, for the opening stages of a war forced upon the United States by Soviet aggression within the next three years.[15] In November 1946, the JWPC had stressed that they did *not* regard a war with the Soviets as likely during the next three years. But the crises in Eastern Europe in early 1948 led to the hasty appointment of an *ad hoc* committee to 'estimate the likelihood of a Soviet resort to direct military action during 1948'. The committee was comprised of representatives of the Central Intelligence Agency (CIA), and the intelligence sections of the Departments of State, Army, Navy, and the Air Force.[16] The committee's assessments, and the debates which they generated, became the basis of a new batch of contingency plans, turned out in 1948 at a frenetic pace (see the glossary).

The *ad hoc* committee delivered its first report on 30 March 1948. It concluded that the Soviets had the military capacity to overrun Western Europe and 'the Near East to Cairo within a short period of time'. However, the Committee concluded, 'the logic of the situation' indicated that the Soviets would not start a war in 1948. But the possibility could not be entirely ruled out. It might still break out, by mistake, due to the Soviets misinterpreting an American move as indicating offensive intentions.[17]

Following this initial assessment, the *ad hoc* committee set up four sub-committees to examine in detail 'the economic, scientific, military, and political advantages and disadvantages that would accrue to the USSR' if it should embark on the conquest of Western Europe and the Near East. The committee's final report, dated 30 July 1948, again estimated that the Soviets would be unlikely to unleash a war prior to 1950, even assuming that the Soviets counted on negotiating a peace leaving them in occupation of most of their conquests. None the less, once again, the possibility of a conflict precipitated 'through accident or miscalculation', was not ruled out.[18]

The advantages that would accrue to the Soviet Union from the con-

[14] Elliott Vanveltner Converse 3d., *United States Plans for a Postwar Overseas Military Base System, 1942–1948*, Unpublished Ph.D. dissertation, Princeton University, 1984, p.214–15.

[15] Condit, *The History of the JCS . . .*, Vol. 2, pp.283–84.

[16] ORE 22–48, Report by Joint Ad Hoc Committee, on 'Possibility of Direct Soviet Military Action During 1948', 30 March 1948, President's Secretary's Files, HST.

[17] Ibid.

[18] ORE 58–48 supra, 'The Strategic Value to the USSR of the Conquest of Western Europe and the Near East (to Cairo) Prior to 1950', 30 July 1948, President's Secretary's Files, [HST].

quest of Western Europe and the Near East would indeed be considerable; the technically skilled manpower at the Soviets' disposal would be doubled, and within 10 years, the committee estimated, 'the joint economic power of the USSR, its Satellites, and the occupied areas would probably equal that of the US'; within five to seven years, Soviet exploitation of Western Europe's scientific institutions might increase their war potential by as much as 50%. Although the Soviets would be unable to pump and transport Middle Eastern oil to the Soviet Union for several years, in the meantime that oil would be denied to the West. And finally, the extension of Soviet boundaries to the Atlantic, and to the Black and Mediterranean Seas would afford them invaluable strategic and logistic advantages.[19]

However, the committee assumed that the Soviets would need a protracted period of peace and stability in which to consolidate and mobilise all these resources. The Soviets were unlikely to enjoy such stability. Furthermore, they might well fear the exposure of their communist ideology to 'the bourgeois fleshpots of Western Europe'. The Soviets could not plan on being permitted to 'digest' their subjugated peoples in peace. A naval blockade alone would pose sufficient economic problems to give the Soviets pause for thought. Above all, the committee concluded that the Soviets were unlikely to undertake a global war before they had accumulated the instruments necessary to deal with the United States: 'the atomic bomb, a long-range air force, and a deep sea Navy'.[20]

Significantly, and perhaps predictably, USAF's Intelligence Department dissented from the main report. In their view, the conclusion that the Soviets would go to war only through miscalculation of American intention, was based on 'Western, not Soviet, logic'. Air Force Intelligence suggested that the Soviets would have no bourgeois compunctions about using either their own people, or the peoples of Western Europe, as hostages to American counter-attacks. The Soviets might not even be convinced that the Americans would employ the atomic bomb. Finally, in the Air Force view, the Soviets, motivated by a deterministic communist ideology, might well regard a new world war as the final, inevitable battle that would bring down the capitalist system, the last obstacle to their own world domination.[21]

USAF, in the course of building up and expanding the Strategic Air Command (SAC), warned against any relaxation of preparations to counter a Soviet offensive. The warning was in fact hardly necessary as all the Intelligence agencies warned of the danger of an 'accidental war'. In November 1948, the National Security Council (NSC) delivered

---

[19] Ibid.   [20] Ibid.   [21] Ibid.

its own report to the President on the dangers of a Soviet offensive, and measures to be taken to counter it. It noted that:

> Present intelligence estimates attribute to Soviet armed forces the capability of over-running in about six months all of Continental Europe and the Near East as far as Cairo, while simultaneously occupying important continental points in the Far East.[22]

The American dilemma was that their military intelligence had no concrete idea of Soviet intentions to use their military potential, nor did their estimates take into account the effects of allied defensive, and counter-offensive measures. The NSC report concluded that whereas they currently had no reliable indications of Soviet intentions to engage in direct conflict with the United States, there remained, for the foreseeable future, the perennial risk of war by mistake:

> . . . through Soviet miscalculation of the determination of the United States to use all the means at its command to safeguard its security, through Soviet mis-interpretation of our intentions, or through U.S. miscalculation of Soviet reactions to measures which we might take.[23]

The NSC recommended a strategy, short of war, that would not cause permanent damage to the national economy, but would:

> reduce the power and influence of the USSR to limits which no longer constitute a threat to the peace, national independence and stability of the world family of nations.[24]

The measures proposed were essentially ideological warfare, to bring those peoples under Soviet subjugation to appreciate the benefits of Western democracy over the communist system. In addition, the NSC recommended the continued development of a military deterrent for as long as the current threat of Soviet aggression persisted.

In the event of war, American war aims would be to push back Soviet influence to the limits of 'traditional Russian territory', and to ensure that any Bolshevik regime left in any part of the Soviet Union did

> not control enough of the military-industrial potential of the Soviet Union to enable it to wage war on comparable terms with any other regime or regimes which may exist on traditional Russian territory.[25]

The *Pincher* studies had identified the atomic bomb as a 'distinct

[22] NSC 20/4, 23 Nov. 1948, President's Secretary's Files, HST.
[23] Ibid. [24] Ibid. [25] Ibid.

advantage' in the strategic air offensive, 'the principal initial effort against the USSR' in case of war. However, given that the JCS themselves did not yet know just how many atomic bombs they actually had in their arsenal, the studies assumed that the atomic element in the strategic offensive would be limited. They also presumed, erroneously, that the Soviets would for some time possess no atomic bombs of their own.[26]

In 1949, at the time the Soviets exploded their first nuclear device, Vannevar Bush (one-time Director of the Office of Scientific Research and Development) was about to publish a book predicting that the Soviets would take another 10 years to develop their own atomic bomb. Fortunately for Bush, the book was still in page proofs, when the Soviet test was detected![27]

One year prior to the Soviets' first nuclear detonation, the American intelligence community was somewhat closer to an accurate estimate, although it was still four years out! An *ad hoc* intelligence committee set up in March 1948, to estimate the probability of war with the Soviets that year reported back in July 1948 that the Soviets would probably explode their own nuclear device in mid-1953. (The committee added the warning that if war did break out, and, as expected, the Soviets quickly overran all continental Europe, that date might be advanced by two years.)[28]

Nor did the Soviet entry into the nuclear club provoke immediate panic. American intelligence estimated that the critical danger period would not arrive before 1954. By that date, the Soviets were expected to have stockpiled some 200 atomic bombs. The Military concluded that it would take some 100 atomic bombs to wreak critical damage to the country. Therefore, given an estimated Soviet ability to get through American defences with some 40–60% of their ordnance, 1954 would be a critical juncture.[29]

---

[26] NSC 20/4, 23 Nov. 1948, President's Secretary's Files, HST.

[27] Cf. George H. Quester, *Nuclear Diplomacy: The First Twenty-Five Years*, New York: Dunellen, 1973, p.35.   [28] ORE 58–48, supra.

[29] (TS) JCS 2081/1, 13 Feb. 1950, CCS 471.6 USSR (11–8–49) sec.2, NA; and NSC 68, 14 April 1950, in FRUS, 1950, Vol. I, p.251. The CIA estimated the Soviet potential production rate of atomic bombs as follows:

By mid-1950: 10 – 20.   By mid-1953: 70 – 135.
By mid-1951: 25 – 45.   By mid-1954: 200.
By mid-1952: 45 – 90.

The number of atomic bombs actually produced by the Soviets has since been estimated at:

1950: 5   1953: 120
1951: 25   1954: 150
1952: 50

Cf. *Bulletin of the Atomic Scientists*, Nov./Dec. 1994, p.59.

The confusion and ambiguity which characterised American nuclear thinking during this period was due in part to the great secrecy in which details about the new device were kept shrouded. Very few planners were privy to details about the bomb, either in respect of its capability, or even concerning how many bombs were in fact operational. Far from determining America's nuclear policy, the JCS 'had some difficulty in discovering what that policy was'.[30]

Until 1948, the atomic bomb was still under the exclusive control of the wartime Atomic Energy Commission. There were no procedures for its release to the armed forces. After prolonged argument inside the JCS, in August 1948, the USAF was given an 'interim' monopoly over the use of atomic weapons. The Air Force was so possessive of the bomb that the Navy, which in the summer of 1946 had begun developing its own plans for a carrier-launched atomic bomber, was forced to defer further development, partly because the Air Force refused even to divulge details concerning the dimensions of the bomb.[31]

General Carl Spaatz, commander of the Air Force from February 1946 to April 1948, recalled later that during his tour of duty there had been only about a dozen atomic bombs operational. The B-29s converted to deliver the atomic bombs were nicknamed 'Silver Plates'. Spaatz recalled that in January 1946, he had disposed of only 27 'Silver Plates', all in the 509th Bomber Group, based in New Mexico. In 1947, there were still only 32 of the specially-converted aircraft.[32]

But in 1947, the United States still had too few atomic bombs to carry out what its planners considered to be the minimum missions necessary. None of the limited stockpile was assembled and operational, and the military personnel who were being trained to take over from the civilians who had assembled them during the war, were not yet fully trained and operational.[33]

President Truman himself was informed about the size of his country's nuclear stockpile only in April 1947. He was startled to discover that it was but a fraction of what he had hitherto believed.[34] The size of the American nuclear arsenal during this period has since been estimated by one scholar as having been:

[30] Schnabel, *The History of the JCS* . . ., Vol. 1, p.273.

[31] Condit, *The History of the JCS* . . ., Vol. 2, pp.184–89; and Herken, *The Winning Weapon* . . ., p.199.

[32] Rosenberg, American Atomic Strategy, p.65; and private communication, Dr Steven Ross, the Naval War College, Newport, RI.

[33] Schnabel, *The History of the JCS* . . ., Vol. 1, p.298.

[34] Quester, *Nuclear Diplomacy* . . ., p.66.

1946: 9 atomic bombs.
1947: 13 atomic bombs.
1948: 50 atomic bombs.
1949: 170 atomic bombs.[35]

None the less, some circles in the American military tended to rely ever more on nuclear weapons. Indeed, the known existence of an American nuclear arsenal, albeit a limited one, induced a new complacency in some circles. On the one hand it was believed that these few weapons would prove decisive; and on the other, it was believed that it would take the Soviets at least a decade to develop and successfully explode their own nuclear device. The American intelligence community later explained away their failure to predict accurately the first Soviet nuclear test (August 1949), by claiming that their estimates had been correct but had been invalidated by espionage rings in the United States, which had given away American atomic secrets.[36]

The first Soviet explosion of a nuclear device produced much reassessment and heart-searching in the West. But the American military remained confident that their own rate of production of nuclear weapons was significantly higher than that of the Soviets. And at the beginning of the 1950s, the Americans achieved a significant breakthrough in the production of nuclear weapons, with the discovery of a more efficient system of using fissionable materials.

But until 1950, planners believed that nuclear weapons would be both expensive and scarce for the foreseeable future. This would have ruled out any 'tactical' use by the Army or Navy. SAC's contingency planning included mass flights of conventional bombers. Plan *Broiler* assumed a massive Soviet air blitz against the UK, in which the Soviets would use up to 6500 bombers. Not only would there not be enough atomic weapons, but certain types of targets were not considered to be suitable for the new weapon. Thus the atomic offensive was planned in the general context of a protracted conventional war. Therefore, the experience gained, and the lessons to be learned from World War Two were believed to be highly relevant to the next war.[37]

The experience of that war had ostensibly demonstrated the futility

---

[35] Personal communication, from Dr Steven Ross; and *Bulletin of the Atomic Scientists*, Nov./Dec., 1994, p.59.

[36] Herken, *The Winning Weapon*, pp.208, 210, 219. It appears that the atomic spies subsequently exposed did not 'give' the Soviets the bomb. At the most, they helped the Soviets advance the date of their first explosion, cf., Phillip Knightley, *The Second Oldest Profession: Spies and Spying in the Twentieth Century*, New York: Penguin, 1988, pp.259, 265–66.

[37] Quester, *Nuclear Diplomacy . . .*, pp. –7; and Poole, *History of the JCS . . .*, Vol. IV, 1950–1952, p.165.

of indiscriminate bombing of urban centres of population. Some studies indicated that the blanket bombing of enemy cities had boosted, rather than impaired, public morale and had increased the civilian population's determination to fight. The enemy's military-industrial infrastructure had continued to function, even if at an ever-declining capacity.

However, after the war, the United States Strategic Bombing Survey had deduced that even if the Allies' strategic bombing campaign had *not* brought the German war machine to a halt by the end of the war, it *would* have done so within a short time, even had Allied ground forces not beaten the Germans decisively. Experience showed that surgical air strikes against the enemy's transportation, petroleum industry, and electrical grid infrastructure had been more effective than 'counter-morale' attacks against enemy cities. The Strategic Bombing Survey concluded that it had been a shortage of aviation fuel that had led to the defeat of the Luftwaffe; and that a more systematic destruction of the German electrical grid would have brought about the collapse of the German war economy.[38]

Given the limited numbers of atomic bombs available and, at least initially, SAC's limited delivery capability, the question of choosing the most 'cost-effective' targets was critical.

B. USAF AND THE NEED FOR OVERSEAS BASES

SAC was established in March 1946. It relied on the four-engined, propeller-driven B-29 bomber. The B-29 had flown its first combat mission in June 1944. Fully-loaded, it had a maximum range of some 3200 miles – i.e., it could deliver a full payload against targets that were just over 1500 miles distant. In 1945, the B-50 was put into production. The B-50 was basically the B-29, with improved engines, and enhanced take-off capability. SAC had nine bomber groups, some of which still used the B-17. Only one unit, the 509th Composite Group, veterans of Hiroshima and Nagasaki, was especially trained to fly the converted B-29s capable of delivering nuclear weapons. By 1947, SAC had expanded to 16 bomber groups, all flying B-29s. But it was still in the slow process of converting its aircraft for 'nuclear operations'.[39]

By the early 1950s, the B-29s and B-50s were being superseded

---

[38] Quester, ibid., pp.8, 37; and Poole, ibid.

[39] For data on the B-29, and the B-50, cf., Iain Persons, ed., *The Encyclopedia of the World's Combat Aircraft*, London: Hamley, 1976, p.26; and Norman Polmar, ed., *Strategic Air Command: People, Aircraft, and Missiles*, Annapolis: The Nautical and Aviation Company of America, Inc., 1979, pp.145–49; also Quester, *Nuclear Diplomacy . . .*, p.34.

gradually by the B-36. The six-engined, propeller-driven B-36 was conceived originally in 1941, in the days when many had believed that Germany was about to prevail over Britain. The new plane was designed originally as a trans-Atlantic bomber that would enable the Americans to bomb Germany from bases in the United States. With a full payload, the B-36 had a range of just over 8000 miles – i.e. it could reach and return to base from targets up to 4000 miles away.[40]

Thirty-six B-36's entered service with SAC in mid-1948. But until the early 1950s, their numbers remained limited, and the B-29s continued to serve as the backbone of the United States' strategic strike force. The following table shows the numbers of strategic bombers available to SAC until the end of 1952:

	31 Dec 49	31 Dec 50	31 Dec 51	31 Dec 52
B-29	386	282	346	417
B-50	99	195	216	224
B-36	36	38	96	154[41]

Only in 1953, did SAC begin to phase out the B-29s and B-50s. In that last year of their active operations, the B-29s were for the first time outnumbered by the B-36s – 110 to 185 aircraft.[42]

The B-36 became the focus of a public feud between the Navy and the Air Force. An official in the Department of the Navy prepared an anonymous document stating that the B-36 was 'a billion dollar blunder', kept in production only because the Secretaries of Defense and Air had financial interests in it.[43]

In promoting its own programme for building a carrier fleet from which to launch the strategic air offensive, the Navy challenged the effectiveness of Air Force strategic bombing. In 1948, the Committee on the National Security Organisation examined the issue. During the course of the hearings, a naval captain stated:

> there were two kinds of air, land-based air and sea-based air . . . land-based air was like a boxer with his feet embedded in concrete.[44]

[40] Polmar, *Strategic Air . . .*, p.154. Persons and Tolmar differ in their data regarding the B-36. Persons, *The Encyclopedia . . .* p.86, states that the B-36 had a range of 8,175 miles, fully loaded; Polmar, p.158, states that the B-36 had a range of 8,000 miles with a partial payload of 10,000 pounds; and fully loaded (72,000 pounds capacity), it had a range of 4,800 miles.

[41] Poole, *History of the JCS . . .*, Vol. IV, 1950–52, p.168.

[42] Polmar, *Strategic Air . . .*, pp.7, 11,13, 17, 20, 24, 28, 31, 35.

[43] Condit, *History of the JCS. . .*, Vol. 2, p.330. The B-36 controversy is surveyed on pp.330–51.

[44] Symington to Sec for Defense Forrestal, 22 Nov. 1948, Symington papers, box 4. HST. The Committee was chaired by Ferdinand Eberstadt. Correspondence on the B-36

Navy criticism peaked in 1949, following the scrapping of its own plans for a 'super carrier', the *USS United States*, which the Navy had hoped would carry nuclear-armed heavy bombers.[45]

The B-36 did not differ significantly from the B-29 in its speed and altitude capabilities. It was considered just as vulnerable to enemy fighters as the B-29. (That vulnerability would be exposed during the Korean war.) It was ostensibly on grounds of this vulnerability that the B-36 was challenged by the Navy. The latter's objections resulted in special Congressional hearings on the B-36, by the House Armed Services Committee. In what became known as 'the Admirals' Revolt', Naval experts objected that the B-36 would be unable to penetrate enemy defences and that, in any case, 'blanket bombing' with nuclear weapons was immoral. However, the Navy's case was flawed deeply by its own evident appetite for a carrier-launched nuclear bomber. Admiral Denfeld, Chief of Naval Operations, claimed that the Navy was being slighted in the defence budget due to an unholy coalition of the Army and the Air Force representatives on the JCS.[46]

The Committee proposed that the B-36 programme be continued but, while regretting the cancellation of the super-carrier, in view of budgetary restrictions, it did not recommend a resumption of its construction. The vociferousness and publicised opposition of the admirals, and their differences with their superior, Navy Secretary Francis P. Mathews, led in October 1949 to the dismissal of Admiral Denfeld, with the deprivation of his seat on the JCS. (In 1950, Gen Marshall was brought out of retirement by President Truman, for a one-year stint as Secretary of Defense, with the mission of promoting unity between the services, and restoring co-operation between the State and Defense departments.)[47]

One possible solution to the limited ranges of the larger part of the USAF fleet, was mid-air refuelling. But hitherto, during World War Two, it had not been considered a practical proposition, given the hundreds of aircraft that sortied on any given mission. However, with the advent of the atomic bomb, the destructive power carried by a single aircraft increased enormously. By the late 1940s, the develop-

controversy is to be found in the papers of Stuart A. Symington, Secretary of the Air Force, (Sept. 1947–April 1950) in the Symington papers, 1946–50, boxes 4 and 5, HST.

[45] On the cancellation of the *USS United States*, cf., Condit, *History of the JCS. . .*, Vol. 2, pp.319–29.

[46] Cf., Condit, *History of the JCS . . .*, Vol. 2, pp.341, 348; and Quester, *Nuclear Diplomacy . . .*, pp.55, 79.

[47] Cf., Condit, ibid., pp.350–51, and the Symington papers, supra; and Forrest C. Pogue, George C. Marshall: *Statesman, 1945–1959*, New York: Viking Penguin, 1987, pp.xvii–xviii, 515.

ment of mid-air refuelling techniques for military purposes had assumed high priority.[48]

By 1947, USAF had begun testing its first medium-range jet bomber, the B-47, with a projected range of 4200 nautical miles. In the mid-1950s, the B-52, the first all-jet long-range bomber (over 8000 miles), came into operational service. The first 18 B-52s were delivered to USAF in 1955, and henceforth began to replace the B-36. By this time, considerable progress had also been made with mid-air refuelling techniques.[49] But during the first decade after World War Two, overseas air bases, for both offensive and defensive purposes, were an essential *sine qua non* of American grand strategy. This was appreciated in all the early post-World War Two strategic studies.

Given the strategists' uncertainty about, and even ignorance of their own country's nuclear arsenal, many had little faith in the West's ability to overcome Soviet conventional superiority. On 18 August 1945, the Joint Strategic Survey Committee (JSSC) was asked by the JCS to study the implications of atomic weapons on future warfare and military organisation. In October, the committee reported back that whereas American industry and population 'were highly concentrated and quite vulnerable to sea-launched bombs, Soviet assets were widely dispersed and far from the ocean'. In the event of war, Soviet air attacks on the United States would have to be intercepted from: 'a system of mutually supporting advance bases extending far out from the homeland'.[50]

As noted already, one of the *Pincher* studies assumed that in the event of a Soviet attack against Europe, American occupation forces stationed there would withdraw from the continent to defensive positions, either in Italy, or in Spain. Another study suggested that the withdrawn forces might be sent to help the British defend Cairo and the Suez area. But by 1950, NSC 68 estimated that in the event of war the Soviets would be able to drop atomic bombs on Britain, and other overseas bases, thereby 'depriving the Western Powers of their use as a base.'[51]

The JCS agreed with the army that the advent of the nuclear era had not reduced the importance of existing conventional forces but had actually increased it. The use of atomic weapons would not permit the 'elimination of the conventional armaments or major modifications of the Services that employ them'. The American nuclear arsenal was still

---

[48] Norstad speech to RAF and RCAF, 24 Jan. 1948, supra.

[49] Quester, *Nuclear Diplomacy* . . ., p.81.

[50] Schnabel, *The History of the JCS* . . ., Vol. 1, p.277.

[51] Staff Studies of certain military problems deriving from the concept of Operations for 'Pincher', JPS 789/1, 13 April 1946. RG 218. CCS 381 USSR (2 March 46), sectn 1. NA; and NSC 68, 14 April, 1950, FRUS, Vol.1, 1950, pp.234–92. The quote is from p.251.

very limited. *Makefast*, the Airforce plan for a global air offensive, completed under the *Pincher* series in September 1946, did not even include a nuclear weapons annex.[52] But at the same time, more forces would now be needed, in order to defend the new nuclear bases that would now become prime targets for the enemy. Paradoxically, USAF itself initially felt threatened by the new weapon, believing that it would obviate the need in peacetime for a large Airforce, since a sudden and decisive blow might now be delivered by very few bombs and aircraft.

In their search for a worldwide overseas base system after World War Two, American planners turned away from the Pacific, 'to the Arctic and the North Atlantic, and then to British, North African and South Asian bases.' But hostile foreign reactions to American requests for base rights, combined with sharply reduced defence budgets led to a 'shift in strategic emphasis from far northern bases to ones along Russia's southern rim,' along the Northern Tier, and in the Middle East. The search for bases within striking distance of the Soviet Union, was motivated also by the need for oil, and the expansion of American commercial transport.[53]

From late 1945, American planners allotted equal importance to British airfields and those along the Soviet Union's southern borders. The authors of the *Pincher* series planned on the basis of the B-29s. The new B-36 bomber, with an effective range of 4000 nautical miles, would alleviate somewhat the need for southern rim bases, closer to the Soviet Union than the British ones. But the new bomber did not become operational until the end of 1948 and, as noted already, its performance specifications came under scathing criticism from the Navy.[54]

Initial plans for a strategic air strike on the Soviet Union, primarily with conventional rather than atomic bombs, identified the Soviet transport system as 'the most vital cog' in the Soviet war machine. However, to make any kind of impact on that system would have required ordnance of preposterous dimensions. It was estimated that it would require about one million tons of bombs 'to destroy even a small portion of the rail network of Eastern Europe alone.' It would have required some 120,000 tons of bombs to destroy any significant percentage of the Soviet steel industry – three times the tonnage of ordnance available! Therefore, the Soviet petroleum industry was identified as the most feasible target vulnerable to bombing from the air. Since some two-thirds of the Soviet petroleum industry were

[52] JSSC report, 30 Oct. 1945, cited in Schnabel, *History of the JCS* . . ., Vol. 1, p.278; and Rosenberg, *American Atomic* . . ., p.64.

[53] Converse, *United States Plans* . . . pp.21–31.

[54] Ibid., p.253; and appendix K to annex II, JP (49) 126, Defe 6/10, 3 Nov. 1949. Public Record Office (PRO).

located in seventeen cities, these were soon identified by American strategists as primary targets.[55]

But detailed planning for the *Pincher* series revealed that an atomic offensive, even on the limited scale planned, was still beyond the capability of the Air Force. Maps appended revealed that several of the 20 cities targeted were from 300 to 500 hundred miles beyond the maximum operational range of the B-29s to be stationed in Britain (although Abu Sueir would have been within range; on the respective distances of Soviet strategic targets from bases in England and Egypt, see Chapter 3). Furthermore, military planners were apparently still unaware that their country as yet had neither sufficient bombs nor bombers to attack even those cities that were within range.[56]

General Eisenhower, acting in 1949 as 'presiding officer' of the JCS, believed that even when they had developed 'a respectable long range strategic bombing force', they would continue to need bases in 'favourable spots', to service the medium range bombers, that would 'always do the bulk of the work.' With the outbreak of the Korean War in 1950, the United States instituted a crash programme for securing rights to develop new air bases; from Canada (Newfoundland and Labrador); from the UK (Libya); from France (Casablanca in Morocco – 1951); and in Spain (1954); and from Turkey (Aadan). Runways at existing overseas bases (England, Guam), were lengthened to accommodate the heavier bombers.[57]

Thus until the mid-1950s, overseas air bases remained essential to allied contingency planning. American planners remained pre-occupied with the problem of delivering their arsenal of bombs to targets that were out of range. As put succinctly by Gen Lauris Norstad, USAF would need 'some measure of assistance from our friends who control important base areas.'[58]

---

[55] Air Plan for *Makefast*, ABC 381 USSR, (2 March 1946), section 3, NA; also Rosenberg, *The Origins of*. . . p.15; and idem, *American Atomic Strategy* . . ., p.64.

[56] Ibid.

[57] Gen. Dwight Eisenhower to Louis Johnson, Secretary for Defense, 14 July 1949, in pre-presidential papers, 1916–1952, box 62, EL; Rosenberg, American Atomic Strategy . . ., pp.79, 81; and Poole, *History of the JCS* . . ., Vol. IV, 1950–1952, p.169.

Eisenhower acted as presiding officer of the JCS from Feb. to Aug. 1949, when President Truman instituted the office of chairman of the JCS.

[58] Norstad speech to RAF and RCAF, 24 Jan. 1948, supra.

C. THE CHANGING PLACE OF THE MIDDLE EAST IN US CONTINGENCY PLANNING, 1946–1950

In November 1946, the JWPC submitted to the JCS a strategic study of the region between the European Alps and the Himalayas. Codenamed *Caldron*, the study included an analysis of allied and Soviet interests in the Near and Middle East. By their very nature, contingency plans for specific theatres tended to stress the special importance of the area under study, in contrast to the more general purview taken by world-wide emergency plans.

The key to victory in a Middle East campaign (yet more so than in the European theatre), would lay with the respective air forces of the antagonists. This was due to the revolutions taking place in aerial warfare and to the inherent logistical difficulties facing a land offensive in the desert wastelands that predominated in the region. There were hardly any metalled highways that were passable in winter. And there was but a single railroad, bypassing Turkey, that connected the USSR with the Cairo–Suez area. This ran through western Iran, via the Basra–Abadan area, thence north-west through Mosul and Aleppo, thence to the Mediterranean, and south along the coastal plain through Palestine, the Sinai desert, to Egypt. Along this line, there were no less than three changes of gauge.[59]

Caldron explained why the Middle East was now regarded by the Soviets as their most vulnerable flank, one to be protected at all costs. This was because:

> The U.S.S.R. had displaced the centre of gravity of her industry to the eastward. This industry, together with the Caucasian oil fields are vital to her war potential.[60]

Conversely, a Soviet denial of the Middle East to the allies would reduce significantly the latter's war-making potential. It would deprive them of the vital oil resources of the region; it would sever the 'lifeline' of the British Empire, through the Suez Canal; and not least, it would critically weaken the allies' counter-offensive potential against the USSR. In the event of war, the Soviets would endeavour to seize the areas lying between the eastern Mediterranean and the Persian Gulf, in order to deny them to the allies 'as possible enemy air, sea and ground offensive bases.' The Soviets would thereby increase substantially the

---

[59] Caldron, JWPC 475/1, 2 Nov. 1946, NA. (Declassified 8 Nov. 1976.) I am deeply grateful to Dr Steven Ross, of the Naval College, Newport, RI, for providing me with this document.　　　　　　　　　　　　　　　　　　　　　　　　　　　　　　[60] Ibid.

security of their vital industrial areas from air attack and/or conquest by a ground offensive.[61]

Northern Egypt and the Sinai peninsula were regarded as key strategic areas in the Middle East. They constituted the land-bridge between Eurasia and Africa. From this area, containing the British bases along the Suez Canal, the allies might support operations in Turkey and the rest of the Middle East, and launch attacks against areas of key importance to the Soviets. Should the Soviets seize these strategic assets, they would be able to deny them to the allies. Not only that, but they would then be in a position to advance west through north Africa, along the southern seaboard of the Mediterranean, and from here, pose a threat to the African continent as a whole. Therefore, *Caldron* concluded:

> the Cairo–Suez area must be held as a minimum Allied requirement and Allied forces must be committed to assure its retention probably even at the risk of losing control of the other strategic areas in the eastern Mediterranean area and the Middle East.[62]

Caldron estimated that, in the event of war, the Soviets would be able to push simultaneously into eastern and western Turkey. They would deploy a total of 75 divisions to the Middle East campaign; some 45 divisions and 900 aircraft in a drive through the Balkans to the Dardanelles; and some 30 divisions and 600 aircraft in a drive through the Caucasus into south-eastern Turkey, Iran, Iraq, Palestine and the Suez Canal. The JWPC estimated that the Soviets would reach Haifa within 40 days and would push the British back into southern Palestine within 60 days. The Soviets were then expected to regroup their forces, and at about D + 120 begin a drive towards Suez with 4 divisions, keeping some 10 divisions in reserve. Unless substantial British reinforcements arrived rapidly on the scene, the Soviets were expected to take the Suez area within another two months.[63]

The inference was quite clear. Given that the Cairo–Suez area was such a key strategic asset for the allies, the Americans would have to come to Britain's aid if it was to be held against a Soviet offensive. Early plans reflected indecision concerning the strategic air bases in the Middle East. This was perhaps due to the fact that these were short-term, almost *ad hoc* plans, prepared under the pressure of events in Eastern Europe, and the fear that the conflict with the Soviets might erupt any day. So many new plans were circulated, frequently revised and modified, with both the Americans and the British allotting every

---

[61] Caldron, JWPC 475/1, 2 Nov. 1946, NA.   [62] Ibid.   [63] Ibid.

new plan with its own separate code name, that confusion reigned at times.[64]

In line with the findings of the *ad hoc* intelligence committee, all contingency plans now conceded the loss of Western Europe to a Soviet onslaught, and stressed American reliance on the atomic air offensive to delay the Soviets. The main difference between the plethora of plans drafted in 1948 concerned the dispositions of forces to be held in the Middle East, and the choice of strategic air bases from which to launch the air strikes.[65]

Due to Britain's continuing dispute with the Egyptians, and the fact that the proposed strategic air base at Abu Sueir had yet to be readied for the heavier B-29s, American planners may be forgiven for having vacillated over the Cairo–Suez area (on Abu Sueir see below, Chapter 5).

During March 1948, no less than three successive short-term worldwide emergency plans were drawn up. The first, code-named *Broiler*, stipulated the British Isles and Okinawa as first preferences for bases from which to launch the strategic air offensive; the Cairo–Suez area appeared as third preference, with Karachi (in Pakistan) now named as a last option, if a base in Egypt could not be secured. In late March 1948, plan *Broiler* was revised and renamed *Frolic*. In *Frolic*, Cairo–Suez was deleted, and Karachi listed as the single third choice.[66]

The JWPC produced yet another revised plan in March 1948, this time code-named *Grabber*. The successive revisions, all within a few weeks, reflected the administration's sense of urgency and vulnerability. Whereas previous war plans had posited that war with the Soviets was unlikely within the coming five years, *Grabber* assumed 'that war could come at any time and would be accompanied by little or no warning'. This led inevitably to a greater reliance upon nuclear weapons. *Grabber* conceded the Middle East to the Soviets and, with it, the strategic air base at Abu Sueir. Any American troops stationed there would be withdrawn, if possible. They would be kept in reserve for an offensive designed to reconquer the area and its oil resources during the second year of the conflict. American planners now expressed a preference for a strategic air base in Pakistan over one in the Middle East. Upon the

---

[64] The bewilderment of British planners is reflected in a memorandum of 1950 which recited the codenames of the various war plans, their revisions, their American counterparts, and the name-changes made necessary when previous code-names had been compromised; cf. ,JP (50), 36, 22 March 1950, in Defe 6/12, PRO.

[65] Ibid., p.289; and David Alan Rosenberg, *Toward Armageddon: The Foundations of United States Nuclear Strategy, 1945–1961*, Unpublished Ph. D. dissertation, Chicago University, 1983, p.107.

[66] Condit, *History of the JCS . . .*, p.286.

outbreak of war, the atomic air offensive was now to be launched from three major air bases, in England, Karachi/Lahore and Okinawa.[67]

Grabber provoked opposition from within the military establishment, particularly from the Navy. Inter-service rivalry lay at the root of the Navy's rebuttal of the Army's pessimistic prognosis of American ability to hold up a Soviet offensive in Europe and the Middle East. The Navy claimed that *Grabber* had placed 'an exaggerated emphasis upon the air-atomic offensive, over-estimated Soviet military capabilities, and ignored the potential contributions of Allied armed forces.' Behind the Navy's opposition lay also its own aspirations to deliver part of the atomic air offensive from its own super-carriers. Finally, the Navy objected also to the surrender of the Middle East oil fields.[68]

However, at an Anglo-American conference held in Washington in April 1948, in order to discuss the British plan for the defence of the Middle East (*Sandown*, on which, see Chapter 6), British planners pointed out to their American counterparts the adverse political reactions that would probably result, both in Pakistan and in India, from a request to develop strategic air bases on their territory. The Americans consequently amended their plans once again, and determined on the Suez/Cairo/Khartoum area as a vital base area in the Middle East. Karachi was relegated to a last alternative. American planners now emphasised the strategic potential of the air base at Abu Sueir, in Egypt (significantly closer to targets in the Soviet Union than were any available air bases in Europe), and of the Middle Eastern oil fields.[69]

In its turn, *Grabber* was replaced by *Halfmoon*, a short-term emergency plan for a war during Fiscal 1949. *Halfmoon* 'reinstated' the Cairo–Suez air base. The American bombing effort would now be distributed between three bases – the UK, Okinawa, and Cairo–Suez, from which the major part of the overseas strategic air offensive was now to be launched. *Halfmoon* planned by D + 12 months to deploy one heavy bomber group from the United States, and ten medium bomber

[67] JP (48) 54 (Final), 10 May 1948, in Defe 6/6. PRO; and Herken, *The Winning Weapon* . . ., p.248, and p.382, fn. 37.

[68] Cf., Condit, *History of the JCS* . . ., Vol. 2, pp.286–87, 319–29; and memo by Chief of Naval operations, Louis Denfeld, 6 April 1948, cited by Herken, ibid., p.253.

[69] Ibid.; and Richard J. Aldrich, John Zametica, 'The Rise and Decline of a Strategic Concept: the Middle East, 1945–51, in Richard J. Aldrich, ed., *British Intelligence, Strategy and the Cold War, 1945–51*, London/New York: 1992, p.254; and David Alan Rosenberg, *The U.S. Navy and the Problem of Oil in a Future War: The Outline of a Strategic Dilemma, 1945–1950*, Naval War College Review, Vol. 29, summer, 1976, p.56.

The Americans dropped all idea of Pakistan when the British warned that the Pakistanis would demand support in the Security Council defence guarantees, economic and financial aid, and American support for their claims in Kashmir, and for universal Islamic interests, especially in Palestine.

groups from overseas bases – five at Cairo–Suez, three in the UK, and two on Okinawa. Due to anticipated Soviet advances against the Middle East, *Halfmoon* planned to send the following 'minimum reinforcements' to the Middle East by D + 6 months: 'two US infantry divisions and six and two-thirds fighter groups.'[70]

Plan *Halfmoon* was approved on 19 May 1948, and circulated to the JCS on 1 September under the name *Fleetwood*. Bowing to the Navy's objections, the new plan provided a larger role for naval forces in blockading Russia's coastline, and bombing Soviet cities. Under *Fleetwood*, the Navy would allocate four of its aircraft carriers to the Mediterranean, from D-day. The allies would now attempt to hold the Soviet offensive at the Rhine, instead of at an unspecified point to the west of that river. Like its predecessor, *Fleetwood* still ceded the Middle East to the Soviets. But it was hoped to deliver a significant, even decisive, blow with the air offensive launched from Abu Sueir, before the Soviets overran the Cairo–Suez area. *Fleetwood* posited a major Allied counter-offensive to regain the Middle Eastern oil fields, to be carried out no later than the second year of the war.[71]

Severe budgetary restrictions also played a significant role in American grand strategy. In May 1948, the same month in which *Halfmoon* was approved, President Truman, concerned about the effects of uncontrolled inflation, imposed a $14.4 billion ceiling on the defence budget for fiscal 1950. The JCS objected that fiscal restrictions would prevent them from maintaining even minimal conventional forces, in order to retain some foothold in Europe, and to carry out limited naval operations in the Mediterranean. In that event, the JCS asserted, 'the only offensive operation the United States could undertake to meet an emergency would be an atomic air offensive from the British Isles and the Cairo–Suez area.' Truman's adamant insistence on the defence budget ceiling thus led American strategists to rely, to an ever-increasing degree, on SAC, and its use of nuclear weapons.[72]

In October 1948, General Curtis LeMay assumed command of SAC. He immediately set about preparing a detailed plan for a nuclear air strike against the Soviet Union. The plan, SAC Emergency War Plan 1–49, notwithstanding Navy opposition, was incorporated by the JCS in plan *Trojan*, (the latest revision of Fleetwood, with an annex outlining the atomic offensive). A rapidly increasing American nuclear

---

[70] Condit, *History of the JCS* . . ., pp.288–92.

[71] Ibid., p.289, and Rosenberg, *Toward Armageddon* . . ., p.266.

[72] Rosenberg, American Atomic Strategy, p.69. There was some irony in the fact that these very same budgetary restrictions forced those who drafted *Fleetwood* to allocate too few bombers even to carry out the atomic air strike, and insufficient ground forces 'to evacuate and move the forward bases from England and Egypt if they were to be endangered by the advance of the Red Army'. Cf. Herken, *The Winning Weapon* . . ., p.255.

stockpile enabled planners to enhance significantly the role of the atomic offensive in their strategy. Whereas the *Pincher* studies had stipulated a nuclear strike on 20 Soviet cities with 50 atomic bombs, by the fall of 1948, *Trojan* provided for an atomic attack on 70 Soviet cities, including Moscow and Leningrad, with their entire assumed nuclear arsenal, estimated at 133 atomic bombs.[73]

First priority was given to the destruction of the 70 Soviet cities. SAC claimed that this would 'so cripple the Soviet industrial and control centres as to reduce drastically the offensive and defensive power of their armed forces.' Second priority was given to 'petroleum refining targets', inside the Soviet Union and on the territories of her satellites. This strike, once Soviet inventories ran down, would 'practically destroy the offensive capabilities of the USSR and seriously cripple its defensive capabilities.' After these operations, air strikes would be made against the Soviets' hydro-electric and inland transportation systems.[74]

When an internal study, the Harmon Report (May 1949, commissioned by USAF), concluded that the planned nuclear air strike would not stop a Soviet occupation of Europe and the Middle East, the JCS were moved to request a major increase in nuclear weapons production. None the less, even the authors of the Harmon Report saw no alternative to the opening nuclear air strike, upon which, somewhat incongruously, they still pinned American hopes of survival against the Soviets. The JCS also pointed out that the report's estimate of a 30–40% reduction in Soviet industrial capacity as a result of the atomic attack, was an overall average, and that the damage to the Soviets' petroleum industry would be far greater.[75]

With the United States's official adherence to NATO, in April 1949, she became committed formally to the defence of Western Europe. Any lingering JCS doubts about the Middle East base were undoubtedly influenced by a directive written on 25 February 1949, by Gen Eisenhower, acting chairman of the JCS:

> The security of the United States requires the pursuance of a definite policy to insure, at the earliest possible moment, the holding of a line containing the Western Europe complex preferably no farther to the West than the Rhine. The

---

[73] Condit, ibid., pp.293–94; and Rosenberg, ibid., p.266. *Trojan* was approved by the JCS at the end of Jan. 1949.

[74] SAC Emergency War Plan, 1–49, 21 Dec., 1948, quoted in Etzold and Gaddis, eds, *Containment* . . ., p.353, and Rosenberg, *American Atomic Strategy* . . ., pp.70–1.

[75] The Harmon Report is cited in Etzold and Gaddis, eds, *Containment* . . ., pp.360–64; see also Condit, *The History of the JCS* . . ., Vol. 2, pp.313–15; and Rosenberg, *American Atomic Strategy* . . ., pp.73, 86.

logical extension of this line involves the United Kingdom on the left flank and the Cairo Suez [area] on the right flank.[76]

Eisenhower realised that the allies would be unable to hold the Rhine with the forces then available. He called therefore for the drafting of a new emergency war plan, to hold a 'substantial bridgehead' in Western Europe, in order to avert the need for an amphibious reconquest of Europe (like the one he had himself commanded in 1944). If even this limited goal proved impossible, he asked the planners to draft plans for a 'return, at the earliest possible moment, to Western Europe . . .'[77]

Eisenhower's directive was apparently responsible for yet another major change in American strategy in the Middle East. For it was in order to attempt to hold that bridgehead, on the Iberian peninsula, that the JCS now decided to switch the American contingent (over three divisions and 160 aircraft) earmarked previously for the Middle East, to North-West Africa. Eisenhower's directive guided those who drafted the successor to *Fleetwood*, plan *Offtackle*, which was seven months in the planning. The new plan anticipated the delivery of 292 atomic bombs, and 17,610 tons of conventional bombs during the first 90 days of a war.[78]

The allies failed to agree on *Offtackle*, which was contested by the British at the annual ABC conference, held from 26 September to 4 October 1949. None the less, after a final revision, it was approved by the JCS in December 1949. Although approved after the establishment of NATO, *Offtackle* made no specific allocation of either bombs or aircraft to the defence of Western Europe.[79] That would not occur until 1952, following the adherence of Turkey to NATO.

Offtackle estimated that the air offensive would destroy:

vital elements of the Soviet war making capacity . . . by inflicting critical damage on petroleum refineries, electric power plants, submarine construction facilities, high octane aviation gasoline production facilities, and other war-supporting industries. In line with the re-deployment of the Middle East contingent, the three bomber groups allocated previously to Egypt, were now re-allocated to Northwest Africa. The Navy's role was curtailed seriously, due to the small number of carriers provided for in the austerity budget. The Cairo–Suez area

[76] Eisenhower memorandum of 25 Feb. 1949, quoted in Condit, *History of the JCS . . .*, Vol.2, p.295.

[77] Ibid., p.296; and Steven T. Ross, *American War Plans, 1945–1950*, London: Frank Cass, 1996, p. 110.

[78] Walter S. Poole, *The History of the Joint Chiefs of Staff: The Joint Chiefs of Staff and National Policy*, Vol. IV, 1950–1952, Wilmington: Michael Glazier, Inc., 1980, p.164.

[79] Ibid., p.297, and Rosenberg, *American Atomic Strategy . . .*, p.74.

was again deleted as a strategic air base. The oil fields of the Middle East would be held only 'if militarily possible'.[80]

Following the communist victory in China (October 1949), the detonation of the first Soviet atomic bomb (August 1949), and the consequent American decision to develop a thermonuclear (hydrogen) bomb in January 1950, President Truman commissioned a study of the implications of all these developments, by a special State and Defense Department study group headed by Paul Nitze, (who in that same month had replaced George Kennan as head of the Policy Planning Staff (PPS)).[81]

The committee's final report, printed as NSC 68, on 7 April 1950, stated that should world war begin in 1950, the United States and her allies would be able to 'provide a reasonable measure of protection to the Western Hemisphere, bases in the Western Pacific, and essential military lines of communication'; but '*an inadequate measure of protection to vital military bases in the United Kingdom and in the Near and Middle East.*'[82] (my emphasis)

The Americans now feared that an enhanced Soviet offensive capacity would narrow the industrial and technological gap between the two Superpowers. In August 1950, in an assessment of Soviet intentions written during the Korean war, the NSC estimated that the Soviets, in addition to being able 'to invade Western Europe and the Near and Middle East, to make direct attacks upon the United Kingdom and Alaska and upon shipping, and to reinforce the communist military effort in the Far East' – would be able also to launch air attacks on a limited scale on the United States and Canada. The Soviet air strike, while not preventing the Americans from launching their own atomic offensive, might well cause attrition to the latter's industrial potential.[83]

NSC 68 has been called 'the most elaborate effort made by United States officials during the early Cold War years to integrate political, economic, and military considerations into a comprehensive statement of national security policy.' NSC 68 was the first strategic assessment to suggest that the Soviets might initiate, and even win a war against the Western allies. The paper urged a substantial increase in United States military preparedness, and spurred the first post-war, rapid expansion of American military forces.[84]

---

[80] Condit, *History of the JCS* . . ., Vol. 2, pp.299–300; and Herken, *The Winning Weapon* . . ., p.296.

[81] President Truman to Secretary of State, 31 Jan. 1950, FRUS, 1950, Vol.I, pp.141–42.

[82] NSC 68, 7 April 1950, ibid., pp.234–92.

[83] NSC Report, 25 Aug. 1950, ibid., p.377.

[84] Etzold and Gaddis, eds, *Containment* . . . , p.383; and Rosenberg, *Toward Armageddon* . . ., p.153.

NSC 68 was not approved by Truman until the end of September 1950. However, the outbreak of the Korean war in June 1950, guaranteed Presidential approval. The new policy document undoubtedly marked a turning-point in the United States' mobilisation of its national resources for possible war against the Soviets.

D. THE ADVANTAGES OF MIDDLE EAST BASES

It has been seen that until the early 1950s, American contingency planning sporadically assumed that a significant part of the strategic air offensive would be launched from airfields in Great Britain, and the Suez–Cairo area.

Further, the strategic importance of the Suez Canal was demonstrated clearly during the Korean war. (For those sections of the US Navy off the West coast of the United States it was, of course, closer to sail west to the Far East. But for those Fleets stationed in the Atlantic and the Mediterranean, and for land forces in Europe, the Suez Canal route was of obvious strategic significance). The war, and the demands it made of the United States, vindicated the Navy's claims 'about the value of mobile, flexible carrier striking forces',[85] and the need for overseas bases. The British, who were about to complete the runway extensions needed by the B-29s at Abu Sueir, had their hopes revived of securing an American commitment to the Middle East.

Furthermore, even when the longer-range bombers did come into service, the Canal Zone air bases remained important both for the launching of medium-range bombers, and as post-strike landing bases. A SAC Emergency War plan approved by the JCS on 22 October 1951 determined that medium-range bombers, flying from the UK, would fly along the edge of the Mediterranean, and deliver 52 atomic bombs on industrial targets in the Volga and Donets basins. On their return flights from their missions, these bombers would make landings at Egyptian and Libyan air bases.[86]

The Cairo–Suez base offered considerable advantages over air bases in the UK. British airfields offered the following benefits: of all the countries of Western Europe, Britain was the one most likely to welcome the return of departed American forces; American B-29s taking off from British bases would be able to attack any part of Western Europe occupied by the Soviets and, in addition, to reach key

[85] Rosenberg, *Toward Armageddon*.
[86] Poole, *History of the JCS . . .*, Vol. IV, 1950–1952, p.170; and Peter L Hahn, *The United States, Great Britain, and Egypt, 1945–1956*, Chapel Hill: University of North Carolina Press, 1991, p.95.

targets such as the Ploesti oil fields in Rumania, and the Donbass industrial region and Moscow. None of the 140 airfields built in Britain during World War Two could yet accommodate the B-29s, but many could be easily and quickly converted. By mid-1947, five airfields had been converted. Four more might swiftly be made operational.[87]

However, the British bases also posed several logistical problems. Weather conditions frequently inhibited flying missions; given that the Soviets were expected to overrun most of Europe, aircraft taking off from Britain would have to expect to overfly hostile, enemy-occupied territory for most of their missions; and most important of all, the B-29s, carrying their normal pay-loads of 10–15,000 pounds, were restricted to an effective maximum flying range of between 1500–2000 miles. This meant that the rich oil-producing area around Baku, and the Soviet industries east of the Ural mountains would be beyond the range of B-29s based in the UK. Finally, the British Isles were expected to hold out against a Soviet offensive for between 45 to 60 days. In contrast, the Cairo–Suez bases were not now expected to fall to the Soviets until from 4 to 6 months after D-day.[88]

Eventually, Allied plans focused on two main air bases in the Middle East, Abu Sueir in Egypt, (for the staging of medium-range bombers) and Dhahran in Saudi Arabia. The negotiations for securing base rights at Dhahran were left to the Americans.[89] The US Navy persisted in its efforts to secure a share in the strategic air offensive. The Navy objected to giving USAF any 'veto power' over the strategic air offensive; and claimed that heavy, land-based bombers 'had reached their practical limit in size and combat radius, compelling the Air Force to plan on one-way flights and unproven refuelling techniques . . .'[90] Apart from Leningrad, every important Soviet target was within range of airfields in Egypt and India. Political difficulties with Egypt raised doubts about Britain's continued tenure of the Egyptian base. Moreover, Abu Sueir still required extensive construction work – runway extensions, and the installation of a new refuelling system for the heavy B-29 bombers. But these were minor problems compared with the strategic advantages offered.

[87] Converse, *United States Plans . . .*, pp.216–17.
[88] Ibid., p.217; and SAC Emergency War Plan, 1–49, 21 Dec., 1948, quoted in Etzold, Gaddis, eds, *Containment . . .*, p.359.
[89] Appendix K to Annex II, JP (49) 126, Defe 6/10, 3 Nov. 1949.
[90] Condit, *History of the JCS . . .*, Vol. 2, pp.178–79.

2 The United States and the Middle East

A. AMERICAN ESTIMATES OF THE SOVIET THREAT TO THE MIDDLE EAST

Allied planners agreed that the Soviets' major objective in a war with the West would be the conquest of Western Europe. But they were also certain that the Soviets would be impelled to undertake a simultaneous conquest of the Middle East. The Soviets would have to attack and occupy those bases close to her borders which posed a threat to those of her own territories and of her satellites vital to her war potential.[1]

The Soviet territories referred to in particular were 'the Caucasian and Ploesti oil fields and the Ukraine and Ural industrial centres'. The Soviets were expected to anticipate, and to try to pre-empt an Allied air offensive against these territories – an offensive designed to deprive the Soviet war machine of its lifeblood. In view of the particular vulnerability of these areas to Allied air attacks from bases in the Middle East, that region must assume the highest priority in Soviet war plans.[2]

A Soviet offensive against the Middle East was expected to advance along two axes; one from the East, through Iran, Iraq, Syria, and through Palestine to Egypt; and a second, from the north-east, through Turkey, then south along the Mediterranean coast, through Syria/Lebanon, and Palestine. The Americans expected the Soviets to attempt to establish airfields along their lines of advance between Turkey and the Suez Canal.

Given Allied, that is British, post-war weakness in the Middle East, it would be of supreme importance to the Soviets to advance rapidly, in order to complete their conquest before the Allies could build up sufficient forces to oppose them. The Soviet offensive would attempt to destroy extant Allied air bases in the Middle East, and to interdict the

[1] Enclosure to Joint Intelligence Committee report, J.I.S. 226/2, 12 Feb. 1946, RG 218 CS 092 USSR (3–27–45) box 153; and JCS 1641/1, 10 March 1946, 'US Security Interests in the Eastern Mediterranean', RG 218, JCS 46–47, CS 092, USSR (3–27–45) section 6, National Archives, Washington DC (hereafter, NA.)

[2] Ibid.

construction of new ones. To achieve this, Soviet armies would have to occupy the Suez Canal and deny the Allies the use of the Persian Gulf.[3]

The British and the Americans agreed essentially on this prognosis. In spring 1949, the COS summarised the objectives of the Soviet Middle East offensive as follows: to give depth to the defence of her southern frontiers; to deny the Allies the use of strategic air bases and oil resources in the Middle East; and to sever Allied sea and air communications that ran through the region, with emphasis on those that passed through Egypt.[4] As might be expected, English and American strategic prognoses about the Middle East were not always in harmony. The British, with their own traditional interests in Africa, feared also that Soviet designs stretched beyond the Middle East – that their strategic goal was to establish in that region a bridgehead from which to launch a campaign for the penetration and conquest of the African continent.[5] Allied strategists also differed on theatre plans for the Middle East. They disagreed over the priority they expected the region to assume in Soviet war plans, and over Soviet prospects of achieving their strategic goals in that theatre.

In 1945, American Planners believed that no major Soviet threat to Europe would develop before 1952. An American Military Intelligence paper, written in December 1945, estimated that the Soviet Union already had the capability to pose a serious threat to, if not actually to occupy all of, western and northern Europe (though not the British Isles), and most of the Near and Middle East (though not the Suez Canal). Even with American aid, the British would be unable to prevent this. By 1952 the British would be unable to avert limited Soviet atomic bombing of their principal urban and industrial centres. (American strategists also forecast that by 1950, the Red Air Force would have the capability of reaching the North American continent.)[6]

In 1945, American planners did not assess the immediate Soviet threat to the Middle East to be as grave as did the British. They expected the Soviets to make considerable progress from the Caucasus, south through the hinterlands of the Middle East. They did not believe that their British ally would be able to prevent a Soviet conquest of the Northern Tier – of Greece, and eventually of most of Turkey. Likewise, Britain might be able to delay, but would not be able ultimately to

    ³ Ibid.
    ⁴ 'Long and Short-term Middle East Strategy', JP (49) 29, 30 March 1949, Defe 6/8; adopted by Chiefs of Staff, in COS (49) 115, 1 April 1949, Defe 5/13; DCC (49) 51, 'Russian and British Interests in the Middle East', 15 June 1949, annex to COS (49) 232, 12 July 1949, in Defe 5/15, pt.1. Public Record Office (hereafter, PRO), London.
    ⁵ Ibid.
    ⁶ JIS 161/6, 17 Dec. 1945, RG 218, Joint Chiefs, CCS 000.1, Gt Britain, section 1, box 608 NA.

check, a Soviet offensive against Iraq – down to Basra and the Persian Gulf.

However, American planners were initially more sanguine about the Soviet threat to the Suez Canal, the ultimate goal of any Soviet attack on the Middle East. The Soviets still lacked significant, modernised naval or amphibious forces. This being the case, the Americans believed that the Soviet land offensive against Egypt would be hampered severely by their need to traverse the deserts of Syria and Iraq, which were lacking completely in all-weather lines of communication. Whatever the route chosen by the Soviets, they would have to reach the Suez Canal via the coastal plain of Palestine, a corridor in which the Soviets would be particularly vulnerable to allied ground, naval and air attacks. It was here, somewhere well to the north of the Suez Canal, that American strategists expected the British to halt the Soviet offensive.[7]

The Americans believed that the key British strategic positions in the Middle East – Palestine and Egypt – would not be susceptible to attacks by the yet-to-be-modernised Red Air Force. Nor were the Soviets capable of any rapid ground offensive. However, the JCS warned against complacency in regard to the future. By 1952, British military strength in the area was expected to have declined considerably, especially in the air. In consequence, the JCS warned that without active American support, the eventual loss of those areas to the USSR would be a distinct possibility.[8]

The Americans' own strategic requirements in the Middle East were narrowed down to buying as much time as possible at the outset of war, during which to launch their opening strategic air offensive from Egypt. Yet during the post-war years, their estimates of the United Kingdom's ability to defend the main base system along the Suez Canal grew progressively more pessimistic. By March 1946, American Intelligence forecast that not only would the British be unable to prevent the Soviet conquest of 'Greece and most of Turkey, including the Dardanelles', or their drive on Basra, in southern Iraq. But they now doubted whether the British could even prevent the Soviets reaching the Suez Canal. In any case, continued British tenure of their Canal base would depend very much upon their ability to come to terms with the Egyptians, an increasingly uncertain prospect.[9]

Soon after the end of World War Two, Palestine became a critical troublespot in the Middle East. By the end of 1945, the British security forces there had been reinforced to 100,000. However, facing a revolt by the Jewish community, they had yet to restore law and order. In

---

[7] Ibid.   [8] Ibid.   [9] J.I.C. 342/2, 27 March 1946, RG 218, box 608. NA.

August1946, with the country in civil turmoil, and its political future still far from clear, an American strategy paper assessed the outcome of a Soviet airborne assault on Palestine. The Americans did not expect the Soviets to attack Palestine during the opening stages of a war, due to the distance between that country and the nearest Soviet air bases in the southern Caucasus and Bulgaria. However, once the Soviets had occupied northern Iraq, as the Americans expected them to do within two to three months, they would be able to airlift some 40,000 troops to Haifa. This Soviet airborne force would be able to hold Haifa for up to 45 days, until joined by reinforcements expected to break through from Turkey via the Lebanon and Syria. American strategists did not believe that the British would be able to pre-empt or hold up Soviet operations.[10]

By mid-1948, the year of crisis in Central Europe, American prognoses about British ability to defend the Middle East on their own had plummeted to their nadir. The JCS believed that the Soviets would be able to conquer Turkey and occupy the Middle East oil lands within one to two months, and the Suez Canal area within four months of the outbreak of war. The JCS believed that this would be the inevitable outcome of a Soviet offensive against the Middle East – unless Britain's allies deployed additional forces in that theatre. But with World War Three expected imminently in Europe, the JCS refused to allot any American forces to the Middle East. To all intents and purposes, the JCS conceded this theatre in advance to the Soviets:

. . . The Joint Chiefs of Staff consider it unrealistic to formulate war plans [for the Middle East] the success of which depend upon the strategic deployment of adequate Allied forces in Mediterranean and Middle East areas prior to the outbreak of war.[11]

B. AMERICAN INTERESTS IN THE MIDDLE EAST

Passing reference has been made already to American interests in the Middle East. These may be summarised as oil, Egypt and Turkey.

Egypt and Turkey were both seen as areas of supreme strategic importance. Each country lay adjacent to, or within flying range of the Soviet Union's vital strategic resources, and across the latter's lines of communication in the event of global war. However, the political status and the military disposition of the Great Powers in Egypt and in

[10] JIS 265/1, 29 Aug. 1946, RG 218, Joint Chiefs, 46–47, CS 092 USSR (3–27–45), box 154. NA.

[11] JCS 1887/1, 19 July 1948, RG 218 Geographic, 1948–50, 381 EMMEA, section 1, box 1, (11–19–47). NA.

Turkey was radically different. The British base in Egypt provided the Allies with a well-established, custom-made strategic facility, under extraterritorial, exclusive British control. In contrast, the allies had no established position in Turkey which, during the recent global conflict, had remained neutral. All contingency planning on Turkey would have to remain on the drawing board, until Congress approved military funding, and until the Turks themselves agreed to an American military presence. No substantial initiatives could be taken until the passage by Congress of the Truman Doctrine, and the concurrent approval of the economic and military aid that went with it, in March 1947.[12]

Thus, during the early period of the Cold War, the United States was dependent particularly upon her British ally for overseas bases. By the autumn of 1946, the two allies had worked out a 'common-user' agreement for their air and sea bases.[13] The British furnished the Americans with a singularly vital strategic asset: air bases from which to launch the strategic air offensive against the Soviets – in England itself, and in Egypt. Therefore, any threat to established British positions in the Near or Middle East, might weaken Britain's position as a Great Power, and would be regarded by the United States as a challenge to its own national security. In this general context the Soviets' post-war refusal to withdraw from Iran, and their demands that the Turks grant them bases at the Straits, were regarded as particularly insidious.

A JCS paper of March 1946, assessed the British position in the Middle East. The paper focused primarily on oil and the British base in Egypt, and reflected American apprehensions about the fortunes of their British ally:

> The two great strategic prizes of the Middle East are oil and the Suez Canal. Control of the Iranian oil fields would materially affect the conduct of military operations in another world war. The British are largely dependent upon Iranian oil, and our own sources of oil are not inexhaustible . . . it would be definitely to Soviet advantage to deny this oil to her enemies. The Suez Canal is one of the most vulnerable points on the British lifeline.[14]

Any disintegration of British power would critically weaken the United States' global disposition. The demise of the British Empire

---

[12] For the thesis that American strategic planning viz. Turkey was the major motive that lay behind the issue of the Truman Doctrine, cf. Melvyn P. Leffler, 'Strategy, Diplomacy, and the Cold War: The United States, Turkey, and NATO, 1945–1952', *The Journal of American History*, Vol. 71/4, March 1985, pp.807–25.

[13] David Devereux, *The Formulation of British Defence Policy Towards the Middle East, 1948–1956*, London: Macmillan, 1990, p.12.

[14] 'United States Security Interests in the Eastern Mediterranean', JCS 1641/1, 10 March 1946, CS092, USSR (3–27–45) sect. 6, RG 218 JCS 46–47. NA.

'would eliminate from Eurasia the last bulwark of resistance between the United States and Soviet expansion'. Should that occur, the strength of the United States, combined with the military potential of her ideological allies might prove insufficient to withstand that of the Soviet Union and her satellites.[15] Therefore, the JCS concluded that even if Soviet demands from the Turks for rights at the Straits did not present any direct threat to American national security, American acquiescence, even to some of those demands, would be detrimental to the American national interest. Such demands, if conceded, would weaken the British position as a Great Power, consequently reducing the effectiveness of the United Nations.[16]

But the Soviets did not constitute the only threat to British hegemony in the Middle East. Britain's position in the region was also jeopardised by indigenous nationalist fervour and, perhaps above all, by her post-war decline as a world power. This decline was demonstrated, more than anything, by her economic collapse at the end of World War Two. An intelligence estimate written for the JCS in mid-1946, suggested that the burgeoning nationalist movements in the Middle East were taking advantage of, and feeding from Britain's own increasingly apparent weakness.[17]

The same intelligence report estimated that in the event of a British withdrawal from the Middle East, all native régimes of the area would be compelled to take renewed stock of the global power balance, in order to determine their own future political and military alignments. American prestige in the region was bound up increasingly with that of the British. However, if the United States acted wisely, she might even benefit from the British demise. If British withdrawal of armed forces were to be accompanied by strong, consistent, constructive US aid, it was believed that US prestige in the Middle East would be greatly increased and this would be accompanied by a very useful increase in the opportunities for American participation in the economic developments of the whole area involved.[18]

As Britain's global position deteriorated, American strategists had to consider what they could do either to prop up or to take the place of, Britain in the Middle East. A protracted debate was conducted between the State and Defense departments about the ability of the United States to support the British military effort in the Middle East (for this

[15]   Ibid.

[16]   Ibid.

[17]   For this and following, see Memorandum for the Chief of the Strategic Policy Section, 'Intelligence study on the possible effects of British withdrawal from the Middle East', 7 May 1946, RG 319 (Army Staff), 092, 1946–48. NA.

[18]   Ibid.

debate, see below, Chapter 8). The State Department alleged that Defense's arguments against an American military contribution in the Middle East were moved by two tactical considerations. First, by the hope that if the United States declined to fight in the Middle East, the British would exert themselves more than would be the case if they knew they could rely on American support. Second, State suspected that Defense's position was biased also by considerations of inter-Service rivalry. If priority was given to the Middle East, it would have a substantial affect on interservice competition for military appropriations. If the Middle East was given a higher priority, and US ground forces committed to its defence, the Navy would have to be given substantial funds to obtain 'very considerable equipment and facilities to supply and defend the sea and air lanes on which such ground forces would be dependent'. Any increase in the Navy's appropriations would have to come at the expense of those budgeted for her rival services.[19]

(i) Oil

The debate among American planners on theatre priorities was also influenced by assessments of peace and wartime needs for Middle Eastern oil. Even if the United States could meet all her own peacetime needs for oil, there was considerable anxiety over how long her own domestic reserves would last. At the end of 1946, a Pentagon report claimed that the total estimated oil reserves of the Middle East were between 20.5 to 50.5 billion barrels. This compared with proven American reserves of 21.5 billion barrels.[20]

It was expected that, in war, the Soviets would attempt to prevent Western use of Middle Eastern oil. If that oil could be proved to be essential to the West for the prosecution of the war, then American strategists would have to make plans, and to allocate forces for defending the Middle Eastern oil fields. Otherwise, American resources might be devoted exclusively to the defence of Europe, and the Middle East could be designated an exclusively-British theatre of operations. It was therefore no coincidence that the Army, which claimed consistently that they would not need (or in any case would have no access to) Middle Eastern oil during hostilities, argued that the United States

[19] Undated paper (probably Dec. 1950, identity of author not given), 'Re-Evaluation of US Plans for the Middle East', annex I to McGhee–Acheson, 27 Dec. 1950, *Foreign Relations of the United States* (hereafter *FRUS*), 1951, Vol. V, pp.10–11.

[20] Cf. Steven L. Rearden, *History of the Office of the Secretary of Defense: The Formative Years, 1947–95*, Washington: Historical Office of the Secretary of Defense, 1984, p.55.

could not afford to divert its limited resources to the Middle East. And predictably, the US Navy, which saw the Middle East as a possible theatre of operations, was as consistent in advocating the need for Middle Eastern oil.

Initial war plans assumed that all of Western Europe would be over-run by the Soviets and, consequently, that the European allies would have low military requirements for oil. However, the economic recovery of Europe – upon which depended its political, economic and social stability, and therefore its ability to withstand the allure of communism – was predicated upon ready and continued access to Middle Eastern oil.

The first Arab–Israeli war, and the risk that it might engulf the entire region, provoked a reassessment of American interests in the region. A brief for the JCS emphasised the critical importance of not antagonising the Arabs, and with them, perhaps the entire Moslem world. The JCS were advised that the Western allies would be unable to pursue their economic recovery if the oil of the Middle East was cut off. In the event of war, without access to Middle Eastern oil, America's European allies would be unable to fight for more than 18–24 months – unless they were to confine themselves to a defence of the Western hemi-sphere.[21]

But in any case, the crises which engulfed Central Europe in the spring and summer of 1948 demanded the first attentions of American planners. It has been argued that these crises left US Naval officers alone in their advocacy of measures to ensure American control of the Middle Eastern oil fields in wartime.[22] This may have been so, but, as will be seen below, by 1950 the State Department supported the Navy with arguments of its own.

The JCS did not believe that the Allies would be able to defend any territories in the Middle East outside of Egypt. A JCS brief drafted at the end of 1948 planned therefore to 'neutralise' enemy (the Soviets and their satellites) oil production in the region by 'air attack, airborne raids, and sabotage . . .'. In any case, even if the Allies did manage to hold on to the Middle East, they would be unable to exploit the region's oil, until they had achieved overwhelming superiority in the air.[23] In other words, whichever country controlled the Middle East oil fields

[21] For this and following, cf. Brief for JCS on 'Future Situation in Palestine and effects on the Middle East', 25 May 1948, RG 360, Secretary of Defense, CD 6–2–47, box 22. NA.

[22] David Alan Rosenberg, 'The U.S. Navy and the Problem of Oil in a Future War: The Outline of a Strategic Dilemma, 1945–1950, *Naval War College Review*, 29, summer, 1976, Vol. 1, p.57.

[23] JCS planning brief of 16 Dec. 1948, as amended on 28 March 1949, cited in T.H. Etzold and J.L. Gaddis, eds, *Containment: Documents on American Policy and Strategy, 1945–1950*, New York: Columbia University Press, 1978, p.353.

in wartime, would be unable to exploit them, due to hostile aerial bombardment.[24]

In 1949, the Navy challenged the Army's assumptions. They pointed out that updated war plans provided for the holding of limited parts of the European continent; and that previous estimates of oil requirements had taken no account either of the sinking of oil tankers, or of the fact that the non-availability of oil from the Middle East would result in the exhaustion of American oil reserves during the course of a long war.[25] In refutation of the Navy's claims, Army Planners pointed out that significant new oil reserves had been discovered recently in the Western Hemisphere. These might rival the size of the East Texas oil fields. And even under current planning, the Allies would still be able to utilise Middle Eastern oil, until a definite Soviet threat to the oil fields materialised.[26]

The State Department, which from the end of 1950 began to press the JCS for at least a token commitment to the Middle East, weighed in with its arguments. First, if the United States were to fight a prolonged war solely on its own domestic oil reserves, they would deplete the fields so much that after the war it would be difficult, perhaps even impossible, to resume normal production. Second, if the United States left the British to stage a token defence of the Middle East alone, while they (the Americans) sabotaged the oil fields of Saudi Arabia, and then withdrew without firing a shot, the political reactions of the Arabs would be devastating. Following such a war, the Americans might not be welcomed back into the region. In consequence, the British would gain a 'strong commercial and political advantage' with the Arab world, and it would prove difficult for the Americans to gain re-entry:

> The peoples we plan to abandon in war are the same peoples we must continue to work with upon liberation and in the post-war period, when access to local resources and facilities would have to be re-negotiated in an adverse atmosphere.[27]

---

[24] JSPC report to JCS, 17 Nov. 1948, 381 TS Case 121/108, RG 319 (Army Staff) 46–48, NA; and meeting of George McGhee with B.A. Burrows (Counsellor, British Embassy, Washington), 24 Oct. 1950, *FRUS*, 1950, Vol. V, p.233.

[25] Memorandum by Col. John S. Guthrie, GSC Exec, Plans and Operations, 6 June 1949, P and O, 463, ME Case 10, RG 319 49–50. NA.

[26] Memo by Col A.G. Viney, Director of Logistics, Assistant Chief Plans Office, to Director of Plans and Operations, 8 June 1949, P & O, 49–50, 463 ME 10/3, RG 319. NA.

[27] Undated memorandum, *FRUS*, 1951, V, pp.10–11, supra.

(ii) Egypt

By mid-1948, American strategists drew pessimistic scenarios about the outcome of a future war with the Soviets. All American resources would have to be devoted to the defence, or reconquest of Western Europe.

However, the Middle East remained an area of critical importance for American interests. The all-important opening strategic air offensive was to be launched from air bases in England and the Middle East. As noted already, air bases in Egypt were expected to hold out for longer than those in the UK.[28]

Thus, even if American planners were unwilling to deploy American ground forces in the Middle East, they did plan on deploying B-29 bombers in Egypt, and hoped that British forces in the Middle East would keep Soviet forces sufficiently distant from the Suez Canal to permit the achievement of the main goals of the strategic air offensive.

As noted, the targets of the strategic air offensive were Soviet petroleum refining complexes and industrial conglomerates, in the Ukraine, south central USSR, and the Ploesti oil fields in Rumania. All three major oil production areas, Baku, the Caucasus and Rumania, lay within bombing range of air bases in Egypt.

This was thought to be understood just as well by the generals in Moscow, as by those in London and Washington. As stated succinctly by Gen Lauris Norstad, head of USAF, in a speech to officers of the RAF and the Royal Canadian Air Force (RCAF), in January 1948:

> If we were to maintain close-in bases from which to reach and destroy the enemy's military strength, we could confidently expect that against such bases our opponent would direct every possible element of his strength to dislodge us.[29]

A JCS study of March 1946 acknowledged that Soviet pressure on the Middle East was motivated by the desire to defend their own vital oil-producing areas. In June 1946, a British Military Intelligence report pointed to Soviet efforts to move their industries eastwards, 'to safeguard the Caucasian oil fields, and to protect the development of Soviet resources from prospective attack'. At the end of the year, American planners stressed that Soviet war designs against the Eastern Mediterranean and the Persian Gulf were motivated primarily by their desire to eliminate as many 'enemy air, sea and ground offensive bases'

[28] Peter L. Hahn, *The United States, Great Britain, and Egypt, 1945–1956*, Chapel Hill: University of North Carolina Press, 1991, pp.74–5.

[29] Speech by Gen Lauris Norstad, 24 Jan. 1948, Norstad papers, speeches, 1948 (1), box 26, The Eisenhower Library (hereafter EL).

as possible. The occupation of these areas would give the Soviets greater defence-in-depth for their strategically vital industrial areas in the south.[30]

In this context, Soviet intentions against the Middle East could in fact be read as defensive. However, this did not allay Allied anxieties about a Soviet offensive against the Middle East. Cold War military planning became tied up in a vicious circle, and developed its own 'chicken-and-egg', iron logic. On the one hand, Western planners understood that the Soviets would read their own intentions accurately, and be forced to adopt defensive, perhaps even pre-emptive measures. But on the other hand, they could not afford, in order to allay Soviet apprehensions, to abandon their own plans for building strategic air bases in Egypt!

In order to carry out the strategic air offensive, a number of airfields in the Middle East would have to be developed further, in order to accommodate the B-29s. At least one of these bases would have to be 'within range of all likely major targets and at the same time, be capable of development to the required standards within a short time.' In addition, Egypt would be required to serve also as a logistic base from which to deploy allied forces to hold up an anticipated Soviet land offensive against the Middle East. In the event of Soviet successes, Egypt would also serve as the base from which the Allies would attempt to reconquer the region, with its oil reserves.[31]

American planners hoped to be able to block the Soviet offensive on the coastal plain of Palestine*, before it reached the Egyptian bases. By this very same reasoning, alternative air bases in Palestine or in Iraq, were eventually ruled out as being too close to the Soviet border, and therefore too vulnerable to the expected Soviet offensive.[32]

The Americans regarded the defence of the strategic base in Egypt as problematical. The Suez Canal zone would be the prime target of the anticipated Soviet offensive against the Middle East. American

---

* The term 'Palestine' has been used throughout to denote the territory held under British mandate until 1948. Strategic planners employed this designation even after the UN Partition Resolution of Nov. 1947, and the Arab–Israeli war of 1948. That war resulted in the partition of Mandatory Palestine between the new state of Israel, and the Kingdom of Jordan, which annexed and ruled Palestine's West Bank until 1967.

[30] Cf. Melvyn P. Leffler, "Strategy, Diplomacy, and the Cold War: The United States, Turkey and NATO, 1945–1952', *The Journal of American History*, Vol. 71/4, 1985, p.813.

[31] General Hollis to the Minister of Defence, 30 Sept. 1948, appendix to COS (48) 138th meeting. PRO; Staff studies of certain Military Problems deriving from Concept of Operations for *Pincher*, 13 April 1946, JPS 789/1, RG 218 CCS 381 USSR (2 March 1946), sect. 1; and JSPC 883/1, 12 July 1948, RG 218 US Joint Chiefs, Geographic File, 48–50, box 17. NA.

[32] Hahn, *The United States* . . . pp.26–8.

planners expected the British to deploy all the forces they could spare from the defence of the British Isles for the defence of Egypt. But they appreciated that the United States would also be required to allocate forces to the defence of that country. In addition to the B-29s and their teams, the Americans would have to provide fighter planes for escort missions, and for the defence of the Egyptian bases themselves. The Americans hoped that the combined Allied forces would be able to hold up the Soviet offensive on the Palestine side of the Sinai desert border. However, the possibility was also taken into account that the Soviets might overrun Allied positions and reach the Canal itself. In that event, the Allies would be forced to use Benghazi in Tripoli as their main air base, and Cyprus and Crete, if available, as staging points.[33] But American strategists concurred with their British counterparts on the vital need to retain 'certain strategic facilities in Egypt during peacetime and rights of re-entry to make full use of these facilities in the event of a threat to the security of the Middle East'.[34]

In 1946, the 'Outline Air Plan for *Makefast*' allocated six B-29 bomber groups for the strategic air offensive against the Soviet Union. They would take off from bases in England, and the Cairo area. This force was expected to destroy 70–80% of the Soviet Union's petroleum production capacity, within the first nine months of the war. After taking into account Soviet reserves, it was estimated that the Soviet army and air force would grind to a halt by the end of the first year of war.[35]

Makefast compared the accessibility of major Soviet strategic targets from air bases in England (Mildenhall) and Egypt (Abu Sueir, in the Cairo area). The study illustrated vividly the geographical advantages of the Cairo area, especially in respect of shorter-range targets, i.e., those within a 1500 mile radius (see details in next chapter).

However, notwithstanding the importance assigned to the Middle East by the JCS, the Americans never contemplated taking over from the ever-weakening British in the region. In April 1947, a JCS paper stressed the limits of American power, and the consequent need to establish priorities between 'areas of peripheral and vital importance to US security'.[36]

It has been suggested that this JCS paper, coming just one month

[33] Staff Studies of certain Military Problems deriving from Concept of Operations for *Pincher*, JPS 789/1, 13 April 1946, RG 218. CCS 381 USSR (2 March 1946), sect. 1. NA.

[34] Brief for Anglo-American staff talks, 24 March 1948, P and O 092, FW 117/2, box 33, RG 319 (army staff). NA.

[35] Brief of Outline Air Plan *Makefast*, signed by R.W.P., 26 Oct. 1946, RG 165. ABC 381 U.S.S.R. (2 March 1946) sect. 3. NA.

[36] JCS 1769/1, 29 April 1947, quoted in Etzold, Gaddis, *Containment*, p.71.

after the Truman Doctrine, appears to confirm that Truman's speech 'was more a rhetorical flourish designed to persuade a parsimonious Congress to approve aid to Greece and Turkey than the blueprint for globalism it appeared to be on the surface'. However, as has been noted, the JCS still regarded the Abu Sueir air base as vital. And, as will be seen below, the JCS also had their own strategic plans for Turkey, plans that were not disclosed to the Congress, but which needed financing that required the approval of that body.[37]

The Pentagon talks held between the British and the Americans in November 1947, resulted in a consensus on the strategic importance of the Middle East. However, the talks also reiterated the 'special responsibility' held by the British for the defence of the area. Egyptian demands for British withdrawal from their bases along the Canal, tabled before the United Nations Security Council since the previous July, were not at issue, and were *not* discussed.[38]

A PPS paper of February 1948, reiterated the view that the security of the Middle East was vital to the American national interest. However, the United States refused to divert any resources to 'duplicate or to take over' those strategic facilities in the region held by the British. Those facilities would in any case be available to the Americans in the event of war. Any attempt to have them transferred formally to American control would not only probably raise 'a host of new and unnecessary problems', but would likely prove unsuccessful.[39]

It needs to be stressed that the lowering of the Middle East's 'strategic profile', was due more to overstretched resources, which dictated harsh choices between priorities, than to indifference or apathy to the region. To the contrary, events in the Middle East during 1947–48 had attracted the closest attention of American planners, and of the State Department – not to mention the Truman White House.

In Palestine, civil war had erupted on the morrow of the UN Partition Resolution of November 1947. It was feared that a general conflict in the Middle East would inexorably draw in the Soviets, and thus open up a 'second front' in that theatre, in addition to Europe. War in Palestine would pose a direct threat to the British base in Egypt. This fear appeared to materialise in May 1948 when, with the end of the British Mandate, five Arab states invaded Palestine, and when in December 1948, the Israeli army crossed into Egyptian territory. On that occasion, President Truman himself, at British behest, issued an

[37] Ibid; and Leffler, 'Strategy, Diplomacy, and the Cold War . . .'

[38] Geoffrey Aronson, *From Sideshow to Center Stage: U.S. Policy Toward Egypt, 1946–1956*, Boulder, CO: Lynne Rienner, 1986, p.7.

[39] PPS/23, 24 Feb. 1948, in *FRUS*, 1948, Vol. V, part 2, Washington DC: U.S. Government Printing Office, 1976, pp.655–7.

ultimatum to the Israelis to withdraw forthwith.[40] (see below, Chapter four.) But Truman's stern warning to Israel was an exceptional, albeit not a unique action. The State Department feared that overt American support (emanating primarily from the White House) for Zionism would alienate not only the Arabs, but the entire Moslem world as well.[41]

A JCS brief warned that if the Allies lost the friendship and respect of the Moslem world, they would forfeit any chance of retaining a foothold in the Middle East – 'the gateway into Africa and a center of air, sea and land communications'. In that event, Turkey would be isolated, and the Americans might also lose their Middle East oil concessions. The JCS stressed:

> If we antagonise the Mohammedan World, we shall not only be unable to obtain the facilities for this base which we require in Egypt but we shall be unable to get facilities in Pakistan (the Eastern alternative) or to obtain a workable trusteeship in Cyrenaica (the Western alternative).[42]

But the war in Palestine was not the only problem that soured relations between the Atlantic allies, and complicated joint strategic planning. Britain's inability to appease Egyptian nationalist forces and to reach agreement on a renewed tenure of the Canal Base, posed harsh dilemmas for American diplomats and strategists.

The Americans were torn between their need for Britain's strategic infrastructure in the Middle East, and their desire not to alienate the Arab world. This meant that they had to do everything possibly to maintain and support the British position in the region, short of making that support public.

A meeting of US Middle Eastern Chiefs of Mission, together with senior State Department officials, and Admiral Robert Carney, commander-in-chief, US Naval Forces, East Atlantic and Mediterranean (CINCELM), which convened in Istanbul in February 1951, concluded:

> It is in the United States' interest that the United Kingdom position be maintained in the Middle East, and strengthened where it serves our interest. This is particularly true with respect to Egypt.[43]

[40] Cf. Michael J. Cohen, *Truman and Israel*, Berkeley: University of California Press, 1990, pp.264–6.

[41] On the Truman White House's support for Zionism, cf. ibid., ch. 5.

[42] Brief for JCS on 'Future Situation in Palestine and its Effects on the Middle East', 25 May 1948, RG 360, Secretary of Defense, CD 6–2–47, box 22. NA.

[43] Record of meeting of Chiefs of Middle Eastern Mission, with Adm Robert Carney and George McGhee, 14–21 Feb. 1951, in *FRUS*, 1951, Vol. V, pp.50–76. The quote is from p.60.

But, on the other hand, they tried to avoid becoming tied so closely to the British as to become tarnished with the latter's colonialist brush. While it was recognised that any erosion of the British position in the Middle East would harm American strategic interests, the United States had no intention of supporting the British at all costs. American support would cease in the event that, as the PPS put it, the British either got themselves 'into a false position', or if American support threatened to incur 'extravagant political committments'.[44]

In 1949, the JCS supported the British in their goal of wresting base concessions from the Egyptians. But they insisted that Anglo–Egyptian negotiations for base rights be 'confined to Anglo–Egyptian interests in the defence of Egypt itself', and that no mention be made of the role to be played by the United States in strategic or military planning concerning the Middle East. The Americans rebuffed all British efforts to involve them in their base negotiations with the Egyptians. The USAF Chief of Staff insisted that the British say nothing about American strategic plans for Abu Sueir.[45]

But by 1948, the Americans had already begun to have their doubts about the projected strategic air base at Abu Sueir, not least because of the political instability of Egypt, and the protracted dispute over British base rights. They had also become increasingly anxious about the vulnerability of the Suez Base to Soviet air attack. The demands upon USAF imposed by the Berlin airlift had reduced the number of aircraft that would now be available for the Middle East theatre. In November 1948, the Joint Strategic Plans committee (JSPC) reported to the JCS:

> the overwhelming superiority in numbers of Russian aircraft than can be brought to bear against the Cairo–Suez bases requires a more rapid build up of air defence forces in this area than now provided in J.C.S. 1844/4.[46]

The JSPC recommended the revision of *Fleetwood*, to include the aspiration to secure a 'base area to the westward of the Cairo–Suez area to which our forces could withdraw and maintain a foothold in Northwest Africa.'[47] This was one of the earliest origins of the switch in American strategic thinking from the eastern, to the western Mediterranean, and presumably influenced Gen Eisenhower, when he took

---

[44] PPS/23, 24 Feb. 1948, *FRUS*, 1948, supra.

[45] Memorandum by Chief of Staff, USAF, 5 May 1949 (approved by the JCS on 11 May 1949), *FRUS*, 1949, Vol. VI, p.219; and Hahn, *The United States . . .*, p.80.

[46] JSPC report to JCS, 17 Nov. 1948, 381 TS Case 121/108, RG 319 (Army Staff) 46–48. NA.

[47] Note by W. G. Lalor, US Navy, secretary to JSPC, 13 Oct. 1948, P and O, 1946–48, 381, sect. VIII-A, TS case 121/100, RG 319 (Army Staff) 46–48. NA.

the temporary post of 'presiding officer' of the JCS, in February 1949 (see above, p.24).

Plans *Frolic* and *Grabber* assumed the loss of the Mediterranean and the Middle East. Instead of the base at Abu Sueir, the new plans proposed an alternative strategic air base near Karachi, Pakistan, and a major base in the Casablanca – Port Lyautey area, Morocco. However, due to the implications of the abandonment of the Mediterranean, and to the political and military problems involved with acquiring the proposed Karachi base, *Frolic* was never approved by the JCS.[48] One version of *Grabber* provided for the withdrawal of all American troops from the Middle East. They were to be held as a strategic reserve, to retake that region, in a campaign planned for the second year of the war.[49]

By the crisis summer of 1948, the JCS had concluded that it would be 'unrealistic' to draft any war plans 'the success of which depended upon the strategic deployment of adequate Allied forces in the Mediterranean and Middle East prior to the outbreak of war.' American planners assigned two roles to their own forces in the Middle East: to launch from Egypt the opening strategic air strike against the Soviets, before the latter overran the region; and to sabotage the region's oil resources, to prevent them falling into Soviet hands. To this end, plan *Halfmoon* provided for the deployment of a group of B-29s in Egypt, and a battalion of US Marines at Bahrain.[50]

At the American–British–Canadian (ABC) planners conference of October 1948, there arose differences over Allied strategic priorities in the event of global war. It was agreed that first priority would be given to protecting the UK. But whereas the Americans now accorded second priority to 'the Western Mediterranean – North African area', including Tunisia, the British accorded second priority to 'the Eastern Mediterranean Middle East area'.[51]

However, notwithstanding the JCS ruling that no American forces could be committed to the Middle East, American planners none the less drafted various plans for the deployment of forces in that theatre – for the contingency that they might ultimately become available. The

[48] JCS 1887/1, 19 July 1948, RG 218 Geographic, 1948–50, 381 EMMEA, sect. 1, box 1 (11–19–47), NA; and Rosenberg, 'The U.S. Navy and the Problem of Oil in a Future War: The Outline of a Strategic Dilemma, 1945–1950', *Naval War College Review*, Vol. 29, summer 1976, p.58.

[49] On *Grabber*, cf. Gregg Herken, *The Winning Weapon: The Atomic Bomb in the Cold War, 1945–1950*, Princeton: Princeton University Press, 1981, pp.248, 382, fn. 37.

[50] JCS 1887/1, 19 July 1948, RG 218 Geographic, 1948–50, 381 EMMEA sect. 1, box 1, (11–19–47), NA; cf. also Devereux, T*he Formulation of British Defence Policy . . .*, pp.22–3.

[51] Joint memorandum by ABC planners, ABC 109, JSPC 757/68, 29 Nov. 1948, 384 TS Case 7/26, box 255, RG 319 P & O, 49–50. NA.

planners were concerned particularly with guaranteeing the safety of the B-29 strategic bombers which, even if not ultimately stationed at Abu Sueir, might still need to stage through there on their return journeys.[52]

In October 1948, with the Berlin blockade crisis at its height, and the Arab–Israeli war still raging, one revise of plan *Fleetwood* allocated extra USAF fighter aircraft to the Cairo area, in order to meet the defence requirements of Abu Sueir. The planners recommended that if the British could not be persuaded to supply the necessary ground forces to defend the Cairo area, shore-based US Marine, or US Navy air units should be deployed for this task. This was proposed in the knowledge that these units would have to be drawn from the US Navy carrier task force charged with securing the Mediterranean Sea.[53]

The mission of the shore-based fighter units would be to defend the skies above the army and air force bases, and to provide air defences and tactical support for the Allied ground forces. In addition, the Americans would deploy a reinforced Marine battalion from the Mediterranean to the Bahrain area, in order to help in the anticipated evacuation of American nationals, and to sabotage the oil installations, to prevent their exploitation by the Soviets.[54]

Dropshot, an American plan circulated in January 1949, for a possible war against the Soviets in 1957, specified that two USAF bomber groups, some 95 aircraft, would strike the Soviet Union from Egyptian bases. By 1957, the British were also expected to have the new V-Bombers deployed in Egypt, to augment the strategic air offensive against the Soviets from the Cairo–Suez area.[55] A further American contingency plan for the Egyptian theatre, dated February 1949, detailed the timetable for a build-up of American forces in the Middle East in the event of a Soviet offensive. The mission of the American Egyptian command would be the defence of the Cairo–Suez area 'from positions east of Suez, between the Canal and the Acre – Sea of Galilee line . . .'[56]

Upon the outbreak of hostilities, US troops would be deployed for the defence of Abu Sueir, and a Marine task force would be landed in Egypt. The Marines' initial task would be to secure the American naval

[52] Ibid.

[53] JCS 1844/13, Recommended revisions of *Fleetwood*, 2 Oct. 1948, RG 319 (Army Staff), 1946–48, 381 TS Case 121/113. NA.

[54] Ibid, and JSPC 883/1, 12 July 1948, RG 218 US Joint Chiefs, Geographic File, 1948–50, box 17. NA.

[55] Plan *Dropshot*, JCS 1920/5, 381 USSR (3-2-46) Bulky Package #3, U.S. Joint Chiefs of Staff, 1948–50, Geographic File, RG 218. NA. See also Anthony C. Brown, *Dropshot: The American Plan for World War III with Russia in 1957*, New York: The Dial Press, 1957.

[56] Memorandum by Major General Maddocks, on 'US Army and Egyptian Theater', 15 Feb. 1949, RG 319 (army staff) P and O, 4950, 381 TR, TS, Case 8/2. NA.

bases in Egypt and, after the first week, to move to the Haifa area. They would establish at Haifa a forward defence for the Cairo–Suez area. An American airborne task force would disembark at Suez at about 40 days after the outbreak of war; its mission would be to secure American air bases in the Cairo–Suez area against ground and air attack, and to provide anti-aircraft defences for disembarking infantry divisions. One infantry division would be landed at Suez at about D + 70, and take command of all American forces by D + three months.[57]

This theatre plan dovetailed in neatly with *Sandown*, the British Middle East theatre plan, drafted during the summer of 1948 by the British Commanders, Middle East (see below, Chapter 4). But the JCS never approved their planners' theatre contingency plans for the Middle East. The US Military had never been very happy with their own dispositions in the Middle East – due to the vulnerability of the sea lanes flowing into that region. As intelligence assessments of the Soviet threat to the area grew more optimistic during the course of 1949, American priorities switched from the Middle East to building up a new base in French North Africa.[58]

In October 1949, at the ABC planners' conference in Washington, the JCS informed their allies that their strategy for a global emergency had changed. They announced that they would build up a new base in North West Africa, in the Casablanca area. Their intention would be to hold all or a part of Spain.[59]

The Middle East was now relegated to third priority in the Americans' plans for global war. Their first priority remained the protection of Great Britain; but their second priority was now the 'maintenance of Allied control of the Western Mediterranean–North African area.' They believed that they should endeavour to retain a foothold in Europe, so as to avoid having to launch an amphibious assault, as had been the case in 1944.[60]

The new base would support operations in the Iberian Peninsula, which would, at best, establish a line up to the Pyrenees. Or failing this, at least establish a line in southern Spain that would secure the western

[57] Ibid.

[58] Eric Grove and Geoffrey Till, 'Anglo-American Maritime Strategy in the Era of Massive Retaliation, 1945–60', in John B. Hattendorf, Robert S. Jordan, eds, *Maritime Strategy and the Balance of Power: Britain and America in the Twentieth Century*, London: Macmillan, 1989, p.276.

[59] Cf David Rosenberg, 'The U.S. Navy and the Problem of Oil in a Future War: The Outline of a Strategic Dilemma, 1945–1950', *Naval War College Review*, 21, summer, 1976, Vol.1, pp.58–9.

[60] For this and the following, see minutes of meeting between JCS and Air Marshal Tedder, 5 Oct. 1949, CCS 337, (72248) S.1, RG 218, 1948–50. NA; also annex to JP (49) 126 (Final), 3 Nov. 1949, Defe 4/26; and annex to COS (51) 686, 28 Nov. 1951, Plan *Cinderella*, in Defe 5/35. PRO.

approach to the Mediterranean. It was hoped that this would neutralise other Soviet threats to north Africa and to the Western Mediterranean, and eventually facilitate a land reconquest of Western Europe. As third priority, the north-west African base might support forces operating in the Eastern Mediterranean–Cairo–Suez area.[61]

Consequently, the Americans now switched the forces they had ear-marked previously for the Middle East to north-west Africa. The British thereby 'lost' three and one-third divisions and 350 tactical aircraft that the Americans had previously committed to the Middle East theatre.[62]

The JCS continued to insist that the Middle East remain an area of 'sole British responsibility', to be defended, at least initially, only with whatever forces the British and the Commonwealth could muster. The American role would consist of aid in keeping open British lines of communication through the Mediterranean, and of delaying, as far as possible, any Soviet advance through Turkey, Iraq and Syria.[63]

The Americans pressed the British to persist in their commitment to the Middle East theatre, which they, the Americans, continued to regard as a high priority. But without American military engagement, the 'plat-form' for the strategic air offensive was left perilously vulnerable.[64]

The Americans' change in strategic priorities was incorporated in a new plan, *Offtackle* (the successor to *Fleetwood*), which was approved by the JCS on 8 November, 1949. *Offtackle* confirmed the downgrading of the Middle East in American priorities. The Navy's role in the Medi-terranean was restricted severely, due to a reduction in the number of carriers it was to be allowed to build under the new austerity defence budget. The defence of the Middle East oil fields would depend on what forces could be spared at the time from other theatres.[65]

The British counterpart was eventually codenamed *Galloper*. Differences over the American withdrawal from the Eastern Medi-terranean led to a delay of several months, before the British JPS finally recommended *Galloper* for the approval of the COS.[66] The commitment of American forces to a Middle East campaign would remain an acute bone of contention between the Americans and the British until 1952, by which time the British themselves had decided to evacuate the major part of their own forces out of the region.

[61] Annex to COS (51) 686, and annex 1 to JP (49) 126, ibid.

[62] Annex to COS (51) 686, ibid.

[63] Enclosure to JSPC 757/63, 11 Oct. 1949, RG 319 P and O, 1949–50, 384 TS Case 7/22, box 255, NA; and JP (49) 133, 14 Oct. 1949, Defe 6/11. PRO.

[64] Cf. Richard J. Aldrich, John Zametica, 'The Rise and Decline of a Strategic Concept: the Middle East, 1945–51', in Richard J. Aldrich, ed., *British Intelligence, Strategy and the Cold War, 1945–51*, London/New York: Routledge, 1992.

[65] Herken, *The Winning Weapon*, p.296.

[66] Grove and Till, 'Anglo-American Maritime Strategy . . .', p.276

None the less, the new American CINCELM, Admiral Richard Connolly, continued extensive theatre planning with British defence officials. His talks focused mainly on protective measures for the British base in Egypt. Connolly pleaded with Washington for additional fighter planes, to be used for the interdiction of the Soviet communications and transport system. This would slow down the advance of Soviet land forces, thereby affording valuable time to carry out the strategic bombing offensive. Connolly pleaded for extra funding to develop suitable airfields, for the expansion of radar facilities, the storage of aviation gas, and the stockpiling of essential military stores and equipment.[67] But his pleas remained largely unanswered.

(iii) Turkey

Historically, the Straits (the Dardanelles and the Bosphorus), which linked the Black Sea with the Mediterranean, has always been a key strategic waterway. Consequently, Turkey's friendship and alliance had been a much sought-after asset. In World War One, the Ottoman Empire had sided with the Germans, and together with them, had paid a substantial territorial price for losing the war. The Ottoman Empire was deprived of its non-Turkish minorities, and modern Turkey, under the leadership of Kemal Atatürk, appeared on the world stage. In the Second World War the Turks had contrived to remain neutral.

The Turks had always feared their Russian neighbour, with its historic strategic *desiderata* of an all-year-round, 'warm-water' sea passage from the Black Sea to the Mediterranean. At the end of World War Two, Soviet demands for bases on the Straits appeared to indicate a resurgence of Czarist Russian expansionism to the south west.

In June 1945, the Soviets demanded of the Turks cession of the provinces of Kars and Ardahan in Eastern Turkey, joint defence of the Straits, (which would require Soviet bases), and a complete revision of the Montreux Convention (1936) governing navigation through the Straits. In early March 1946, there arrived in Washington ominous intelligence reports of Soviet troop concentrations and war preparations in the Balkans. (In the same month, Soviet forces were advancing on Tehran, to enforce their demands for oil concessions in northern Iran).[68]

The Turkish (and to a lesser extent, the Iranian) crises of 1945–

---

[67] Ibid.

[68] Cf. Plan *Griddle*, J.W.P.C. 467/1, 15 Aug., 1946, 381 Turkey (15 Aug 46) (new case), NA; and Schnabel, *History of the JCS* . . ., Vol. 1, pp.57, 108; and Eduard Mark, 'The War Scare of 1946 and its Consequences', *Diplomatic History*, p.6. (forthcoming – I thank Dr Mark for showing me his article in draft form).

46 alerted American planners to the Soviet threat along the Northern Tier of the Near and Middle East, and focused their attention on the strategic importance of those theatres as international intersections of air and sea routes.[69]

Until the spring of 1946, American planners had paid scant attention to the Middle-Eastern theatre. While the United States had considerable oil concessions in Saudia Arabia, the Middle East itself was not defined as a vital national interest, and there were no American plans to defend the region. Following the intelligence reports on Soviet war preparations against Turkey in early March 1946, Secretary of State Byrnes asked the JCS for an appraisal of the situation in Turkey.[70]

Beyond the regional aspect of the Soviet–Turkish crisis, Soviet pressure on Turkey was regarded by the Americans as an indirect threat to the British Empire, their only substantial ally in Europe. The JCS warned that any action that threatened Britain's control of the Eastern Mediterranean, the Suez Canal, or its share of the Middle East oilfields, would in effect pose a threat to Britain's position and status as a Great Power. They reasoned that Soviet bases at the Straits would not by themselves be able to guarantee the passage of Soviet shipping into the Mediterranean. The Soviets, therefore, were unlikely to stop at the Dardanelles, but would probably seek further bases, in the Aegean and the Eastern Mediterranean.[71]

Should the Soviets secure control of the Straits and the Aegean Sea, thus presenting a direct threat to the 'vital Suez Canal–Aleppo–Basra triangle', Britain would either have to fight, 'or accept eventual disintegration of the Empire'.[72] And if the British Empire disintegrated:

> . . . Soviet prospects for gaining control of Eurasia would be greatly enhanced, and the United States might be left vulnerable and exposed.[73]

Until the close of the 1940s, notwithstanding her manifest post-war weakness, Britain was still regarded by the Americans as, 'by a vast margin, the most valuable and dependable' of her allies. Anglo-American unity was considered to be one of the major deterrents to Soviet aggression. British troops were considered to be of a fighting quality comparable to American. In American strategic plans, 'British or British-controlled or British-influenced strategic areas, extending

[69] Devereux, *The Formulation of British Defence Policy* . . ., p.10

[70] Mark, 'The War Scare . . .', p.7.

[71] Leffler, 'Strategy, Diplomacy, and the Cold War . . .', p.811.

[72] JCS 1641/3, 13 March 1946, RG 218 JCS 46-47, CS 092 (3-27-45), sect. 6. NA; also Schnabel, *History of the JCS* . . ., Vol. 1, p.109-10.

[73] Leffler, 'Strategy, Diplomacy, and the Cold War . . .', p.811; Mark, 'The War Scare . . .', pp.6–7.

from the UK itself through the Eastern Hemisphere', were considered
to be of critical value. The cost of US aid to Britain was considered to
be a bargain, considering the security and strategic benefits the
Americans received in return. Should the British be forced, for
economic reasons, to reduce their overseas commitments, and the size
of their armed forces, the Americans reasoned that this would require
'an immediate increase in their [own] international strategic commitments . . . or the acceptance of highly increased security risks'.[74]

By the end of May 1946, the Soviets had withdrawn all their troops
from Iran, save for a few in Azerbaijan, that had been left to guard
supplies not yet evacuated.[75] But the Turkish crisis graph still fluctuated
wildly. American, and especially British intelligence reports reported
alarming Soviet troop build-ups in Bulgaria, threateningly close to the
Turkish border. However, by late June, new intelligence reports of
Soviet troop withdrawals from the Balkans calmed the Washington
establishment.[76] But on 7 August 1946, a further Soviet note to Turkey,
again demanding a joint defence of the Straits and of the Montreux
convention, while coming as no surprise, threw Washington into a
mood of crisis. This triggered the so-called 'war scare', which some
historians have since tagged as marking the beginning of the Cold War.

President Truman asked Acting Secretary of State Dean Acheson to
initiate an inter-departmental study on the Turkish question. Eight
days later, on 15 August, a grim meeting was held at the White House,
with the President, Acheson, Secretary of the Navy Forrestal, Acting
Secretary of War Kenneth C. Royall, and Services representatives in
attendance. The inter-departmental study tabled for discussion advised
that the Soviets might have aggressive intentions against Turkey, and
that the only thing that would deter them would be 'the conviction that
the United States is prepared, if necessary, to meet aggression with
force of arms'.When asked by Acheson, Truman confirmed that he
understood that this might mean war.[77]

The Turkish and Iranian crises convinced American officials that
World War Three might break out at any time – not because the Soviets
were planning for, or able to wage a global conflict with the West, but
because their policy of intimidating smaller states might precipitate a
general conflagration, if the Soviets misjudged the West's determination to protect the interests of its allies.[78]

[74] Intelligence report, SR-25, 7 Dec., 1949, in PSF, box 261, The Harry S. Truman
Library (hereafter HST).
[75] Mark, 'The War Scare . . .', p.10.
[76] Ibid., p.13.
[77] *FRUS*, 1946: 7, pp.840-42; cited in Mark, 'The War Scare . . .', p.1.
[78] Cf. Mark, p.3.

There has been some difference of opinion among historians as to the authenticity of the August 1946 war scare. On the one hand, it has been claimed that notwithstanding Soviet strong-arm tactics against the Turks, and alarmist intelligence reports from the field about Soviet troop concentrations, no major threat to Turkish territorial integrity actually materialised. The inference of this argument is that the Truman administration exaggerated the Soviet threat, in order to justify its demands for funds to construct American bases in Turkey.[79] On the other hand, it has also been claimed lately that the Soviet threat was all too real, and that Stalin was persuaded to pull back his forces only by his own Intelligence, which provided him with inside reports of Truman's determination to fight over Turkey, as expressed by the President at the 15 August meeting.[80]

Whatever the case, the JCS were not afforded the benefit of hindsight. Given the information available to them at the time, they could not simply disregard or dismiss the threat to Turkey. And even if the Soviets did stand down their troops in the autumn of 1946, this did not necessarily gurantee that they would not be returned, or that the Soviets would not try to exert pressure at another point (i.e., in Berlin, in 1948).

In 1946, the JCS believed that Turkey held the key to the defence of the Middle East. The fate of the latter theatre would depend upon the extent and efficacy of Turkish resistance to a Soviet offensive.

The JCS asked the Secretaries of War and Navy to offer concrete economic and military aid to the Turks. Their memorandum was passed through military channels to Secretary Byrnes, who approved the despatch of economic aid. As for military aid, the state department advised that this should be continued through British channels, although if necessary, the US might furnish the British with the arms for the Turks.[81]

The Turkish crisis in 1946, also provided the catalyst for the first American strategic studies, the *Pincher* series, and to the first contingency plan for World War Three, plan *Griddle*, for the defence of

[79] From May–Sept. 1946, the Soviets in fact reduced their force levels in Europe in Europe from two million to about 1.5 million men, and, inside the Soviet Union itself, from five to 2.7 million; cf. Leffler, 'Strategy, Diplomacy, and the Cold War . . .', p.811.

[80] Stalin's source was Donald Maclean (one of the 'Cambridge Five' spies), who ironically was sent to Washington by the British Foreign Office to determine exactly that question – how determined were the Americans to defend Turkey? Cf. Mark, 'The War Scare . . .', pp.15, 22.

However, Mark's argument is slightly flawed by his own finding that the perceived Soviet threat to Turkey was due largely to inaccurate British appraisals of their own Intelligence reports; cf. Mark, p.21.

[81] James F. Schnabel, *History of the Joint Chiefs of Staff*, Vol.1, 1945–1947, Wilmington: Michael Glazier Inc., 1979, pp.113–15, 119–20.

Turkey. The *Pincher* studies defined a new strategic role for Turkey: the longer that country was able to resist a Soviet attack, the longer American B-29s based at Abu Sueir in Egypt (on which, see Chapter five), would be able to bomb targets in the Urals, beyond the range of bombers based in Britain.[82]

In mid-1946, American planners estimated that, by 1949, the Soviets would be able to deploy 75 divisions for the assault on western and northern Turkey – an operation that would in fact require only 46 divisions. They estimated that as a part of a Soviet general offensive against Turkey, their main effort in the East would be 'a 10 division tank and infantry attack through Iran and northern Iraq into south-eastern Turkey and the Levant states'. This assault would aim to conquer Mosul and Alexandretta. This would cut Turkey's L of C to Syria, and at the same time prevent 'foreign aid from reaching the Turks by the overland route from Palestine'. In addition to this 10-division thrust, the planners expected the Soviets to deploy an additional force of five divisions against Haifa and Suez.[83]

On 10 September 1946, General Carl Spaatz, commander of USAF, was directed to prepare a plan for 'the immediate initiation of strategic air operations to the eastward'. Within a record time of just 20 days, USAF had drafted the appropriately-named plan *Makefast*, for the conventional aerial bombing of the Soviets' petroleum industry from bases in the UK and in Egypt.[84]

In February 1947, the British decided to withdraw military aid from Greece and Turkey. This both underlined the vulnerability of Europe to Soviet communism, and impelled the Americans to take concrete steps to advance contingency plans for Turkey that had been under consideration since 1945.[85]

It would appear that the American response, the Truman Doctrine of March 1947, was issued not so much to secure funding for the defence of Turkey against any immediate Soviet threat, but in order to build up that country militarily as a strategic base against the Soviet Union. The argument used in Washington by the administration was the evident fact that Turkey's strategic significance for the allies also lay in its constituting a buffer against the expansion of the Soviets into the Near and Middle East.

[82] Mark, 'The War Scare . . .', pp.9, 18.

[83] JCS 1641/3, 13 March, 1946, sect. 6, RG 218, JCS 46-47, CS 092 USSR (3-27-45); J.I.S. 253/1, 26 July 1946, RG 218, Joint Chiefs, 46-47, CS 092 (3-27-45), sect. 12, box 154; and *Griddle*, J.W.P.C. 467/1, 15 Aug. 1946, 381 Turkey (15 Aug 1946), (new case). NA.

[84] 'Outline Air Plan for *Makefast*', 1 Oct. 1946, RG 341, PO 381 (10 Sept. 1946), entry 335, Box 380, NA; cf Mark, 'The War Scare . . .', p.19.

[85] John Lewis Gaddis, *The Long Peace: Inquiries into the History of the Cold War*, New York/Oxford: Oxford University Press, 1987, p.41; and Hahn, *The United States . . .*, p.25.

At the meeting with the majority and minority leaders of Congress in February 1947, at which Truman and senior members of his administration secured the advance approval of the Congress for the new programme of aid to Greece and Turkey, Secretary of State Marshall justified that aid as follows:

> If Greece should dissolve into civil war it is altogether probable that it would emerge as a communist state under Soviet control. Turkey would be surrounded and the Turkish situation . . . would in turn become still more critical. Soviet domination might thus extend over the entire Middle East to the borders of India . . . It is not alarmist to say that *we are faced with the first crisis of a series that might extend Soviet domination to Europe, the Middle East and Asia.*[86]

Whereas the Turkish army by itself was not expected to hold out for long against a Soviet, or Soviet satellite attack, the Americans hoped that once modernised, with American aid, Turkish forces would be able to hold up the Soviets long enough to enable Turkey's allies to activate key bases in the Near and Middle East, from which to launch attacks against vulnerable targets in the Soviet Union.[87] In March 1949, a NSC report to the President summarised American strategic objectives in Turkey as being to build up in that country:

> A Turkish military establishment of sufficient size and effectiveness to insure Turkey's continued resistance to Soviet pressure; the development of combat effectiveness to the extent that any overt Soviet aggression can be delayed long enough *to permit the commitment of U.S. and allied forces in Turkey in order to deny certain portions of Turkey to the USSR.*[88]

But American strategists moved beyond the 'buffer' concept, i.e., Turkey serving as a trip-wire to hold up a Soviet offensive against the Middle East. The more the British position in Egypt deteriorated, the more the Americans looked to Turkey as an alternative, substitute strategic base, on the Soviets' 'southern rim'.

Since the autumn of 1945, American planners had studied Turkey's potential as an air base from which to launch part of the air offensive against the Soviets. In August 1946, while Truman discussed with Acheson, (Under Secretary of State) Forrestal (Secretary of Defense) and Royall (Secretary of the Army) how they could persuade American public opinion that it was in the national interest to send military aid to

[86] Quoted in Forrest C. Pogue, *George C. Marshall: Statesman, 1945–1959*, New York: Viking/Penguin, 1987, p.164. Pogue's emphasis.

[87] Cf. CIA Report, ORE 50, 'The Current Situation in Turkey', 20 Oct. 1947, President's Secretary's files, HST.

[88] NSC 42/1, 'U.S. Objectives with respect to Greece and Turkey to counter Soviet threats to U.S. Security', 22 March 1949, President's Secretary's files, HST (my emphasis).

Turkey, the Joint War Plans Committee at the Pentagon was com-
pleting a strategic study on Turkey, entitled *Griddle*. This underlined
that country's strategic importance as a base from which to launch an
offensive against the Soviet Union, in the event of war.[89]

Griddle listed the following strategic advantages that would accrue to
the allies from a base in Turkey, preferably in western Anatolia:

a. It would remove 'a threat to the vital Suez area and the land route
to North Africa'.

b. Allied aircraft would be able to operate from it 'at greatly reduced
distances with consequent higher effectiveness against the vital areas of
the U.S.S.R.'

c. 'Moscow, and all Soviet territory to the south (including the
Caspian Sea) would come within range of Allied fighters.'

d. 'Some seventy per cent of the U.S.S.R. oil resources would be
within range of Allied fighter aircraft.'

e. 'A staging base would be available for VLR [very long range] aircraft operating from bases in Egypt.'

f. The base would enable the allies to control the Straits, thus deny-
ing the Soviets exit from the Black Sea.

g. 'The threat against the LOC through the Mediterranean to the
Cairo–Suez–Haifa area would be greatly reduced.'[90]

From as early as September 1945, American planners had targeted
the Soviets' vulnerable southwestern flank. First priority was given to
the oil-producing areas of the Caucusus and Rumania; second priority
was allotted to 'industrial complexes in the Urals, Ukraine, Upper
Silesia and Czechoslovakia, Moscow and Mukden areas'.[91]

By the time that the Truman Doctrine was issued, nearly all civilian
and military officials already concurred on the need to supply military
equipment and aid to the Turks. Not only would a strategic air base in
Turkey (closer in to vulnerable Soviet targets than the Egyptian base)
serve fighter escorts for bombing runs on the Soviet Union. But Turkey
could also field ground forces that would at the very least slow down a
Soviet offensive against the Middle East. The Turks might also interdict Soviet shipping, and lock up Soviet submarines inside the Black
Sea.[92]

But the Turkish armed forces would need substantial quantities of
American arms, equipment and training. In 1946, American planners
reported that the Turkish air force was 'ineffective . . . poorly trained,
and equipped with only 662 obsolescent and obsolete aircraft'. The
Turkish Navy could not be 'considered an effective fighting force in

---

[89] Plan *Griddle*, J.W.P.C. 467/1, 13 Aug. 1946, 381 Turkey (15 Aug 1946) (new case), NA;
and Leffler, 'Strategy, Diplomacy, and the Cold War . . .', p.813.   [90] Plan *Griddle*, ibid.
[91] Leffler, 'Strategy, Diplomacy, and the Cold War . . .', pp.813–14.   [92] Ibid., p.815.

terms of modern warfare'. Consequently, the Turks planned to base their defence on their ground forces, of which they had some half a million on active service, and a further one million on reserve status.[93]

The Americans also wanted to use their aid as a lever with which to persuade the Turks to correlate their military planning with their own. American strategy was concerned not so much with maintaining Turkish territorial integrity, as with persuading the Turks to adopt a strategy that would cause the maximum delay to a Soviet offensive against the Middle East. American planners foresaw that the Soviets would attempt to defeat Turkey with a three-pronged attack, 'across the Bosphorus, the Black Sea, and the Caucasus'. The Americans did not believe that the Turks would be able to resist the Soviet onslaught. But they feared that the Turks would attempt to make an all-out stand at the Bosphorus, and quickly lose most of their army in the process. Instead of this, American strategists wanted the Turks to carry out an orderly withdrawal, harass the Soviets by guerrilla activity behind their front lines, and 'make a final, large-scale stand in southern Turkey in the Iskenderon pocket'.[94]

Much of the American military aid given to Turkey during the period under discussion was designed to endow the Turkish army with the 'mobility and logistical capability' to support American strategy in the region. In the summer of 1947, after Congress had in May approved $400 million in aid to Greece and Turkey under the Truman Doctrine, a US Survey Group visited Turkey. The Group recommended that $100 million of this sum allotted to Turkey be spent on 'modernizing and training the Turkish armed forces and to alleviating the heavy financial burden of maintaining those forces, some 40–50% of their defence budget'.[95] American investment in the construction of strategic roads and air bases in Turkey reached substantial dimensions. By the end of 1950, US military aid to Turkey had reached $271 million, of which $105 million alone had been authorised for FY 1950. The appropriation for FY 1951 was $67.4 million, with a supplemental appropriation of $87 million.[96]

American advisers in Turkey conducted courses at eight Turkish military schools, in 'artillery, motor transport, armour, infantry, signal, ordnance, antiaircraft, and field medical services.' By the autumn of 1948, the Americans had supplied the Turkish army with over '50,000

---

[93] Plan *Griddle*, J.W.P.C. 467/1, 15 Aug. 1946, 381 Turkey (15 Aug 1946) (new case), NA.

[94] Leffler, 'Strategy, Diplomacy, and the Cold War . . .', pp.817–19.

[95] CIA Report, SR-1/1, 22 Dec. 1948; and NSC 109, 11 May 1951, President's Secretary's files, HST; also George Lenczowski, *The Middle East in World Affairs*, third edition, Ithaca: Cornell University Press, 1962, p.148.

[96] NSC 109, 11 May 1951, HST.

measurement tons of equipment, including heavy ordnance, vehicles, and training supplies'; they had delivered 11 surface vessels (of which 8 were minesweepers) and four submarines to the Turkish Navy.[97]

After the Turkish Army, the Turkish Air Force was the largest recipient of American aid. By the Fall of 1948, the Turkish Air Force had taken delivery of 180 P-47s, 30 B-26s, and 86 C-47s'; heavy engineering equipment for the construction and maintenance of airfields, and over '30 million long tons' of supplies and equipment. (There was a difference between the metric ton, as used by the Americans, which weighed 1000 kilograms and the 'long' and 'short' ton as used by the British; a 'long' ton weighed 1016 kilograms, whereas a 'short' ton weighed 907 kilograms.) The US 1950 Military Defence Materiel Programme for Turkey provided for the delivery to Turkey in 1951 of limited numbers of jet fighters, including 25 P-84Es.[98]

The United States also invested great effort in constructing new, and rehabilitating old Turkish airfields. American funds were earmarked to develop two new air bases at Adana and Antalya; to bring the airfields at Diyarbekir, Kayseri and Eskisehir up to operational level; and to supply housing and utilities to other airfields at Bandirma, Erzincan, Afyon and Balikesir. As a result of renovations carried out with American funds, the Ploesti and Baku oil fields came within range of the P-47s and the B-26s stationed at Turkish air bases.[99]

The Turkish General Staff was of the opinion that a Strategic Air Force was beyond its capabilities. In the event of war, Turkish-flown aircraft would be restricted to tactical operations and local air defence. The American Military wanted to 'institutionalise strategic coordination with Turkey', so as to guarantee the use of Turkish airfields by American strategic bombers in wartime.[100]

But there were political, as well as military hurdles to be overcome. The Turks were reluctant to align themselves openly with the West until the Americans agreed to guarantee to come to their aid in the event of a Soviet attack. Until such a commitment was forthcoming, the Turks would not permit overt military construction work likely to attract Soviet attention (and Soviet bombers in the event of war).

[97] Fifth State Department report to Congress, undated, on Assistance to Greece and Turkey for period ending 30 Sept. 1948, Harry S. Truman Official file, HST.

[98] Ibid., and Leffler, 'Strategy, Diplomacy, and the Cold War . . .', pp.817–18; and *FRUS*, Vol. V, 1950, p.1295, n.9.

[99] Memo by John H. Ohly, Deputy Director, Mutual Defense Assistance, Department of State, to Major General Lyman L. Lemnitzer, Director of Military Assistance, Department of Defense, 26 April 1950, *FRUS*, ibid., p.1250; and US Embassy, Ankara, to Turkish Minister for Foreign Affairs, 4 May 1950, ibid., p.1256.

[100] CIA report, SR-1/1, 22 Dec., 1948, PSF, HST; and Leffler, 'Strategy, Diplomacy, and the Cold War . . .', p.819.

The Americans themselves were aware of the contradictions inherent in building up Turkey as a Western offensive base, while at the same time refusing to grant the Turks an American security guarantee. In the closing days of 1948, two American military missions visited Ankara. Both were received by the Turkish President, Ismet Inonu. The latter complained that it was unjust that the Americans were extending more help to the countries of Western Europe than to Turkey. Inonu conveyed the following message to President Truman:

> Turkey is like an oasis in the desert. We have no reliable friendly forces on any side . . . We need assurance now that we would not be abandoned should Turkey be attacked . . . We feel that on every appropriate occasion, the U.S. should declare that Turkey will not be abandoned, then Turkey will feel itself doubly strong.[101]

In April 1949, Secretary of State Dean Acheson wrote a memorandum for the National Security Council on the construction of airfields and the stockpiling of aviation fuel in Turkey. He acknowledged that the JCS considered these to be essential for the strategic air offensive. But he advised caution, in view of American reticence in admitting Turkey into NATO, or otherwise to guarantee her territorial integrity. It would be unwise, Acheson wrote, 'to press Turkey to agree to any action that would expose her more to pressure from the Soviet Union'. The construction of forward air bases, and the storage of aviation fuel in Turkey, would be regarded by the Soviets as a direct threat to their security, and might provoke further Soviet pressure on the Turks and, perhaps, even on Iran. Such construction might also lead the Soviets to 'the erroneous conclusion that the North Atlantic Treaty is aggressive in intention and operation'.[102]

The administration took all possible care to hide from Congress (and from the public), the fact that US military aid to Turkey in fact served American strategic *desiderata*. Major General Lyman L. Lemnitzer, director of the Office of Military Assistance at the Department of defence, had to report to the Budget Bureau of the Congress. He was

[101] Inonu to Truman, 17 Dec., 1948, NLT (PSF-Subj.) 402, HST. The first American mission, headed by Secretary of the Army, Kenneth C. Royall, visited Ankara from 17–19 Dec. 1948. The mission included Ambassador George Wadsworth, Gen. Lawton Collins, VCOS, US Army, and Major General Horace McBride, Chief of the US Army Group, American Mission for Aid to Turkey.

The second mission, headed by Vice Admiral Arthur Radford, Chief of Naval Operations, visited Ankara from 19–21 Dec. 1948. Again, Wadsworth accompanied Radford to the meeting with Inonu. Cf. wditorial note, p.217, *FRUS*, 1948, Vol. IV.

[102] NSC 36/1, Acheson to National Security Council, 15 April 1949, President's Secretary's files, HST; reprinted in *FRUS*, 1949, Vol. VI, p.1655.

instructed by the State Department on the imperative need to make it appear that the work carried out in Turkey was on behalf of Turkey, 'compatible with the needs of the Turkish airforce, and not for the United States . . .'. Lemnitzer was directed also that his testimony should be limited to a general statement that US funds were being used 'for the rehabilitation of certain Turkish airfields' in order to permit their 'fullest efficient use by the Turkish Air Force of the equipment we have given them.' He was to avoid giving details about the size, and locations of the airfields they were building and, if possible, to give his testimony only in executive session.[103]

In October 1950, Turkey and Greece were invited to become associate members of NATO. This allowed them to be included in NATO planning for the Mediterranean. The US Department of Defence agreed also that 'informal assurances' be given Turkey that 'a Soviet attack against it would probably mean the beginning of global war', and would draw an commensurate reaction by the United States and her allies.[104] But generalities and platitudes failed to assuage Turkish fears of Soviet attack. The Turks would not agree to full strategic coordination with the United States until they were admitted into NATO as a full member. However, since 1948, American attentions had been focused on, and its resources devoted exclusively to, Western Europe. They continued to oppose the admission of Turkey (and Greece) into NATO, and any arrangement that 'would require the commitment of United States forces to defend Greece and Turkey (or Iran) in the event of hostilities'.[105]

The Turks, who still felt 'exposed and vulnerable', remained unwilling to take one-sided risks for the Western allies. The US administration had to confront the fact that the Turks were likely to remain neutral in a future conflict. They would probably defend themselves if attacked by the Soviets. But if the latter did not attack Turkey initially, the Americans might lose a valuable strategic base, in which they had already invested considerable funds and military equipment.[106] Until 1951, all Turkish pleas to be admitted into the Western defence alliance were rebuffed. In addition, until the summer of 1951, the British vetoed Turkish entry into NATO. The British regarded Turkey as a Middle

---

[103] James Bruce, Director Mutual Defense Assistance Program, State Department, to Maj Gen Lemnitzer, 28 Feb. 1950, p.1234, and Ohly to Lemnitzer, 26 April 1950, p.1250, *FRUS*, 1950.

[104] Louis Johnson, Secretary of Defense, to Secretary of State Acheson, 11 Sept. 1950, *FRUS*, 1950, Vol. III, p.279.

[105] State Department position paper, 11 Sept. 1950, approved by Defense Department, prepared for use by delegation to Foreign Ministers' tripartite meetings in New York, 12–19 Sept., 1950, Ibid, p.283.

[106] Leffler, 'Strategy, Diplomacy, and the Cold War . . .', p.820.

Eastern power, which should fight in the Middle East, under a British theatre commander. This affronted Turkish national pride, since they considered themselves to be a European power.

Several factors were instrumental in persuading the Americans to agree to grant Turkey full NATO membership in the summer of 1951. First, American fears that Turkey would 'veer towards a policy of neutralism'. At a meeting with the Turkish President, Celal Bayar, on 12 February 1951, George McGhee learned at first hand of the Turks' disappointment with the Americans.

McGhee paid tribute to the strategic importance and military strength of Turkey, noting especially its recent contribution of a brigade to the allied side in Korea. Turkey's strength had been highlighted, added McGhee, 'by the revelation of the comparative weakness of the Middle East as a whole'. He tried to explain that until NATO was firmly established, at full strength, the United States would be unable to extend its current commitments. But the Turkish President was not assuaged. Turkey wanted '*to give a guarantee, and it would like to receive a guarantee*'.[107]

The general consensus at a meeting of Middle East chiefs of mission, from 14–21 February 1951, attended by McGhee, was that until some commitment was extended to Turkey, they could not be certain that Turkey would declare war on the Soviets unless attacked first. Such a commitment was a *sine qua non* to assure:

> Turkey's immediate cobelligerency, utilization in collective security action of the military potential which Turkey is building, and immediate United States and Allied utilization of Turkish bases in the event that the United States is engaged in hostilities . . .[108]

Admiral Carney (CINCELM), pointed out that the potential military contributions of Turkey, Greece and Yugoslavia would prove vital to the European campaign, in that 'they would undoubtedly involve the commitment of significant Russian forces.'[109]

A PPS memorandum written in the summer of 1951 suggested that the Turkish army might be deployed along two major fronts, east and west of Turkey. In the west, the Turkish commander in the Dardanelles–Bosphorus theatre might become part of the southern

---

[107] Memorandum of conversation by William M. Rountree (Director of Office of Greek, Turkish, and Iranian Affairs, 12 Feb. 1951, *FRUS*, 1951, Vol. III, pp.468–70 (emphasis in original).

[108] Conclusions of Middle Eastern Chiefs of Mission, Istanbul, 14–21 Feb. 1951, *FRUS*, 1951, Vol V, p.52.

[109] Summary of the Strategic implications of the Istanbul conference, Feb. 1951, by Admiral Robert C. Carney, CINCELM, ibid., p.103.

flank of Gen. Eisenhower's European command (SACEUR); Turkish forces in the East, guarding the Outer Ring mountain passes blocking Soviet access to the Middle East via the Caucasus, would become part of the proposed British Middle East Command (MEC). (Eisenhower, who had apparently yet to familarise himself with Anglo-Turkish animosities, advocated deploying all the Turkish effort to the Middle East Command, on the grounds that it would be 'militarily impracticable' for him to supervise the Turkish effort from SHAPE.)[110]

Following the Istanbul conference, held in March 1951, the State Department undertook a study of 'the desirability and feasibility of the United States entering into reciprocal security arrangements with Turkey and Greece.' The study concluded that the Turks would take certain measures of strategic importance to the United States, only if the Americans gave them a direct security guarantee. Such measures included persuading the Turks to mine the Straits and allowing the United States to 'use air and other bases which the Joint Chiefs of Staff consider essential.' Those bases developed by the United States in Turkey would be of only limited value to the United States unless they could be assured of immediate Turkish belligerency in the event of Allied hostilities with the Soviets. Without such a security guarantee, Turkey would be unwilling to commit further combat units to the allies, and would refuse to join any mutual defence pacts with its neighbors. If the guarantee was not given soon, there were grounds for the belief that Turkey would 'veer toward a policy of neutralism'.[111]

On 30 April, the JCS informed Secretary of Defense Marshall, that 'from the military point of view . . . United States security interests demand that Turkey and Greece be admitted as full members of the North Atlantic Treaty Organisation'. This recommendation was approved by President Truman on 24 May 1951.[112]

One of the main obstacles to the admission of Turkey into NATO was British opposition. But during the course of the summer of 1951, a 'package deal' of sorts was finally reached between the British and the Americans. Since the summer of 1950, the British had been trying to resolve their conflict with the Egyptians by replacing their own base rights with a new MEC, in which British, American and Egyptian forces would defend the Canal base, under a British Supreme Commander (SACME). In return for agreeing to the admission of Turkey and

---

[110] Memorandum by John Ferguson of the PPS, 6 July 1951, *FRUS*, 1951, Vol. III, p.553; and Eisenhower to Gens Juin, Slim and Bradley, 9 Oct. 1951, in Louis Galambos, ed., *The Papers of Dwight David Eisenhower*, Vol. XII, Baltimore/London: Johns Hopkins University Press, 1989, p.627.

[111] Secretary of State Acheson to Secretary of Defense Marshall, 24 March 1951, *FRUS*, 1951, Vol. III, pp.502–4.

[112] Editorial note, ibid., pp.524–25.

Greece into NATO, the United States agreed to join the British as co-sponsors of the MEC, and to join the British in selling the new scheme to the Egyptians (on this still-born project, see below, Chapter 8).

By mid-1951, the massive military build-up that had resulted from NSC 68, and the progress made in the institutional organisation of NATO, endowed the administration, including the Pentagon, with a new determination and confidence.[113] On 20 September 1951, at its seventh session, meeting in Ottowa, the NATO Council extended formal invitations to Greece and Turkey to join the organisation as full members.

Now that they had been admitted into NATO, the Turks were expected to play their role in American strategic plans. In September 1952, in a conversation with Turkish Prime Minister Menderes, the American Secretary for Air, Finletter, indicated that he hoped that now that Turkey was a member of NATO, 'the possibility existed that Turkish air bases, which the US had helped to build, would at some time be required for the use of other NATO forces, including those of the US'. The Secretary reassured the Turkish Prime Minister that the United States would not seek exclusive use of the Turkish air bases, and put forward the dubitable thesis that the Americans' use would not in any way 'infringe upon Turkish national sovereignty'.[114]

By the end of 1951, the Americans were convinced that the British were a spent force in the Middle East. They appreciated that there would be an inevitable delay in the build-up of British and Common-wealth forces in the Middle East in the event of war. Once the Americans had lost confidence in their British ally's ability to fulfil their projected role of commanding and leading the Allied defence of the Middle East, Turkey became 'the logical country to take over primary responsibility . . .'[115] In the event of war, the Turks would field the major part of the ground forces needed for the defence of the Middle East. And Turkey, rather than Egypt, would serve as the launching platform for the strategic air offensive.

The year 1951 thus saw the beginning of a novel American involvement in the Middle East, one that focused on Turkey. MEC notwithstanding, the American military effort, planning, and funds, were projected henceforward to the Northern Tier, rather than as hitherto, to the British base in Egypt. Before turning to a detailed analysis of these developments, however, we will turn to an examination of the fundamentals of Britain's post-war policy and strategy in the Middle East.

[113] Leffler, p.822; and Hahn, *The United States . . .*, p.109.
[114] McGhee memorandum of conversation between Secretary for Air Finletter and Turkish Prime Minister Menderes, 24 April 1952, McGhee Papers, HST.
[115] PPS memorandum by John Ferguson, 6 July 1951, supra.

3 The Middle East in British global strategy

A. BRITAIN'S POST-WAR SELF-IMAGE AS A GREAT POWER: THE NUCLEAR DETERRENT

The development of Britain's independent nuclear deterrent was due perhaps as much to political factors as to military ones. The Labour government elected in July 1945 assumed from the outset that Britain would remain a great power. American respect, and aid, could be assured only by Britain building herself up as the major European power. Foreign Secretary Bevin regarded the United States as 'a well-intentioned but inexperienced colossus'. He recognised her overwhelming economic and military strength but he believed apparently that with the aid of the colonies' material resources (especially those of Black Africa), Britain might yet aspire to equality with the United States and the Soviet Union.[1]

Thus it was the very fact of Britain's weakness that, paradoxically, 'reinforced the tendency to think imperially'. The reaction of the Labour government to the sterling crisis of 1947 was to revert to 'a highly insulated imperial economy'. It was a form of protectionism under which Britain, her Dominions (excluding Canada), her remaining colonies, and certain associated states, set up a free trade zone between them, with high tariff walls against foreign imports, especially dollar goods.[2]

The more intelligent British mandarins appreciated that Britain would have to readjust herself to the new bipolar world of the two Superpowers. However, this did not have to lead to the abandonment of Empire, or aspirations to continued grandeur. As put so well by John Darwin, all it meant was:

---

[1] Cf. Ronald Hyam, ed., *The Labour Government and the End of Empire, 1945–1951*, Series A, Vol. 2, Part I, p.xlix.

[2] John Darwin, 'British Decolonization since 1945: A Pattern or a Puzzle?' *Journal of Imperial and Commonwealth History*, Vol. 12, 1983–84, p.197.

. . . the selective shrugging off of commitments, the enforced retreat from exposed positions, coupled with the hope, more perhaps than the expectation, that the heart of the system was still sound.[3]

Bevin believed in Britain's ability to erect and lead a Euro-African 'third world force', that would be able to act on the world stage independently of the Americans and the Soviets. Bevin's 'half-baked pie in the sky' (his views were shared in October 1948 by the new President of the Board of Trade, Harold Wilson), was to 'organise the middle of the planet' – Africa, Western Europe, the Middle East and the Mediterranean – into a pre-eminent world power! With the United States devoid of the very precious minerals in which Africa abounded, Bevin believed that within four to five years, the Americans would be eating out of British hands![4]

But during the post-war years the British suffered a series of economic and currency crises. Already, in August 1945, Truman's peremptory cessation of Lend-Lease precipitated the first post-war economic crisis, one that led the British to run cap in hand to Washington, where they were bailed out by an American loan to the tune of $3.75 billions. But the American loan could not solve Britain's underlying economic problems, or instil long-term international confidence in the British currency. The crisis of confidence in 1949, which led to devaluation that summer, was spurred largely by the United States' own first post-war recesssion, and by sterling's weakness abroad. However, by early 1950, the British economy had made an apparently startling recovery, only to be battered again by the demands of the Korean war. That conflict provoked the severest burst of universal inflation since World War Two, and an equally universal acute shortage of raw materials. Britain's economic problems were complicated by a sharp rise in her defence budget, from £830 million in 1950–51, to £1,300 million for 1951–52. British defence expenditure, as a percentage of the total budget, rose from about 7% in 1949, to 10½% by 1952. As a result of all this, the British balance of payments lurched from a comfortable surplus of £300 million in 1950, to a deficit of over £400 million in 1951. (This deficit was due in part to the Iranian seizure of the Abadan oil refineries.)[5]

It was only after the economic crisis of October 1949, that Bevin personally finally conceded the inevitability of Britain's future eco-

[3] Ibid., p.198.

[4] John Kent, 'Bevin's Imperialism and the Idea of Euro-Africa, 1945–49', in Michael Dockrill, John Young, eds, British Foreign Policy, 1945–56, New York: St Martin's Press, 1989, pp.47, 66, 70.

[5] On the British economy, cf. J.C.R. Dow, *The Management of the British Economy, 1945–60*, Cambridge: Cambridge University Press, 1965, pp.45–6, 55–7, 63.

nomic dependence on the Americans. However, in 1954, when delivering the Reith Lectures for that year, Sir Oliver Franks, just returned from four-and-a-half years' service as British ambassador to the United States, told his audience that he always had taken for granted, and still did take for granted, that Britain would continue to be 'a Great Power'.[6]

After the war, Labour refused to acquiesce in an American nuclear monopoly. It regarded the possession of nuclear weapons as an essential appurtenance of a first-class power, and thought it unseemly to be dependent upon any foreign agent. As stated by the historian of Britain's independent nuclear deterrent, British possession of the atomic bombs:

> did not simply duplicate American power; they conferred a special international status on their possessor . . .. A British demurral of the bomb would have been equivalent to contracting out of Great Power status. Further, the British believed that success in the development of their own nuclear weapons would 'impress the United States and enhance her own special status as an ally'.[7]

In 1955, the British White Paper on Defence made Britain's policy of nuclear deterrence official. However, the real decision had been taken much earlier.

In 1946, the British COS still believed that the defence of the Empire would 'not be radically altered by new developments in methods or weapons of warfare'. They did not yet have enough data to predict the effect of the tactical use of nuclear weapons, although they did foresee that nuclear attacks on the enemy's bases and stores depots might well cripple his offensive capacity.[8] In any case, it was too early to rely on a decisive airborne nuclear offensive – if only because current nuclear stockpiles were minimal, and the COS certainly had no idea of how many atomic bombs the Americans had. In the late 1940s, the COS did not devote any serious thought to the ways in which nuclear weapons would change modern warfare. Field Marshal Bernard Montgomery (CIGS from June 1946 to October 1948) failed to comprehend the impact of nuclear weapons on conventional strategy, and to all intents and purposes ignored the ramifications of the atomic bomb. If war did come, it was expected that its outcome, as in World War Two, would depend upon a massed ground forces campaign. As to the defence of British global interests, the COS retained, at least initially,

[6] Oliver S. Franks, *Britain and the Tide of World Affairs*, London: Oxford University Press, 1955, p.6.

[7] Margaret Gowing, *Independence and Deterrence: Britain and Atomic Energy, 1945–1952*, Vol. 2, *Policy Execution*, New York: St Martin's Press, 1974, pp.499–501; also Richard N. Rosencrance, *Defence of the Realm: British Strategy in the Nuclear Epoch*, New York/London: Columbia University Press, 1968, pp.41–42.

[8] COS memorandum of 2 April 1946, in DO (46) 47, Cab 131/21, PRO.

the traditional strategic conception of an imperial system based upon India, with the Middle East as its natural fulcrum.[9]

The nuclear deterrent made its first 'formal' appearance as an element in British global strategy in a secret COS paper in the Spring of 1952. But the decision to manufacture the atomic bomb had been 'taken most deliberately and under cover of the greatest possible secrecy' early in January 1947, by 'Gen 163', an ad hoc forum of six senior Ministers: Prime Minister Attlee, Foreign Secretary Bevin, Lord President Morrison, Minister of Defence Alexander, Dominions Secretary Addison, and Minister of Supply Wilmot.[10]

The British exploded their first atomic device in October 1952, just one month before the Americans carried out their first hydrogen bomb test. Extra funds (mostly secret, not revealed in official defence estimates) were soon channelled into the development of Britain's own hydrogen bomb, and in the V-bomber series to deliver it. The COS believed that more dependence on nuclear weapons would provide the answer to the Soviets' conventional superiority, would permit drastic reductions in conventional forces, and consequently in the defence budget. At a lecture delivered to senior members of the British army in November 1954, Field Marshal Bernard Montgomery, at the time Deputy Supreme Allied commander of Europe, stated:

> I want to make it absolutely clear that we at S.H.A.P.E. are basing all our operational planning on using atomic and thermo-nuclear weapons in our defence. With us it is no longer: 'They may possibly be used.' It is very definitely: 'They will be used, if we are attacked.'[11]

But without a strategic, or long-range air-force, the most deadly nuclear arsenal was irrelevant. Only the Americans had both an operational atomic bomb, and the means wherewith to deliver it. At the close of World War Two the American B-29s were the only aircraft operational that had the range to reach Soviet targets. Allied war plans posited that the strategic air offensive would be carried out by some 400 American aircraft, operating from airfields in Britain, the Egypt-Aden area, and Okinawa. Plans for that offensive would remain within the exclusive realm of the American JCS, for not only did they alone dis-

[9] Alun Chalfont, *Montgomery of Alamein*, New York: Atheneum, 1976, p.288; and David R. Devereux, *The Formulation of British Defence Policy Towards The Middle East, 1948–56*, London: Macmillan, 1990, p.2; and Rosencrance, *Defence of . . .*, p.56.

[10] Gowing, *Independence and Deterrence*, Vol. 1, Policy Making, 1974, pp.179–82; and Julian Murray Lewis, *British Military Planning for Post-War Strategic Defence, 1942–1947*, Ph.D. thesis, Oxford University, 1981, p.304, note 1.

[11] Field-Marshal Bernard L. Montgomery, 'A Look through a window at World War III', *The Journal of the Royal Service Institution*, Vol. XCIX, No. 596, Nov. 1954, p.508.

pose of the aircraft, but only they knew, supposedly, how many atom bombs were available.[12] So much did the British consider the air offensive to be 'an American show', that the British Treasury baulked at paying for the extension of the runways at the Abu Sueir air base in Egypt (see the following chapter), on the grounds that the extra expenditure was for 'an American base'.

Britain's own first jet bomber, the Canberra, was on the drawing board already in 1944, made its maiden flight in May 1949, and became operational under Bomber Command in 1951. However, the Canberra was a twin-engined light bomber, not designed to carry nuclear weapons. With a range of just 2000 miles, it was a tactical, not a strategic bomber, even if it did remain England's 'chief bomber standby' until the late 1950s.[13]

It was not until 1955, that the first of Britain's own strategic jet bombers entered operational service. It was the four-engined Valiant jet bomber, the first of three in the V-Bomber series. (The delta-winged Vulcan became operational in July 1956, and the Victor in November 1957.) The pre-jet age Lancaster and Lincoln heavy bombers (the latter became operational in 1946) had neither the range to reach targets deep inside the Soviet Union, nor would they have survived against the new generation of Red Air Force jet fighters. The only jet aircraft flown by the RAF was the Meteor day fighter, which had already proved inferior to the German jet fighters during World War Two.[14]

The British Government had commissioned the Valiant in January 1947 (the same month in which the government decided to manufacture the atomic bomb). The Labour government had been ready to leave the strategic bombing of the Soviet Union to the Americans, while concentrating on the air defences of Great Britain, and tactical missions from Middle Eastern bases. In its search for a nuclear deterrent force, the RAF had faced its most acute problem in securing authorisation for the development of a strategic bomber. Greater political and economic pressures were mobilised against aircraft development than were mobilised against the atomic programme. The programme for the development of long-range bombers lacked the immediate sense of urgency which attended the development of nuclear weapons. But the Conservative Party and the RAF itself exerted strong pressure to build up a British strategic bomber force.[15]

---

[12] Annexe to Plan *Speedway* (the October 1948 revision of the Anglo-American worldwide emergency plan, to D + six months), COS (48) 210, 16 Dec. 1948, in Prem 8/745. PRO.

[13] Alfred Goldberg, 'The Military Origins of the British Nuclear Deterrent', *International Affairs*, vol. 40/4, Oct. 1964, pp.605, 610. The Canberra was in fact converted to carry a small atomic bomb, and did become the RAF's first atomic jet bomber.

[14] Owen Thetford, *Aircraft of the Royal Air Forces since 1918*, London: Putnam, 1988; and Goldberg, ibid, pp.604–5.   [15] Goldberg, ibid., pp.600–1, 609.

The V-Bombers were supposed to endow Britain, within a decade, with an independent capacity to penetrate enemy defences and drop atomic bombs on remote targets, no matter what opposition might be encountered. The British built their own strategic bomber not because of any fear of a rupture with the United States, but because of their calculation that 'certain targets, vital to Britain, would not be hit in the first round of the American strategic air strike against the Soviet Union'. However, as noted by one scholar, the V-bombers, together with the nuclear weapons they were designed to deliver, did also endow the RAF, and Great Britain as a whole, with 'a sense of prestige and power that was probably not justified by its true capability to influence the course of international events.'[16]

In November 1947, the British Government authorised the development of a new, interim jet bomber, a straight-winged aircraft, designated the S.A.4. Its purpose was to fill the gap between the Lincolns and the V-bombers. However, it was soon appreciated that the new aircraft would not meet the goals required of it. The project was cancelled at the end of 1949, a victim of economic retrenchment. The cancellation was facilitated by the good progress being made on the Valiant, and by the loan from the Americans of 88 B-29s (designated Washington B.1), which at the time still constituted the backbone of SAC. (The first of the B-29s arrived in England in March 1950 and were incorporated into RAF Bomber Command.)[17]

The first two groups of American B-29s, flown by American crews, had in fact arrived in Britain at the height of the Berlin crisis, in July 1948. At the same time, two other groups were sent to West Germany. By November 1948, a third American bomber group arrived in England, bringing their numbers to a total of 90 American-operated B-29s. (An Anglo–American agreement governing the operation of American aircraft from British bases was not in fact reached until October 1951.)[18]

[16] Ibid., p.618; and Rosencrance, *Defence of the Realm*, 1968, pp.12, 55–6, 104, 167.

[17] Goldberg and Rosencrance give the number of B-29s delivered to Britain (designated 'Washington B.1') as 70. This was the number anticipated by the British government. But American aviation histories give the total number of aircraft finally loaned as 88; cf. Norman Polmar, ed., *Strategic Air Command: People, Aircraft, and Missiles*, Annapolis: The Nautical and Aviation Company of America, Inc., 1979, p.148, and Ray Wagner, *American Combat Planes*, New York: Doubleday, 1982, p.402. Britain returned all the B-29s to the United States by 1954, a year before the first Valiant squadrons became operational. Goldberg, *The Military Origins . . .*, pp.606–8, 610.

[18] Goldberg, ibid., 608; and Rosencrance, *Defence of . . .*, p.74. The B-29s were sent to Europe as a warning to the Soviets. The documents now reveal that the B-29s sent to Europe were not in fact loaded with nuclear weapons, nor were they modified to carry the atomic bomb. Cf., Gregg Herken, *The Winning Weapon: The Atomic Bomb in the Cold War, 1945–1950*, Princeton: Princeton University Press, 1981, p.259.

The presence of American strategic bombers on British soil, under exclusive American control, raised acutely sensitive problems for the Labour administration, especially with the outbreak of the Korean War in June 1950. The government feared that the war might expand into a global conflict. The British side – which was privy neither to the Americans' atomic secrets, nor to the circumstances in which the latter would launch the strategic air offensive – feared that American-flown, nuclear-armed B-29s might be launched from British soil, and provoke a nuclear retaliation on Britain, without the British government even being consulted on the American decision, or the British people ever knowing what their country had done to warrant the Soviet attack. British anxieties on this point undoubtedly contributed to her determination to build up her own independent nuclear deterrent.

In January 1951, Air Marshal Sir John Slessor, Chief of the British Air Staff, was despatched to Washington to discuss operations in Korea. He was also instructed to question the Americans on their 'strategic air plan', especially about the use of the B-29s stationed on British soil. Foreign Secretary Bevin maintained that it had been 'implicit' in the agreement to station the American B-29s in the UK that his government would be consulted about their use, and that this understanding underpinned British agreement to the presence of the American planes in the UK, and to the provision of facilities for them. Bevin felt a 'personal responsibility' for ensuring that no misunderstanding existed on 'the use to which the United States air forces in the United Kingdom might be put', and felt that he would have not discharged that responsibility:

> while the British Government has no information as to the strategic plan in support of which these aircraft might be used at very short notice nor how far this plan accords with their own.[19]

Thus it is not to be wondered that, following the Korean War, the British V-bomber project was given accelerated impetus, under a massive rearmament programme adopted by the Labour Government. The new V-bombers would compare favorably with the American B-52 and B-58. The British fleet, small but élite, with a reputed range of over 4000 miles, was supposed, by the late 1950s, to be able to reach the majority of important targets inside the Soviet Union. (It was something of an irony that the V-bombers came into full operational use just when the two Superpowers were beginning to complement their own strategic bombers with ballistic missiles.)[20]

---

[19] Bevin to British Embassy, Washington, 13 Jan. 1951, FO 800/456. PRO.
[20] Goldberg, *The Military Origins . . .*, pp.615–17.

Allied war plans posited that by the beginning of 1951, USAF would deploy three groups (45 aircraft in each) of long-range strategic bombers from the United Kingdom, comprising B-29s and B-50 bombers (the former had a range, fully-loaded, of 3,250 miles, compared with the B-50's fully-loaded range of 4,900 miles). By mid-1952, this number was supposed to rise to six long-range bomber groups, a total of 270 aircraft. With fighters and other aircraft, there would be a total of 1506 American aircraft stationed on British soil.[21]

Until the late 1950s, British Bomber Command was charged primarily with the defence of the United Kingdom and the Middle East.

B. THE DEBATE ON RETAINING THE MIDDLE EAST.

In contrast to the United States, Britain had long-standing commercial and strategic interests in the Middle East, built up during centuries of Ottoman rule, under the privileges afforded by the Capitulations. In order to defend those interests, Britain, together with France, had from the nineteenth century occupied various Mediterranean and Middle Eastern provinces of that Empire: France had occupied Algeria in 1830, Tunisia in 1881, and in 1904, had received British assent to their primacy in Morocco, as part of the colonial deal that went with the *entente cordiale* of that year.

Britain had occupied Egypt in 1882 in order (initially, at least), to defend Western property and citizens. But the Suez Canal soon became, after the Dardanelles, the most important international strategic waterway. The British occupation of Egypt developed its own dynamic and, although not originally intended as such, had during World War One turned into a long-term Protectorate, whose principal *raison d'être* became to secure the short passage to India via the Suez Canal. When the Turks joined the German side in World War One, Britain's traditional 'Eastern Policy' (that of propping up the decaying Ottoman Empire) became obsolete.[22]

As a result of the final demise of the Ottoman Empire during the course of World War One, and the conquest of the Middle East by British arms, both France and Britain had secured mandates over the states newly carved out from the territories that had been known as Greater (or Ottoman) Syria, and Mesopotamia. Britain received the

---

[21] Cf., DO (51) 2, 2 Jan. 1951, Cab 131/11; and D.(52) 25, 14 June 1952, in Cab 131/12.PRO.

[22] On Britain's 'Eastern Policy', cf., Elie Kedourie, *England and the Middle East*, London: Bowes & Bowes, 1956, Ch. 1.

mandates for Iraq, Transjordan and Palestine; France for the Lebanon and Syria.

After World War One, the British Military had not been over-enthused with the extra burdens imposed by their newly-acquired Middle Eastern Mandates. They had referred to them, disdainfully, as 'the new provinces'. Churchill, as Secretary of State for War (1919–21), and then Colonial Secretary (1921–22), had repeatedly urged Prime Minister Lloyd George to return the Mandates (including Palestine) to the Turks. The Conservative establishment, and typically Winston Churchill, had always regarded Britain's overseas possessions as assets which had put the 'Great' into Great Britain. But for Churchill, the Middle East had always taken 'back seat' to India and Black Africa. Egypt, and the Suez Canal had been a means rather than an end in itself.[23]

Britain's tenure of Egypt proved vital during both world wars. The Suez Canal was the main artery of the Empire, and it ensured her ability to bring colonial forces from India to the Middle East and to Europe. During the course of World War Two, the oil resources of the Middle East had for the first time assumed vital military and strategic importance. During that war, the volume of oil extracted from wells in the Middle East had increased by 52 per cent. A considerable proportion of this increase came from recently-developed American concessions. Britain also had substantial economic interests in the Middle East. She annually exported goods to the region to the value of £150 millions, and imported substantial amounts of high-grade Egyptian cotton. The revenues from her oil concessions in the region were a significant factor in maintaining a healthy balance of payments.[24]

After World War Two, the COS, in marked contrast to their predecessors in 1919, regarded the Middle East as an integral part of an empire that was essential to guarantee Britain's continued status as a first-class power. The Military's position clashed directly with that of the Labour Prime Minister, Clement Attlee. Attlee had his own agenda, and high up on it were the resuscitation of the British economy and the establishment of the welfare state that his Party had promised to the electorate during the war. Attlee clashed with his Chiefs of Staff over global strategic priorities, in particular, over the need to retain tradi-

[23] Cf. Michael J. Cohen, *Churchill and the Jews*, London: Frank Cass, 1985, especially pp.62, 96–97.

[24] Hyam, *The Labour Government . . .*, Part I, p.lviii. On the importance of Middle East oil from this period, and on increasing American interest, cf. Aaron David Miller, *Search for Security: Saudi Arabian Oil and American Foreign Policy, 1939–1949*, Chapel Hill: University of Chapel Hill Press, 1980; George E. Kirk, *Survey of International Affairs, 1939–1946: The Middle East in the War*, London/New York: Oxford University Press, p.25, note 1; and Devereux, *The Formulation of . . .*, p.9.

tional British positions in the Mediterranean and Middle East. Attlee, in some ways a reincarnation of President Wilson (in 1919), looked forward to a peaceful world, where nations' interests would be secured peacefully under the auspices of the United Nations. This body would mediate and resolve international disputes.

Attlee was committed less to the traditional empire than to social reform at home. In addition, Labour politicians were in general more sensitive than the Military to anti-colonialist, nationalist opposition across the Empire, and less willing than the latter to cling to traditional strategic footholds against the wishes of the local population. As a consequence, the first two years of the Labour government's term in office witnessed a marathon internal debate as to whether Britain should hold on to her traditional positions in the Mediterranean and Middle East. On the one side, there was the Prime Minister, supported by his Chancellor of the Exchequer, Hugh Dalton. On the other, the Chiefs of Staff, ably and decisively supported by the Minister for Defence, Alexander, and the pugnacious, influential Foreign Secretary, Ernest Bevin. The clash between Dalton and Bevin over military spending became the most serious conflict within the Labour Cabinet, reflecting both a clash over national priorities, and over departmental interests. This clash continued betwen the two even after Attlee conceded the argument over the Middle East.[25]

Even if the Labour administration was willing to shed imperial burdens that the national economy could no longer sustain, the coalition of Bevin and the COS was no more willing than the Conservatives to surrender Britain's Great Power status. Bevin's long-term ambition was to transform the Middle East into a prosperous economic federation that would replace the Indian market for British goods, thereby compensating the British economy for the loss of the 'jewel in the crown'.[26]

In May 1947, three months after the Cabinet's decisions to evacuate India, and to refer Palestine to the United Nations, Bevin reassured the House of Commons on the government's determination to maintain the country's Great Power status:

> So far as foreign policy is concerned, we have not altered our commitments in the slightest . . . His Majesty's Government do not accept the view . . . that we

---

[25] On Bevin, cf. Sir Alan Bullock, *The Life and Times of Ernest Bevin*, Vols. 2 and 3, London: Heinemann, 1960, 1967; on the clash between Dalton and Bevin, cf., Ben Pimlott, *Hugh Dalton*, London: Jonathan Cape, 1985, pp.498–500. Dalton resigned office in November 1947, after a 'technical' leak of Budget secrets.

[26] John Kent, 'Bevin's Imperialism and the Idea of Euro-Africa, 1945–49', in Michael Dockrill, John Young, eds, *British Foreign Policy*, 1945–56, New York: 1989, p.53.

have ceased to be a Great Power, or the contention that we have ceased to play that role. We regard ourselves as one of the Powers most vital to the peace of the world, and we still have our historic part to play.[27]

Attlee had made no secret of his radical views, even before his electoral triumph, which was announced in late July 1945, during the proceedings of the Peace Conference at Potsdam. (Attlee attended initially as potentially the next Prime Minister, and formally, as care-taker Prime Minister Churchill's 'friend and counsellor'.) At Potsdam, Attlee objected to Foreign Secretary Eden's pessimistic view of the Soviets' intentions. He pleaded: 'We ought to confront the Russians with the requirements of a world organisation for peace, not with the needs of the defence of the British Empire'. Eden, as some authorities have suggested (and presumably the Chiefs of Staff too) regarded such sentiments as 'international outpourings of the worst kind'.[28]

As has been noted already, one of the major allied concerns in 1945 was Soviet demands of the Turks for bases at the Straits. The British Chiefs of Staff, like their American counterparts, regarded the Soviet demands as revealing offensive intent. In contrast, Attlee regarded Soviet moves as defensive in essence. He failed to see how the British, who themselves effectively controlled another international strategic waterway – the Suez Canal – could preach to the Soviets about inter-national control of the Straits. (One scholar has suggested that, in 1946, one of the reasons the British proposed their own unilateral evacuation of Egypt, was in order to keep the Soviets out of the Straits.)[29]

Admiral Andrew Cunningham, First Sea Lord and Naval representa-tive on the Chiefs of Staff Committee, probably reflected the view of his colleagues when he confided to his diary:

> Atlee [sic] has apparently written what appears to be a damned silly letter to the P.M. saying we ought not to oppose a great country like Russia having bases anywhere she wants them. What an ass![30]

Attlee's victory at the polls presumably shocked the Chiefs of Staff as much, if not more than anyone else. Now they had to contend with Attlee as their titular commander-in-chief, and until December 1946, in his capacity as Minister of Defence, as their political supremo.

[27] Speech of 16 May 1947, H.C. Deb., Vol. 437, col. 1965.
[28] Quoted in Raymond Smith, and John Zametica, 'The Cold Warrior: Clement Attlee reconsidered, 1945–7', *International Affairs*, Vol. 61/2, spring 1985, p.241.
[29] Cf., John Kent, 'The Egyptian Base and the Defence of the Middle East, 1945–54', in Holland, Robert, ed., *Emergencies and Disorder in the European Empires after 1945*, London: Frank Cass, 1994, p.46.
[30] Diary entry of 23 July 1945, quoted in Smith and Zametica, p.242.

The debate on the Middle East was opened by Attlee less than one month after his election victory, in a memorandum he addressed to the Cabinet on the future of the Italian colonies. Attlee maintained that the Empire had been created by British sea power. However, their naval strategy, which had hitherto guaranteed British control over a vast Empire, 'by means of a Fleet based on island fortresses', had now been rendered obsolete by the advent of modern air warfare.[31]

Given their inability to defend their own Empire, Attlee further shocked the Chiefs by implying that the United Nations should now act as trustee for their imperial interests:

> The British Empire can only be defended by its membership of the United Nations Organisation. If we do not accept this, we had better say so.
>
> If we do accept this we should seek to make it effective and not at the same time act on outworn conceptions. If the new organisation is a reality, it does not matter who holds Cyrenaica or Somalia or controls the Suez Canal.[32]

The CIGS, Viscount Alanbrooke, recorded that the COS were 'shaken by Attlee's new Cabinet paper in which apparently the security of the Middle East must rest in the power of the United Nations.'[33]

During the spring of 1946, Attlee developed further his new theory on the obsolescence of British sea power. In February 1946, at a meeting of the Cabinet's Defence Committee, he challenged one of the most cherished of British strategic assumptions – that British forces had to guarantee access to the Mediterranean and the Middle East.[34] In a paper written in early March 1946, Attlee asserted that whereas in the era of naval power, they had been able to maintain the Mediterranean route to India by holding Gibraltar and Malta, and by retaining the friendship of Egypt – they would now need to provide very large air forces and bases. The country simply could not afford the very large sums involved. Attlee proposed no less than a revolution in imperial thinking:

[31] CP (45) 144, 1 Sept. 1945, in Cab 129/1, PRO; reproduced in Hyam, *The Labour . . .*, Series A, Vol. 2, Part III, pp.207–8.

[32] Ibid.; also Smith and Zametica, 'The Cold War Warrior . . .', p.243.

[33] Quotation from Alanbrooke's diary, 3 Sept. 1945, in Smith and Zametica, ibid.

[34] DO (46) 5th meeting, 15 Feb. 1946, Cab 131/1. PRO.

The Cabinet's Defence Committee was established in 1946 to replace the Committee of Imperial Defence. Established by Attlee, the Defence Committee met on a regular basis, unlike other Cabinet committees which met when circumstances required. It was the central body responsible for reviewing strategy, and for co-ordinating the departments concerned in preparation for war. Ministers who attended regularly were the Prime Minister, the Minister of Defence, the Lord President of the Council, the Foreign Secretary, Chancellor of the Exchequer, the service Ministers, and the Ministers of Labour and Supply. Other Ministers attended as called upon. The Chiefs of Staff attended all meetings. Cf. Darby, *British Defence Policy . . .*, p.19; and Kenneth Harris, *Attlee*, London: Weidenfeld & Nicolson, 1982, p.402.

We must not, for sentimental reasons based on the past, give hostages to fortune. It may be we shall have to consider the British Isles as an easterly extension of a strategic era [*sic* area?] the centre of which is the American Continent rather than as a Power looking eastwards through the Mediterranean to India and the East.[35]

The Prime Minister's paper provoked a sharp debate. The COS warned that if Britain evacuated the Middle East, the Soviets would move in to replace them. Britain would then lose all control or influence over the entire Mediterranean area, from Egypt in the east to the Iberian peninsula in the west. Moreover, the COS feared that once the Egyptians suspected that the British were unable to maintain their position in the Mediterranean, they would reconsider whether to continue to grant base facilities to the British in the Canal Zone.[36]

British planners believed that their position in the Mediterranean enabled Britain to 'bring influence to bear on Southern Europe, the soft underbelly of France, Italy, Yugoslavia, Greece and Turkey'. Without that physical presence, they felt, those countries might well succumb to communist rule. In that event Britain might also lose her position and assets in the Middle East, including Iraqi oil, now one of Britain's greatest resources, and a major source of foreign earnings.[37]

But Attlee remained preoccupied with the political and military ramifications of Soviet suspicions of British intentions in the Middle East in general, and of Egyptian nationalist opposition in particular. In view of the protracted dispute with the Egyptians over base facilities, Attlee suggested that the headquarters of the British command and communications system in the Middle East be moved south, into Africa – from 'foreign', to 'British' territory. He regarded Kenya as an ideal alternative to Egypt.[38] (On this, see Chapter 5)

It has been suggested that Attlee's challenge to sacrosanct strategic doctrine, and the debate which ensued, forced the COS to draw up a radical revision of traditional strategy in the eastern Mediterranean and the Middle East; that in order to convince the Prime Minister of the need for remaining in the Middle East, the COS now produced the novel thesis that the air bases in that region were vital for the strategic air offensive against the Soviets, and that: 'The concept of bombing the Soviet Union from the Middle East was an inspired and powerful new argument which was to remain at the heart of British strategic planning

---

[35] Attlee memorandum on Defence in The Mediterranean, Middle East and Indian Ocean, DO (46) 27, 2 March 1946, Cab 131/2. PRO; reproduced in Hyam, *The Labour Government*, Series A, Vol. 2, Part III, pp.213–14.

[36] DO (46) 40, 13 March 1946, in Cab 131/21. PRO.

[37] Ibid.

[38] Ibid.

for some time.'[39]

The 'intellectual origins' of this new departure in COS thinking may be traced to Group Captain M. R. MacArthur, the Deputy Director of Policy at the Air Ministry. MacArthur's argument ran as follows: the arguments used hitherto to convince Attlee of the need for the retention of the Middle East, had become obsolescent, and had reached the 'right answers . . . for the wrong reasons'.[40] MacArthur argued that the next war would be provoked by 'land-grabbing' Russia, and the Allies would be 'forced to cry halt and declare war on her'. But the Allies would not be at all ready for war, and in any case, their shortage of manpower ruled out any thought of a land attack on the Soviet Union, at least not during the early stages of a war. The air offensive, 'either by aircraft or projectile', would not only be their sole strategic weapon, but their 'only means of effective defence'. Therefore, they had to have air bases close enough to the Soviet Union to enable them to reach major strategic targets inside that territory. In this context, the Middle East was essential as a launching platform for the strategic air offensive.[41]

With some dexterity, the Joint Planners adopted and adapted MacArthur's argument. Not only was the air offensive their only strategy in the event that the Allies were themselves 'forced' into a war; but the possession of the capacity to launch such a strike was the sole weapon wherewith to ensure the very survival of the the United Kingdom itself: 'the threat of attack by air or long range weapons will be our one effective military deterrent to Russian aggression.'[42] The COS stressed Britain's own vulnerability to air attack, and devastation by new scientific weapons. They argued that the only strategy that might save the United Kingdom would be an immediate air offensive, and that the only area from which they could effectively reach the Soviets' vulnerable south-eastern flank was the Middle East.[43]

Thus, it is claimed, within a single week:

the entire character of British planning had been transformed . . . The Middle East now derived its value from its proximity to the Soviet Union and as a barrier guarding the main support area of Africa south of the Sahara. Defence in depth and an early attack were the twin pillars of COS Middle East strategy.[44]

[39] Cf. Richard Aldrich, John Zametica, 'The Rise and Decline of a Strategic Concept: the Middle East, 1945–51', in Richard Aldrich, ed., *British Intelligence, Strategy and the Cold War, 1945–51*, London/New York: 1992, p.246.

[40] ibid, pp.243–44; and Note by Group Captain M. R. MacArthur to Director of Plans, 25 March 1946, Air 9/267. PRO.

[41] Ibid.

[42] Aldrich, Zametica, 'The Rise and Decline of a Strategic Concept . . .', p.244.

[43] DO (46) 80, *British Strategic Requirements in the Middle East*, Cab 131/3, quoted in ibid.

[44] Ibid, p.245.

Attlee's paper may well have prompted a more precise definition of Britain's strategic goals in a global war, and of the role of the Middle East in such plans. Strategic analysts on both sides of the Atlantic were still probing for a viable global strategic plan (initial American staff studies for global war, the *Pincher* series, were begun only in March 1946).

However, it would appear to be somewhat far-fetched to imply that it was primarily Attlee's iconoclasm that opened the eyes of the COS (and of the American JCS) to the only available response to the Soviets' overwhelming conventional superiority – the [American] strategic air offensive; and to the logistic advantages of Middle Eastern air bases. Neither must one ignore the element of special pleading for the Air Force in MacArthur's paper. In fact, the origins of the strategic air offensive response may be discerned clearly in a paper written back in March 1943, by the British Post-Hostilities Planning Committee. This paper had pointed to the potential post-war danger of 'Russia's over-whelming superiority in land forces', which would enable the Russians, should they so desire, to move rapidly through Western Europe. The same paper had pointed to the very evident fact that since northern Iraq was but 300 miles from Russian airfields in the Caucusus, the main threat to British interests from the Russians was in the Middle East.[45]

Had not the Americans begun as early as 1941 to develop the B-36 as a long-range bomber, in order to carry out a strategic air offensive (albeit, at the time, against Nazi Germany)? And was it too much of a flight of the imagination to see in 1943 (or in 1945?) that the same aerial threat could be posed in both directions? Gen 'Hap' Arnold, commander of USAF during World War Two, had certainly grasped this point (above, Chapter one).

The debate between the Prime Minister and his Chiefs of Staff was rejoined early in April 1946. In a memorandum dated 2 April, the COS reiterated that Britain's presence in the Mediterranean was vital to her status as a Great Power.[46] (As has been seen, this was a view shared by American military planners at that time.)

At a meeting of the Defence Committee held three days later, Foreign Secretary Bevin supported and elaborated upon the COS position. The British presence in the Mediterranean served purposes other than purely military, which were vital to the country's position as a Great Power. Through that presence, they were able to bring political influence to bear on southern Europe, and the Balkans. If they left the Mediterranean, the Russians would undoubtedly move in to take their

---

[45] PHO (43) 1(0), 8 March 1943, quoted in Lewis, *British Military . . .*, pp.103–4.
[46] Chiefs of Staff (COS) memorandum, 2 April 1946, DO (46) 47, Cab 131/21. PRO.

place, and the Mediterranean countries, along with the economic benefits which Britain derived from commerce and trade with them, would
be lost to the nation.[47]

At a further meeting of the Defence Committee at the end of May
1946, Attlee again raised the Kenya project. He doubted whether
Britain had the resources to maintain all of its current positions in the
Middle East, and asked the COS to examine which of them, in the
event of war, it would be vital to hold on to.[48]

In June 1946, Field Marshal B. L. Montgomery was appointed as
CIGS. Montgomery's wartime glory and stature were soon dissipated
at Whitehall. He fell out both with his fellow Chiefs of Staff and his own
Army Council. Mutual contempt and personal antipathy shaped
Montgomery's relations with his Service colleagues on the COS. This
was due largely to Montgomery's total lack of grace, his 'unsophisticat-
ed analysis and the dogmatic way in which he expressed it.'[49] He
crossed swords with almost every member of the Labour Cabinet with
whom he had any contact. It has been stated of Montgomery that he
formed part of a trio at the War Office, together with the Minister,
Emmanuel Shinwell, and the latter's Parliamentary Under Secretary,
George Wigg. Each of the trio:

> disguised quick minds behind gruff, bluff, contentious remarks, and all of them
> were suspicious and critical of political colleagues.[50]

But Montgomery did introduce a new assertiveness into the Chiefs of
Staff position, even if at times he had to threaten his colleagues with
resignation to get his own way.[51] Shortly after being appointed CIGS,
he wrote a paper explaining why the Middle East had been classified by
the COS as one of Britain's 'main support areas':

> We must fight for the Middle East, which, with the United Kingdom and North
> Africa, would provide the bases for the launching of a tremendous air offensive
> against the territory of any aggressor from the east. The Army must maintain
> a Corps H.Q. in the Middle East, available to go off anywhere to handle an
> emergency.[52]

The Prime Minister's question about priorities in the Middle East
was taken up by the JPS. In two separate papers, they now stressed the

[47] DO (46) 10th meeting, 5 April 1946, Cab 131/1, quoted in Lewis, *British Military . . .*,
p.270.
[48] See DO (46) 17th meeting, 27 May 1946, Cab 131/1. PRO.
[49] Chalfont, *Montgomery . . .*, p.291.
[50] Peter Slowe, *Manny Shinwell*, London: Pluto Press, 1993, p.237.
[51] Chalfont, *Montgomery . . .* p.291.
[52] Fieldmarshal B.L. Montgomery, *Memoirs*, New York: Da Capo Press, 1982, p.390.

importance of the Middle East for the future survival of the home country itself. If they were to restrict the exploitation of the nation's resources to the defence of the United Kingdom alone, any prospective enemy would be able to devote his undivided efforts against the homeland, unimpeded by any dangers to his own flanks. Britain would be exposed to piecemeal attrition through attack by long-range weapons and aircraft that would pierce its defences. The inventory of direct strategic losses that would result from the abandonment of the Middle East would include: 'irreplaceable air bases' (this loss would permit the Soviets to secure their most vulnerable flank); 'the world's greatest potential source of oil', and the cession to the Soviets of 'a formidable base from which to attack Britain's main support areas'. In response to Attlee's insistence on military cutbacks, the JPS reasoned that:

> The forces needed to guard against the resultant threat from a Sovietised Middle East would be no smaller – though a good deal less favorably placed – than those needed for the defence of the Middle East itself.[53]

The paper was approved by the COS, and taken up with Attlee at a special forum of the Prime Minister and the COS, convened on 12 July 1946. The COS spelled out for Attlee the points made by the JPS. Montgomery opened the debate with the assertion that their best means of defence would be 'an immediate attack on vital Russian points from the Middle East'. Air Marshal Tedder added that the Soviet attack on Britain would be reduced by the factor of those forces the Soviets would have to divert in order to deal with Egypt. But Attlee was not convinced. Referring to the Germans' record in World War Two, he doubted if a British counter-attack from the Middle East would significantly impair the Soviets' offensive potential against the British Isles.[54]

However, Allied planners were agreed that if the Americans did enter a war against the Soviets, their first offensive would be the airborne strategic attack from bases in the Middle East. In other words, any British withdrawal from the Middle East would prejudice the prospects of a crippling, opening American strategic assault on the Soviet military infrastructure.

But Attlee was still not convinced. He was preoccupied above all with creating the right climate for international conciliation. His prime concern was that, in view of the impending resumption of the Peace conference in Paris, 'it would be most dangerous to create suspicions in the mind of the Russians that we were threatening her security in the

---

[53] JP (46) 108, 11 June 1946, Cab 84/82, cited in Lewis, *British Military . . .*, p.283.

[54] COS (46) 108th, 12 July 1946, Cab 21/2086, quoted in Aldrich, Zametica, p.248; and Lewis, *Military Planning . . .*, pp.284–5.

Middle East.' At a further meeting of the Defence Committee, held one week later, he reproached the COS with the jibe that in any case, no country would provide Britain with bases if they suspected that she had aggressive intent.[55]

The differences between Attlee and the COS came to a head at the end of 1946, with the deterioration of the situation in Greece and Turkey. Once again, at the heart of the debate lay the two sides' respective world outlooks in regard to Soviet intentions. The COS, like their American counterparts, believed that once the Soviets gained control of the Straits, Turkey's value as a strategic bulwark to the Middle East would disintegrate, and that British positions in Palestine and Egypt would be exposed. By contrast, Attlee remained convinced that the only solution to Britain's relations with the Soviets lay in conciliation and agreement.[56]

At the beginning of 1947, Prime Minister Attlee was almost isolated in his opposition to the retention of Britain's traditional position in the Middle East. But in a key exchange of private notes with his Foreign Secretary, Attlee beat a tactical retreat. He complained that the latest COS appreciation would involve the country in 'heavy military commitments', which they had to consider in relation to their 'man power and economic resources'. He still regarded the Military's Middle East strategy as one of despair, of supporting 'a congeries of weak, backward and reactionary States'. He expressed his grave doubts as to its efficiency. Once again, he pleaded that before committing themselves to that strategy, they should try to reach an agreement with the Soviets, 'after consideration with Stalin of all our points of conflict'.[57]

Two days later, on 7 January 1947, at a COS staff conference attended by the Prime Minister and the Foreign Secretary, the Middle East was again discussed. The COS defined the principles upon which the defence of the UK should be based:

(a) protecting the Commonwealth's means to fight a major war until an offensive could be developed . . .

(b) holding bases for the offensive.

To achieve these objectives, British forces were first to defend the United Kingdom, second to maintain sea communications, and third to keep a 'firm hold' on the Middle East.[58]

---

[55] Ibid., and minutes of Defence Commitee 19 July 1946, Cab 131/1. PRO.

[56] DO(46) 9th meeting, 27 March 1946, Cab 131/1; COS(46) 277, 13 Nov. 1946, in Cab 80/103, also R17592, FO 371/58659. PRO.

[57] Attlee – Bevin, 5 Jan. 1947, FO 800/476. PRO.

[58] Cf. Eric Grove and Geoffrey Till, 'Anglo-American Maritime Strategy in the Era of Massive Retaliation, 1945–60', in John B. Hattendorf and Robert S. Jordan, eds, *Maritime Strategy and the Balance of Power*, London: Macmillan, 1989, p.275.

In the Chiefs of Staffs' opinion, should any of these three 'pillars' of British strategy collapse, the whole edifice of Britain's global strategy would crumble.

Attlee reiterated his view that Soviet foreign policy was benign, 'based entirely on the need for self-preservation'. He lectured on the central theme of his private note to Bevin. In a broadside against a central pillar of Allied contingency planning, he accused the COS of looking on the Middle East principally as 'an offensive base from which to attack Russia'. He himself was not persuaded that British facilities in the Middle East were necessary for the defence of the Commonwealth, and again pressed the idea of transferring Britain's main base in Egypt to Kenya.[59]

In any case, continued Attlee, even if Soviet expansionist ambitions were as extensive as apprehended, he doubted whether the Allies had sufficient resources wherewith to support Iraq or Iran against a Soviet attack. He personally doubted if the Soviets were covetous of Allied oil interests in the Middle East, since under their own territories lay over one third of the world's then known oil resources. He believed that the Soviets would agree to the Allies exploiting 'a similar proportion of the world's supplies in the Middle East'. But such an agreement would not be forthcoming if provocative moves by Britain in the Middle East fanned Russian suspicions of 'an ultimate capitalistic war on her'.[60] This latter point, a recurrent theme in Attlee's argument, was in fact concurred in by the JPS on both sides of the Atlantic. They assumed that in any global offensive, the Soviets would make a pre-emptive strike against the Middle East, in order to neutralise the allied potential for attacking them at their soft under-belly, in the Caucasus and in Rumania.

Lord Tedder, Chief of the Air Staff, referred to the essential role of the strategic air offensive from the Middle East. He maintained that they could rely on the Americans to send forces quickly to the Middle East in the event of a Soviet attack. But Attlee had apparently derived his own 'lessons of history' from the American record in two world wars. In a private letter addressed to Bevin the previous month, Attlee had warned:

> There is a tendency in America to regard us as an outpost of America, but an outpost that they will not have to defend. I am disturbed by the signs of America trying to make a safety zone around herself while leaving us in Europe in No Man's Land.[61]

[59]　COS (47) 6th meeting, 7 Jan. 1947, Defe 32/1, Secretary's Standard File. PRO.
[60]　Ibid.
[61]　Attlee to Bevin, 1 Dec. 1946, FO 800/475, PRO; reproduced in Hyam, *The Labour Government . . .*, Series A, Vol. 2, Part III, p.222.

At the 7 January meeting, he told the COS that unless the Americans took on specific obligations in the region in peacetime, the British would have to absorb and repel the initial Soviet assault on their own. He insinuated that the despatch of American troops to the Middle East would depend upon the date of American entry into the war. Attlee wanted the Americans to undertake now a commitment equal to that of their own in the Middle East. As noted already, this was something the Americans consistently refused to do.

The Prime Minister was not persuaded by COS arguments on the strategic importance of the Middle East. However, he did concede that 'the best form of defence was the ability to retaliate', and agreed that their policy in the region might be described 'more as a deterrent than as provocation'. But Attlee still insisted that it would be premature for Britain to plan on remaining in the Middle East as a long-term policy. He averred that once they discovered what the Soviets really wanted in the region, an international agreement could be arrived at. As usual, Chancellor of the Exchequer Dalton backed the Prime Minister. Due to Britain's grave economic position, Dalton urged the reduction of all overseas commitments to an absolute minimum.[62]

The continuing clash between the Prime Minister and the COS threw Foreign Office officials into consternation. They spoke of the disasters that would befall the country if the Middle East was evacuated, and the consequent harm to their status in Europe. They warned that the United States would despair of Great Britain, and that all this would 'heighten the probability of a world war in which we should be massacred'.[63] On 9 January, in a private note, Bevin warned Attlee that evacuation of the Middle East 'would be Munich over again'. After their abandonment of India and Burma, a retreat from the Middle East would indicate to the world that they were abdicating their position as a great power. The United States would write them off, and it would weaken the United Nations. Echoing Kennan's 'long telegram', Bevin stated that the present rulers of the Soviet Union were ideologically committed to a universal communist crusade, one that must involve conflict with the capitalist world. He argued that even if they did not believe that the Soviets harboured aggressive intentions, the latter would be unable to resist moving into the Middle East vacuum that a British evacuation would leave.[64]

---

[62] COS (47) 6th meeting, 7 Jan. 1947, Defe 32/1, Secretary's Standard File. PRO.

[63] Minute by Pierson Dixon (Bevin's private secretary), 8 Jan. 1947, on Foreign Office staff meeting, attended by Sir Orme Sargent, Sir William Hayter, and Messrs Howe and Warner. FO 800/476. PRO.

[64] Bevin to Attlee, 9 Jan. 1947, ME/47/4, ibid.; reproduced in Hyam, *The Labour Government . . .*, Series A, Vol. 2, Part III, pp.227–9.

Later that same day, 9 January, Bevin and Attlee met alone to thrash out the issue. Attlee finally agreed that there would be no further withdrawals of forces from the Middle East in excess of programmes contemplated already. However, this was but a tactical retreat. Attlee still opposed the COS strategic conception of using the Middle East as an offensive platform from which to attack the Soviets. Bevin and Attlee agreed that this concept would be discussed at a further discussion with the COS.[65]

At around this time, Montgomery delivered a private threat to the Prime Minister, warning that if he persisted in overriding the Service Chiefs on this issue, they would resign *en bloc*. Attlee, like his formidable predecessor, Winston Churchill, could not have remained indifferent, when faced with a determined, combined front of his senior Ministers and the COS.[66] At a further staff conference between Attlee and the COS, held just six days later, on 13 January, the Prime Minister did appear to reverse his prior position. He now conceded the need to rest future defence policy on the three fundamental principles of global strategy, as outlined first by Montgomery at a conference held with Defence Minister Alexander, on 23 December 1946, and reiterated at the staff conference of 7 January. Attlee apparently conceded the need, to retain a firm hold on the Middle East, for counter-offensive purposes.[67]

Some scholars have claimed that Attlee's concession on 13 January (when he 'inexplicably endorsed the Chiefs of Staff strategy') marked the end of the debate on Britain's Mediterranean strategy, because Attlee capitulated to Montgomery's threat that the COS would resign.[68] But it would appear to this writer that Bevin's, rather than Montgomery's, was the principal influence on Attlee. Both Attlee and Bevin

[65] Dixon minute, 10 Jan. 1947, ME/47/4, ibid.

[66] Montgomery, *Memoirs*, pp.390–1.
On Prime Minister Churchill's relations with the Military (and his trauma following his ejection from the Cabinet for his part in the Dardanelles débacle in 1915), cf., Cohen, *Churchill and . . .*, pp.6, 218–19.

[67] Staff conference of 13 Jan. 1947 in Defe 4/1; and meeting of 23 Dec. 1946, in COS(46) 187th. Cab 79/54, PRO. Both also cited in Lewis, *British Military . . .*, pp.300–1, and Aldrich, Zametica, p.253.

[68] Cf., Ritchie Ovendale, *The English-Speaking Alliance: Britain, the United States, the Dominions and the Cold War, 1945–1951*, London: Allen & Unwin, 1985, p.52; Also Smith, Zametica, 'The Cold War Warrior . . .', p.251, who claim that 'It would appear from the timetable of events that Attlee received this information on Sunday, 12 January', i.e., the day before the crucial meeting. But they adduce no evidence for the said 'timetable of events'; it is in fact impossible to deduce from Montgomery's own memoirs exactly when he delivered the resignation threat to the Prime Minister. Zametica repeats this argument in Aldrich, Zametica, 'The Rise and Decline . . .', p.252.

had grown used to dealing with their 'bristling and pugnacious CIGS', who had developed the threat of resignation into something of an art.[69]

Whatever the case, the combined pressures of the Foreign Secretary and the CIGS had their effect. For the present, Attlee's campaign to reduce the British military presence in the Middle East had indeed been blocked. But in fact, Attlee was far from convinced. The COS themselves harboured few illusions that the Prime Minister was truly converted. In late January 1947, the Future Planning Section of the COS produced the first draft of its long-term study of 'Future Defence Policy'.

Their paper adduced a new element into the strategic importance of the Middle East. Given that Western Europe was now thought to be indefensible, the Allies' counter-offensive bases might be sited in one or more of four possible locations; the United Kingdom, French North Africa, the Middle East, or India. French North Africa and India were dubious propositions, due to political uncertainty. This left only the British Isles and the Middle East. Admittedly, the air base in Egypt was recommended only for a transitional period, for so long as the Soviets lacked the means of eliminating the United Kingdom itself quickly. The Egyptian base might be counted upon until 1956–57. By that time, the planners believed, 'the Russian stock of atomic weapons would suffice to cause the collapse of the United Kingdom before any Middle Eastern counter-offensive mounted from Egypt could possibly take effect'. After that date, they might try to utilise Aden, Malta, and perhaps Cyrenaica in combination, until the longer-range bombers became operational.[70]

A further claim made by the COS study was that the Middle East was the only area from which the British, if attacked first, could immediately launch a counter-attack, with a view to limiting the weight of the Soviet offensive. This was vital not only to the immediate defence of the UK itself, but also to that of her sea lanes, and of the resources upon which the Commonwealth depended to defend herself.[71] But this draft was not ready in final form for presentation to the Prime Minister until March, too late to forestall three Cabinet decisions of long-term strategic significance, all taken in mid-February, all of which had direct ramifications for Britain's position in the Middle East.

The Cabinet decided to withdraw from India by June 1948; to refer the Palestine question to the United Nations; and to inform the

---

[69] Chalfont, *Alamein* . . . pp.291, 295. Interestingly, Chalfont does not mention this particular resignation threat of Montgomery's.

[70] See Lewis, *British Military* . . ., p.320. An early draft of this document, COS (47) 5, 'Future Defence Policy', 23 Jan. 1947, Defe 5/3, does not contain the passages cited here. The final version of this document, dated May 1947, from which Lewis quotes, (pp.369–81), was retained by the Cabinet Office.   [71] COS (47) 5, ibid.

Americans of their intention (due primarily to financial reasons) to terminate British economic and military aid to Greece and Turkey by the end of March 1947. The decision to end aid to Greece, and to continue with very limited aid to the Turks, was conveyed the same month to the Americans. The British decision prompted the issue of the Truman Doctrine the following month, which elicited a Congressional grant of $400 million to Greece and Turkey.[72]

For those historians not familiar with the documents on the planned strategic offensive from the Egyptian base, it has proved hard, if not impossible, to conceive why the February decisions, especially the withdrawal from India, did not bring a change in British strategic thinking on the Middle East. Thus, with the apparent wisdom that comes with hindsight, Philip Darby wrote in 1973:

> In retrospect the need for reappraisal seems so obvious that at first sight it is difficult to understand how Indian independence could pass leaving little more than a ripple on the placid surface of British political and strategic thinking.

Darby castigated British planners for failing to scale down British commitments in the region, and to redefine their country's goals, and to adjust her imperial role to 'the conditions of the post-imperial order'. He has accused the Chiefs of Staff of having confined their attentions 'to the problem of re-building an imperial strategy from what remained of the pre-war pieces'. The reason for this failure to address new imperial realities, in Darby's opinion, lay in ingrained 'patterns of thought which only slowly lost their hold on decision-making in Whitehall'.[73]

Attractive and elegant as this thesis might appear to be, it simply does not accord with the facts. Even when the Suez Canal was no longer needed for communications with India, the bases along its banks continued to be of critical strategic importance in Allied contingency planning for a global war against the Soviet Union.

John Kent, a British scholar who did have access to the documents, has recently suggested that British imperialism in the Middle East was simply 'more of the same', the clinging to the appurtenances of Great Power status:

[72] Rosencrance, *Defence of* . . ., pp.62–3; and Peter G. Boyle, The British Foreign Office and American Foreign Policy, 1947–48, *Journal of American Studies*, Vol. 16/3, Dec. 1982, pp.373–89. Between 1944–47, Britain had expended $540 million on Greece, and between 1938–1947, $375 million on Turkey. On British aid to Greece and Turkey, see Terry H. Anderson, *The United States, Great Britain and the Cold War, 1944–1947*, Columbia/London: University of Missouri Press, 1981, pp.167–69.

[73] Philip Darby, *British Defence Policy East of Suez, 1947–1968*, London: Oxford University Press for the RIIA, 1973, pp.15–16.

... the British military at the end of Second World War did not seek to retain a military presence in the Middle East in order to defend the region; rather, they sought to defend Britain's position as an imperial power through the maintenance of a military presence in the Middle East, which for most of the first post-war decade was connected to the base in Egypt.[74]

This thesis is the more curious, since Dr Kent is cognizant of British contingency planning for the defence of the Middle East against a Soviet offensive. Even so, pointing to the evident surrealistic aspects of British strategy (i.e., the lack of forces with which to implement it), Dr Kent concludes that the Cold War simply became 'a useful means of justifying a British presence in the Middle East . . .'.[75]

But this is to gainsay the very evident gravity with which post-war leaders, both civil and military, regarded the Soviet threat. The metamorphosis which had taken place in British strategic thinking about the Suez Canal is articulated clearly in a seminal memorandum written by Foreign Secretary Bevin in November 1950. Noting the change in the strategic role of the Egyptian base since the signature of the last Anglo-Egyptian treaty, in 1936, Bevin stated:

> The strategic emphasis has in fact shifted since 1936, and our primary strategic requirement is now not so much the defence of the Suez Canal itself, as the maintenance of a base in Egypt capable of rapid expansion on the outbreak of war, in order to support a major campaign in the Middle East and the defence of the base against air attack.[76]

The COS believed that the February 1947 decisions had eroded the foundations of Britain's global strategy. They forecast doom and disaster. CIGS Montgomery complained that the decision to withdraw from India had been taken without even consulting the COS. In early March, the COS produced a paper cataloguing all the recent strategic setbacks: the reference of the Palestine question to the United Nations (a move whereby Britain risked losing its hold on that country altogether); the decision to cut off aid to Greece which, unless the Americans stepped in, would probably consign that country to communist control; the lack of progress in securing strategic rights in Cyrenaica, and the decision to quit India in June 1948 (subsequently

[74] John Kent, 'The Egyptian Base and the Defence of the Middle East, 1945–54', in Robert Holland, ed., *Emergencies and Disorder in the European Empires after 1945*, London: Frank Cass, 1994, p.47.

[75] Ibid., p.53.

[76] Memorandum to the Cabinet by the Foreign Secretary, CP (50), 283, 27 Nov. 1950, Cab 129/43. PRO.

brought forward by one year). Added together, these decisions 'would rule out prospects of fighting in, and for the Middle East in war'.[77]

The COS feared that any power vacuum left by the British would be exploited by the Soviets. British withdrawal might encourage countries previously within the British sphere of influence to gravitate into the Soviet orbit. Egypt might succumb to communist influence, which in turn would make Britain's position in the Sudan untenable. India might go the same way, and the repercussions would reverberate throughout Africa, with grave damage to Britain's traditional position throughout that continent.[78]

The COS still regarded the Middle East as a vital strategic 'land-bridge between continents'. Moreover, the value of the region as a counter-offensive base assumed yet more significance, once it became apparent that the air bases in India could not be relied upon even for the short-term.[79]

The COS Planning Staff's 'Review of Defence Problems' was completed in final draft at the end of March, circulated by the COS as 'The Overall Strategic Plan' in May, and discussed and approved finally at a staff meeting with Attlee and Bevin on 11 June 1947. It was only at this latter meeting that the Prime Minister finally conceded to COS demands about the supreme importance of holding on to Egypt.[80] The final report stressed the need for Britain to develop, or secure long-range bombers. Once the operational range of their aircraft was significantly extended, 'the outstanding military importance of the United Kingdom and the Middle East as offensive bases would drastically decline.' They would then be able to counter-attack the Soviets from a wide circle of British, or American-owned bases, 'from Alaska and the Far East to Ceylon, Kenya and Newfoundland'.[81]

The COS stressed that Britain must be prepared to take offensive action at the outset of any war with the Soviets. Such a war would reach a climax rapidly, and the United Kingdom itself could not be 'guaranteed for any considerable period against attacks by modern weapons, still less by weapons of mass destruction.' The best bases for this counter-offensive were now reduced to three – the United Kingdom, the Middle East and, 'if possible North-West India'.

[78] Cf., Ovendale, *The English-Speaking* . . ., p.52.

[79] DO (47) 23, 7 March 1947, Cab 131/4. PRO.

[80] Both the COS memorandum ('The Overall Strategic Plan'), as well as the minutes of the 11 June meeting were witheld by the Public Record Office. Their release was apparently secured by Julian Lewis, supra.

[81] 'Review of Defence Problems', COS (47) 5 (0) Final, 31 March 1947, Defe 5/3. PRO, cited in Lewis, *British Military* . . ., p.323. (Lewis' footnote reference is given on p.302.)

The primary task of the Army, the paper noted, was to man the anti-aircraft defences and to aid the civil power in the United Kingdom, as well as to guard the Middle East base. But such was the importance allotted to the Middle East by the Overall Strategic Plan that the COS now gave priority to the security of the Middle East base even over the provision of anti-invasion forces for the United Kingdom itself.[82] In essence, the COS were proposing that the government run the lower risk of a Soviet airborne invasion of the United Kingdom, in order to provide a better chance of success for the Allies' strategic air offensive from the Middle East against the Soviet Union.

The COS paper was discussed at a special staff conference of the COS, with Attlee and Bevin, on 11 June 1947. Attlee still remained sceptical as to whether the Middle East was in fact defensible, and whether the weight of the Soviet attack on the United Kingdom would be reduced significantly by the counter-offensive launched from the Middle East. But Bevin came down firmly on the side of the COS, averring that the Suez Base might even deter the Soviet Union from war. He insisted that the Soviets were so anxious about their vulnerability on their southern flank that the British presence in the Middle East 'would act as a definite check on Russian aspirations and would make her hesitate before embarking on a major war.'[83]

The COS claimed that the Middle East was unique, in that it was the single area from which successful British opposition could be mounted with relatively small forces. They pointed out that the more the Russians developed oil fields further to the east, the more urgent the Allies' need for forward bases from which to launch attacks against this most important element of the Soviet war machine.

Faced with unanimity among all those present at the special conference (Chancellor Dalton had not been invited), Attlee finally agreed to the Overall Strategic Plan. However, due to fear of provoking the Soviets if the plan leaked out, he stipulated that it was to be given a strictly limited circulation, and that no mention be made of the Soviets by name in the follow-up papers, which would receive a wider circulation. The COS conceded Attlee's circulation restrictions on the plan, so long as its contents were approved.[84]

Attlee had bowed finally to the majority, led by the COS and Bevin. But not due to conviction. In a private letter to Bevin, written on 10 August 1947, Attlee remonstrated:

[82] The Overall Strategic Plan, May 1947, D0(47) 44, and COS (47) 102 (0), both retained in Cabinet Office; reprinted in Lewis, *British Military* . . ., pp.369–381.

[83] COS (47) 74th, retained by PRO, but cited by Lewis, *British Military* . . ., p.341.

[84] Lewis, *British Military* . . ., pp.341, 343.

I cannot see how the fact of our needing a Commonwealth base in the Middle East gives us any ground for demanding that that base should be in Egypt, a foreign Sovereign State. We have no case to retain more troops than we are allowed under the Treaty. Our only defence is the difficulty of removal in the time at our disposal . . .. The Chiefs of Staff must press on with alternative arrangements.[85]

The Overall Strategic plan now became the basis of Britain's global strategy. Britain's own survival in a future war was now seen to rest on the Middle East base. In addition, her Middle Eastern oil concessions were still considered a long-term strategic asset, one that made a significant contribution to the British economy. A Foreign Office paper written in May 1952 (six months after the British had been evicted from Abadan) pointed out:

The Middle East contains 45% of known world oil reserves, and produces about 20% of the world's current crude oil supplies. Large British investments and export markets are involved . . . In war, it could provide a platform from which air attacks on the southern industrial areas of the Soviet Union could most easily be mounted.[86]

However, even if the the COS had overcome Attlee's opposition to the Middle East garrison, political and economic factors would ultimately vindicate his misgivings. The economic cost to Britain of holding on to the Middle East without American military support, became prohibitive. Attlee may have 'lost' the strategic debate against the COS in 1947, but it took only a few short years to vindicate the Prime Minister's prescience about post-imperial Britain's incapacity to maintain a substantial military presence in the Middle East.

To this would be added intransigent Egyptian nationalist opposition, which finally convinced the Allies that they could no longer rely on secure access to the Suez base even in peace time, much less in an emergency. At the turn of the new decade, British strategic conceptions in the Middle East began to undergo a radical change. But even when the COS were finally persuaded of the inevitability of evacuating Egypt, the aspiration to secure re-entry rights and access to strategic bases in that country immediately upon the outbreak of war remained a basic goal of British planning.

Where Attlee's rhetoric had failed to win the day, economic and political realities dictated the eventual turn of events in the Middle East. Nothing illustrates this better than the progressive reduction of the British garrison in that theatre.

---

[85]   Attlee – Bevin, 10 Aug. 1947, FO 800/457, PRO. The COS estimated that it would take three years to remove all equipment, stores, and installations from the Canal Base.
[86]   Minute by J.C.W. Bushell, 1 May 1952, E1056, FO 371/98253. PRO.

C. REDEPLOYMENT IN THE MIDDLE EAST

At the beginning of July 1945, in the somewhat euphoric post-VJ-Day period, Edward Grigg (later Lord Altrincham), Minister of State Resident in the Middle East, proposed to the Conservative Cabinet that Britain maintain a post-war Middle East garrison of no less than seven Divisions – two in Palestine, one each in Cyprus, Egypt, and Transjordan; with the remaining two divisions to be split between Cyrenaica and East Africa. The War Office rejected Transjordan and Cyrenaica altogether, and stated that Britain would be able to maintain no more than a single Brigade in Cyprus. Their counter-proposal was for just five Divisions in the Middle East, three in Palestine and two in Egypt.[87]

The participants in this debate displayed no prescience about Britain's pending post-war economic bankruptcy, or the burgeoning indigenous nationalist movements in the region. No one at that time saw any apparent reason why the imperial glory that had been should not continue ever after. When the British Foreign Office objected even to the War Office's five-Division proposal, it was on the grounds that the garrison it proposed exceeded by far the force levels they were allowed (or had agreed) to hold in Iraq and Egypt, under their treaties with those countries.[88] But the Foreign Office did not apparently foresee any difficulty with stationing two Divisions in Palestine.

The initial euphoria was soon shattered. Within two months of the Foreign Office demurral, the Egyptians were demanding total evacuation of the British Canal Base, and a Jewish Revolt in Palestine threatened the rule of British law in that country. In less than three years hence, the British had evacuated Palestine.

By the end of 1945, British security forces in Palestine, which had numbered some 50,000 at the end of the war, had reached 80,000. These included a parachute division brought in from Germany. By 1947, at the peak of the revolt, 100,000 British troops and police were tied down by an insurgent Jewish community. In February 1947, having failed to secure American support for various plans to solve the impasse in that country, the British referred the Palestine problem to the United Nations. By the summer of that year, the British Cabinet had decided to relinquish their Mandate, and to evacuate Palestine. On

[87] Grigg memorandum, *Imperial Security in the Middle East*, 2 July 1945, CP (45) 55, Cab 66/67, and Minute by Charles Baxter, Head of the Eastern Department at the Foreign Office, 25 Aug. 1945, E6528, FO 371/45252, PRO; these are quoted in Habibur Rahman, 'British Post-Second World War Military Planning for the Middle East', *The Journal of Strategic Studies*, Vol. 5/4, 1982, p.517.

[88] Baxter minute, ibid.

29 November 1947 the United Nations resolved to partition Palestine into Arab and Jewish states. By the following May, the British had evacuated the last of their personnel, and the British occupation of Palestine, having lasted exactly 30 years, was at an end.[89]

The final British evacuation of Egypt, where Britain had more vital, and longer-standing interests, would take seven years longer.

As noted already, the Foreign Office were anxious to reduce troop levels to those determined by their treaties with Iraq and Egypt. The Treasury seized on the same argument. In August 1948, Chancellor Dalton remonstrated with Foreign Secretary Bevin and Minister of Defence Alexander. He complained that current troop levels in Egypt were in excess of those they had agreed to in the 1936 treaty. And he warned that he would find it impossible 'to find the gold or dollars for the maintenance of British troops in Egypt after December 1948.'[90] (On the costs to the British Exchequer of the Egyptian Base, see Appendix 1).

As early as spring 1949, the COS were placed on notice by the Cabinet that defence expenditure over the coming three years would be reduced to below £700 million per annum. A COS working party reported back in June on the implications of the budget cuts. The Navy would be hit the hardest; they would able to retain only small forces in the Mediterranean and in the Persian Gulf, and none permanently East of Suez, apart from Hong Kong. The army would have to be reduced from 391,000 to 290,000 men by 1953, and the Royal Air Force from 213,000 to 185,000 men. In the event of war, just two divisions would be mobilised, and despatched either to Europe or to the Middle East. Britain's total Middle East garrison would be no more than 42,500.[91]

From a very early stage, it became apparent that Britain would need significant American, or Commonwealth support in order to hold on to her traditional positions in the Mediterranean, the Middle East and the Persian Gulf. In November 1949, the Americans announced that they were withdrawing the three-and-one-third divisions and 350 tactical aircraft that they had previously allotted to the Middle East (see Chapter 2). The Americans informed the British that they and their Commonwealth allies would have to assume responsibility for this theatre.[92]

The COS urged high-level talks with member countries of the Commonwealth, in order to mobilise contingents for the Middle East.

---

[89] Cf., Michael J. Cohen, *Palestine and the Great Powers, 1945–1948*, Princeton: Princeton University Press, 1982.

[90] Note by Ernest Bevin, 5 Aug. 1948, FO 800/457. PRO.

[91] DO (49) 48, 21 June 1949, in Cab 131/7. PRO.

[92] Cf., COS (51) 759, 18 Dec. 1951, Defe 5/35. PRO.

At a Commonwealth Prime Ministers' conference in October 1948, Pakistan had expressed some willingness to despatch forces, though it was feared that her enthusiasm had mostly to do with Moslem antipathy to Israel. South Africa was concerned more with her African hinterland. She made a general offer of aircraft for service in the Middle East, although there were doubts about the technological modernity of her air force. At further bilateral talks with each member country, Canada had refused to commit any forces to the Middle East, and the Australians had remained non-committal.[93]

The Australians still chafed at Britain's 'great betrayal' in the Far East during World War Two, and preferred to align themselves with the Americans. From 1950, insurgency in Malaya concerned Australia and New Zealand far more than the Middle East. Their final answer to British appeals came in September 1951, with the signing of the ANZUS pact – 'a Pacific security agreement embracing Australia, New Zealand and the United States, but not Britain.' Although Britain chafed somewhat at being excluded, she was not entirely displeased, hoping that the American guarantee would release Commonwealth troops for the Middle East. The ANZUS pact was the consummation of a 'trend initiated by the fall of Singapore in 1942', and the British themselves came to appreciate the reality that 'unless Australia and New Zealand felt fully secure at home they would not contribute to a Commonwealth defence of the Middle East'.[94]

Two months later, the COS noted that they still remained without any Commonwealth commitment to the Middle East. Australia was making its contribution contingent upon the situation in Malaya. And in any event, no Commonwealth units could be deployed in the Middle East before 1954.[95]

The essential difference separating American and British global strategy remained the question of the priority given to the Middle East. By 1950, the Americans allotted a higher priority to the Pacific theatre than to the Middle East. The British were unable to fathom out how the Americans could simply write off this critical theatre. The CIGS, Field Marshal Slim, commented that had Britain lost the Middle East in the last world war, she 'would almost certainly have been defeated.'[96]

From 1950, faced with Egyptian intransigence, American and Commonwealth equivocation, and economic impecunity, the COS

---

[93] Aldrich, Zametica, *The Rise and . . .*, pp.258–60, 265; on British efforts to secure Commonwealth aid in the Middle East, see also Devereux, *The Formulation of . . .*, Ch. 3.

[94] Cf., Aldrich, Zametica, ibid., p.265, and Devereux, ibid., p.90; and Hyam, *The Labour Government . . .*, Part I, p.lx.

[95] Annexe to COS (51) 686, 28 Nov. 1951, Defe 5/35. PRO.

[96] COS 169th. 16 Oct. 1950, Defe 4/36. PRO.

drew up plans for a drastic reduction in the Middle East garrison. This was also due to an 'adverse ratio between infantry serving at home and overseas'. In January 1950, the British held some 15 battalions in the Middle East. The COS planned to bring home seven of these, including the three in Italian Somaliland, the two in Eritrea, and the single battalion in Aqaba, Jordan. Eight battalions of the 1st Division would be left in the Middle East. These, it was hoped, would be sufficient to cover internal security needs, and to fulfil initial treaty commitments to Jordan, if the latter was attacked by Israel. One Infantry Brigade from the 1st Division, with its affiliated field regiment, was to be held in the UK as a mobile reserve. In the event of an emergency, it would, it was hoped, rejoin its Division in the Middle East within six weeks.[97] (For the mobile reserve concept, see Chapter 9.)

The projected role of the Egyptian base in the Allied strategic air offensive was reflected in the relative levels of British ground and air forces still stationed in Egypt at the end of 1950. The dominance of air force personnel is readily apparent. British force levels in Egypt in that year were over three times that permitted by the 1936 Treaty. The Land Striking Force numbered some 7000, compared with 10,000 in the Royal Air Force and air defence units; in addition, there were over 13,000 Headquarters and Base troops associated with the GHQ, MELF. (In addition, there were also some 8000 Mauritian troops guarding the base.)[98]

However, British fighting forces in the Middle East, on their own, were hopelessly inadequate for carrying out even the most minimal of the contingency plans then being drafted for the defence of that theatre against a Soviet attack. In March 1951, Gen Robertson, the C. in. C. Middle East, told the Chiefs of Staff that during the opening stages of a war, before the arrival of Commonwealth reinforcements, the deficiency in land forces would be 'of the order of seven divisions'. As for the RAF, Air Marshal Baker told the same meeting that in the air, they fell so far short of parity with the Soviets, 'that there was no early solution in sight'. They did have two good forward air bases, in Iraq and in Jordan, but their 'only' problem was 'to find the air forces'.[99]

In November 1951, the COS approved a new plan, *Cinderella*, to succeed *Galloper*. They now estimated that to hold the minimal defence line in front of the Egyptian base would require two divisions, within the first month of a war, and five divisions, including one armoured division, by the end of the third month. However, current British plans for

---

[97] COS (50) 52, 21 Jan. 1950, in Air 20/2463. PRO.

[98] Memorandum by Foreign Secretary Bevin, CP (50) 283, 27 Nov. 1950, Cab 129/43, PRO.

[99] COS (51) 166, 30 March 1951, Defe 5/29.

the Middle East hinged on a single Division, the 3rd., which was soon to be returned to the UK. In its place, the 2nd Territorial Division, stationed in the UK, was to be earmarked for service in the Middle East, and was expected to arrive there by the end of the fourth month of war.

As the COS noted, with superb understatement, all this meant a 'grave deficiency' in infantry after D + 6 months, and a 'grave lack of armour before D + 150 days'. Current British plans would leave a deficiency of 300 aircraft on D Day itself, rising to 700 by the sixth month of war. The COS were able to devise only makeshift measures. They had to rely on the Territorial Divisions in the UK. They decided to employ the Parachute brigade deployed in the Middle East as infantry. In addition, they proposed the withdrawal of two Vampire Fighter/Ground attack squadrons (each equipped with 16 aircraft) from the Far East to the Middle East. (The squadrons concerned, Nos. 28 and 60, were not in fact ever moved to the Middle East.)[100]

These improvisatory measures were no sooner drafted than they were superceded by developments in Egypt. In the Fall of 1951, as negotiations between the UK and the Egypt collapsed, the country degenerated into chaos. Reinforcements had to be rushed in from the UK. British and Egyptian security forces clashed, as an indigenous guerilla campaign mounted attacks on British forces, sabotaged British installations, and organised labour boycotts. The violence in Egypt peaked on 25 January 1952, with large-scale clashes between British and Egyptian security forces. The next day, the mob torched and ransacked Cairo.[101] (See below, Chapter 9.)

Three days after the sacking of Cairo, CIGS Slim warned the Cabinet that any further conflict with the Egyptians might require the despatch of reinforcements from the UK. However, as he also noted, they did not in fact have any additional troops to send out, since the entire strategic reserve had already been despatched to Egypt. Slim feared that the lack of any reserve at home might encourage insurgency in other parts of the world, to which they would be unable to respond.[102]

At times, it appears almost as if the planners in London were divorced from realities in the Middle East itself. In December 1951, at the height of the crisis in Egypt, the JPS drew up yet another plan for troop dispositions in defence of the Middle East against a possible Soviet attack. It planned on the deployment of no less than two infantry

[100] Annex to COS (51) 686, supra. For the information on the two Vampire squadrons, I am most grateful to Mr Mungo Chapman, of the Department of Research and Information of the Royal Air Force Museum, London.

[101] Cf., Peter L. Hahn, 'Containment and Egyptian Nationalism: The Unsuccessful Effort to Establish the Middle East Command, 1950–53', *Diplomatic History*, II/I, Winter 1987, p.37, and Devereux, *The Formulation of . . .* pp.63, 137–8.

[102] CC (52) 8th. 28 Jan. 1952, Cab 128/24. PRO.

divisions and one armoured division, as well as a mobile force of about two brigades. And this, less than one month after the JPS had noted that the Commonwealth had yet to make any firm commitment to the Middle East, and that no American units would be available in that theatre for at least the first two years of a war.[103]

Quite clearly, as had been the case in Palestine, British force was unable to quash, or cope with indigenous demands for independence. By the end of 1951, the garrison in Egypt had been reinforced from 33,500 to 64,000 troops; and 20,000 more were on their way.[104] It was the largest concentration of British forces anywhere across the globe, and constituted a burden that Britain could no longer shoulder. Moreover, as CIGS Slim had warned, if they stretched out their forces too thinly across their remaining possessions, indigenous opposition would take advantage.

As noted recently, and succinctly by one scholar:

> As the crisis of power became more a crisis of prestige the issue was whether scuttling would retain more prestige and influence than refusing to scuttle; to remain would be too costly in both manpower and money.[105]

The paucity of British resources, as noted in these last pages, should be borne in mind when we come to discuss (in Chapter 5), Britain's vain attempts to wrest from the Egyptians a new treaty to guarantee her base rights along the Suez Canal. But first, a closer look at the military and strategic importance of Palestine will be taken.

---

[103] Annexe to COS (51) 755, 18 Dec. 1951, Defe 5/35, and to COS (51) 686, 28 Nov. 1951, supra. PRO.
[104] Cf., Kent, *The Egyptian Base . . .*, p.51.
[105] Ibid., p.60.

4 The strategic and military importance of Palestine

A. THE PALESTINE–EGYPT NEXUS

At the end of World War Two, the strategic importance of Palestine was reassessed in the light of the transformed strategic role of the region as a whole, and of Egypt in particular. The strategic assets of Palestine, as summarised by British planners, were as follows:

a. Palestine was the natural position from which to defend the Suez Canal against an attack from the north.
b. Palestine constituted a potential base in which to hold troops in excess of those the Egyptians would permit to be stationed on their soil, by virtue of the 1936 treaty.
c. Palestine lay across the Lines of Communication (L. of C.) along which the Allies would have to move their forces northwards, in order to meet and block a Soviet offensive against the Middle East.[1]

Allied planners agreed that the coastal plain of Palestine would be the scene of the decisive battle between Soviet and Allied forces in the Middle East. This was due primarily to topographical factors. In order to reach the Canal overland, the Soviets would be forced to pass through Palestine. They would be unable to traverse the arid Arava desert area between the southern edge of the Dead Sea and Aqaba – since this area had few tracks or roads, and was guarded on either side by mountains. All routes through the north of Palestine were dispersed between 'the defiles and passes formed by the Lebanon and Ante-Lebanon, and the Palmyra hills, the Jebel Druze . . .' Therefore, any sizeable Soviet force would be:

> . . . canalised in Palestine into the bottleneck formed between the Dead Sea and the Mediterranean, in the area of Ramallah.[2]

[1] Cf., annex to JP (46) 100, 23 May 1946, Cab 84/81; DO (46) 67, 25 May 1946, Cab 131/2, and DO (46) 80, 18 June 1946, Cab 131/3. PRO.
[2] War Office note on *Sandown*, COS (48) 123, 16 Oct. 1948, Defe 5/8. PRO.

After World War Two, the COS took it as axiomatic that Britain would retain its mandate over Palestine. That country was the only one in the Middle East in which they were free to make whichever military dispositions they cared to. Apparently, the COS expected that pan-glossian state of affairs to continue indefinitely.

Palestine was regarded as the optimal military disposition from which to defend Egypt. This had been a cardinal element in British strategy since the early part of World War One. The Turks' success in reaching the Suez Canal in February 1915 (with German aid) had shattered the ruling strategic orthodoxy, which hitherto had held that the Sinai desert was intraversable by a modern army. Indeed, there is no little irony in the fact that in issuing the Balfour Declaration in November 1917, the British had gone to great lengths, and to no small degree of subterfuge, in order to install the Jews in Palestine, largely so that they might guard their (the British) position at the Suez Canal.[3]

From 1946 on, the COS stressed repeatedly the importance of Palestine as constituting 'the core of the natural defences of Egypt against an attack from the north'. Palestine and Egypt were considered to be inter-dependent strategically – it would be difficult to hold Egypt unless they controlled Palestine as well. Indeed, claimed the COS, unless they retained 'full military rights' in Palestine, allowing them in peace-time to take whatever measures they deemed necessary, they doubted if they would be able to defend the Middle East at all. American planners concurred; if the British withdrew from Palestine, the Allies would have to abandon plans to retain the Middle East, to aid the Turks, and to initiate strategic air offensives against the Soviets, and they would find it difficult to deny intact oil facilities in the Middle East to the Soviets.[4]

In April 1946, the COS warned that should the Soviets ever gain control of the Egypt–Palestine axis, the ramifications would stretch way beyond the Middle East:

> Control of the area Egypt–Palestine would provide the Russians with a ready-made base area which could be built up by short sea route from Russia itself and which then would enable them to extend their influence both westward and southward into Africa. Such an extension would prejudice our position both in North-West Africa . . . and in the Indian Ocean. It would be the first step in a direct threat to our main support area of Southern Africa.[5]

[3] On these aspects, cf., Meyer Vereté, 'The Origins of the Balfour Declaration', _Middle Eastern Studies_, Vol. 6/1, Jan.1970, pp.48–76, and Michael J. Cohen, _The Origins and Evolution of the Arab–Zionist Conflict_, Berkeley: University of California Press, 1987, Ch. 2.

[4] Annex to JP (46) 100, and DO (46) 80, supra; and Brig. William L. Ritchie to Gen. Carl A. Spaatz, 28 April 1947, Carl Spaatz papers, box 28, Library of Congress.

[5] COS paper, 'Strategic Position of British Commonwealth', DO (46) 47, 2 April 1946,

In addition, the COS advised that if they failed to reach an agreement with the Egyptians to accommodate on their territory an Allied head-quarters for regional defence, they would need to locate it in Palestine instead.

All these themes were repeated by the COS in January 1947, in a vain attempt to avert the Cabinet decision to refer the Palestine problem to the United Nations. The COS made a last-ditch plea for the indefinite retention of mandatory rule in Palestine. They argued that any defence plan for the Middle East must rest upon Egypt, 'an essential base both for the defence and for the air counter-offensive'. However, they continued, Egypt could be defended effectively against attacks from the north only if they also held Palestine, Egypt's defensive bulwark. Only Palestine could furnish the strategic depth necessary for the defence of the Egyptian base. In peacetime, Palestine's strategic role would be to accommodate part of Britain's Middle East garrison; in the event of war, it would serve as a fighter base.[6]

Palestine's strategic importance lay also in its position on the land and air routes to Trans-Jordan and Iraq. At the outset of any future war, the COS would need to have ready in Palestine those forces and air bases considered necessary to meet the Soviet threat to the Middle East. They would also require absolute freedom to move troops and equipment around the country at will. The base installations required by British planners in Palestine were listed by the COS as follows: the use of Haifa as a supply port, and an airfield system in central Palestine; they would also require army bases in the districts of Haifa, Lydda, and Gaza, and in the sub-districts of Tulkarem, Nazareth and Beisan; and finally, they would require access to the oil refined in Haifa's refineries.[7]

But in evident reference to the current turmoil in Palestine, the COS laid down two overriding *desiderata*: first, Palestine could be of no strategic or military value unless order was restored; and second, any political solution in Palestine must be such as to retain for Britain the goodwill of the Arab world.[8]

On 7 January 1947, a meeting was held between the COS, Attlee and Bevin, to discuss the Palestine problem. The Secretary of State for Defence, Viscount Alexander, stated that Palestine was currently the

Cab 131/2. PRO. quoted in Wm. Roger Louis, *The British Empire in the Middle East, 1945–1951*, Oxford: Clarendon Press, 1984, p.28.

[6] For this and following, see annex to JP (47) 1, 5 Jan. 1947, PRO.

[7] Annex to JP (47) 1, supra; and JP (49) 29, 30 March 1949, Air 20/2463. PRO. A custom-made British-constructed airfield network was available, around Lydda and Akir, just south of Rehovot.

[8] Ibid., annex to JP (47) 1; and Michael J. Cohen, *Palestine and the Great Powers*, Princeton: Princeton University Press, 1982, p.211.

only alternative garrison for those troops that they were not allowed to hold in Egypt in peacetime. In wartime, Palestine offered the Allies a position of great strength, being flanked by the Mediterranean to the west, by mountainous terrain to the north and north-east, and by waterless desert to the east. Alexander, and the First Sea Lord, Sir John Cunningham, reassured the Ministers that once peace was restored to Palestine, a small force, of no more than two divisions, would be able to retain the British position in the Middle East.[9]

COS estimates of the force levels needed to hold their position in the Middle East would appear to reflect wishful thinking, a sublime insouciance in the eye of a storm, or perhaps an attempt to calm anxious Ministers? At that time, in January 1947, the nearly 100,000 British troops and police stationed in Palestine were having little success in restoring law and order to that small country.[10] The Egyptians had yet to come out in open revolt against the British.

American planners also were cognizant of Palestine's strategic importance. They noted its key geo-strategic position, at a focal point of the Eastern Mediterranean–Middle East area. The main land routes (both road and rail) between Turkey and the Cairo–Suez area passed through mandatory Palestine. In addition, the major land routes from the Caspian region of the Soviet Union to Egypt, via Iran, Iraq and Saudi Arabia, as well as the major pipelines carrying oil from the Middle East to the Mediterranean, all passed through, or ran adjacent to what was by now Israeli territory.[11]

However, the JCS regarded Israel's strategic assets as being by far inferior to the 'more highly developed and more accessible Cairo–Suez area some two hundred miles to the West'. They took note of the 'fine, but small, artificial harbour at Haifa', and the 'excellent, although limited, system of well-developed airfields and bases.' The JCS appreciated that these bases would be of great use to the allies in interdicting a Soviet offensive against the Middle East, and that in Soviet hands, they could interfere seriously with allied operations in this theatre.[12] However, like their British counterparts, the JCS also

[9] Secretary's Standard file, COS (47) 6th meeting, 7 Jan. 1947, Defe 32/1. PRO.

[10] An American Intelligence report dated Oct. 1947 estimated the size of British forces in Palestine as being 83,000, including the British-controlled TransJordan Frontier Force. ORE–49, 20 Oct. 1947, PSF, box 254, HST. However, it is generally believed that by the end of 1945 the British had brought their Palestine garrison up to 100,000, to deal with the Jewish insurrection. The American Intelligence report possibly did not count the Palestine Police.

[11] Cf. PPS/19, 19 Jan. 1948, *FRUS*, 1951, V: Part 2, pp.546–47, and JCS 1684/28, 1 April 1949, CCS 092 Pal (5–3–46), sect. 7; and RG 330 (Secretary of Defense) box 22, CD 6–2–47, 16 May 1949. National Archives (NA).

[12] NSC 47, 16 May 1949, *FRUS*, 1949, Vol. VI, pp.1009–12.

appreciated that the sum total of Israeli strategic assets could never match those possessed by the Arab world.

B. THE FIRST ARAB-ISRAELI WAR, AND THE ESTABLISHMENT OF ISRAEL

Initially, the Americans and the British agreed that the Jews would lose the war against the Arabs in Palestine. In late November 1947, one week before the UN Partition Resolution, and *before* civil war erupted in Palestine, an American Intelligence estimate proferred the following prognosis:

> The Jewish forces will initially have the advantage. However, as the Arabs gradually coordinate their war effort, the Jews will be forced to withdraw from isolated positions, and having been drawn into a war of attrition, will gradually be defeated. Unless they are able to obtain significant aid in terms of manpower and materiel, the Jews will be able to hold out no more than two years.[13]

In Washington, the JCS leaned heavily on the 'expert' opinion of a varied array of men in the field – not least, ex-State Department officials, who had moved on to lucrative positions with the oil conglomerates, with the specific task of acting as an anti-Zionist lobby in Washington. Not untypical was the briefing given by Col (Res.) William A. Eddy (ex-State Department, currently ARAMCO official) to the JCS on 20 December 1947, in which he forecast that the Arabs were about to soundly beat, if not massacre, the Jews in Palestine. On 20 January 1949, with Israel triumphant on the field of battle on all fronts, Eddy communicated directly to General Greunther, chairman of the JCS. Unable to reconcile himself to a military outcome so different from his own prognostication of just over a year before, Eddy insisted that the Jews' victory was ephemeral, and was due to their having 'cheated'. He still had no doubts that the Arabs would triumph ultimately.[14]

British military experts initially held similar opinions. At a meeting with Bevin in December 1947, CIGS Montgomery assured the Foreign Secretary that '. . . in the long run the Jews would not be able to cope

[13] ORE (Office of Research Estimates) 55, 20 Nov. 1947, PSF, box 264, HST. The Office of Research Estimates functioned from 1946–1950, when it was succeeded by the Office for National Intelligence Estimates (NIE).

[14] On Col. Eddy's activity, see Michael J. Cohen, William A. Eddy, 'The Oil Lobby and the Palestine Problem', *Middle Eastern Studies*, Vol. 30/1, Jan. 1994, pp.166–80; also Philip Baram, *The Department of State in the Middle East, 1919–1945*, Philadelphia: University of Pennsylvania Press, 1978, pp.75–6.

with the Arabs and would be thrown out of Palestine unless they came to terms with them'.[15]

However, once the war began, the British, able to observe at first-hand the military prowess and standard of organisation of both sides, soon revised their opinion. By the end of February 1948, the last British High Commissioner in Palestine, Sir Alan Cunningham, was predicting that the Arabs would be unable to prevent the Jews from establishing themselves in their own state on the coastal plain. The COS concurred in his view.[16]

As the prospect of a Jewish state emerged as a military and political reality, the British were forced to reassess their own strategic interests in the region. In addition, notwithstanding the American and British consensus on Palestine's strategic importance, President Truman's support for the Zionist cause, in particular his instant recognition of the new state of Israel, on 14 May 1948, in the face of State Department objections, produced acute friction between the allies.[17]

By 1947, the British were traumatised by their mandatory experience with the Jews in Palestine. In contrast, and notwithstanding the wartime pro-Axis activities of Egyptian and Iraqi nationalists, they regarded the Arabs as being more reliable clients, and more amenable than the Jews to their own strategic interests in the Middle East.

In May 1948, at the outset of the first Arab–Israeli war, British diplomats in Arab capitals inundated the Foreign Office with 'cogent' arguments as to why it was in Britain's best interest to support the Arabs, and why it was detrimental to her interests for a Jewish state to be established in the heart of the Arab world. These communications were not entirely free of antisemitic undertones.

From Beirut, E.W. Houston-Boswall warned that a Jewish state in Palestine 'could well become the Achilles heel of our whole defence system', and would never be strong enough to be of use to Britain if faced with 'a hostile Arabia'. He advised therefore, quite bluntly, that:

> . . . we should make up our minds on which side our own bread (and nobody else's) is buttered. We need the Arabs and they need us – though most of them are too timid to say so openly . . .[18]

In language reminiscent of a classic imperialist paternalism,

---

[15] Bevin, CIGS interview, 22 Dec. 1947, E12325, FO 371/61583. PRO.

[16] Cunningham to Martin, 24 Feb. 1948, E4291, FO 371/68537, and COS memorandum, 28 Feb. 1948, E3549, FO 371/68538. PRO.

[17] On Truman's support for Zionism, and Anglo–American friction concerning the establishment of the state of Israel, cf., Michael J. Cohen, *Truman and Israel*, Berkeley: University of California Press, 1990.

[18] E.E. Houston-Boswall, Michael R. Wright, 9 May 1948, E8737, FO 371/68386. PRO.

Houston-Boswall averred that it would now not be too difficult to persuade the Arabs where their best interests lay. Writing before the invasion of Israel by the Arab states on 14 May 1948, he believed that if the Arabs, due to their 'gross incapacity and lack of discipline for the last six months', had proved unable to resist some 30–50,000 'well-trained and disciplined Jews', they would appreciate that: 'they could not have much hope of survival as a race, let alone independent States, against an attack by, say, two or three Russian divisions . . .'[19]

He believed that the key to deriving the optimum from the impending conflict would be to arm Abdullah up to the hilt, to enable the latter 'to get the Arabs out of their present predicament'. The British would thereby not only earn the gratitude of the Arabs, but prove to them that it paid to be Britain's ally.[20]

Houston-Boswall's ideas were undoubtedly provincial, but did represent a section of British officialdom in the Middle East. Certainly, the Foreign Office was more sensitive to the general Arab disparagement of Abdullah as a British stooge, and to the risks of getting caught in the crossfire of inter-Arab rivalries. The Foreign Office also had to work within the restraints of Britain's alliance with the United States. However, the pervading distrust and resentment of the Jews, in contrast to the somewhat condescending paternalism adopted toward the Arabs, were, with but a few exceptions, universal among British officialdom.

Four days after the Arab States' invasion of Israel, John Troutbeck, head of the British Middle East Office at Cairo, wrote a yet more rancorous letter to the Foreign Office against the Jewish state. (As will be seen below, Troutbeck's tone would change, following Israel's triumphs on the field of battle.) Evidently 'in the heat of battle', Troutbeck warned that the Jewish state 'would bring bitterness and unrest and, wherever the Jew was in control of an Arab population, the worst form of oppression'.

He warned that the Jewish state would be bound to expand, and if it succeeded, the Arabs would 'just be slaves, under masters more brutal and soulless than anything they have yet known'. He could not conceive of Britain ever 'getting any return from the Jews', whatever she might do for them. He concluded that 'on the grounds of justice, of benefit to the Middle East as a whole, and of our own interests', they should do all they could to prevent the Arabs being defeated by the Israelis.[21]

The State Department initially took a similar view of the conflict, even if its views were perhaps not so emotion-laden. In January 1948, the PPS warned against taking any steps to help the establishment of

---

[19] Ibid.
[20] Ibid.
[21] John Troutbeck (Cairo) to Michael Wright, 18 May 1948, E8738, ibid.

the Jewish state. The PPS did not believe that Israel could survive for long, and warned that any one-sided aid to the Jews would be regarded by the Arabs as 'a virtual declaration of war by the U.S. against the Arab world.'[22]

One of the main contentions upon which the British based their opposition to Israel was the alleged danger of it becoming a communist state. From the very inception of their mandate over Palestine, they had tended to taint the Zionists as communist-oriented. The spectre of what has been coined 'the communist bogey' was raised against the *Yishuv* (Jewish community) in Palestine throughout the mandatory period.[23] Both Houston-Boswall, and Troutbeck duly warned that Israel was likely to be dominated by the communists.

Ostensibly, there was some circumstantial evidence for such stereotyping; many of the early Zionist pioneers originated from Russia and Eastern Europe; Soviet-oriented Zionist-socialist parties in Palestine comprised a significant minority; and finally, the Soviets had not only supported Israel diplomatically, at the UN, in 1947; but during the 1948 war, had also sanctioned the shipment of Soviet-manufactured arms to Israel, via Czechoslovakia.

The 'communist bogey' was the argument used most frequently by the British when urging their American allies not to support Israel. Following the Soviet decision to support the partition of Palestine into Arab and Jewish states, in October 1947, Bevin asserted, in a private letter to a colleague, that the Soviets were convinced that within a very short period, they would be able to pour into Palestine 'sufficient indoctrinated Jews to turn it into a Communist state'. He chided that 'The New York Jews have been doing their work for them'.[24]

At a lunch given by Bevin to the senior staff of the US embassy in London, at the end of December 1948, he warned that the Negev desert had to be awarded to the Arabs, since there was a distinct possibility that Israel might become a communist state 'within five years'.[25]

The Foreign Office and the State Department, in their common opposition to Israel, saw eye to eye on the alleged risk of Israel turning communist. The American intelligence community lent credence to such charges. For example, in late November 1947, a US Intelligence estimate alleged that Soviet agents were already being smuggled into Jewish Palestine, within the Displaced Person (DP) quotas. The report

[22] PPS/19, 19 Jan. 1948, *FRUS*, 1948, Vol. V, Part 2, pp.546–7.

[23] Cf Bernard Wasserstein, *The British in Palestine: The Mandatory Government and the Arab-Jewish Conflict, 1917–1929*, London: 1979; and Louis, *The British . . .*, pp.43–4.

[24] Bevin, Hector McNeil, 15 Oct. 1947, FO 800/509. PRO. Quoted in Louis, ibid., p.43.

[25] Holmes (US charge in UK) report to Lovett on luncheon meeting given by Bevin, 20 Dec. 1948, in *FRUS*, 1948, Vol.V, Part 2, pp.1683–84.

predicted that from Palestine, the agents would 'scatter' into the other Arab states, where they would attempt to organise 'democratic movements', similar to those the Soviets had already organised in Greece and Iran. In May 1948, a further intelligence estimate warned that there was 'a real danger that Communism may gain a firm hold in Israel'.[26]

But Truman dismissed such charges out of hand, as being politically-biased. In May 1948, he told an aide 'Don't pay any attention to the communist charge, they are always making it . . .' Truman felt that the heads of his State Department (Marshall and Lovett) were led astray too much by their subordinates, to whom he referred disparagingly, as the 'striped pants boys'.[27]

The State Department even sent a special envoy to Israel, specifically to study the danger of communist infiltration. But he found little evidence. By January 1949, American intelligence had downgraded the risk of Israel turning communist. It was still assumed that the Soviet satellite states were trying to infiltrate communist agents into Israel. But it was also recognised that the Communist Party in Israel was minuscule in size, just 2000 members, and that the Israeli government itself was free of communist influence.[28]

C. THE WAR OVER THE NEGEV

During the first Arab–Israeli war (1948–49), the Allies also found themselves in disagreement over the future political disposition of the southern half of Palestine, the Negev desert. The latter's strategic significance lay in its being the land-bridge between Egypt and Transjordan, and thus a vital artery for the allied L. of C. from the Egyptian base, to potential battlegrounds to the north, and north-east. The British, who had left Palestine in a state of undeclared war with the Jewish community there, feared that a Jewish Negev would impose an alien wedge between its strategic outposts in Egypt and the rest of the Arab world.

When the UNSCOP partition plan allotted the Negev desert to the Jews, both the Foreign Office and the State Department worked for the

[26] ORE 55, 20 Nov. 1947, PSF, box 264, HST; and Brief of 25 May 1948, RG 360, Secretary of Defense, CD 6–2–47, box 22. NA.

[27] Cf., Cohen, *Truman and . . .*, p.215.

[28] Memorandum by Maj. Gen. Ray T. Maddocks, GSC, Director of Plans and Operations, 14 Jan. 1949, RG 319 (army staff) 091.Israel, 1949–50, box 160. NA.

Israel's first elections were held on 25 Jan. 1949. Ben-Gurion's Mapai party won 35.8 per cent of the votes; the Left-Wing Mapam party came next, with 14.7 per cent, and then the United Religious Party, with 12.3 per cent; the right-wing Herut party, headed by Menachem Begin, won 11.5 per cent of the vote.

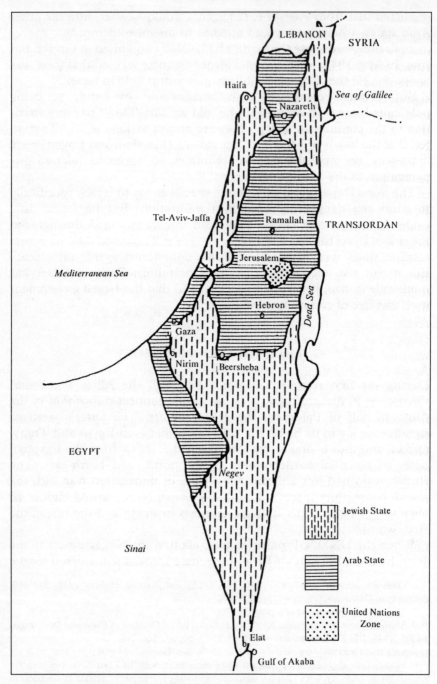

Map 1: The UN Plan for the Partition of Palestine, November 29, 1947

transfer of this area to the proposed Arab state. However, following the personal intervention of the Zionist leader, Dr Chaim Weizmann ('who perceived the strategic importance of the area as a southern outlet to Africa and the East'), Truman overruled the State Department. It is to be doubted whether Truman acted from any cognizance of the strategic significance of the Negev – it is more likely that he acted from a desire to do a favour for the Zionists, and their elder statesman. In any case, the outcome was that the partition plan adopted by the UN on 29 November 1947, awarded the Negev to the Jewish state.[29]

Whereas the British reconciled themselves to the establishment of a Jewish state in a part of Palestine, they could not reconcile themselves to the Negev falling into 'unreliable' Jewish hands. Harold Beeley, Bevin's principal adviser on Palestine, undertook a campaign to persuade the Israelis, and their American patrons that the Arabs would never agree to a Jewish state that included the Negev.

On 6 June, during the first UN-imposed truce of the Arab–Israeli war, Beeley told the head of NEA, Loy Henderson, that the Arabs might just agree to the existence of a Jewish state, on condition that they were also given the Negev, the land-link between Arab capitals. In return for this, the British would support the transfer of the Galilee (allotted to the Arabs by the UN Resolution) to the Jews. At a meeting with the Israeli envoy in London, on 1 July Beeley insisted that 'the Arabs could not agree to Egypt being cut off from direct land contact with the rest of the Arab States.'[30]

This author has not discovered any evidence to verify that the British first consulted the Arabs themselves, before volunteering in their name to hand over to the Jews the fertile, predominantly-Arab populated Galilee area, in return for the virtually-empty, barren Negev desert. In seeking to secure the strategically-important Negev desert for the Arabs (i.e., for themselves), soil fertility, and population distribution were minor considerations for the British.

During the second phase of the Arab–Israeli war the so-called '10-days war' in July 1948, the Israelis captured and consolidated their hold on parts of western, and southern (or Lower) Galilee.[31] For the

---

[29] On Truman's intervention with the State Department, at the personal bequest of Dr Chaim Weizmann, the Zionist leader, cf., Cohen, *Palestine and . . .*, pp.289–90.

[30] Note of conversation with Harold Beeley, by Loy Henderson, 6 June 1948, *FRUS*, V, Part 2, pp.1099–101; and Memorandum by Ivor J. Linton, on meeting with Beeley, 1 July 1948, in Yehoshua Freundlich, ed., *Israel Documents, Vol. 1, May–Sept. 1948*, Jerusalem: Hamakor Press, 1981, p.272.

[31] The Lower Galilee was conquered by Israel from 9–18 July 1948. The northern part was conquered during a four-day campaign at the end of October. On the military operations, cf., Netanel Lorch, *Israel's War of Independence, 1947–1949*, Hartford: Hartmore House, 1968.

British, this conquest presented a golden opportunity to 'retrieve' the Negev for the Arabs.

During the last days of July 1948, the Foreign Office drafted an official plan for a 'revision' of the UN partition plan, along what the Foreign Office called the 'lines-of-force' frontier. An exchange of territories would be made; Israel would receive the Galilee (which she had just conquered), although it had *not* been awarded to her by the UN plan. In return, Israel would relinquish all the southern Negev (which she had *not* yet conquered) although it *had* been awarded to her by the UN plan.

In August 1948, Bevin sought American agreement to a permanent crystalisation of the current ceasefire borders. If the Americans agreed to this, Bevin suggested that the Allies make their views clear to the UN mediator, the Swedish Count Bernadotte. They would urge the latter to attach a map to his next report, indicating clearly the lines-of-force frontier that pertained at the end of the fighting. Concurring in the British plan, Lewis Douglas, the US ambassador in London commented: 'compulsion sometimes offers a firmer basis for a workable peaceful settlement than theoretical plans'.[32]

On 9 August, Secretary Marshall received Dr Ralph Bunche, the American deputy to the UN Mediator for Palestine, Count Folke Bernadotte. Bunche reported that Bernadotte (who had already issued one abortive report in June) wanted this time to secure prior Anglo–American support for his next proposal. The UN Mediator felt that once he had secured an Anglo–American consensus behind him, then both the Jews and the Arabs, while protesting violently, would eventually reconcile themselves to the new plan. He was in fact thinking along lines identical to those held at the Foreign Office:

> . . . [the] Jews should be given valuable lands in Western Galilee which they now
> hold by virtue of military conquest but in return for this acquisition should
> permit Arabs to take over most of the Negev.[33]

Three days later, Secretary Marshall informed the British of his agreement to their proposal of a joint, informal approach to the UN Mediator. The State Department believed that the basis for an agreement between Israel and the Arabs should now be the transfer of Jaffa (awarded to the Arabs by the UN plan) and all, or a part of western Galilee to Israel, in exchange for all or a part of the Negev to the Arabs.[34]

[32] Ambassador Lewis Douglas (London) – Secretary of State, 2 Aug. 1948, *FRUS*, 1948, V, Part 2, pp.1266–71; and Ilan Asia, *The Core of the Conflict: The Struggle for the Negev, 1947–1956*, Jerusalem: Yad Izhak Ben-Zvi Press, 1994, pp.60 ff. [Hebrew]

[33] Marshall, Lewis, 13 Aug. 1948, *FRUS*, ibid., p.1309.

[34] Marshall, Douglas, 12 Aug. 1948, ibid., pp.1303–5.

On 26 August, the British Cabinet confirmed Bevin's new stratagem. The most convenient way for Britain to secure its strategic requirements in the Negev would be for the UN Mediator to endow them with the aura and authority of UN sponsorship. Prime Minister Attlee was absent from the Cabinet meeting, sick in hospital. When he returned to work, Bevin informed him that the new *démarche* was so secret that the Cabinet had decided that only its own members should receive copies of Bevin's cabinet memorandum. However, added Bevin, the matter was of such importance to the Chiefs of Staff and the Middle East Command that he requested permission to circulate it to the Defence Committee, and to the Middle East Command at Cairo.[35]

In mid-September 1948, an American (Robert McClintock), and a British (John Troutbeck) senior official met secretly with the Count Bernadotte on the island of Rhodes. Their purpose was to 'consult' with him on the preparation of his second plan for a solution of the Palestine problem. Bernadotte and Troutbeck agreed on the transfer of the entire Negev to the Arabs, from Majdal (Ashkelon) eastwards. But McClintock suggested that the Israelis might receive 'a token salient into the Negev', down to the Beersheba–Gaza road (this road was a key section of the strategic route between Cairo and Transjordan). Bernadotte objected, firstly on the grounds of equity – the Jews would receive the 'rich Galilee', and should not be rewarded with any salient to the Negev, even if in Arab hands it would always remain 'a worthless desert'; second, Bernadotte was calculating on information he had received that the Israelis themselves were divided on this question, with Shertok and other moderates feeling that giving up the Negev for the Galilee was in fact 'a good bargain'.[36]

McClintock himself agreed with Bernadotte and Troutbeck, and promised to recommend their proposal to the State Department. But he made it quite clear that he could not commit the American administration. He advised that since the Negev held such significance for the Jews, it might be 'political good judgement' to compromise (given Truman's support for the Zionists), and to give Israel a token salient there.[37] Such a compromise would help the State Department to secure Truman's agreement to the exchange-of-territory deal.

Bernadotte's plan was completed on 16 September 1948. It duly met

[35] Cf., Asia, *The Core of . . .* pp.62–63. Bevin's cabinet memorandum is CP (48) 207, 25 Aug. 1948, in Cab 28/13. PRO.

[36] Troutbeck and McClintock held two days of talks with Bernadotte on the island of Rhodes, from 13 Sept. 1948. cf., Cohen, *Truman and . . .*, p.237; Louis, *The British . . .*, pp.549–50; and Asia, *The Core of . . .*, p.64. See also McClintock's report in Stanton Griffis (US ambassador, Egypt) – Secretary of State, 15 Sept. 1948, *FRUS*, 1948, V, Part 2, pp.1398–401.

[37] Griffis – Secretary of State, ibid.

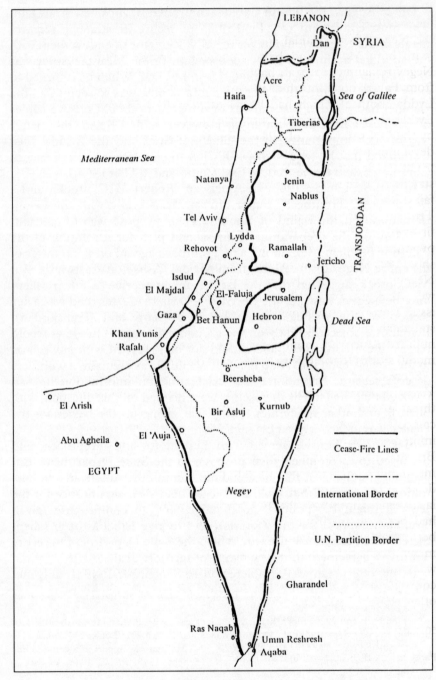

Map 2: The Cease-Fire Lines in Palestine, April, 1949

British strategic *desiderata* in southern Palestine. Following the current 'lines-of-force' frontiers, his plan awarded the Galilee to the Jews, and the Negev, from Majdal south-east to Faluja (Plugot), to the Arabs (with both Majdal and Faluja, and the strategic roads crossing the Negev remaining in Arab hands). The Arab state's border would run from Faluja north-north-east up to, and would include Ramleh and Lydda (both of which had been conquered by Israel in July). From Lydda, the frontier would continue east, according to the line laid down by the UN resolution of 1947.[38] But the plan was thwarted by further developments, political and military.

On 21 September, US Secretary of State Marshall issued a public statement to the effect that the UN Mediator's plan offered 'a generally fair basis for settlement of the Palestine problem'. But President Truman (running as underdog in a campaign to be elected for the first time as President in his own right) was unable to resist domestic pressures from the Zionist lobby. He intervened to state that Israel should receive not only the Galilee, but also those parts of the northern Negev they had already conquered. On 25 October, having received word that his rival for the Presidency, Governor Dewey, was about to issue a pro-Israel statement, Truman went further and issued a press statement that all but refuted his own Secretary of State, and in effect nullified American support for Bernadotte's plan. He stated that any modifications to the UN partition plan must be acceptable to Israel.[39]

Second, on 15 October, Israel opened a new offensive (Operation *Yoav*) against Egyptian forces in the Negev. Notwithstanding the threat of sanctions pressed by Britain at the UN, Israel pursued its campaign in two phases, in October and December 1948. One of the immediate reasons for the Israeli operation was their prescience that the British, with American support, would implement Bernadotte's recommendations on the Negev. In addition, Israeli Intelligence reported a deterioration in the Egyptian garrison's position in Palestine. And lastly, since June 1948, the 21 Jewish settlements in the northern Negev had been cut off from the Jewish state by Egyptian forces deployed between Majdal and Faluja. Unless the Israeli army acted, these settlements might have soon been starved into surrender or evacuation. (It was on the ostensible grounds of Egyptian harassment of their supply convoys to these settlements that the Israelis opened their October offensive.)[40]

[38] On Bernadotte's plan, cf Cohen, *Truman* . . ., pp.237–8; Louis, *The British* . . ., pp.547–50; and Asia, *The Core of* . . ., pp.65–6.

[39] *FRUS*, 1948, V, Part 2, p.1415; and Acting Secretary of State to US delegation to UN, Paris, 23 Oct. 1948, idem, p.1508; and Cohen, *Truman and* . . ., p.253.

[40] Cf., Ilan Pappé, *Britain and the Arab-Israeli Conflict, 1948–1951*, London: Macmillan, 1988, p.59. Between 23 Aug. and 21 Oct., in Operation *Dust*, the Israelis had changed round

During the first phase of the Negev campaign, from 15–22 October 1948, the Israelis relieved their settlements, and conquered Beersheba, thus cutting off Egyptian forces in the Hebron area from their rear bases in the southern Negev. In the West, Israeli forces broke through to Bet Hanun, near the Mediterranean coast. At this point, a ceasefire was imposed, under threat of UN sanctions. The Israelis prepared to conquer the east and south-west sections of the Negev.[41]

On 13 November, US ambassador Douglas was summoned to Chequers, the official country residence of British Prime Ministers. Douglas was confronted by Prime Minister Attlee, and the CIGS, Lord Tedder. Attlee warned that his government felt that the current situation in Palestine 'present[ed] dangers as great and immediate to world peace and to Anglo–American co-operation as Berlin or any other present problem'. Tedder warned that the Israeli advances into the Negev presaged a threat to Aqaba, Transjordan's southern port. The British warned that any Israeli infringements of either Jordanian or Egyptian sovereignty would force them to come to the defence of their Arab allies. Indeed, Israeli infringements of UN-imposed truces were placing in jeopardy the very future of the United Nations. But perhaps worse still, if Britain intervened militarily against Israel, the Allies could find themselves supporting opposing belligerents in the Middle East.[42]

The Israelis' incursions into the Negev since October 1948, and the threat that the next phase of the fighting might bring them into the Sinai desert, prompted a COS analysis of the strategic importance of the Negev, in mid-December 1948.

The Negev was described as an area through which vital communications would pass, and in which vital airfields had to be developed in war. The Egypt–Palestine railway passed through this area, as did the main arterial roads from Egypt to the north-east – through Rafah to Gaza, El Auja to Beersheba and Hebron; and the route from Egypt to Aqaba passed through Sinai, to the southern tip of the Negev, at the Gulf of Aqaba, and thence northwards, inside the Negev, for about 10 to 15 miles.[43]

On 20 December 1948, shortly before fighting was renewed in the Negev, Bevin invited a delegation from the US Embassy, headed by ambassador Douglas, to a 'Palestine luncheon' at his official residence. Bevin expressed his disappointment over the lack of Anglo–American

their forces in the northern Negev, and brought in fresh supplies and ammunition – all in preparation for the Oct. offensive.

[41] Pappé, ibid., p.60, and Louis, *The British . . .*, p.555.

[42] Report of meeting in Marshall – Acting Secretary of State, Robert A. Lovett, 15 Nov. 1948, in *FRUS*, 1948, Vol. V, Part 2, pp.1585–89; also Cohen, *Truman and . . .*, pp.262–3.

[43] Annex to COS (48) 208, 15 Dec. 1948, Defe 5/9. PRO.

collaboration in the Middle East – in contrast to the position in Europe. The COS analysis on the Negev, written five days before, evidently served Bevin as background material for the presentation he now made to the Americans on Britain's strategic requirements in that desert. Since Israel might turn communist 'within five years', maintained Bevin, the key strategic roads in the area would have to remain under Arab control:

> To have a communist Israel lying athwart vital strategic roads in ME such as Auja–Beersheba, Gaza–Beersheba and El Kuntilla–Aqaba, would be a serious blow to UK strategic plans for area.[44]

In the light of recent events on the battlefield, Bevin now conceded that provided these strategic roads, together with the airfields in the Gaza Strip, remained 'safely in Arab hands', Britain would not mind Israel obtaining part of the Negev. Ambassador Douglas retorted that since the British military now agreed that Israel possessed 'the strongest indigenous military force in the Middle East', it might be propitious to consider ways in which Israel could be kept friendly to the West. Hector McNeil, Minister of State at the Foreign Office, responded that whereas Israel might eventually become an 'important asset in Middle Eastern defence', for the present, Egypt and Transjordan were definitely 'better bets than Israel'.[45]

But further events on the field of battle overtook Anglo–American consultations. On 22 December 1948, fighting broke out again in the Negev, after the Israelis, during secret negotiations with the Egyptians, had rejected the latter's demands that they relinquish newly-conquered Beersheba. During this round of the fighting, on 28 December, the Israelis crossed the international border into Sinai. Israeli strategy was to outflank the Egyptian garrison at El Arish (a forward Egyptian air base), thus cutting off those Egyptian forces in the Gaza Strip from their rear bases. They penetrated some 20 miles into Egyptian territory, and captured the main road from Beersheba to Bir Asluj. In the process they took control of two vital strategic crossroads, at al Auja, on the international border, and at Abu Agheila, some 20 miles inside Egyptian territory (al Auja lay astride the road from Jerusalem through Sinai to Cairo; Abu Agheila commanded all the access roads from Israel into the Sinai desert and Egypt – see map 2).[46]

The Israeli advances presented a severe test for British nerves,

[44] Julius C. Holmes (US Charge in UK) – Robert Lovett, Acting Secretary of State, 22 Dec. 1948, *FRUS*, 1948, V, Part 2, pp.1680–5.

[45] Ibid.

[46] Cf., Louis, *The British . . .*, p.564; Cohen, *Truman and . . .*, pp.263–64, and Pappé, *Britain and . . .* p.62. My thanks also to Col (res.) Uri Algom, for clarifying this point for me.

and brought the latter perilously close to direct military intervention, ostensibly in fulfillment of their treaty obligations to Egypt. The British military had prepared a contingency plan, codenamed *Clatter*, to come to Egypt's aid, in the eventuality of an Israeli infringement of Egyptian sovereignty.[47]

As the British saw matters, Israel now not only occupied crossroads of key strategic importance to them, but also posed a challenge to their own credibility in the Arab world.

When British intelligence discovered that Israel had crossed into Sinai, they rushed reinforcements to Aqaba. Two battalions were brought up from East Africa to the Suez Canal, and some naval units were alerted. Although no threat to the Canal was perceived, the British authorities at Cairo pressed London to take advantage of the Israeli crossing into Sinai in order to invoke the 1936 Anglo–Egyptian treaty.[48] Cairo wanted British military intervention, to achieve what the Egyptians themselves were patently incapable of doing – ejecting the Israelis from Sinai and the Negev by force.

The Foreign Office appealed to the Americans to restrain the Israelis, and to convey an ultimatum that unless all Israeli forces were withdrawn from the Sinai desert forthwith, Britain would be left with no choice but to intervene. The consequences for Middle East stability and for Anglo–American relations were potentially disastrous. Truman directed his envoy in Tel Aviv, James MacDonald, to advise the Israelis of the British ultimatum, and to add his own personal warning that he, the first to recognise the new state and a sponsor of Israel's current application for admission to the United Nations as 'a peace-loving state', might be forced to reconsider his policy. He demanded Israel's immediate withdrawal from Sinai, as minimum proof of Israel's peaceful intentions. Upon receipt of Truman's cable, MacDonald conveyed its contents to Moshe Sharett, Israel's Foreign Minister, in Tel Aviv. MacDonald then travelled from Tel Aviv to Tiberias, on Lake Galilee, that same day, New Year's Eve, in order to deliver Truman's warning in person to Ben-Gurion, the Israeli Prime Minister. Ben-Gurion ordered a withdrawal behind the international border that same day.[49]

Israeli troops were supposed to have been back in the Negev by 2 January 1949. But they did not in fact complete their withdrawal until 8 January. On 3 January 1949, Ben-Gurion was advised by his diplomats in Washington that a British combat unit was on its way to Aqaba, and that a second unit was contemplated for Gaza. An Israeli military spokesman claimed to have learned of British military manoeuvres in

[47] Cf Pappé, ibid., pp.65–7.
[48] Ibid., pp.63–65.
[49] Cohen, *Truman and . . .* pp.264–7.

Tripolitania, in preparation for landing operations in the Negev. The British consul at Haifa tried to reassure the Israelis that Britain had no intentions of making war on them. But the latter interpreted British movements as portending direct military intervention if the Security Council rejected British demands for an Israeli withdrawal. The British were also threatening to lift their arms embargo on Jordan and Egypt.[50]

In early January 1949, the RAF was scrambled over the Sinai desert, in order to check if the Israelis had withdrawn, to locate and assess the strength of their forward positions, and to test the fledgling IAF. On 7 January 1949, the RAF flights were intercepted by fighters of the IAF. Five RAF Spitfires were shot down by the Israeli aircraft, for no losses on the Israeli side.[51]

During this last week of the Arab–Israeli war, the Atlantic allies debated the consequences of the Arab–Israeli war for their strategic interests in the region. Whereas the British had stopped short of attempting to drive the Israelis back by force to the northern Negev, they now urged the Americans to exert diplomatic pressure to achieve the same goal. The debate focused on the question of the future political disposition of the Negev.

John Troutbeck, one of whose duties as head of Britain's Middle East Office in Cairo was strategic planning for the region, sent the following assessment to Bevin on 4 January 1949. By this point in time hostilities between Egypt and Israel were all but over, and the Israelis were withdrawing their forces back across the international border from Sinai. Troutbeck's views had undergone something of a revolution since the previous May, as a result of events on the battlefields in Palestine. He now drew the conclusion that the UN and the Arab states were 'broken reeds'. But which options did this leave the British? All they could usefully do would be to defend the territorial integrity of their allies, Transjordan and Egypt, if Israel attacked either of them. However, in Troutbeck's opinion, Israel had no intention of posing that challenge. He hoped that Britain might even now still manage to salvage a strategic corridor through the southern Negev, from Egypt to Aqaba. (The Israelis had yet to establish any position on the Gulf of Aqaba).[52]

The British ambassador at Cairo, Sir Ronald Campbell, took a more extreme view than Troutbeck. In an apocalyptic telegram, sent to

---

[50] E. Elath, E. Ben-Arzi to Ben-Gurion, Sharett, 3 Jan. 1949, *I.D.* 1949, Vol. 2, No. 289, p.340; and Pappé, Britain and . . ., p.64.

[51] The Egyptians themselves opposed the RAF flights, since their agreement to British aircraft defending Egyptian skies would have implied their recognition of the continued validity of the 1936 treaty. Cohen, ibid., pp.267–8. Pappé, *Britain and . . .* pp.63–5.

[52] Troutbeck to Bevin, 4 Jan. 1949, E156G, FO 371/75334, quoted in Louis, *The British . . .*, p.566.

Bevin on 10 January 1949, Campbell advocated British military intervention:

> Nothing to my mind is more certain than that if the Jews are permitted to seize
> and hold the whole of the Negeb not only will our strategic position in the whole
> region be hamstrung but politically we shall be pretty well bankrupt in this part
> of the world.
>
> . . . it will take force other than Egyptian or Arab to keep Jews out of Negeb, at
> least to keep line clear of Beersheba–Hebron–Jerusalem road:
>
> British and American interests identical in keeping this road open in event
> another war – but United States too preoccupied with other issues to see this, so
> we might have to do it alone . . . since our vital interests are so closely involved
> and our forces are on the scene, it will . . . almost certainly be up to us to take
> necessary action, preferably with American backing, but possibly alone, if the
> Middle East is, in fact, to be saved.[53]

On 11 January 1949, Bevin sent two urgent cables to his ambassador
in Washington, Sir Oliver Franks. The latter was instructed to appeal
urgently to the Americans to close ranks with their ally on the issue of
the strategic roads from Egypt to Transjordan. Specifically, Bevin
pleaded that Israel's southern border in the Negev should be fixed
north of the Gaza–Beersheba–Jericho road. He also wanted the
Americans to join him in forcing Israel to obey those UN resolutions (of
4, 16 November, and 29 December 1948) calling upon her to withdraw
to the 14 October lines. Bevin entreated the Americans not to expect
the British to stand by idly while their influence in the Middle East was
eroded away.[54]

On the next day, ambassador Franks secured meetings with both
Truman and with Under-Secretary of State Lovett. The outcome of
these meetings was that the British were finally disabused of any
thoughts of coercing Israel to retreat to the northern Negev. Truman
appeared oblivious to the strategic importance of the Negev in Allied
war plans. He told Franks that the Negev was 'a small area not worth
differing over', and that he saw no possibility of dividing it up. Truman
could not understand why the British were so anxious about it![55]

On the same day, Franks met with Lovett at the State Department.
He encountered a novel (from this quarter), more positive attitude
towards Israel. This may have had something to do with the fact that
Secretary Marshall (with whom Truman had quarrelled over the Zionist

[53] Sir Ronald Campbell (Cairo) to Foreign Office, 10 Jan. 1949, E454, FO 371/75334,
PRO; quoted in Cohen, *Truman and . . .*, p.270.

[54] Acting Secretary of State Lovett to UK embassy, 13 Jan. 1949, in *FRUS*, 1949, VI,
pp.658–61; and Asia, *The Core . . .*, pp.77–8.

[55] Franks to Bevin, 13 Jan. 1949, E615, FO 371/75334, PRO; also Cohen, *Truman and . . .*,
pp.270–1, and Louis, *The British . . .*, pp.566–7.

question), had after the elections been replaced by Dean Acheson. The latter was closer to Truman, and enjoyed his confidence.[56]

When Franks quoted Bevin's arguments, and Britain's doubts about Israel's future political disposition, Lovett responded that the British were following an unrealistic policy of trying to contain the Israelis even at the risk of estranging them permanently. Lovett suggested that the best way of securing allied strategic requirements in the region 'was to win the Israelis over into the Anglo–American camp and not to alienate them permanently'.

In unprecedented harsh language, Lovett alleged that the British were trying to confine Israel in a straitjacket, besieged by 'a circle of weak Arab enemies kept in a ring only by British armed assistance'. This was a policy calculated to turn Israel hostile to the West, and to push her into the Soviet orbit.[57] As for the strategic roads in the Negev, Lovett insisted that they would be of no use to the allies if Israel was hostile to the West. Lovett continued:

> . . . the major problem . . . was not on which side of the frontier the land route from Egypt to Transjordan and beyond lay, but rather to ensure as far as possible that Israel was a democratic state and to orient it westward.[58]

When Franks put Bevin's question, what were the Americans prepared to do to help in the Middle East, he received the stinging reply that the Americans were doing 'a great deal', but the UK had perhaps 'been doing too much in a non-constructive sense'. Lovett castigated British troop movements to Aqaba, and blamed the British for the recent (7 January) dog-fight between Israeli and British aircraft over the Negev. Lovett suggested that this series of moves might well be regarded by the Israelis as threatening, and hardly calculated to encourage them to believe that the British were looking for peace. The Americans believed that with the Egyptians and the Israelis about to sit down together at Rhodes for UN-sponsored peace talks, and when Israel was talking peace with other Arab states, it would be highly unfortunate 'if any [British] action should prevent these developments from coming to fruition'. The Americans now believed firmly that instead of using the UN Security Council to oust the Israelis from the Negev, as the British wanted, the Allies should allow the parties concerned to negotiate a peace settlement on their own.[59]

[56] On Marshall's quarrel with Truman over the post-haste recognition of Israel in May 1948, when Marshall declared that if Truman recognised Israel, then he, Marshall would not vote for the President in the next elections, see Cohen, *Truman and . . .*, pp.212–15.

[57] Franks to Bevin, 13 Jan. 1949, E615, supra.

[58] Franks to Bevin, 13 Jan., E613, FO 371/75334. PRO; also quoted by Louis, *The British . . .*, p.570.   [59] Lovett, UK embassy, 13 Jan. 1949, supra.

So the Labour government recoiled from what was the brink of war with Israel. It had been assailed at home by a violent press and parliamentary reaction to the Spitfires incident. Even the Conservative Opposition was apprehensive that the demonstration of force at Aqaba might escalate into a conflict that might end badly for Britain. In private, some Conservatives told Bevin that they held him personally responsible for the British pilots' deaths, and threatened to go public with their charges.[60]

In any case, the government would have found it hard to explain to their electorate why, having withdrawn from Palestine just seven months before, they had taken the country to war against the Israelis, in defence of Egypt, 'a dubious, discredited, and somewhat reluctant ally'. And finally, as the Israelis learned, the British had been pressed by the Americans to 'take positive steps to liquidate hostilities' in the Middle East, and warned that if they took the Spitfires incident to the Security Council, they would be isolated.[61]

But the Foreign Office was unable to relinquish its antagonism to Israel with good face. In its own bitter myopia about Jewish triumphs in the Negev, it dismissed American policy on Palestine as being dictated by Truman's subservience to Jewish influence. A proposal that either Bevin or Attlee himself visit Washington to persuade the president in person, was dismissed out of hand by the Permanent Under-Secretary, Sir Orme Sargent:

> A weak, obstinate and suspicious man as is the President would I am certain bitterly resent such an attempt to influence him unduly.
>
> . . . we must do our best to hold the position single-handed until President Truman begins to see straight and free himself from the Jewish pressure to which he has succumbed.[62]

In contrast to the American hypothesis that they should cultivate Israeli friendship, some senior officials still tended to write off Israel as an ephemeral nightmare. There was an element of bitter 'sour grapes' in British derision of American assessments. The Foreign Office believed that the Americans were narrow-minded and 'unduly optimistic' about Israel aligning herself with the West. Troutbeck commented that the Americans' 'present blindness to the strategic implications of their policy' was a 'strange phenomenon'.[63]

---

[60] Linton (London) to Sharett, 22 Jan. 1949, *I.D.*, 1949, Vol. 2, no. 349, pp.391–2.

[61] I. J. Linton to M. Sharett, 11 Jan. 1949, ibid., no. 309, p.358; and Pappé, *Britain and . . .* pp.63–5.

[62] Minute by Sir Orme Sargent, 17 Jan. 1949, E1273, FO 371/75336, PRO, quoted in Cohen, *Truman and . . .*, p.272.

[63] Troutbeck to Foreign Office, 16 Jan. 1949, FO 800/488. PRO.

Foreign Office officials believed that those immigrants who did succeed in reaching Israel from behind the Iron Curtain would be 'picked communists'. Even Israeli neutrality, although preferable to communism, would hardly meet Britain's strategic needs. It was predicted that Israel would prove to be unviable economically, and that once the drama was removed from the Palestine question, American funds would dry up.[64]

However, given the Americans' refusal to co-operate with the UK against Israel at the United Nations, the only means left of ejecting the Israelis from the Negev would be to adopt Campbell's proposal to intervene militarily themselves. However, as will be seen shortly, the C. in C.s Middle East were about to warn London that such a 'military adventure' was too fraught with unquantifiable risks, and beyond British resources. And, politically, the British public, which in 1947 had pressed the government to 'bring the boys home from Palestine', was hardly likely to support a war against Israel.

Ultimately, the Foreign Office had to face up to realities, and the limitations on Britain's autonomy imposed by her alliance with the United States. As noted by one scholar, 'by pretending still to be the masters of the Middle East, the British tended to lose sight of the overriding importance of retaining American goodwill'.[65] American sponsorship of Israel had brought the British up against a dead end. Henceforth, they would need to seek an accommodation with the Jewish state.

D. THE COMPLETION OF THE NEGEV CAMPAIGN

For once, the senior staff of the Foreign Office lagged behind their own military in their assessments of Israel's future role in the Middle East. Even as Bevin's emotional appeals were being rebuffed by Washington, the British C. in C.s Middle East were coming to the very same conclusion as the Americans, on purely military grounds. On 12 January 1949, a conference was convened in Cairo on the strategic implications of the Arab–Israeli war. In attendance were Sir William Strang, Permanent Under-Secretary at the Foreign Office, ambassador Campbell, John Troutbeck, and the C. in C.s Middle East.

The meeting signified a seminal turning-point in British strategic thinking on the Middle East. For the first time, it was appreciated that British strategic interests in the Middle East could not be met by

---

[64] Franks to Bevin, 17 Feb. 1949, E2480, and summary of Foreign Office views by John Beith, 22 March 1949, E6145, in FO 371/75054. PRO.

[65] Louis, *The British . . .*, p.567.

reliance on the Arab world alone. If the British did secure an Arab-held land bridge through the Sinai desert and the southern Negev, to Aqaba, this would enable them to rush forces to the eastern front, in the event of a Soviet offensive through Persia and Iraq. But the Cairo–Aqaba route would not have been of much use in the event of a Soviet offensive from the north and/or north-west – through Turkey, and/or Syria. For that contingency, they would need transit rights across Israeli territory. With or without the Negev, Israel held vital strategic assets that would be essential for the Allies in the event of war.

The Middle East commanders stressed that if they ever had to advance north from the Egyptian base, they would require the friendly collaboration of all the inhabitants of Palestine, so as not to have to fight their way through hostile territory. Even if they secured all of the Negev for their Arab patrons, their strategic requirements would still not have been met. For in the event of war, they would need to 'advance into the heart of Palestine'. Therefore, the C. in C.s concluded:

> On the assumption that Israel has come to stay, this means that we must make it our aim eventually to get on friendly terms with Israel.[66]

The C. in C.s appreciated the difficulties of Anglo–Israeli relations – the current hostility of the majority of Israel's population towards the UK; and the danger of Israel opting for the communist camp, or remaining neutral. However, Britain's strategic interests now required that they acquire the friendship of both Israel and the Arab world (naturally, the friendship of Egypt, where Britain's main Middle East base was situated, remained of paramount importance).[67]

The meeting also apparently discussed the possible consequences and implications of a British military intervention against Israel in the Negev, as proposed by ambassador Campbell. Their views were forwarded to the Foreign Office by John Troutbeck, a few days later.

Troutbeck could not 'too strongly endorse' Campbell's warning that if the Israelis retained their hold on the Negev, the British would be 'pretty well bankrupt' in the Middle East. Nor did he dismiss the possibility that they, the British, might be faced with the dilemma of 'either seeing the Jews in possession of the Negeb . . . or of turning them out ourselves.' But he warned the Foreign Office about the potential risks of such an operation.[68]

a. The scale of any military intervention would not depend entirely on

---

[66] Troutbeck to Sir Michael Wright, 14 Jan. 1949, E999, FO 371/75367. PRO.

[67] Ibid.

[68] Troutbeck to Foreign Office, 16 Jan. 1949, FO 800/488. PRO.

the British, and they could not be certain of limiting it to pushing the Israelis back to the 14 October lines.

b. If they indeed secured their military objective, they could not be sure how long their forces would have to maintain it, until an international settlement was reached. Israel might refuse to make peace, especially if backed by the Soviets, and possibly by the Americans.

c. Such an operation would require using an L. of C. through Egyptian territory. But the Egyptians might not welcome a situation that would make it universally apparent that 'the British Army had thus come to their rescue.'

d. If the British took over the Negev, with the Gaza area, they might find themselves saddled with the responsibility for the welfare of over 200,000 refugees.

In conclusion, Troutbeck asked, evidently rhetorically, whether Britain, on her own, had:

> . . . the manpower, the money, the material and everything else that would be needed to carry such an adventure to a successful conclusion?[69]

But Israel had yet to occupy the southern Negev, down to the Gulf of Aqaba. Until she did, in March 1949, the British still entertained hopes of retrieving enough of the southern Negev for the Arabs to maintain the land-bridge between Egypt and Transjordan. At the beginning of February 1949, the JPS in London assessed the strategic pros and cons of the Negev remaining in Arab or Israeli hands. The theme dominating their report was the uncertainty of Israel's future ideological disposition, in contrast with what the British apparently still took for granted – the enduring benign disposition of the Arabs.

The planners still believed that Britain's strategic interests would be served best if the *Arabs* retained control of the southern Negev and central Palestine. Their first consideration was that if the Arabs occupied these areas, the UK would enjoy a foothold from which she would be able, in war, to re-occupy the rest of Israel more quickly. Not only would the southern Negev guarantee the land route from Egypt to Transjordan, but in peacetime, the British might be able to construct a number of airfields in this area. The planners recognised the fact that in Israeli hands, communications and military facilities in the Negev would be developed more rapidly. However, they did not feel able to rely upon future Israeli collaboration – even if, in the event of war, the Israelis' goodwill would be vital to Britain, and their hostility would 'seriously prejudice' British plans. But, as always, Britain's overriding

[69] Ibid.

consideration remained the retention of Arab goodwill, especially that of Egypt.[70]

In Cairo, ambassador Campbell tried to persuade the UN's Palestine Conciliation Commission about the importance of the strategic routes running from Egypt north through the Sinai and Negev deserts. The American delegate, Mark Ethridge, doubted whether the final settlement would leave the Auja–Beersheba–Hebron road in Arab hands, and asked whether a road south of the Dead Sea would not meet Britain's strategic needs? Campbell demurred, stated that there were geographical difficulties, and stressed the importance of the northern route, as 'providing the best and most rapid military communication'.[71]

On 24 February 1949, the Egyptians and the Israelis signed an armistice agreement. Just over one week later, on 5 March 1949, an Israeli force set off to secure the southern Negev, and to establish a foothold on the Gulf of Aqaba. The British were about to lose their last L. of C. from their Egyptian base through to the north-east. But they had learned the 'lessons' of the Israeli incursion into Sinai in December, and the consequent diplomatic exchanges with the Americans. They therefore now took every precaution to ensure that this time their forces did not risk becoming involved in hostilities with the Israelis.

Initially, the British believed that Israeli troop movements were tactical, designed to exert pressure on Transjordan, with whom Israel was currently negotiating armistice terms. The main concern of the COS was that Israel might cross into Transjordanian territory, and engage British troops at Aqaba. Britain's sole interest now was to defend the strategic port of Aqaba, and Transjordan's territorial integrity. She had no intention of fighting in what had been mandatory Palestine, least of all in that area of it allotted by the UN to Israel.

The cabinet took extraordinary precautions to avert a clash. It despatched detailed orders to the Aqaba garrison, making it eminently clear that they were not to engage the Israeli force, unless it opened fire on them first. (In the event that the Israelis crossed into Transjordan, but did not open fire, British forces were to push them back across into the Negev, if possible, without resorting to force.) No doubt bearing in mind the RAF's casualties over the Sinai desert on 7 January, strict orders were also given that the two Auster spotter aircraft stationed at Aqaba were not to fly over Palestinian territory. Moreover, in the warning they conveyed to Israel, the British cautioned the Israelis only against attacking their Transjordanian ally.[72]

[70] JP (49) 11, 11 Feb. 1949, Defe 6/8; discussed by COS on 16 Feb. 1949, COS (49) 26th., Defe 4/20. PRO.

[71] Campbell to Foreign Office, 18 Feb. 1949, FO 800/488. PRO.

[72] Asia, *The Core . . .*, pp.86–7.

The inference was, quite clearly, that the British would not oppose Israel establishing herself on the Gulf of Aqaba, provided she remained within the borders of mandatory Palestine. The single exception to the British instructions was a warning given the Israelis that if any of their aircraft flew over British positions, for whatever reason, they would be engaged by the RAF.[73]

This time, the British kept the Americans advised of events in the southern Negev which, they maintained, were in breach of the Security Council resolutions. Ambassador Franks told Secretary Acheson that the British would only return fire in self-defence if attacked first. There was some discussion as to whether the Israelis had in fact crossed the border into Transjordan. (The Israelis claimed that they had been engaged by an Arab Legion patrol, moving illegally within Israeli territory.) But even Franks, who claimed that the Israelis had engaged Jordanian forces, inside the latter's territory, conceded that his latest information was that the Israelis had broken off the engagement, and were returning westwards, back into Palestine. Acheson repeated the words of caution already issued by his under-secretary, Lovett. He expressed his confidence that the British at Aqaba would act with restraint, and 'not allow any minor incident to set off the balloon.'[74]

In a personal telegram, Bevin apologised to Kirkbride in Amman for their failure to act against the Israeli force, either against its progress toward the Red Sea, or against its incursion into Transjordanian territory. The government appreciated by now that nothing short of 'British intervention in force inside Palestine' could have possibly stopped the Israelis establishing themselves on the Red Sea, and that neither the Americans, nor any in the Commonwealth would have supported them. Bearing this in mind the government had deemed it 'essential not to stir up opinion too much either in this country or in the United States'. Kirkbride conceded that there was no urgent need to reinforce British forces in Transjordan, given that the Israelis apparently had no intention of invading that country on a large scale. However, he did urge that it would be appropriate to send ammunition to the Arab Legion, who were about to take over the Iraqi section of the West Bank front.[75]

On 10 March 1949, the Israeli force reached a point on the Red Sea called Umm Reshresh. They raised a makeshift sheet with the Star of

[73] I.J. Linton report on meeting on 9 March with Michael Wright (Foreign Office), *I.D.* 1949, Vol. 2, No. 425, pp.482–3.

[74] Note of telephone conversation between Ambassador Franks and Secretary Acheson, 10 March 1949, Acheson conversations, box 73, HST. For the Israeli claim, cf., Israeli memorandum sent to British Foreign Office, 11 March 1949, *I.D.*, 1949, Vol. 2, no. 432, pp.488–9.

[75] Bevin to Kirkbride, 10 March 1949, and Kirkbride to Bevin, 12 March, FO 800/477. PRO.

David inked in on it, and renamed the point Elath. Israel had established its own independent egress to the Indian Ocean and to the Far East. As fate would have it, this vital strategic concern of Israel cut across an historic route from Cairo, via Amman to Damascus, the so-called 'King's Highway'.

As with many strategic conceptions, British hopes for a land bridge from Egypt to Transjordan lived on long after realities on the ground had turned them into an anachronism. On 23 March 1949, two weeks after the Israelis had established themselves on the Gulf of Aqaba, Bevin asked the Minister for Defence, Viscount Alexander, whether in the event that the final Palestine settlement left the Auja–Beersheba–Hebron road in neither Egyptian nor Transjordanian hands, Britain should develop the 'Suez–Aqaba–Amman track as an all-weather road capable of carrying heavy transport?'[76]

In a paper circulated to the Washington embassy and to all diplomatic posts in the Middle East, at the beginning of April 1949, the Foreign Office once again tried to salvage something from the shambles of Britain's strategic interests in southern Palestine. It was conceded, finally, that Britain was 'very unlikely in present circumstances' to secure the road from Egypt to Transjordan running through Beersheba. The best alternative, it was now suggested, would be:

> a road starting at El Kubri on the Suez Canal and running to Aqaba across Sinai via Nakhl and El Thamad, and running on from Aqaba via Ma'an and El Hasa.[77]

But the problem with this route, as ever, was that in order to secure it for their Arab protegés, it would be necessary to deny Israel access to the Red Sea, at the southern tip of the Negev. But, by now, even the Foreign Office appreciated that Israel would not surrender access to the Gulf without a fierce fight. One official suggested that Israel might be persuaded to grant transit rights along the sections of the road that ran through her territory.[78] But this idea was premature, given the tense state of Anglo–Israeli relations. It would take two more years before the British dared to raise with the Israeli government the idea of transit rights across its territory (on which see Chapter 7).

---

[76] Bevin to Minister of Defence, 23 March 1949, FO 800/477. PRO.

[77] Foreign Office to Washington and all Middle East posts, 1 April 1949, E4322, FO 371/75349. PRO.

[78] Minute by John Beith, 2 April 1949, E4531, FO 371/75332. PRO.

5 The Egyptian base – and alternative options

A. NEGOTIATING A STRATEGIC ASSET

It will be recalled that the Military's argument on the need to maintain a presence in Egypt was based on the following considerations. The Allies would need to use Middle East air bases as launching platforms for their strategic air offensive against the Soviets; the latter were expected to launch a land and air offensive against the Middle East, both to interdict the Allied air offensive, to protect their left flank, when attacking Western Europe (their main objective), and to seize British strategic assets in the Middle East, culminating with the base complex in Egypt. Therefore, in the event of any global war, the Middle East would be a major theatre of operations, even if secondary to the European theatre.

As noted already, the British expected the Soviet offensive against the Middle East to be launched along two axes; the first from the north, through Turkey, and thence south through Lebanon and Palestine; and the second, from the East, through Iran, northern Iraq, Syria and Palestine.

The Turks might be able to defend themselves, or at least to delay the Soviets until Allied reinforcements arrived. But there were no indigenous military forces of any consequence in the Arab world. The Arab armies could not even delay a Soviet land offensive. (In 1948, the Turkish army was estimated to be roughly the size of half the population of Saudi Arabia!) Therefore, with a typically paternalist, imperialistic logic, the British argued in August 1948:

> In the foreseeable future . . . the only way to defend the Arab countries against attack by a great power is for the Arabs to grant us facilities in time of peace that will enable us to go to their help immediately they are attacked.[1]

---

[1] B.A. Burrows (Foreign Office) – R. Speaight (Cairo), 17 Aug. 1948, E10346/103/G, FO 371/68386. Public Record Office [PRO]. This 'paternalism' seems all the more ironic in retrospect, after the Anglo-French Suez adventure of 1956.

Even in 1951, by which time the British were reduced to negotiating the terms of their withdrawal from Egypt, the COS insisted that minimal British forces had to stay on in peacetime. This was because they had no faith whatever in the Egyptians' ability to maintain the base facilities in operational order in peacetime.[2]

The British base along the Suez Canal comprised 38 army camps and 10 airfields. In 1945, it was the single largest military base in existence, anywhere across the globe. In 1946, the COS described Egypt as 'the political and industrial centre of the Middle East and the key point in vital communications'.The security of Egypt in war was considered 'vital to the defence of the Middle East as a whole'. Egypt was the only country that had port facilities which provided access to both the Mediterranean and the Indian Ocean, 'the communications, man-power and industrial infrastructure necessary to support forces of the size required for the defence of the Middle East', and airfields from which offensive air operations could be maintained.[3]

If the Soviets conquered Egypt (after having first taken over Turkey and the Straits), they would enjoy a custom-made base, which could be built up easily by the short sea passage from the Soviet Union itself. From here they would be able to extend their influence westward to North Africa and Western Europe, and southward into Africa.

In 1950, when the Cabinet ordered the COS to examine possible alternatives to the Egyptian base, the CIGS, Field Marshal Sir William Slim, insisted that a COS paper on global strategy be amended, to include the statement: 'Egypt was the key strategic area of the Middle East and the retention of the Egyptian base was indispensable.' With Britain fighting a rearguard battle with the Egyptians even to secure rights of immediate re-entry in case of war, the COS insisted that 'Egypt was the only really suitable location for the Middle East base in peace and war and that the difficulties of establishing an alternative base elsewhere in peace were almost insuperable.'[4]

However, since 1948, it had become increasingly apparent that the Egyptians would in no circumstances agree to the stationing of British combat units, or even the nucleus of a regimental Middle East headquarters in Egypt in peacetime. From that point on, British negotiations with the Egyptians focused on securing rights to retain a 'nucleus operational and administrative base organisation' in Egypt, one capable

[2] Memorandum, 'British strategy v. Soviet attack', COS (51) 759, 18 Dec. 1951, Defe 5/35. PRO.

[3] J.P. (46) 100, 23 May 1946, Cab 84/81; and D.O. (46) 67, by COS, Admiral Sir John Cunningham (First Sea Lord), Air Marshal Lord Tedder (Chief of Air Staff), Lt Gen Sir F.E.W. Simpson (Vice C.I.G.S), 25 May 1946, Cab 131/2. PRO.

[4] COS (50) 149th, 13 Sept. 1950, Defe 4/35; and JP (50) 124, 4 Oct. 1950, Defe 6/14. PRO.

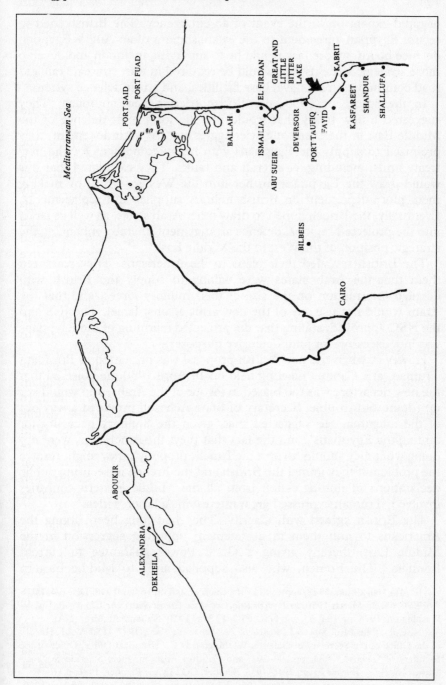

Map 3: The British Base at the Suez Canal

of rapid expansion in the event of an emergency. The British tried to secure Egyptian agreement to the establishment of an Anglo–Egyptian defence board, whose task would be to supervise, maintain and develop those strategic airfields that would be required in war, strategic rail and road communications, naval base facilities, and an air defence system.[5]

In the spring of 1950, the British tried a new approach. They suggested a new treaty that would provide for a joint defence of the Middle East in the event of Soviet aggression. As an inducement, they promised to supply the Egyptians with heavy equipment for the new treaty units, including jet aircraft and tanks. They calculated that this would draw the Egyptians further into the Western orbit, by making them more dependent on British military supplies and replacements. Eventually, the British hoped to draw other Arab states, as well as Israel into the projected regional defence arrangement, thereby enhancing the strategic position of the West in the Middle East.[6]

The British revealed their plans to the Americans. They reassured them that the Arab states were willing to supply the British with detailed information on the size of their military forces, and that the Arabs would not use any of the new arms against Israel. The JCS and the NSC approved, stating that the projected rearming of the Egyptians was 'not excessive for joint defensive purposes'.

However, when the new British proposal was presented to President Truman, at a Cabinet meeting held on 14 April 1950, he objected that the new departure was too biased in favour of the Arabs, and would stir up (domestic) trouble. Secretary of State Acheson provided a way out of the dilemma. He suggested that, given the 'military necessity for arming the Egyptians', and the fact that they, the Americans, were not doing what they should 'to arm the Israelis properly', they might resolve the problem if they joined the British and the French in securing public declarations of non-aggression from all the Middle Eastern countries involved. Truman expressed great interest in Acheson's idea.[7]

The British agreed with alacrity. They had long been urging the Americans to join them in a statement opposing aggression in the Middle East, thereby giving a Great Power guarantee to current frontiers.[8] The French, who also supplied arms to Middle Eastern

[5] JP (47) 160, 13 Jan. 1948, approved by the chiefs of staff on 16 Jan. 1948. Defe 6/4. PRO.

[6] NSC 65, 28 March 1950, in *Foreign Relations of the United States (FRUS)* 1950, Vol. V, Washington: 1978, pp.131–35, and NSC 65/2, 10 May 1950. National Archives (NA).

[7] NSC 65, ibid. Also, Steven L. Rearden, *The Formative Years, 1947–1950*, Vol.1, History of the Office of the Secretary of Defense, Washington D.C.: Historical Office, Office of the Secretary of Defense, 1984, pp.200–201, and Geoffrey Aronson, *From Sideshow to Center Stage: U.S. Policy Toward Egypt, 1946–1956*, Boulder, CO.: Lynne Rienner, 1986, p.16.

[8] Cf., Furlonge minutes, of 27 March 1950, E1023/10, FO 371/81907, and of 5 May 1950, E1023/89, FO 371/81910. PRO.

countries, were invited to join in, and thus was born the much-vaunted Tripartite Declaration of May 1950.

But the Egyptians refused categorically to concede the British demand for 'joint defence in peacetime' (Britain's own ulterior calculations were apparently not entirely lost on them). Notwithstanding persistent British efforts to explain to the Egyptians the seriousness of the Soviet threat to the Middle East, the latter were concerned more about the Israelis than the Soviets. British concessions – an offer to share with the Egyptians the maintenance and command of the country's British-built defence facilities, and even to renounce British responsibility for the security of the Suez Canal – were all rejected.[9]

In September 1950, the British replaced 'the carrot' with the 'stick'. By this point, British national pride had become involved – popular feeling rankled at supplying heavy arms to a state which obdurately insisted on discontinuing British base facilities. In the hope of inducing a more co-operative attitude on the part of the Egyptians, (and also, in part, due to arms shortages in Britain itself) the British suspended shipment of an old order of 16 Centurion tanks. When the government tried later to ease the suspension on the tank shipments, the British Parliament intervened and forestalled the move.[10]

But British sanctions did not bring the hoped-for result. Instead, on 16 November 1950, King Farouk, in a speech from the throne, called for 'the complete evacuation of the Canal Zone and the unity of Egypt and the Sudan'. Farouk went on to declare the Anglo–Egyptian Treaty of 1936 'null and void'.[11]

At times, the Americans found themselves in an acute dilemma regarding the British position in Egypt. On the one hand, their own global strategy dictated support for the British position. On the other, they felt that their standing in the Middle East would be compromised if they became tainted with the British imperialist brush.[12]

Still hoping to break the deadlock with the Egyptians, the British now pressed the Americans to help them out of their impasse. But the Americans refused to allow the British to mention to the Egyptians any American strategic interest in their country. The British were forced to swallow any irritation they may have felt at 'moralising American

[9] Memorandum to the Cabinet by Bevin, 27 Nov. 1950, CP (50) 283, in Cab 129/43. PRO.

[10] H. Freeman Mathews, Deputy Under Secretary of State to James S. Lay, Executive Secretary, National Security Council, 24 Jan. 1951, *FRUS*, 1950, Vol. V., Washington: 1978, pp.186–87; and David R. Devereux, *The Formulation of British Defence Policy towards the Middle East 1948–56*, London: Macmillan, 1990, p.29.

[11] Devereux, ibid., p.29.

[12] Peter L. Hahn, *The United States, Great Britain, & Egypt, 1945–1956*, Chapel Hill: University of North Carolina Press, 1991, pp.88–9.

criticisms of British colonialism'. They believed that such sentiments, when expressed openly, had encouraged Egyptian intransigence and undermined their own negotiating position.[13]

The Korean war (which began in June 1950), enhanced the importance of the Suez Canal in Allied strategy. The Americans shipped large amounts of troops and war materiel through it to Korea. The JCS now regarded British control of the Suez Canal in a new perspective, even if they still baulked at any direct American political involvement, or military commitment.[14]

In late 1950 the Americans at last agreed to a new, joint approach to the Egyptians. This would eventually take the form of a new proposal, the Middle East Command (MEC, on which, see below, chapter 8). However, the Americans never allowed the British to inform the Egyptians that the base at Abu Sueir was earmarked for the war-time use of American B-29s.[15]

But the Egyptians would not contemplate a continued British military presence, under whatever guise, and refused to consider any new agreements until British forces evacuated the country completely. Under Ministerial pressure, the COS commissioned the JPS to examine alternatives to Egypt, for the eventuality that Britain would be forced to leave the country in 1956, the year in which the 1936 Anglo–Egyptian treaty was due to expire.[16]

By the end of 1950, British politicians, if not yet the Military, had become convinced of the need to evacuate Egypt. The Cabinet was influenced by the ambassador in Cairo, Sir Ralph Stevenson, who advised that the Egyptians would never acquiesce in any form of continued British military presence on their soil. Although King Farouk had confided in private that he did not want British forces to leave, the Egyptian government insisted on British evacuation within 'a fairly short period'; at the most – not more than twelve months. Foreign Secretary Bevin concluded that the maximum they could now get from the Egyptians would be permission to leave their base installations and matériel in Egyptian hands in peacetime. The Egyptians might guarantee immediate re-entry rights in wartime.[17]

An alternative base would have to be found immediately for the British striking force. Among the proposals made by Bevin were Libya, the Gaza Strip, and Cyprus. The only alternative to immediate

[13] Peter G. Boyle, ed., *The Churchill–Eisenhower Correspondence, 1953–1955*, Chapel Hill: The University of North Carolina Press, 1990, p.24.

[14] Devereux, *The Formulation of . . .*, p.40.

[15] Bevin memorandum on Egypt, 27 Nov. 1950, CP (50) 284, in Cab 129/43. PRO.

[16] JP (50) 124, 4 Oct. 1950, Defe 6/14. PRO.

[17] Bevin memorandum, CP (50) 284, 27 Nov. 1950, Cab 129/43. PRO.

evacuation, in Bevin's view, was to stay on in Egypt regardless, under the protection of the 1936 Treaty, until 1956. By that date, it might be hoped that either the Soviet threat would have diminished, or that the Egyptian government would have become more aware of it.[18]

Roger Allen, head of the African Department at the Foreign Office, believed that the days were past when the British could maintain imperialist bases against the rising tide of local nationalism:

> It would be difficult to find legal or moral justification for insisting on the continuance of a British base on foreign soil against the wishes of the country concerned, and the political repercussions of such an attitude are incalculable.[19]

By the autumn 1952 (by which time the MEC, and its successor, MEDO, had become moribund), for the first time, some elements in the COS came round to the view that the Egyptian base might not be essential. It was becoming apparent that traditional British strategy in the Middle East – that based on Egypt and the Suez Canal – had become anachronistic and unrealistic.

A meeting of the COS, on 21 October 1952, failed to produce a consensus on the strategic need for Egypt. Air Marshal Sir John Slessor, commander of the RAF, elaborated on the new factors which had transformed Egypt's centrality in Allied Middle Eastern strategy. With Turkey's adherence to NATO, and the projected pruning of British Middle Eastern forces down to just one division (with no more than two further divisions to be dispatched as reinforcements during the first six months of war), it was likely that a war in the region would be fought further forward, to the north east, than had previously been thought (on the new 'Levant–Iraq' strategy, see below, Chapter 10).

Slessor doubted therefore if the Egyptian base was still essential, and suggested that they consider Alexandretta and Basra as alternatives. The Navy representative, Sir Guy Grantham, contended that on the broader view, Egyptian goodwill was essential, and 'the base would be of little value surrounded by a hostile Egypt'.[20]

But Major General Chilton, Vice Quarter-Master General, stated that even if only three British divisions were to fight in the Middle East during the first six months of war, the Egyptian base would remain essential. This was because they could not rely on keeping the Mediterranean open in wartime, and in any case they would not have the shipping to transport the stores that would be needed even for a three-division force.

[18] Ibid.

[19] Minute by Roger Allen, 16 March 1951, JE1194/30, FO 371/90177. PRO.

[20] For this and following, cf., minutes of COS meeting, 21 Oct. 1952, in Defe 4/57, and copy in Air 20/7435. PRO.

CIGS Slim supported General Chilton, stating that in war, British forces in the region would have to be reinforced, and as they grew in size, it would be vital to reactivate the base in Egypt. Even if the Egyptian base was not absolutely essential at present, access to it in war would greatly enhance Britain's chances for a successful defence of the Middle East.

Roger Allen of the Foreign Office pointed out that all negotiations with Egypt until now had been predicated on the assumption that the base there was essential. It now appeared, he continued, that 'although a base would clearly be a tremendous asset, it was not necessarily still indispensable to the defence of the Middle East.'[21]

The meeting decided that a review should be made of strategic plans for the defence of the Middle East, based on the assumption that the base in Egypt would not be available (though a benevolent Egypt might permit use of the Suez Canal), and that the Mediterranean might be closed.

Thus doubts were voiced about the very foundation-stone of British strategy in the Middle East – whether the Canal Base was vital to the defence of the Middle East. In a letter to the ambassador at Cairo, Allen argued that it would be 'ridiculous' to persist in negotiations with Egypt, in order to:

> secure a fully operative base in Egypt if it turned out that such a base was no longer militarily essential.

The COS did not believe that the Egyptians would be able to keep the base in a fully-operative state in peace-time. But retaining the base under full British control, as the COS still insisted, could be achieved only against Egyptian opposition. Allen concluded that this course might be politically acceptable, or necessary, only if the COS could assure the government that they must do so, 'or risk the loss of the Middle East'.[22]

The COS still insisted that this was indeed the case. But they urged that no indication of their need for Suez be given to the Egyptians, before studies of alternative base sites, then being carried out urgently, were completed.

There still remained a gap between the military and the politicians. In effect, the COS were willing to relinquish Egypt only if suitable alternatives could be found. But by mid-1952, it had been concluded that no feasible, practical alternative bases could be developed in the

[21] Ibid.

[22] Roger Allen – Sir R. Stevenson (Cairo), 23 Oct. 1952, JE1194/104G, FO 371/96979. PRO.

region. Following the debate in October 1952, the COS circulated a memorandum in December, which returned to the traditional view that in the entire Middle East, only Egypt could meet Allied strategic requirements in the region. All alternatives were ruled out:

> nowhere else in the Middle East could existing facilities be expanded to form a substitute except at prohibitive cost. Furthermore, only in Egypt can a base be found which could be used if the Mediterranean were closed to our convoys.[23]

But by 1953, the COS had to accept the inevitability of evacuation. Their objective in Egypt was reduced now to ensuring conditions that would guarantee immediate re-occupation and reactivation of the base in the event of war. When Anglo-Egyptian negotiations resumed in 1953 (the Americans refused British entreaties to join in, or to exert economic pressure on the Egyptians), talks stalled on how many maintenance 'technicians' the British would be allowed to leave behind, if they would be allowed to wear military uniforms, and the conditions for British re-entry in the event of war.

The impasse was broken in February 1954, when Nasser replaced Neguib as President of Egypt (on the Free Officers' revolution of July 1952, see Chapter 9). Agreement was reached in July of that year. The British gave way on the question of uniforms, more of a symbolic than strategic significance; and the Egyptians ceded the British request for re-entry rights in the event of a Soviet attack on Turkey. British troops were to withdraw within 20 months, and the duration of the agreement (signed in October 1954) was determined ultimately as seven years.[24]

Economic stringencies had in fact played a major role in Britain's overseas deployments. This may be illustrated by a comparison between an American estimate, and projection of future British dispositions in the Middle East, drafted in 1946, and actual British reductions in 1952.

In the middle of 1946, an American intelligence report estimated that the RAF had a total of 294 fighter aircraft and 134 bombers in the Middle East, Greece and India; that the British army had a total of 270,000 ground forces in the Near and Middle East – 30,000 in Greece (withdrawn by the end of 1947), 96,000 in Egypt, 70,000 in Palestine (withdrawn in May 1948), and 16,000 in Iraq. The report estimated that by 1 August 1947, British forces would be reduced to their postwar goal of 150,000, concentrated mostly near the Suez Canal.[25]

---

[23] Memorandum by Air Marshal Sir John Slessor, Field-Marshal Sir John Harding (CIGS), and First Sea Lord Sir Robert McGrigor, appendix to COS (52) 683, 15 Dec. 1952. PRO.

[24] For details on the negotiations, see Laila Amin Morsey, 'The Role of the United States in the Anglo–Egyptian Agreement of 1954', *Middle Eastern Studies*, Vol. 29, No. 3, July 1993.

[25] JIS 265/1, 29 August 1946, Joint Chiefs of Staff, 46–47, CS 092 USSR (3–27–45), box 154, RG 218. NA.

The reality turned out to be somewhat different from that of the intelligence forecast. In some contrast to American prognoses, a British redeployment plan of September 1952 provided for a Middle East garrison of just 32,900, with a Marine commando brigade to be stationed at Malta.[26]

In regard to relative Soviet and Allied Air force levels in the Middle East, in July 1950, the British expected that within the first six months of war, the Red Air Force would commit 270 fighter and fighter/ground attack aircraft, and 360 medium bombers. To face these, the British hoped to muster 290 fighter/ground and attack/reconnaissance aircraft, and 60 light and medium bombers. At that time no assistance was expected from USAF.[27]

Britain's 'Moment in the Middle East'[28] – Suez notwithstanding – was over. However, the continuing centrality in Allied strategic planning of the British base in Egypt, in particular of the strategic air base constructed at Abu Sueir, cannot be over-emphasised.

B. THE STRATEGIC AIR BASE AT ABU SUEIR

In 1948, Anglo-American talks on the Middle East produced agreement that the base at Abu Sueir was the most suitable for meeting the needs of the strategic air offensive. American planners concluded that 'Egypt's strategic location, her comparatively well-developed air facility system, and her potential sites for future airfield development' would make that country an essential strategic asset in the Middle East.[29]

Abu Sueir's main strategic advantage over English bases lay in its closer proximity to Soviet strategic targets. A far higher percentage of those targets lay within short-range of the Egyptian base, even if the percentages did even out somewhat when it came to long-range targets.

Of the forty most important Soviet petroleum refineries and urban areas targeted by *Makefast*, the American plan for a global war offensive (October 1946), their ranges respectively from the Mildenhall base in England and from Cairo were as follows:

	1500 miles	2000 miles	2500 miles
England:	5	16	30
Cairo:	12	20	32

[26] Devereux, *The Formulation of . . .*, p.107.

[27] DO (50) 58, 21 July 1950, in Cab 131/9. PRO.

[28] The phrase is, of course, Elizabeth Monroe's – *Britain's Moment in the Middle East*, London: Methuen, 1965.

[29] Hahn, *The United States . . .* p.74.

With regard to the percentage of Soviet petroleum refining capacity within striking distance from England and Cairo, the logistical comparison is yet more striking:

	1500 miles	2000 miles	2500 miles
England:	12%	25%	96%
Cairo:	72%	94%	99%[30]

Given the shorter ranges of the strategic bombers available until the early and mid-1950s, the advantages of Abu Sueir over English air bases are readily apparent.

According to *Makefast*, one task force of B-29 bombers would be sent to Britain within one to two months of the outbreak of war, and a further task force to Cairo within four months. In addition, the United States would despatch to Cairo a tactical Air Force, consisting of eight Fighter groups, four light bomber groups, a tactical reconnaissance group, and three troop carrier groups. It was hoped that this force would destroy 70–80% of the Soviets' petroleum refining capacity within nine months. The Soviets were believed to have scanty petroleum reserves of not more than three months supplies for their armed forces under combat conditions. Once those reserves were spent, the Soviet armed forces would be paralysed by the end of the first year of war.[31]

The percentages of Soviet oil refining capacity within effective range of the B-29s to be stationed at Mildenhall and Cairo are shown in the following table:

	No. plants:	% of total crude capacity	% of total Av Gas capacity
Mildenhall:	13	4	47
Cairo:	16	69	34
Total:	29	73	81[32]

The British calculated that, of all the existing bases available in the British treaty zone in Egypt, Abu Sueir was the most economical to develop and prepare for the reception of the heavy B-29 bombers. Abu Sueir would require the least expenditure in labour and money. The development of an alternative base in Cyprus was considered but proved to be much more expensive. The British determined to ask the Americans to meet the 'hard currency costs' of the work involved at

[30] 'Outline Air Plan for *Makefast*', 1 Oct. 1946, RG 165, ABC 381 USSR (2 March 46), sect. 3. NA.
[31] Ibid.
[32] Ibid.

Abu Sueir. But in view of the urgency of the project (the work itself would take longer to carry out than the warning period now expected from the Russians), in September 1948 the COS asked the Treasury to approve an immediate start to construction. It was hoped that the Americans would eventually agree to bear their share of the costs.[33]

Abu Sueir's main runway was too short to accommodate the B-29 bomber. In the Fall of 1948, Abu Sueir was capable of accommodating only medium-range bombers. This meant that until at least D + 3 months, the effective limit of strategic air operations would be 1500 miles. Therefore, there were no important strategic targets which could be reached from Cairo/Suez, which could not be reached from either the UK or Okinawa. However, as the US Plans and Operations division (P and O) noted, this still left 'two very important target complexes' that could not be reached from any of the three base areas. But once the main runway at Abu Sueir was lengthened, this base would offer a significant strategic advantage over US bases in the UK or at Okinawa.[34]

However, a start to the further development work needed was held up, due to the failure of the British and Americans to agree on their relative shares of the funding. On 13 November 1948, US Secretary of Defense, James Forrestal, and General Alfred Greunther, chairman of the JCS, met with their British opposite numbers, A. V. Alexander, Defence Minister, and the COS, Field Marshal Sir William Slim, in order to discuss the sharing of the costs of the work at Abu Sueir. The British expected the Americans to pay an equal share for the necessary improvements. But the Pentagon, hard hit by austerity cuts at home, insisted that the British pay the whole bill.[35] The result was impasse and further delay to the development work.

The British authorities in Egypt had already secured the agreement of the Egyptian government to supply the necessary materials and facilities (the Egyptians were not informed as to the true purpose of the improvements proposed for Abu-Sueir). They thought that it would be a shame not to seize the opportunity on hand. Without the extension of the runways at Abu Sueir, there would be no base for the B-29s in the Middle East, and the British were most concerned about the effect of this on their Middle East theatre plan, *Sandown*.[36]

The long-range plan was to develop four air bases in Egypt, including

---

[33] General Hollis (Secretary, British Chiefs of Staff) to Ministry of Defence, 30 Sept. 1948, in COS (48) 138th, Defe 4/16. PRO.

[34] 381 Case 121/83, P and O 381 TS, 7 Oct. 1948, RG 319 (Army Staff) 46–48. NA.

[35] Ibid.

[36] Memorandum on Egyptian airfields, 8 March 1949, P and O, 49–50, 686 TS (8 Mar. 49), box 264, RG 319 (Army Staff). NA.

the one at Abu Sueir. The total eventual cost was estimated at £7,717,000 ($31,000,000). During Fiscal year 1950, £1 million would be required for the work on the four bases, £800,000 of which was to be spent on Abu Sueir. But the British Air Ministry failed to secure Treasury approval of the British share of the total cost, £1.8 million. The Treasury argued that it could not endorse an appropriation of funds for USAF requirements without the agreement of both governments on the source of funding. When the Treasury learned that the Americans were unlikely to earmark any money from their current budget for the first year's work at Abu Sueir, it withdrew the £400,000 which it had already allotted as the British share.[37]

US Secretary of Defense Forrestal asked the NSC to approve negotiations with the British on the provision of the required funds. In response to the NSC's query, Forrestal forwarded the Joint Chiefs' consensus that the further development of the Abu Sueir air base (together with four extra airfields in England) was indeed 'in the national interest'. The NSC endorsed the proposal, and on 18 April 1949, President Truman signed NSC 45/1, which recommended the immediate opening of talks with the British 'at the highest level', in order to settle the issue of funding for the further development of the Abu Sueir base.[38]

In May 1949, the British Secretary of State for Air, Arthur Henderson, secured the agreement of the Defence Committee to the further development of five airfields in the Canal Zone and one at Aden, at a total cost of some £3.5m. Henderson explained that the urgent airfield development in Egypt was not essential for RAF purposes. British heavy bombers that would need longer runways would not become operational for several years. The B-29s that the British were to receive from the Americans would not be operated from the Middle East, since this role had been allotted to the Americans. But British self-interest, the very survival of the British Isles themselves, dictated that they begin construction work at Abu Sueir prior to the Americans' final agreement to share the costs. Abu Sueir, Henderson explained, was vital for the 'American strategic bomber offensive', upon which the British themselves were largely dependent to defeat the Soviets.[39]

[37] Secretary of Defense Forrestal to Sidney Souers, executive secretary to the NSC, 17 March 1949, *FRUS*, 1949, Vol. 1, 1976, pp.286–7; and memorandum on Egyptian airfields, supra.

[38] Forrestal to Souers, supra; and NSC 45/1, 'Airfield Construction in the United Kingdom and the Cairo–Suez Area', 15 April 1949, President's Secretary's Files, HST; and Aaronson, *From Sideshow . . .*, p.9.

[39] Annex to D.O. (49) 37, 9 May 1949, Memorandum by Secretary of State for Air, 'Works Services in the United Kingdom and Middle East Required for the United States Air Force', Cab 131/7. PRO.

The function of the Middle East airfields, 'would be to provide bases for United States bomber forces and supporting units to operate against Russian targets' which could not be reached from the United Kingdom. Later on, Abu Sueir's role would also be to accommodate medium- and long-range USAF bombers operating out of other bases, for refuelling and servicing, on their way out, and on their return from their missions.[40]

Henderson told the Defence Committee that it was 'particularly urgent' to begin the work at Abu Sueir, for there was currently no airfield in the Middle East which could handle fully-loaded B-29 aircraft. Henderson estimated that in 1949 alone, the work at Abu Sueir would cost some £400,000.[41]

Henderson considered the work to be so vital that he urged that it be started immediately, without prejudice to the discussions with the Americans, which he expected to take some time. He submitted that if the Americans did not eventually agree to bear their share of the costs, the Air Ministry itself would bear the whole amount, from savings to be made from the Ministry's budget. The Defence Committee agreed that construction should begin at Abu Sueir immediately on a 'full "post-strike" base for USAF bombers in the event of war.'[42]

The additional construction work involved extending and strengthening existing runways; the addition of aircraft standing areas, extra fuel tankers, extra accommodation for USAF personnel; the installation of 'a high speed refuelling system', and facilities for 'prestocking U.S.A.F. servicing equipment and vehicles'.[43] In June 1949, the two allies arrived at a cost-sharing agreement. The Americans undertook to assume at least one-third of the costs of developing the Abu Sueir field.

The JCS insisted that the development work at Abu Sueir had to be carried out 'under the guise of potential British use'. In order to avoid any publicity about the American share in the financing of the construction work at Abu Sueir, it was agreed that the American funds would be transferred to Britain as part of American aid to Western Union defence.[44]

[40] Memorandum by the Secretary of State for Air, Lord de L'Isle and Dudley for Prime Minister Churchill, 18 Feb. 1953, Prem 11/483. PRO.

[41] Annex to D.O. (49) 37, 9 May 1949, supra.

[42] Ibid.

[43] Memorandum from Chief of the Air Staff, Sir John Slessor, to Secretary of State for Air, July 1953, in Air 20/7448. PRO.

[44] Slessor, to Secretary of State for Air, July 1953, ibid.; DO (49) 13th., 13 May 1949, in Cab 131/8, PRO; undated annex, attached to PPS/56, 4 Aug. 1949 on Military Rights in Foreign Territories, *FRUS*, 1949, Vol. 1, 1976, pp.369–70; and Hahn, *The United States . . .*, pp.79–80.

Whereas current US strategy envisaged the early loss of the Middle East, the Abu Sueir base none the less remained a high priority. It was hoped that an opening atomic air offensive could be launched from Egypt before the Soviets overran the Middle East. But even once authorised, the construction work at Abu Sueir still encountered delays, and fell behind American contingency planning for a global conflict with the Soviets. American planners not only demonstrated their impatience, but began to lose their faith in the ultimate reliability of the Egyptian base.

A war plan drafted by SAC in the summer of 1949, noted that the atomic air offensive might have to be limited to airfields in the United States and Britain, 'principally because of the lack of suitable operational bases in the Cairo–Suez area'.[45]

By September 1949, the American Joint War Plans committee had reduced the requirements of SAC in the Suez-Cairo area from six airfields to one – at Abu Sueir. The planners urged that the work there be speeded up. They believed that this should be possible, in view of the reduced expenditure now required for the pre-D-Day improvements at Abu Sueir ($3.2 millions, down from the readjusted $16.2 millions estimated for developing the six airfields). They recommended the development of Abu Sueir as a 'medium bomber airfield for a post-strike staging base' for SAC aircraft. They hoped that the British would soon complete the developments needed 'to bring the Abu Sueir airfield up to medium bomber standards'.[46]

Later that same month, September 1949, Admiral Connolly, the US Commander-in-chief, Atlantic and Middle East (CINCELM), warned the JCS that the development of the necessary facilities for SAC at Abu Sueir might require up to two years, and that unless work was begun immediately, the build-up of SAC forces might have to be delayed to an unforeseeable extent. This might 'well affect the over-all concept of strategic air force operations'.[47]

But the question of funding had not been the principal reason for the delays in the work at Abu Sueir. Completion had been held up also due to the repeated stalling of base negotiations between the British and the Egyptians. The British Foreign Office had imposed a moratorium on

---

[45] ACEWP 1–49, 23 August 1949, cited in Gregg Herken, *The Winning Weapon: The Atomic Bomb in the Cold War, 1945–1950*, New York: Knopf, 1980, p.390, n.47.

[46] RG 319 P and O, 49–50, box 263, 600.1, TS case 8, 21 Sept. 1949. NA. Hahn, *The United States . . .*, p.77, states mistakenly that in 1949 US Planners revised contingency plans to exclude the air offensive from Egyptian bases, since budget austerities made it doubtful that the United States would be able to defend the Eastern Mediterranean.

[47] Mediterranean and Middle East theatre plan, 13 Sept. 1949, appendix to JCS 2034/1, 29 Sept. 1949, RG 318, army staff, P and O, 49–50, 381 NE TS. NA.

heavy expenditures in Egypt, due to the uncertainty of continued British tenure of the Suez Canal bases.[48]

Difficulties with Egypt led the COS to consider the construction of an alternative base for very heavy bombers on the island of Cyprus, by that time 'the only territory in the Middle East . . . unfettered by treaties'. Britain's most advanced bomber at that time, the Lincoln, with a range of just 750 miles, was unable to reach 'worthwhile Russian targets' (in the Dombas region and the Caucasian oil fields) from Abu Sueir. But the Lincolns might reach them from Cyprus, which was just that much closer than Egypt. At a time when Britain was developing its own independent nuclear deterrent, a base in Cyprus might also give her a semblance of strategic independence of the United States.[49]

The Cyprus project was first examined by the COS in July 1947, but rejected on grounds of expense. But in April 1948, the Air Ministry asked the COS to examine the possibility of constructing a very heavy bomber air base on Cyprus. The Ministry estimated that, owing to the limitations in range and performance of their current bomber fleet, for the next ten years, it would be possible to reach only the more important Soviet targets from the Middle East. They asserted that Cyprus was 'better situated than any possible alternative country in the Middle East for use as an advanced base', and estimated that it would take just two years to construct an air base on the island.[50]

In view of the protracted impasse with Egypt, the COS approved the project in principle, but also ordered a study of the problem of defending Cyprus against the Soviets, in the event of war. During the course of the next year, enough preliminary work was carried out at the site to permit the 'detailed planning, drawing and costing' which was necessary for the financial approval for the first phase of construction. But in September 1949, due to 'financial stringency', the project was shelved. Cyprus remained the most favoured location, 'on all but financial grounds'. But no further work was ever undertaken.[51]

As for Britain's 'strategic independence', by the end of 1949, the United States had agreed to 'loan' 88 B-29s to the United Kingdom. The first batch arrived in England in March 1950. (See Chapter 3.) Egypt remained the sole option for a strategic air base in the Middle East, and for the next few years, the B-29 remained the main 'work-horse' of the Allied air forces.

[48] Minute by Assistant Chief of the Air Staff, 'Deployment Plan – M.E.A.F.', April 1951, Air 20/7435. PRO.

[49] Cf., Richard J. Aldrich, John Zametica, 'The Rise and Decline of a Strategic Concept: the Middle East, 1945–51', in Richard J. Aldrich, ed., *British Intelligence, Strategy and the Cold War, 1945–51*, London/New York: Routledge, 1992, p.256.

[50] JP (48) 39 (S), 10 April 1948, Defe 6/5. PRO.

[51] Ibid; COS (49) 289, 5 Sept. 1949, Defe 6/5, PRO; and Aldrich, Zametica, *supra*.

Construction work at Abu Sueir had still not been completed by the end of 1950. By that time, costs were running at £1,500,000 per year. The Americans, whose interest in the base was apparently diminishing, (in part, due to their pre-occupation with the Korean war, and in part to their despair of the British ever reaching a new base agreement with the Egyptians) had yet to pay their agreed share of the costs. The British Ministers concerned became embittered, and pointed out repeatedly that they would not have undertaken the work for RAF purposes alone.[52]

Further negotiations were scheduled with the Americans. The British side was instructed to try to get the Americans to pay the costs of all the air-base facilities that they (the Americans) required in the United Kingdom, and of the work at Abu Sueir. Minister of Defence Emmanuel Shinwell believed that the Pentagon still allotted the highest strategic priority to Abu Sueir. However, he warned that due to their difficulties in obtaining the necessary appropriations from Congress, their military would be most unlikely to agree to British demands. Therefore, the British negotiating team was instructed to compromise, as any deadlock with the Americans would have the gravest consequences for the UK.

Disagreement with the Americans would not only delay the completion of airfields which were of the highest strategic importance to the UK herself, but might also have a 'disastrous effect on Anglo–American military and political relations'. It might provoke the Americans to cut back assistance in the form of Mutual Aid supplies, and/or the anticipated receipt of the 70 B-29s which the Americans had agreed to sell to England under the Mutual Dfence Assistance Program.[53]

In April 1951, the Foreign Office authorised the completion of 'an integrated air defence system' in Egypt. Even if Britain was forced eventually to evacuate Egypt, the COS still hoped to secure from the Egyptians re-entry rights in the event of war. And if the Egyptians did concede re-entry rights, the British could not plan on returning early enough in advance of the outbreak of war in order to refurbish their bases before operations began. Therefore, it would in any event be vital

[52] JP (50) 124, 4 Oct. 1950, in Defe 6/14; and memorandum by Minister of Defence, Emmanuel Shinwell, DO (50)17, 10 March 1950, in Cab 131/9. PRO.

[53] Ibid. As regards airfield construction for USAF in the United Kingdom, a compromise was reached whereby the Americans agreed to do the work themselves, with their own uniformed engineer battalions. This cut down the estimated UK share of the costs to £3.7 million compared with a previously authorised British share of £5 million. Cf., Memorandum by Foreign Secretary Ernest Bevin, 'Facilities for the United States Air Force', D.O. (50) 25, 12 April 1950, in Prem 8/1566, PRO; and Philip C. Jessup to James S. Lay, Executive Secretary, NSC, 31 Oct. 1950, President's Secretary's Files, Harry S. Truman Library [HST].

to improve essential bases up to minimum operational standards before they evacuated Egypt. It was decided not to invest money in constructing expensive domestic accommodation. But authorisation was given to begin work immediately on minimum essentials, such as 'runways, hard-standings, taxi-tracks, etc.' This applied especially to Abu Sueir, the base from which the opening atomic strike against the Soviet Union was to be launched.[54]

The RAF was about to make its own contribution to the Middle East theatre, with the introduction of its first medium-range jet bomber, the Canberra. The RAF's Plan H (1951) provided for a force of five Canberra squadrons to be stationed in the Middle East by December 1953. The Canberras, due to become operational in May 1951, had a shorter range than either the B-29 or the B-36. They were to be deployed in forward positions, in Iraq and Jordan.[55] However, by the mid-1950s, the Canberras would in any case be superseded by the V-bomber series.

In Spring 1952, the American military still dangled before their British counterparts pious hopes that their government would share in the costs of development work at Abu Sueir. At a meeting between the British Air Staff and American Air Force Generals Griswold (3rd Air Force) and McConell, the latter reiterated that USAF was 'most anxious to complete the work at Abu Sueir and to be able to use it as a pre-strike base in war'. The Americans promised to press Washington to forward the £669,045 they owed as their share of current costs, as well as for their share of the costs of the whole project. This time, with Egypt in a most volatile state, the British Air Staff demanded that they secure official American endorsement and agreement to pay their share before the British embarked on the last stage of the project, estimated to cost a further £700,000.[56]

However, the British government also looked on the Abu Sueir project in its wider strategic and economic context. The Secretary of State for Air referred to the wider benefits that Britain was deriving from military co-operation with the Americans, specifically in the United Kingdom itself. He pointed out that the planned deployment in

[54] Minute by Assistant Chief of the Air Staff, 'Deployment Plan – M.E.A.F.', April 1951, Air 20/7435. PRO. Perhaps the Foreign Office decision was facilitated by an earlier agreement with the Americans, in Feb. 1951, whereby the latter agreed to finance 50 per cent of the redevelopment work on British airfields that USAF heavy bombers were to use (a previous agreement had set the American contribution at two-thirds!). Cf., Meeting of Defence Committee, 21 Feb. 1951, in DO (51) 3d., in Cab 131/10, PRO.

[55] Minute of 13 July 1951, Air 20/8544. PRO. The Air Staff urged an immediate start to development work at projected air bases at Habbaniya, Shaibah, Mafraq and Amman, especially as the Air Force might have to leave Egypt earlier than expected.

[56] Minute by Deputy Chief of Air Staff, 14 May 1952, in Air 20/7448. PRO.

the United Kingdom of USAF units represented an accretion of strength 'out of all proportion to its cost' to them. The USAF bombers stationed in the country were 'part of the main deterrent to Russian attack', and in the event of war, would form an integral part of the Allies' offensive and counter-offensive. Furthermore, the US fighter squadrons already in the country were the only aircraft yet capable of dealing with the Soviet MIG.15s. For the RAF to provide an equivalent force would cost the Exchequer at least £100 million, or 'five times what the United Kingdom will spend on its share of the U.S.A.F. works programme – and, in fact . . . far beyond our resources both in man-power and material.'[57]

Ironically, it was during 1952, the year in which Egypt was racked by civil disturbances, that the major part of the construction work was carried out at Abu Sueir. By the end of that year, the essential base facilities had been completed, at a cost to the British Treasury of some £1.75m. In all, some £2m had been expended by the British on this single airfield.[58]

Two extended runways, a perimeter track and nearly all the hard stands were completed. However, due to the unstable political situation in Egypt, it had proved 'politically impracticable' either to lay the fuel pipeline from Abu Sueir to Fanara, or to construct the airfield refuelling system necessary for the heavy bombers. Neither did the British feel able to comply with American requests to store the equipment required (pipes, fuel hydrants and pumps) at Abu Sueir, so as to be readily on hand in the event of war. (The British could not even afford the man-power needed – estimated at 50 men – to guard the American equipment and, with evacuation an imminent prospect, they did not want the embarrassment of having to move out of Egypt not only all of their own equipment, but the Americans' too.)[59]

---

[57] Note by the Secretary of State for Air, Lord de L'Isle and Dudley, D.(52) 25, 14 June 1952, Cab 131/12. PRO. At the end of 1950, Allied plans provided for the stationing of the following USAF units in England:

Three Groups (of 45 aircraft each) of B-29 and B-50 long-range strategic bombers.

Three squadrons (20 aircraft each) of refuelling-in-flight tankers.

One group of 75 F-84E escort fighter aircraft.

One group of 75 F-86 defence fighter aircraft.

Within the first three months of war, these were to be built up to seven groups of medium bombers, seven squadrons of tanker aircraft, five groups of escort fighters, four groups of defence fighters, two groups (36 aircraft each) of RB-29s and RB-50s – strategical reconnaissance aircraft, one group of 48 B-45 light bombers, and one group of 48 C-54 and C-82 troops carriers. Cf., Secretary of State for Air to Prime Minister, 15 Dec. 1950, Prem 8/1566. PRO.

[58] Secretary of State for Air to Prime Minister Churchill, 18 Feb. 1953, Prem 11/483; and brief on Abu Sueir, March 1953, Air 20/7435, PRO.

[59] Air Ministry, London, to HQ Middle East Air Forces, 13 Jan. 1953; and Chief of Air Staff to Secretary of State for Air, July 1953, Air 20/7448. PRO.

In January 1953, when informed of British diffidence concerning the supply of any further facilities at Abu Sueir, General Hoyt S. Vandenburg, Chief of Staff, US Air Force, replied that he quite understood the British difficulties, and was suspending the shipment of any further materiel to Egypt, pending an agreement between her and Britain. At the same time, he reaffirmed that USAF would:

> . . . continue to have both a short and long term requirement for S.A.C operations at Abu Sueir, since this is the only facility in this area possessing any degree of capability to support this type of operation.[60]

In 1953, notwithstanding the unstable domestic situation in Egypt, and developments along the Northern Tier (see below, Chapter 9), USAF still required Abu Sueir, 'for full operational use within a few days of the outbreak of war', or at the very least, as a post-strike landing and refuelling site for heavy bombers taking off from the British Isles. By 1953, the RAF also intended using Abu Sueir, for staging bombers to delay the Soviet offensive against the Middle East, through the Caucasus, and the passes leading into Iraq and Turkey.[61]

Thus the situation at Abu Sueir at the beginning of 1953 was as follows: the airfield, having undergone extensive development work, was still required by USAF and the RAF as a strategic bomber base. However, even with the newly-extended runways in service, the base was still not ready for heavy bombers, with their especially large fuel requirements; there were no bulk storage tanks, no special fuel pipeline to the base, and no fuel distribution system on it.[62]

In 1953, negotiations were still taking place on the conditions for Britain's evacuation from Egypt. The RAF suggested that the Egyptians, apparently still in the dark, now be told what Allied wartime requirements of the base were.[63] However, it would seem that the British never did reveal to the Egyptians Allied contingency plans for Abu Sueir.

In any case, in October 1954, the British finally agreed to evacuate their base in Egypt. Britain's Middle East headquarters had already been moved to Cyprus, in December of the previous year.

---

[60] Ibid.

[61] Brief on Abu Sueir, March 1953, Air 20/7435; Secretary of State for Air to Prime Minister Churchill, 18 Feb. 1953, Prem 11/483. PRO; and Hahn, *The United States . . .*, p.141.

[62] Brief on Abu Sueir, March 1953, ibid.

[63] Ibid.

C. REDEPLOYMENT FROM EGYPT: THE KENYA AND GAZA PROJECTS

It should be emphasised that all redeployment plans were no more than peacetime stopgaps. Egypt remained the focus of British strategic planning for war in the Middle East and, even when British evacuation was agreed upon, was to be re-occupied as soon as possible after the outbreak of hostilities. Ultimately, negotiations with the Egyptians centred, and eventually stalled, on the determination of the terms upon which the British would be allowed to maintain that base in peacetime, and re-occupy it in wartime. (On COS consideration of Israel as an alternative base to Egypt, see below, Chapter 6.)

The Kenya and Gaza schemes illustrate two different aspects of ways in which the British searched desperately for *ad hoc* alternatives to the Egyptian base. Kenya was promoted by Attlee in particular, as an alternative Middle East stores depot and communications centre, in place of those in Egypt.

i. Kenya

The idea of transferring elements of the British base in Egypt to Central Africa was examined immediately after World War Two. At a Cabinet meeting held on 4 October 1945, the CIGS, Field Marshal Lord Alanbrooke, revealed that the Mombasa area in Kenya was being considered as a possible base. However, there were logistical difficulties, since Mombasa was not served by any road or rail communications.[64]

Attlee raised the idea again at the Defence Committee in March 1946, during a debate on whether to maintain Britain's current commitments in the Middle East. The COS appointed a sub-committee (of the Principal Administrative Officers) to recommend alternative sites to Egypt in which to store those stocks that the British might be forced to evacuate from Egypt. One of the proposals raised was again Mombasa, in Kenya.[65]

Foreign Secretary Bevin also gave serious consideration to the Kenya base idea. Like the COS, he was not inclined to replace Britain's major bases in the Middle East and the Mediterranean with one in Kenya.

---

[64] CM 36 (45) 6, 4 Oct. 1945, Cab 128/1, PRO; quoted in Habibur Rahman, 'British Post-Second World War Military Planning for the Middle East', *The Journal of Strategic Studies*, Vol. 5/4, 1982, p.522.

[65] DO (46) 27, 2 March 1946, in Cab 131/2; and COS Principal Administrative Officers' report, CSA (46) 91, 9 Sept. 1946, in Air 20/2461. PRO. the latter document is cited in Michael J. Cohen, *Palestine and the Great Powers, 1945–1948*, Princeton: Princeton University Press, 1982, p.38.

Nor did he agree with Attlee's idea of placing 'a large barrier of desert and Arabs between the British and the Russian Empires'. However, in 1946, the idea of an extra defence line on the African continent appealed to Bevin, who still entertained visions of Britain as a world power, fuelled by African raw materials and manpower.[66]

Furthermore, given the continuing impasse in the negotiations with the Egyptians, Bevin supported the Prime Minister in his desire to lower Britain's 'strategic profile' in Egypt, even if he did not agree on withdrawing from the Middle East altogether. Indeed, unless Britain succeeding in convincing the Egyptians that she was able and willing to maintain her position in the Mediterranean, the Egyptians would be disinclined to concede any of Britain's strategic requirements on their territory.[67]

Bevin was apprehensive about Britain's precarious situation in Egypt. He was acutely concerned that Britain's command and communications centre in the Middle East was located on 'foreign' territory, i.e., in Egypt. He believed that in order to avert pressure being placed on her from time to time, Britain should locate her 'whole heart and centre of command' on British territory. In his opinion, for this purpose, Kenya was as good as British territory. Mombasa might be an ideal site for a central Imperial command headquarters. The Canal Zone might then be regarded as a forward base.

Bevin believed not only that Britain would be able to defend the Middle East from these positions, but also that the Kenya position would strengthen their position with South Africa, whose main source of recent trouble had been east Africa. Finally, he believed also that east Africa held the key to the defence of the Indian Ocean. Behind Bevin's reasoning at this point lay the belief that the Egyptians might prove more amenable to compromise, once they became convinced that the British were not so desperately dependent upon their military bases along the Suez Canal. He even suspected that the Egyptians were being intransigent only because they believed that the British had no alternative. Once they heard that the British wanted to move their communications centre to British territory, they might beg the British to stay on![68]

With the Foreign Secretary's support, Attlee initiated an investigation into the costs of the Kenya project. At a meeting of the Defence Committee at the end of May 1946, with Attlee, Bevin, and the COS

[66] John Kent, 'Bevin's Imperialism and the Idea of Euro-Africa, 1945–49', in Michael Dockrill, John Young, eds., *British Foreign Policy, 1945–56*, New York: St Martin's Press, 1989, pp.53–4.

[67] For this and following, see Bevin memorandum, DO (46) 40, 13 March 1946, Cab 131/2. PRO.   [68] Ibid.

attending, Attlee again questioned the need for locating their theatre military headquarters as far forward as the Suez Canal or Palestine. Attlee suggested that for security reasons, their main headquarters should not be so close to the anticipated battlefield. Sensitive to Egyptian and Soviet sentiment, Attlee feared that the siting of such a large Service headquarters along the Canal would advertise British intentions and provoke Soviet suspicions about their motives for retaining military installations and forces in the Middle East. Chancellor of the Exchequer Dalton supported the Prime Minister. He favoured the Kenya project, primarily due to the relief he expected the move to bring to Britain's adverse sterling balance with Egypt (accumulated during the war in defence of that country).[69]

But the COS were adamant against moving the main Middle East base out of Egypt. Relying on the experience of the last war, they insisted that full control of a major conflict required that the central command headquarters be positioned as close as possible to their centre of communications. Egypt was the central axis for all Middle Eastern and imperial communications, and political activity. It would be impossible to control naval operations in the Mediterranean from any headquarters further south.[70]

Attlee was encouraged by Bevin's apparent readiness to discard old strategic concepts. Reading into Bevin's statements more than their author had intended, Attlee wrote to him at the end of 1946:

> I agree wholeheartedly with you that the real line of the British Commonwealth runs through Lagos and Kenya. The Middle East is only an outpost position.[71]

In January 1947, at a staff meeting of the COS, attended by Attlee and Viscount Alexander, the recently-appointed Defence Minister (20 December 1946), the Prime Minister tried to take the Kenya project one step further, now going beyond what Bevin had been prepared to agree to. He proposed that Britain's main base in Egypt be transferred to Kenya. The COS may have been willing to consider building a stores depot in Kenya, to accommodate materiel that would possibly have to be evacuated from India, Palestine, and ultimately, even from Egypt. But they protested vehemently against transferring Britain's main base away from Egypt.[72]

[69] For this discussion, see DO (46) 17th meeting, 27 May 1946, Cab 131/1. PRO.

[70] Ibid.

[71] Attlee to Bevin, 1 Dec. 1946, FO 800/475, PRO; reproduced in Ronald Hyam, ed., *The Labour Government and the End of Empire, 1945–1951*, Series A, Vol. 2, Part III, p.221.

[72] For this and following, cf., COS (47) 6th meeting, 7 Jan. 1947, Defe 32/1, Secretary's Standard File. PRO.

Alexander warned that any British withdrawal into Africa would invite Soviet infiltration into the resulting Middle Eastern power vacuum. He reiterated the JPs' argument that in the long run, a retreat into Africa would cost the British far more than would the retention of their present position in the Middle East.

However, as noted above (Chapter 3), in the summer of 1947, Attlee finally conceded the COS demand that Britain retain its positions in the Middle East. At the same time, in June 1947, the Cabinet decided to establish a store depot at MacKinnon Road in Kenya, 60 miles inland from Mombasa. As agreed with the COS, the depot was earmarked for holding whatever military supplies could be saved from Egypt and India, when Britain evacuated those two countries. In September 1947, 300 Royal Engineers were brought to Kenya from Egypt, to begin construction work. At the same time, rail and road networks between Cairo and Mombasa were improved. In 1948, some 1800 Italian workers were brought in to help with the work.[73]

In January 1948, Bevin tested out another one of his ideas on Minister of Defence Alexander. This time, it was a new conception of forward and rear bases in north and east Africa. Cyrenaica might be considered as an alternative to Egypt, and Aqaba as an alternative to Aden, with Mombasa to be built up as a 'vital rear base'. The Sudan, protecting the back door to Egypt, might also be developed, as an important source of manpower. Bevin accused the COS of having focused too narrowly on Egypt and Palestine. No record has been found of Alexander's reaction, and we now know that nothing ever came of this particular inspiration of Bevin's. As noted by one scholar of British imperialism, almost without exception, Bevin's 'exuberant schemes proved on investigation to be unworkable.'[74]

Likewise, the logistical problems involved in establishing a base or store depot in Kenya soon became all too apparent. Many of these problems were encountered during construction; road and railway transport was poor, water had to be piped in, there was a paucity of skilled labour, and living conditions were unfit for Europeans. The MacKinnon Road project, codenamed 'Leader', was dropped eventually in 1950, after some £2 million (of a budgeted £8 million) had been expended on it. A statement published by the East Africa Command explained that the army no longer required additional

---

[73] Philip Darby, *British Defence policy East of Suez, 1947–1968*, London: Oxford University Press for RIIA, 1973. pp.36–7.

[74] Conversation between Bevin, Alexander, and Foreign Office officials, on board HMS *Victory*, 15 Jan. 1948, FO 800/477. PRO; and Hyam, *The Labour Government . . .*, Series A, Vol. 2, Part 1, p.l.

storage depots, and that MacKinnon Road was too isolated to meet the requirements of a major base.[75]

ii. The Gaza project

The Gaza Strip was never intended to provide an alternative site for the main base in Egypt. The Strip was considered as an alternative base for the Strike (or Covering) Force, the combat troops then stationed at the Canal base, whose mission was to check and hold up a Soviet offensive against the Middle East. In the event of a Soviet attack, this Force, originally designated as Brigade strength (approximately 5000), would advance rapidly northwards, to meet and hold up Soviet forces as far to the north of the Canal as possible; in addition, in peacetime, it would cover the main Middle Eastern base in Egypt.[76]

As talks with the Egyptians dragged on without resolution, the British naturally searched for alternative bases in the region. It needs to be emphasised, once again, that, from the outset, the Gaza Strip, just like Kenya, was to have provided only a partial substitute for the facilities Britain enjoyed in Egypt. The Gaza Strip could never hope to compete with Egypt's industrial infrastructure, or its ports and communications facilities.

Initially, in November 1947, in the wake of the government's decision to pull out of Palestine, British planners considered the establishment of base facilities on the east bank of the Suez Canal, in the Sinai desert. The idea was to transfer part of the Egyptian base – troops, administrative installations and stores.

At the end of November, the COS approved a Joint Planners' study which pointed to the serious logistic deficiencies of the Sinai peninsula.

The Sinai desert had just one Ordnance Depot, at Rafah, on the Palestine frontier; and just one site for accommodating troops, a 'skeleton camp' on the east bank of the Canal. The desert had no appreciable water supplies, therefore considerable water works would be needed before any troops could be moved in. Sinai had no ports, and poor roads. To operate a base in Sinai would require the continued use of Egyptian ports, and extensive road construction in the desert. The

[75] Hyam, ibid., p.lx; Devereux, *The Formulation of . . .*, pp.18, 42; and Darby, *British Defence Policy . . .*, p.36.

[76] Minute by Geoffrey Furlonge, 1 July 1950, EE1202, FO 371/82220. PRO. The Gaza Strip, as a separate political entity, had been created during the Arab–Israeli war of 1948. An Egyptian column advancing along the coast of Palestine, from Gaza to Tel Aviv (under the command of Brigadier Muhammad Neguib, and Major Gemal Abdel Nasser) had been cut off here and surrounded by Israeli forces. The 1949 Egyptian–Israeli Armistice Agreement had left the coastal strip, (from just south of Ashkelon to Rafah) in Egyptian hands.

planners noted also that there was no skilled, and little unskilled labour on hand. These deficiencies would require huge expenditures to make good. And money spent in the Sinai desert would be at the expense of other projects then under way (such as the Kenya Stores Depot, and the construction of accommodation in Cyprus and Cyrenaica for the troops to be withdrawn from Palestine).[77]

All these reservations applied equally to another project studied by the JPS, that of building a strategic bomber base in Sinai. The construction of even a few landing strips in Sinai, together with radar coverage and air defences, would have enabled the British to fly troops and stores in and out, remote from watchful, highly-sensitive Egyptian eyes. But again, the administrative difficulties and the expenditure required were prohibitive.[78]

The conclusion of an armistice agreement between Israel and Egypt in the Spring of 1949, prompted two further studies by the COS, on the potential of the Gaza Strip to accommodate part of the British garrison in Egypt.

At the end of the Arab–Israeli war, in March 1949, Bevin asked Secretary of Defence Alexander to commission a study of the Gaza Strip. On the assumption that Egypt retained the Strip, Bevin asked Alexander if Britain should seek any military facilities there?[79]

One week later, at the beginning of April, the COS reported back that the forward deployment of fighting formations in the Gaza–Rafah area would be invaluable since, in the event of war, Britain would have to move forces into and through Palestine. A base in the Gaza Strip might serve also as an 'overflow' for troops from the Canal Zone that were in excess of the limits provided for by the treaty with Egypt. Likewise, it would be invaluable to develop in the Strip forward airfields from which tactical aircraft might operate immediately upon the outbreak of war.[80]

A further COS paper, circulated at the end of April, analysed the strategic assets of the El Arish–Rafah–Gaza coastal strip. The Strip's strategic significance lay in the fact that it (and Palestine) lay astride Allied lines of communication from Egypt to the anticipated Middle Eastern battlefield against the Soviets (and conversely, across the path of a Soviet offensive against the Suez Canal). For this reason, the attitude of Israel to the presence of British forces, and a British base on her borders, was from the outset understood to be a critical factor. Israeli agreement to the transit of British forces across her territory in time of

[77]   COS (47) 238, 20 Nov. 1947, Air 20/7203. PRO.
[78]   Ibid.
[79]   Bevin to Alexander, 23 March 1949, FO 800/477. PRO.
[80]   For this and following, cf COS (49) 116, 1 April 1949, Air 20/2463. PRO.

war, 'with the minimum amount of trouble' would remain an over-riding strategical desideratum.[81]

The COS recommended that in peacetime Britain should build in northern Sinai those facilities that would enable a rapid forward deployment of Allied forces in the event of hostilities. They stressed the current lack of any logistical infrastructure, the need for road and railway communications, tactical airfields, and a 'skeleton air defence organisation'.

They pointed out that apart from the east bank of the Canal, the El Arish–Rafah area was the only sector of Sinai that could accommodate British forces. They believed that a British fighting force stationed in that area would be 'well placed to re-enter Palestine' in the event of war. If Gaza was eventually included in Egyptian territory, the usefulness of the Sinai area would appreciate significantly. However, in the final account, the Sinai desert was not considered to be of sufficient strategic importance to justify the expenditure required.[82]

In 1950, the British Military Command, Middle East, again turned its attention to the Gaza Strip. This was because the Egyptians themselves suggested that the evacuation of British troops to the Strip might provide a solution to the continuing impasse in their talks on the evacuation of the Suez Canal base.

The idea was put to CIGS Field Marshal Montgomery by the Egyptian Commander-in-Chief, Gen Haidar Pasha, in June 1950, during a visit by the former to Egypt. An evacuation of British forces from Egypt to Gaza, the Egyptians believed, might 'satisfy the Egyptian public on the score of evacuation'.[83]

If the major part of British fighting forces was moved from Egypt to Gaza, the Egyptians would be able to tell their people that 'all British operational troops had been withdrawn from Egypt proper, and that only technical units had remained behind'. The bulk of British troops in Egypt would remain there, but, as the Foreign Office noted, 'it is our presence, rather than reduction in their numbers which appears to be the main stumbling block'.[84]

By 1950, Egyptian interest in the Gaza Strip had worn thin. The heavy expenses that the Egyptians had incurred in the administration of the Strip persisted as an economic dead weight long after any glory, or patriotic fervour over Palestine had faded. By 1951, it was reported that the administration of the Strip was costing the Egyptian government £85,000 per day. Egypt had not planned to be left with the Strip as its

---

[81] COS (49) 146, 27 April 1949, Defe 5/14; and COS (49) 116, supra. PRO.
[82] COS (49) 146, ibid.
[83] Minute by Geoffrey Furlonge, 1 July 1950, EE1202, FO 371/82220. PRO.
[84] Ibid.

sole conquest in the war against Israel, and significantly, had not annexed it. It was almost common knowledge that the Egyptians would welcome some face-saving device to evacuate Gaza. In November 1951, an Egyptian diplomat confided to his Israeli counterpart that his government would not view the loss of the Strip as a disaster.[85]

Notwithstanding the formidable economic, administrative, and politico-legal problems which beset the Gaza scheme, it received a fresh lease of life when the new Conservative government under Winston Churchill took office at the end of October 1951, barely two weeks after Egypt's unilateral abrogation of the Anglo–Egyptian treaty of 1936. On 17 November, Nuri Pasha, the Prime Minister of Iraq, called upon the new Foreign Secretary, Anthony Eden. Nuri, evidently acting as an unofficial go-between for the Egyptians, stated that the British might find it easier to reach a settlement if they offered to transfer their combatant troops from the Canal Base to the Gaza Strip. Nuri added that the Egyptians 'would be glad to get rid of' the Strip, since it was costing them £E50,000 a day to maintain it.[86]

Churchill was informed that both the Foreign Office and the COS had examined the Gaza option 12 months before. Notwithstanding the strategic advantages that had been perceived, the scheme had been shelved, due to the need to secure the Israelis' agreement, and due to the heavy costs of building installations and accommodations in the desert (in 1950 these had been estimated at £11 million for a Brigade Group); and the need to take care of the 200,000 Arab refugees. However, Sir William Strang, head of the Foreign Office advised that Eden had asked the COS to have another look at the project, since it might indeed provide a way out of the impasse with Egypt; and since the Israelis might now acquiesce, especially if they were associated with the projected MEC.[87]

Following the severe riots against British forces in Egypt, in January 1952 (see below, Chapter 9), the question of defending British interests against Egyptian insurgency became a key question for the British. The Military now calculated that in peacetime (after the British had

---

[85] Conversation of 17 Nov. 1951, between Foreign Secretary Antony Eden, and Iraqi Foreign Secretary Nuri Said, reported in William Strang to Prime Minister Churchill, 23 Nov. 1951, annex to COS (51) 725, 6 Dec. 1951, in Defe 5/35. PRO; and S. Divon – Walter Eytan, 8 Nov. 1951, in *Documents on the Foreign Policy of Israel*, 1951, Vol. 6, editor, Yemima Rosenthal, Jerusalem: Graph Press, p.472. Divon, an Israeli delegate to the United Nations, reported on a meeting with Mahmud 'Azmi, a member of the Egyptian delegation, reputed to have influence with the Egyptian Foreign Minister.

[86] Sir William Strang to Churchill, 23 Nov. 1951, Prem 11/92. PRO. The note in the Prime Minister's file quotes the figure of £E50,000 per day. This same note, when added as an annex to COS (51) 725, appears as £E85,000. This author was unable to ascertain which was the correct figure. [87] Ibid.

officially evacuated Egypt), a strike force in Gaza would be admirably poised to exercise a stabilising influence on the Middle East as a whole and upon Egypt in particular.

As put indelicately by CIGS Slim, the Force would be 'sufficiently close to the Canal to enable us to exert pressure on Egypt for the proper control of our Base.' Without such a base in Gaza, the CIGS believed that 'there would be little to prevent a future Egyptian Government from using the [Canal] base for its own purposes hostile to us and our Allies.'[88]

However, some officials balked at evacuating Egypt under duress, even if only to near by Gaza. Some were less sensitive than others to Egyptian nationalist opposition. There was considerable opposition from the Air Force. The air attaché at Cairo felt that the best site for both Air Force and Army Headquarters was in Cairo, not only for purely military/strategic purposes, but also for reasons of internal security. He objected to any redeployment to Gaza, on the grounds that:

> . . . if the Egyptians should turn hostile when we are engaged in a major war in these parts, we should be better sitting on EGYPT'S head than standing on the edge of her skirt.[89]

The RAF felt that too little account had been taken of the air factor. If an army base was constructed at Gaza, it would be out of the protective reach of fighter squadrons based in Egypt. So the construction of any army bases in Gaza, which would present new targets to the enemy, would also require the construction of air bases from which fighters could defend the new base. The RAF estimated that they would need at least two airfields in Gaza, and warned that 'modern aerodromes, with all their communications, are elaborate expensive things'. Not only this, but the dispersal of the RAF's aircraft would complicate the command and control aspects of its operations. The RAF would have to operate from several centres, instead of from a single, compact army and air force base like the one it currently enjoyed along the banks of the Suez Canal.[90]

The COS examined the strategic-military pros and cons of the idea, while the Foreign Office examined the legal-political ramifications. In the wings, Treasury officials winced as the bill for the Gaza project escalated.

The COS believed that Gaza might offer significant strategic/military

[88] D (52) 1st, 12 March 1952, in JE1194/12, and CIGS note on Redeployment, 20 March 1952, in JE1194/13, FO 371/96972. PRO.

[89] Minute by Patrick Campbell, Air Attaché, 7 Feb. 1952, FO 141/1467. PRO.

[90] Ibid.

advantages as a base for the Strike Force. This had in the summer of 1950 been increased from a Brigade to an armoured division. Under the new 'forward strategy' that was developed from mid-1952 (see Chapter 9), the strike force was assigned a specific mission. In the event of war, it would advance immediately to the Iraqi/Syrian desert, in order to contain Soviet forward reconnaissance elements, and to buy the time in which to deploy the extra forces required to defend the Middle East and the Egyptian base. The Strike Force had to be located either to the East of the Suez Canal, or close enough to cross it in time to head off any Soviet advance.[91]

The CIGS had his doubts. He feared that the strategic advantages offered by Gaza would have little long-term value if they could not be guaranteed by security of tenure. There would be little point in investing much effort and money only to encounter in Gaza in a few years time the same troubles that were currently forcing the British out of Egypt.[92]

The legal status of the Strip was complicated. Upon the termination of the Palestine mandate in 1948, it had become *res nullus* (legally, a 'non-entity'). The Egyptians had made no attempt to annex the territory, after occupying it in 1948. The British Attorney General believed that the Egyptian occupation could not be regarded as unlawful. However, given their declared policy of 'liberating' Palestine for the Arabs, the Egyptians could hardly grant permanent base rights to the British in Gaza. Thus, while there was no reason to fear that any other power would want the Strip in the foreseeable future, the British could not hope to obtain any legal right of tenure. For so long as the Egyptians occupied the Strip, the British would enjoy base rights only at the Egyptians' pleasure.[93]

There remained the question of eventual sovereignty over the Strip. If the British did establish a base there, the Egyptians would have to be able to claim that it was not on Egyptian territory. It did not appear likely that the Egyptians themselves would want to annexe the Strip; but any British attempt at formal annexation would most probably arouse opposition both among the Arab States and at the UN. But if it was not to be Egyptian territory, then whose would it be?[94]

The 'legal solution' proposed by the Foreign Office was that Britain

[91] Annex to JP (50) 89, 'Redeployment to Gaza', 11 August 1950, Defe 6/13; and CIGS note on Redeployment, 20 March 1952, JE1194/13, FO 371/96972. PRO.

[92] CIGS note, 20 March 1952, Ibid.

[93] Furlonge minute, 1 July 1950, EE1202, FO 371/82220. PRO.

[94] Discussion of 19 Sept. 1950, between Michael Wright (Assistant Under-Secretary at the Foreign Office), and State Department officials, 19 Sept. 1950, *FRUS*, 1950, Vol. V, Washington, 1978, pp.297–99; and D.V. Bendall minute, 28 March 1952, EE1201/3G, FO 371/96972. PRO.

should take over from the Egyptians complete administrative responsibility for the Strip and, like the latter, establish *de facto* control, without claiming any formal legal title. If they managed effectively to occupy Gaza, the British would have a claim to sovereignty at least as good as the Egyptians did now. The key to the British position in Gaza would be the degree of agreement, or acquiescence in their occupation which they could secure from Egypt, Israel and the Arab states.[95] Seeing that the Egyptians themselves had suggested the Gaza idea, the key question remained, what would Israel's reaction be?

The British had not parted on the best of terms with the Israelis when they had evacuated Palestine in May 1948. They now feared that the Jews would regard the presence of British troops astride their southern border as a form of encirclement (together with the British presence in Jordan, which might extend to Palestine's West Bank, now annexed by Jordan). But on the other hand, in the event of a continuing state of war between Israel and Egypt, the Israelis might regard the intercession of British troops between them and the Egyptians as a more practical guarantee than the 1950 Tripartite agreement. (In fact, Ben-Gurion feared that if the British established a base in Gaza, they would demand transit rights across Israel to Jordan.)[96]

Some in the Foreign Office believed that if both the COS and the Egyptians favoured the Gaza scheme, they should go ahead with it, even in disregard of Israeli opposition. Yet the COS themselves stressed the strategic need for establishing good relations with Israel. The defence of the Middle East would depend upon the Allies' ability to move through that country quickly and unopposed in an emergency.[97]

Israeli objections to the future stationing of British troops in Gaza would probably be as vehement as they had been to the stationing of British troops in Palestine's West Bank, in 1949, after Abdullah's annexation of that territory (even if, as the Israelis had admitted, their protests had then been mainly for domestic reasons). The Israelis had expressed concern that the British might extend their treaty rights with Jordan to the newly-annexed territory. The British had then assuaged the Israelis with two statements in the House of Commons (on 23 December 1949 and 27 April 1950) to the effect that they had no intention of setting up bases on the West Bank.[98]

It was generally agreed that Israel might just agree to a British base in

[95] Bendall minute, 28 March 1952, supra.

[96] Michael Wright to Sir Ralph Stevenson (British ambassador to Egypt), 30 June 1950, EE1202/3, FO 371/82220. PRO; and Ben-Gurion diary entry, 24 Feb. 1952, BGA; also, Ilan Asia, *The Core of the Conflict: The Struggle for the Negev, 1947–1956*, Jerusalem: Izhak Ben-Zvi Press, 1994, (Hebrew) pp.117–18.

[97] Wright to Stevenson, ibid. and COS (49) 146, 27 April 1949, Defe 5/14. PRO.

[98] Furlonge minute, 1 July 1950, EE1202, FO 371/82220. PRO.

Gaza, but only as part of a package deal that included a peace agreement with Egypt, and a British commitment to treat Israel on a basis equal to that of the Arab States. Those conditions, admitted Geoffrey Furlonge (head of the Foreign Office's Eastern Department), were unlikely to pertain in the near future. Therefore, they would either have to abandon the Gaza project, or risk seriously damaging their relations with the Israelis.[99]

The Foreign Office deferred to the COS restriction that it would be unwise to take any step that 'might drive the Israelis to refuse transit facilities to our forces in time of war'. Further, it was appreciated that the base at Gaza would be of little use unless relations with the Israelis were cordial enough to permit manoeuvres on both sides of the border.[100] It remained to sound out the Israelis on the idea (see Chapter 7).

The Americans too hoped that the Gaza project might provide a solution to the Anglo–Egyptian impasse. They offered their services in approaching the Israelis. Michael Wright, Under-Secretary of State at the Foreign Office, accepted the American offer of help, provided they did not give away to the Israelis the fact that Gaza was under active consideration. George McGhee, Assistant Secretary of State for Near Eastern Affairs, believed that Israel might acquiesce in a British base in Gaza, if coupled with a peace treaty with Egypt. The Israelis badly wanted a treaty with the Egyptians, and might well agree to a British military presence in the Gaza Strip as the price. For their part, the Egyptians could balance the treaty with Israel against the British evacuation.[101]

However, even before State Department officials had received Foreign Office permission to sound out the Israelis discreetly, Emmanuel Shinwell, British Minister for Defence, had already raised the issue with them directly. On 1 September 1950, Shinwell, himself a Jew, who was on friendly terms with the Israelis, broached the subject with Mordechai Kidron, a Counsellor at the Israeli Legation in London. When asked by Shinwell what the Israeli reaction would be to the establishment of a British base at Gaza, Kidron responded that under present circumstances, it was bound to be negative. (It was at this meeting also that the Israelis were first asked about a visit to Israel by the British C. in C. Middle East Land Forces, General Sir Brian Robertson. On the visit itself, see below, Chapter 7.)[102]

[99] Furlonge minute, 22 August 1950, EE1202, FO 371/82220. PRO.

[100] Ibid.

[101] Minutes of informal Anglo-American discussion, 19 Sept. 1950, *FRUS* 1950, pp.297–9.

[102] Kidron to Michael Comay (Head of British Commonwealth section in the Israeli Foreign Office), 1 Sept. 1950, in *Documents on the Foreign Policy of Israel*, Vol. 5, 1950, ed., Yehoshua Freundlich, Jerusalem: Keter, 1988, pp.516–17.

In January 1951, Sir William Strang, Permanent Under-Secretary of State at the Foreign Office, approached Eliahu Elath, the Israeli Minister in London, with the proposal that Gen Robertson visit Israel the next month, with a view to including Israel in Allied defence plans for the Middle East. Strang stated that the British were looking for some kind of an alliance with Israel, preferably on a regional basis – but if that wasn't possible, they would agree to a bilateral one. When Elath asked what the British wanted from Israel, Strang replied that they were looking for Israeli consent to the setting up of British bases in Gaza (possibly with a corridor from it linking Jordan to the Mediterranean), and in Israel.[103]

The Israelis were interested first and foremost in receiving military and economic aid from the West, in order to build up their own military infrastructure. However, as Elath reported home, the British appeared to be interested more in military bases in Gaza and Israel, than in Israel's military or industrial potential. Elath regarded the British initiative as so important, that he flew back to Israel to report personally to Prime Minister Ben Gurion. The latter was incensed by the British proposal, and reprimanded Elath for taking the extraordinary measure of returning to Israel to deliver it personally. As for the British desire for bases, Ben-Gurion thought it was a transparent stratagem for a British return to their old imperial positions, and dismissed the idea out of hand.[104]

It might have been thought that the legal and political problems would have caused the cancellation of the Gaza project by the end of 1950. How could the British contemplate the huge expenses involved in constructing a permanent base in Gaza, on a basis of *de facto* occupation, in the hope that an Egyptian–Israeli peace treaty would dissipate Israeli opposition?

But the intractability of the Egyptian impasse left the COS no option but to search around for alternative base sites in the region, in to which to 'offload' the troops that would need to be evacuated from Egypt. In November 1951, Strang secured Churchill's permission to proceed with an examination of 'the possibility of transferring the combatant troops in the Canal Zone to the Gaza Strip'.[105]

Israel's agreement to the project was still considered to be 'if not essential, at least highly desirable'. But the Foreign Office believed that the political developments which had taken place during the course of 1951, now augured well for Israeli assent. As a result of the Korean

---

[103] Elath report on meeting with Strang on 15 Jan. 1951, in *Documents on the Foreign Policy of Israel*, Vol. 6, pp.31–4.

[104] Ibid., note 7, p.33.

[105] For this and following, cf., COS (51) 725, 6 Dec. 1951, Defe 5/35. PRO.

War, Israel had 'come a great deal closer to identifying herself openly with the West'. In addition, during 1951, the Americans had joined Britain in sponsoring the MEC, in which Turkey, the Arab world and, eventually, Israel herself were to be members. (See below, Chapter 7.) If the Israelis were confronted with a MEC, composed of representatives of the United States, France and Turkey, as well as the UK, they were hardly likely to veto a base required by that Command in the Gaza Strip. With an excess of sanguinity, the Foreign Office even hypothesised that with the support of the MEC, they 'should be prepared in the last resort to take a chance with Israeli reactions and simply go ahead with our plans in the Gaza strip despite their objections.'[106]

Foreign Secretary Eden apparently believed that the removal of British combatant troops from Egyptian soil, to a barren desert strip which in fact constituted a burden to the Egyptians, might soften the latter's intransigence. He asked the COS to confirm whether it would still be practicable to move the combatant troops from the Canal Zone to the Gaza Strip – on the understanding that by doing so they would obtain Egypt's agreement to the retention of Britain's administrative base in the Canal Zone, and to join the MEC.[107]

Churchill supported Eden, and in March 1952, ordered a COS study on the estimated costs of moving elements of the British base from Egypt to Gaza and Cyprus.[108]

During the Spring of 1952, the project was studied at length by British Military Headquarters in Egypt, and by the COS. The COS appointed a 'Working Party on Gaza Redeployment'. They still believed that the only reasonable chance of holding on to the Middle East lay in a redeployment plan based on the use of the Gaza Strip. However, any British base in Gaza must enjoy a long-term security of tenure, and must be preceded by the 'removal' of the refugees.[109]

Whereas the political/legal problems involved in the Gaza Strip project had not 'defeated' the plans of successive Labour and Conservative governments, the economic, logistic and human problems would. First and foremost, there was the problem of the density of the indigenous population of the strip.

The working party did not initially rule out the Gaza project, but it did note the 'considerable administrative and financial difficulties' involved. In addition to the Strip's 80,000 indigenous inhabitants, some 200,000 refugees from the war in Palestine had poured in since 1948. And all this in an area of approximately 150 square miles, some

106 Ibid.
107 Ibid.
108 DO (52) 1st, 12 March 1952, JE1194/12, FO 371/96972. PRO.
109 COS (52) 172, 20 March 1952, Defe 5/38. PRO.

25 miles long and from two to four miles wide. There was little or no prospect of resettling the refugees elsewhere. They were currently being fed by UNRWA, and living in derelict huts, erected by the British during the Mandate. If Britain took on a long-term occupation of the Strip, she would be unable to avoid responsibility for the refugees.[110]

On the credit side, the local population would provide a cheap labour force of some 50,000 people. The working party decided to ask Military Headquarters in Egypt to assess the space actually available in the Strip. British Headquarters, Middle East Land Forces (MELF) at Cairo reported that it would be medically essential to move out the refugees from all areas to be occupied by British troops. But those refugees were currently occupying camps in the only areas of the Strip that appeared suitable for British Forces – the only ones that had adequate water resources. MELF calculated that if some 20,000 British troops and their families were moved into the Strip, the effective population density in the Strip would approach something like 3000 per square mile. In such a hot climate this would be unacceptable. Therefore, no base could be built in Gaza without first moving the refugees elsewhere.[111]

On 25 April 1952, the Foreign Office reported to the COS on an offer by Syrian President Husni al-Zaim to resettle in his country '500,000 refugees from Gaza, Jordan and the Lebanon'. The Syrian offer gave rise to some ephemeral hopes of solving the refugee problem in Gaza. But it was doubted if the refugees themselves would agree to leave the strip. The COS noted also that even if the refugee problem was solved, they still needed to obtain transit rights for their troops, from both Egypt and Israel. But nothing ever came of the Zaim offer, and in August 1952, President Zaim was himself deposed.[112]

Apart from the 'refugee problem', there were numerous other logistical problems. The operation of a strategic base from Gaza would require improvements to the water supply, the construction of new airfield, road and rail links – not to mention accommodation and facilities for an Armoured Division and its equipment.[113]

---

[110] Strang to Prime Minister, 23 Nov. 1951, annex to COS (51) 725, 6 Dec. 1951, Defe 5/35; and meeting of Working Party on Gaza Redeployment, 28 March 1952, Defe 7/27. PRO.

[111] Meeting of Working Party, ibid.; and MELF to Ministry of Defence (for COS), 2 April 1952, Defe 27/7. PRO.

[112] COS (52) 57th. 25 April 1952, Defe 4/53, PRO. Husni Zaim was President of Syria from April–August 1952. On his offer to take in the Palestinian refugees, see Avi Shlaim, 'Husni Zaim and the Plan to Resettle Palestinian Refugees in Syria', *Middle East Focus*, Vol. 9/2, 1986.

[113] Cf., COS (52) 177, 24 March 1952, Defe 5/38; and Strang to Prime Minister, supra. PRO.

By 1952, the Army's Middle East redeployment plan envisaged a total MELF garrison of 48,600; one armoured division in the Gaza area, and an infantry division dispersed between Cyprus, Tripolitania and Malta. It was estimated that the construction of a permanent cantonment in Gaza would take up to ten years, and that even an interim tented scheme would take 12 months. The Gaza project would also require Israeli and Egyptian assent to overflying and ground transit rights for troops and equipment, as well as the grant of training areas on their territories.[114]

All these construction and logistical problems would prove to be pro-hibitively expensive. Because of the desert conditions, it would be far more expensive to maintain troops in Gaza than at the Canal Zone. They would have to be supplied from the Canal along a 180-mile desert road. The general costs of building a cantonment at Gaza would be some 50% higher than for a similar construction at the Canal.[115]

In February 1949, the cost of stationing a Brigade Group in Gaza had been estimated at £11 million. By mid-1951, total estimated costs for the redeployment of the Middle East base from Egypt were running to £97 million; £41 million until 1956, and £56 million thereafter. Since a capital expenditure of £38 million would in any case be needed for the Middle East over the next few years, the direct costs arising from redeployment would be £59 million.[116]

But the COS clung stubbornly, and in all seriousness to the Gaza project. In March 1952, they asked the Cabinet's Defence Committee to confirm that:

> A redeployment based on the use of the Gaza Strip is the only one which offers a reasonable chance of holding the Middle East.[117]

The COS asked that in the next round of negotiations with the Egyptians, the cession of the Strip to Britain, or the granting to her of a long-term lease to it, should be made a 'cardinal point'. (All this, of course, was contingent on the removal of the refugees, a point taken for granted by the COS.)[118]

But by the summer of 1952, when the Churchill cabinet re-estimated the costs of the Gaza scheme – which by now was for the accommoda-tion of a mobile armoured Division and a Brigade Group – they had soared to £100–120 million! Some at the Foreign Office suggested that

[114] COS (52) 214, 18 April 1952, Defe 5/38. PRO.

[115] Annex to JP (50) 89, 11 August 1950, in Defe 6/13. PRO.

[116] Ibid.; and minute by Defence Minister Shinwell, 8 June 1951, and Shinwell to Prime Minister, same date, JS1194/44, FO 371/90177. PRO.

[117] COS (52) 172, 20 March 1952, Defe 5/38. PRO.

[118] Ibid.

the only solution was to seek American financial aid. But in August 1952, Churchill finally shelved the plan as being 'financially unbearable'.[119]

The Treasury, which had regarded the War Office's 'lunatic plans . . . with the most profound horror', was genuinely relieved by Churchill's veto.[120] Gaza was finally eliminated from British redeployment plans for the Middle East.

British plans now provided that their Middle East HQ would be established on Cyprus. The major part of the combat troops in Egypt would be held as a Strategic Reserve in the UK, to be flown out to the Middle East in the event of war. This solution had been offered by Lt. General Brownjohn, VCIGS, as early as in August 1950. Brownjohn had then argued that Britain needed a strategic reserve ready to move to any trouble spot at short notice. In view of their numerous overseas commitments the only appropriate location for such a reserve, he believed, was the home country itself.[121]

In 1952, it was appreciated that the aircraft needed to fly out the Strategic Reserve from England to the Middle East would not be operational for a further five years. But by 1952, new strategic considerations were taking the place of old ones. These were the entry of Turkey into NATO, the evolution of a new Northern Tier policy (see below, Chapter 9); and the introduction of thermonuclear weapons, and new, faster, and longer-ranged aircraft, that could deliver ordnance with greater certitude, over greater distances.

British strategic thinking had been influenced profoundly by the demonstrations of the Soviets' nuclear (and later thermonuclear) potential. These made the Middle East appear more like a strategic liability than asset. The Allies began to doubt whether they would even have the time in which to launch their opening strategic air offensive. The 80,000 British troops stationed at Suez were now thought to be within range of a Soviet nuclear strike. And finally, they were now needed more urgently as a strategic reserve at home.[122] But perhaps, above all, as even the Military were beginning to appreciate, a strategic base that was preoccupied with defending itself against the local popu-

---

[119] Churchill minute to Foreign Secretary, 19 August 1952, and minute by R.T. Ledward, 23 Aug. 1952, JE1194/79, FO 371/96977. PRO.

[120] I.P. Bancroft to R.M.J. Harris, 4 April 1952, T225/1051. PRO.

[121] Confidential annex to COS (50) 135th, 22 August 1950, Air 20/8113; Minute by R.C. Mackworth-Young, 9 May 1952, JE 1194/43, FO 371/96974; COS (52) 388, 29 July 1952, JE 1194/71, FO 371/96976; and Cabinet meeting of 3 Dec. 1952, Prem 11/487. PRO.

[122] The Americans exploded their first Hydrogen bomb in Nov. 1952; the Soviets exploded theirs in August 1953; also Devereux, *The Formulation of . . .* p.157.

lation could not in the long term usefully fulfil its main mission.[123] The Egyptian guerrilla campaign, which included the withdrawal of native labour from service jobs at British bases, and the additional threat to the army's water and food supplies, had sapped the Army's morale and rendered the Base all but inoperable.

Basically, two problems – political and financial – ruled out the redeployment of British forces from the Egyptian base to any Middle Eastern alternative.

Firstly, neither Israel nor any other Arab state was prepared to grant base facilities, of any kind. And secondly, there was no room left in the British budget for the expenses involved in building an alternative base, or even in keeping up the same peacetime force levels that had been the rule in Egypt.

By 1952, when the COS asked the Foreign Office to consider the long-term political effect of moving out of the Middle East, the latter believed that it was no longer a case of guaranteeing Allied strategic interests in the event of war with the Soviets, but mainly of preserving British 'face' as a Great Power:

> From a long-term point of view there is much to be said for pulling as many troops as we can out of the Middle East, and so removing a major irritant to our relations with Middle East countries. On the other hand their presence there increases our prestige, and lends strength to our diplomatic arm. It boils down to whether we really want to keep our troops in the Middle East in order to fend off the Russians, or whether one purpose, if not the main purpose, of keeping them there is to safeguard our position in those countries.[124]

---

[123] Cf., Cohen, *Palestine and the Great Powers*, p.35, and Boyle, *The Churchill–Eisenhower Correspondence* . . ., p.24.

[124] R.C. Mackworth-Young minute, 9 May 1952, supra. Interestingly, in 1952, the British did not apparently consider the logistical problems of re-taking Egypt by force, against *Egyptian* resistance. When the attempt was made in 1956, the mobile forces available proved 'altogether inadequate'; cf., Darby, *British Defence Policy* . . . pp.95–6.

6 British plans for the defence of the Middle East

A. THE PLACE OF THE MIDDLE EAST IN BRITAIN'S GRAND STRATEGY

Since 1948, the American–British–Canadian (ABC) planners had drafted three worldwide emergency plans (i.e. for World War Three). The British versions were called *Doublequick* (for a war by July 1949), *Speedway* (for a war by July 1950) and *Binnacle* (for a war by July 1951). (For the American codenames see the Glossary, and Chapter 1). Plans *Doublequick* and *Speedway* accepted the early loss of the European continent to the Soviets as inevitable, and pinned Allied hopes primarily upon the strategic air offensive, to be launched from air bases in the United Kingdom, Egypt and Okinawa.[1]

In 1948, British global strategy was based on the following fundamental principles. The highest priority was given to the RAF. First and paramount was the defence of the UK itself. Therefore first priority was given to the strengthening of the RAF's fighter aircraft. Such was the vulnerability of the UK that the COS determined that none of Britain's day fighter squadrons would be stationed in overseas theatres.[2]

Second only to the defence of the home country came the protection of the sea lanes that linked the country with its far-flung empire. The Middle East lay third in the UK's order of priorities. This was because Britain's fleet of heavy bombers then in operation didn't possess the range to reach Soviet territory, except from the Middle East. Over half of the British bomber force would operate out of bases along the Canal Zone. Even so, the RAF would be able to fulfil its missions against the Soviet Union only if it was re-equipped with the American longer-range B-29s.[3]

British planners did not believe that the Soviets would be able or

[1] Plan *Cinderella*, Annex to COS (51) 686, 28 Nov. 1950, Defe 5/35. PRO.
[2] Air Ministry memorandum, 6 April 1948, Air 20/8101. PRO.
[3] Ibid.

inclined to devote as many military resources to the Middle East as they would to their offensives against western and southern Europe. They appreciated the gravity of the Soviet threat to the Middle East, but did not concur with American estimates concerning the speed of the Soviet advance on the Suez Canal. They agreed that the Soviets would over-run Persia, Iraq and the Saudi Arabian oil fields within the first few months of a war. But they argued that the Soviets would first have to consolidate their hold over their conquests before they were able to turn their attention to the final offensive against Egypt.

British strategists agreed with their American counterparts that air interdiction was the key to the defence of the Middle East. The Allies' single effective deterrent to Soviet aggression, in view of the latter's 'great numerical superiority in land forces . . . geographical position and economic self-sufficiency', would be 'the threat of attack by air or long-range weapons'. However, as noted already, for this very same reason, the British believed that the Middle East would feature prominently in Soviet war strategy. At the very least, Soviet planners would be forced to move against Allied strategic air bases in the Middle East, in order to eliminate the threat to their vital resources from this flank. The COS believed that the Soviets would not limit themselves to air strikes, but would mount a land offensive, to ensure physical possession of the entire complex of army, air and naval bases that lay at the Allies' disposal in the Middle East, especially in Egypt.[4]

In March 1948, British Military headquarters, Middle East, at Fayid, in Egypt, conducted a war game, codenamed *Intermezzo*, on the conduct and outcome of a war in the Middle East against the Soviets, in May 1958. The exercise focused on the strategic importance of the Persian Gulf. The 'lessons' drawn from the exercise were somewhat pessimistic. The Middle East commanders doubted whether Allied tactical air attacks against Soviet lines of communications would significantly hamper their advance. Strategic bombing of Soviet industrial centres to the north of the Caucasus might eventually interdict the Soviets' logistic supplies, but were unlikely to seriously affect the Soviets' initial offensives.[5]

But some at the Foreign Office believed that the C. in C.s' Middle East were over-anxious about the anticipated Soviet land offensive. One commented, somewhat precociously:

> It seems to me rather unrealistic to assume that the Russians would launch an elaborate land attack across several deserts in order to capture the Suez Canal.

[4] COS memorandum, DO(46) 47, 2 April 1946, in Cab 131/21. PRO.
[5] JP (48) 19, 12 Feb. 1949, Defe 6/5; and note of April 1948, in E4319, FO 371/68378. PRO.

They don't want the Canal for themselves but only to deny it to us. The obvious answer seems to be a few atomic bombs.[6]

Whatever the logic in the Foreign Office's cynicism, it lay beyond the comprehension of Britain's planners. The latter saw it as their duty to prepare plans for all contingencies – and the prospect of a Soviet Middle East land offensive, aimed at the Suez Canal, lay at the heart of their concerns.

A staff study prepared in May 1948 by British headquarters Middle East based on the lessons of exercise *Intermezzo*, stated that Britain's 'minimum requirements' in the event of war would be:

(a) A powerful air force operating from a belt of modern and secure airfields in EGYPT, CYPRUS and along the north coast of AFRICA, with the task of strategic bombing, interdiction on the enemy's Lines of Communication, and defence of our vulnerable areas.

(b) Security of sea communications in the MEDITERRANEAN for maintaining the airfields . . . continuous fighter and anti-submarine cover for shipping . . . for this, bases at Malta and Alexandria are essential.[7]

B. PLAN SANDOWN

In July 1948, the COS directed the C. in C.s Middle East to draw up an operational plan for the defence of the Middle East. The new plan, the first of its kind, was codenamed *Sandown*. The strategic air offensive, to be delivered at the outset of the war, was to be carried out by the American B-29s. Until 1949, the British still entertained pious hopes that airfields for this offensive would be developed also in Cyrenaica, Aden, and perhaps the Sudan.[8]

However, as noted already, Abu Sueir, in Egypt was the only strategic based prepared for the B-29s, and even here, the infrastructure for the special refuelling facilities required for the heavy bombers was not yet installed.

Sandown was drawn up on the assumption that the Americans would come to Britain's aid in defending the Middle East against a Soviet offensive. British forces would be based on the Suez Base, using Canal ports; American forces would be based on the Nile Delta, using Alexandria (which would continue to serve also as a base for the British Navy).[9]

---

[6] Minute by J. E. Cable, 7 April 1948, E4319, ibid.

[7] Staff study *Intermezzo*, by C. in Cs Middle East, COS(48) 111, 13 May 1948, Defe 5/11. PRO.

[8] JP(49) 59, 11 July 1949, Defe 4/23; COS(48) 144, 1 July 1948, Defe 5/11; and CC (48) 31 Aug. 1946, Air 8/1602. PRO.

[9] COS(48) 144, ibid.; and CC (48) 86, ibid.

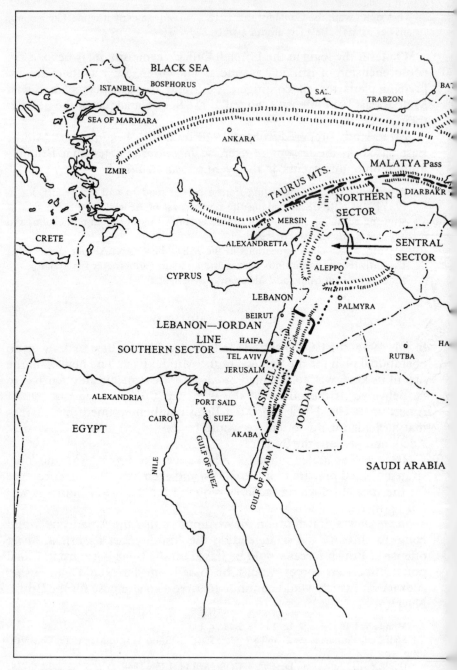

Map 4: *Sandown*: British Plan for the defence of the Middle East,
Aug. 1948

British planners saw the major role of their own forces in the Middle East, with American (and ultimately, Commonwealth) aid, to be the tactical blocking and attrition of Soviet land and air forces advancing on the Middle East, and the final elimination of Soviet land forces on the coastal plain of Palestine. British strategists delineated four possible defence lines on which to hold up and break a Soviet offensive against the Egyptian base (see map 4).

1. The optimal defence line was the so-called *Outer ring* This line ran along the 'mountain passes leading into southern Turkey and western and southern Persia as far as Bander Abbas' (on the Straits of Hormuz, the exit from the Persian Gulf into the Indian Ocean). Holding this line would retain within Allied control all the lands of the Middle East except for Turkey and Persia. It would ensure also Allied access to Middle Eastern oil fields.[10]

   However, the COS determined that in the short term the preparation and maintenance of this line was beyond British resources. The defence of the Outer Ring required the early deployment of air and land forces which simply were not yet available. Finally, the necessary military infrastructure, bases and logistic backing for the forces required, could not be built or supplied in the foreseeable future. At best, it was hoped that these might become available ten years hence, in 1957![11]

   In the meantime, the planners concluded, that Britain would have to suffice with doing everything in her power, 'by diplomatic and economic means' to forestall a Cold War penetration of these areas by the Soviet Union.[12]

2. Next, there was the *Inner ring*. This line ran from Aqaba on the Red Sea, northwards, to the east of the Jordan, and Baalbeck valleys, through Jordan and Syria to Turkey, to a point just west of the Malatya Pass; thence it ran west along the Taurus mountains, to Alexandretta, at the north-eastern corner of the Mediterranean. The Inner Ring ran along positions with natural defences, with intervening open desert areas suitable for the deployment of armoured forces. Its main advantage, was that it would force the Soviets to channel their offensive along restricted desert communications leading to the Palestine coastal plain, and thence to the Suez Canal; in the southern sector, there was only the Baghdad–Amman pipeline road; in the north, the Mosul–Aleppo railway; and in the central

---

[10] Ibid. and JP (49) 29, 30 March 1949, Defe 6/8. PRO.

[11] Annex to COS (51) 755, 18 Dec. 1951, Defe 5/35. PRO.

[12] JP (49) 59, supra, and DCC (49) 51, 15 June 1949, annex to COS (49) 232, 12 July 1949, Defe 5/15, pt. 1. PRO.

sector, just two caravan routes leading to Aleppo and Homs. Finally, the Inner Ring strategy was based on the assumption that the Turks would engage and hold up the Soviets along the northern sector.[13]

3. The third option was the *Lebanon–Jordan* line (also variously known as the 'Palestine–Lebanon line' or, the 'Tripoli–Homs' line). The Lebanon–Jordan line ran from the Mediterranean coast eastwards, from a point just north of Beirut, parallel to the main lateral road from Beirut to Damascus, thence south through Lake Tiberias and the Jordan Valley, along the 'parallel mountain ranges of the Lebanon and Anti-Lebanon running north and south on each side of the Jordan and Baalbeck valleys,' down to Aqaba.[14]

The Lebanon–Jordan line would cover much of Lebanon and mandatory Palestine, with small areas of western Syria and Transjordan. This line, whose defensive positions were more dispersed, would be difficult to defend, and would require almost as many forces as those needed for the defence of the Outer Ring.[15]

However, the Lebanon–Jordan line provide some defence-in-depth for Israel [a critical issue, as that country's military co-operation was needed], and would retain the major airfields of the Levant in Allied hands.[16]

4. Finally, there was the *Ramallah* line. This ran east from Tel Aviv through Ramallah, to Jericho, then south through the Dead Sea and along the Jordan rift valley to Akaba.[17]

As noted already, the COS favoured the Ramallah position since any Soviet offensive against the Suez Canal would be forced to traverse Palestine through 'the bottleneck formed between the Dead Sea and the Mediterranean, in the area of Ramallah.'[18]

But the key advantage of the Ramallah line was that it could be held by far fewer forces, with significantly less administrative backing than the other lines. However, any strategy based on this line had great disadvantages; it was perilously close to the Suez Canal; and it would mean giving up most of the Middle East oil fields in advance.[19]

The planners were quite aware of the political problems that the Ramallah line would cause. This line depended upon the military collaboration of a country, Israel, the northern half of whose territory was to be abandoned in advance. However, they were forced to conclude that for the short-term, lack of forces and resources would compel the Allies to fall back on this strategically and politically problematic, but most economic and practical defensive position.

[13] Annex to COS (51) 755, 18 Dec. 1951, Defe 5/35. PRO.
[14] Annex to JP (50) 94 (Final), 22 Sept. 1950, Defe 4/36. PRO.
[15] JP (49) 59, 11 July 1949, Defe 4/23. PRO.
[16] Ibid.   [17] Ibid.   [18] Ibid.   [19] Ibid.

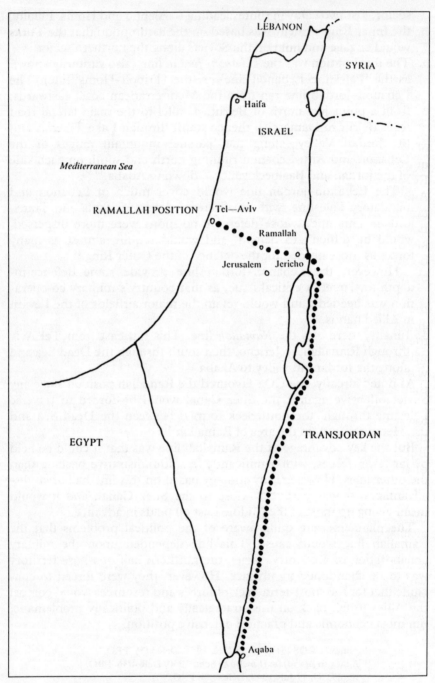

Map 5: The Ramallah Line: Detail of Plan Sandown

Sandown posited that the decisive battle for the Egyptian base would be fought on this 'last-ditch' defence line in the middle of Palestine. They would have to limit their aim:

> to defending Egypt by holding the enemy in Palestine, the last acceptable position being the Ramallah–Tel Aviv line from which there must be no withdrawal.[20]

The planners were themselves so sceptical about *Sandown*'s chances of success that they foresaw the possibility that the Soviets would quickly break through the Ramallah line, and pose a direct threat to the Egyptian base itself. If that happened, they would have to call upon the American strategic bomber force to divert aircraft from their strategic targets inside the Soviet Union, to Soviet tactical targets in the Middle East, in order to hold up the advance of the Red Army. No one really knew which Soviet battlefield targets would be suitable for strategic bombing, but advance bases and supply depots along their lines of communication were mentioned.[21]

A problem of equal gravity was *Sandown*'s inherent assumption that the indigenous states of the region would welcome Allied ground and air forces with open arms, permit the construction of the Ramallah line, the billeting of huge Allied forces on their territory, and contemplate with equanimity the ravaging of their economies and countryside by a war waged between the Great Powers. All this notwithstanding the fact that at the end of 1948, a British intelligence report estimated that the most they could expect was that the Arab states would be better disposed towards the Allies than to the Soviets, and that the Allies might expect to deploy their forces without meeting any active indigenous opposition. But even if neither the Arabs nor the Jews of Palestine were expected to offer resistance to an Allied entry into their country, the report warned against planning on the co-operation of either community.[22]

Sandown suffered also from other glaring flaws. The most serious of these were: the failure to provide adequately for the defence of Egypt against air attack – RAF Middle East was seriously lacking in fighter and ground attack aircraft; the somewhat naive assumption that there would be 'a 28-day precautionary period', prior to D-Day, during which the Allies would be able to redeploy their forces in the Middle East; and perhaps most serious of all, *Sandown* was based on the pious, soon-to-be-dashed hope of receiving prompt and considerable American military aid in the Middle East.[23]

[20] JP (49) 29, supra.
[21] JPS (48) 57, Aug. 1948, Air 8/1603. PRO.   [22] JP (48) 109, supra.
[23] Summary of plan *Sandown*, JP (48) 106, 7 Oct. 1948, Defe 6/6, and COS (48) 123, 16 Oct. 1948, in Defe 5/8. PRO.

Sandown was in fact premised upon the supposition that the Americans would provide the *major* part of all three Allied services during the first year of a war in the Middle East. At the close of 1948, the COS even suggested that they concur in American wishes that the SACME should be an American officer. They argued this on the following grounds: that Field Marshal Montgomery held the chair of the Western Europe C. in C.'s committee; that the C. in C. MELF must in the first instance be British; and most important, since the appointment of an American SACME might resolve the Americans' 'considerable doubts . . . about the wisdom of attempting to hold the Middle East', and ensure early and substantial American reinforcements for this theatre.[24]

Because of the paucity of British forces in the Middle East, no major subsidiary operations could be ventured. All available land and air forces would have to be concentrated to meet the main Soviet land threat to Egypt. Thus large areas of the Middle East, including the Persian Gulf and most of the oil fields, would be abandoned and left without Allied cover or support.[25]

Sandown elaborated upon the projected build-up of Allied forces, and British strategic goals for the first six months of war in the Middle East.

The first month: the British would deploy a mobile force of one brigade group and two armoured regiments whose task would be to delay and hold up the Soviet advance as far to the north of Lebanon, Syria and Iraq as possible. RAF aircraft operating from Habbaniya, Iraq, with three ground attack squadrons and one fighter reconnaissance squadron (a maximum of 56 aircraft) would begin bombing Russian communications. However, the RAF believed that their own aircraft were inferior by far to those flown by the Soviet Air Force, and planned to withdraw them as soon as possible from Iraq, to airfields in Palestine, once those were ready for them. *Sandown* provided also for the arrival of a group of 30 B-29 strategic bombers in Egypt during the third and fourth weeks of the war.

The second month: It was hoped that substantial Allied reinforcements would arrive during this period. These would bring ground forces up to two British divisions, one armoured, and one infantry. During this period, American forces would be built up to one division of infantry, and one airborne regiment. These were to prepare defensive positions on Palestine's eastern border, in order to repel anticipated Soviet thrusts from Syria and Iraq. British forces would cover the sector in front of the Jericho–Ramallah–Jerusalem line; the Americans would cover the Tiberias (Lake Galilee) area. The RAF's missions would be

[24] COS (48) 209, 16 Dec. 1948, Defe 5/9. PRO.
[25] For this and following, see JP (48) 106, ibid.; and Devereux, *The Formulation of . . .* p.22.

tactical: to achieve local air superiority, to harass and delay the advance of Soviet ground forces, and to give support to Allied ground forces.

During this second month of the war, the Soviets were expected to secure a base in the Baghdad–Mosul area, from which they would attempt to launch an offensive eastwards to the Mediterranean, via the north-eastern desert routes and the Mosul–Aleppo railway, to the Mediterranean coast.[26]

The third month: during this period, British planners hoped to reinforce the Middle East with a second infantry division and infantry brigade. They hoped that by the end of this phase, the preparation of the Ramallah defensive line would be nearing completion.[27]

The fourth month: This period was expected to be critical. By now, Soviet forces deployed against Syria and Palestine were expected to have been built up to a strength of up to six divisions. The Allies would be preparing to make their last-ditch stand on the Ramallah line. British planners believed that the campaign in the Middle East would now turn on the issue of air superiority. To achieve this, the Allies would need something in the order of 400 fighter and ground attack planes, operating from bases in Palestine (mainly south of the Ramallah line). This force would mount an all-out offensive against the Red Air Force, in order to secure control of the skies. Allied air forces would then be able to disrupt Soviet lines of communication, and bludgeon their forces on the ground.[28]

The fifth and sixth months: During this period, further Allied reinforcements – a third British infantry division and armoured brigade, and a second US infantry division – were to be thrown into the critical battle in Palestine. These reinforcements would most likely be deployed on the Ramallah position. In all, at the end of the first six months, British planners counted on being able to commit to the critical battle in Palestine a force of four and two-thirds British Divisions, three-and-a-half American, and '250 British, 150 Commonwealth, and 350 U.S. aircraft'.[29]

Against the just over eight Allied divisions the British hoped to have deployed by the end of the sixth month, it was expected that the Soviets would have available up to nine divisions, with possibly an additional two divisions from Turkey. (British planners warned also that Soviet divisions were something in the order of 20% stronger than their own.) Once the Soviet force had overcome any local opposition, which was expected to be minimal, it would pose a direct threat to the Suez Canal.[30]

[26] COS views on *Sandown*, JP (48) 109, 3 Dec. 1948, Defe 6/7. PRO.
[27] JP (48) 106, supra. [28] Ibid; and JP (48) 106, supra.
[29] Ibid. [30] JP (48) 131, 18 Nov. 1948, Defe 6/7. PRO.

C. ANGLO–AMERICAN DIFFERENCES ON THE MIDDLE EAST

As Allied global war plans began to take shape, Anglo-American differences over British responsibility for Middle East, and their respective military contributions to the campaign in that theatre sharpened. As noted already, the unfounded assumption of a substantial American military contribution to the Middle East campaign was a serious lacuna in *Sandown*.

At the ABC planners conference held in Washington, in October 1948, the British pleaded with their American counterparts to assume some responsibility for the Middle East. The Americans responded with the charge that the British exaggerated the Soviet threat to the Middle East, and that *Sandown* took no account of Allied air interdiction of the Soviet advance. Nor had the British taken into account the effect of Allied strategic bombing of the Soviet Union itself. By this point, the Americans had revised their own prior estimates of the speed of the Soviet advance to Suez:

> From November to April flood conditions in the Tigris–Euphrates Valley and heavy snows in the Iranian mountain passes would virtually deny all routes through these areas to Russian columns.[31]

Therefore, during the winter season, the Soviets would probably be unable to reach Palestine in any significant force until they had overrun Turkey. And finally, the Allies would have the ability throughout the year to delay the Soviet advance, by sabotaging the Iranian mountain passes, and interdicting from the air the Soviet columns advancing through the Mosul–Aleppo–Baghdad front.[32]

British planners in fact conceded that *Sandown* had taken no account of the potential effect of the strategic bombing of Soviet bases facing the Middle East.[33]

From 18–26 October 1948, the ABC planners convened at the Pentagon for the annual updating of plans for global war against the Soviets. The British side intended to present plan *Sandown* to their American colleagues. Before leaving London, the COS asked the War Office staff to examine whether, given the forces they were likely to have at their disposal, they could not move their last-defence line further north, from the Ramallah area, to the Tripoli–Homs region (i.e to the 'Palestine–Lebanon' Line).[34]

---

[31] P and O 381 TS, case 121/83, 7 Oct. 1948, RG 319 (Army Staff) 46-48. NA.
[32] Ibid.
[33] JP (48) 106, supra.
[34] For this and following, cf COS (48) 123, 16 Oct. 1948, Defe 5/8. PRO.

The War Office stressed that the Middle East C. in C.s intended to hold up the Soviets for as long as possible 'on successive positions in the mountains of the Lebanon and North Palestine and in the Syrian Desert.' But the Ramallah line remained the final prepared defensive position, to which there would be no withdrawal unless and until Allied forces were absolutely compelled to do so. And from this line there would be no retreat!

The JPS pointed to the significant advantages (over the Ramallah line) of holding the Soviets at the more northern Tripoli–Homs area. The more northern line would leave the ports of Haifa and Beirut in Allied hands; and Soviet land and air forces would be kept further from the main British base in Egypt. And finally, the Allies would have the advantage of forcing the Soviets to fight their way through naturally strong, more defensible positions; on the other hand, if the Allies conceded these positions to the Soviets in advance, then they, the Allies, would themselves have to fight against a Soviet defence of those same positions, if and when they were strong enough to mount a counter-offensive to retake the Middle East.

However, as noted already, British strategy was determined not by the topographical advantages of the best defensive line, but by the forces available to defend it. It was estimated that it would require between eight and ten divisions (two to three armoured, and six to seven infantry), as well as three armoured car regiments and the Arab Legion to defend the Tripoli–Homs position against the offensive that the Soviets were expected to mount by the sixth month of the war.

In contrast, the Allies would require just four to five divisions to defend the 'shortened line and secured flanks' of the Ramallah line. According to *Sandown*'s projections, the Allies would have just four infantry divisions and one armoured brigade by the sixth month of the war.[35]

The COS asked the C. in C.s Middle East what the effect would be on their planning if Turkey entered the war (either of her own volition, or if attacked by the Soviets). In October 1948, the British Middle East commanders concluded that *Turkish resistance would not make any significant difference to the Middle East campaign* (my emphasis). The Turks themselves would be exclusively preoccupied with the defence of their own soil, and the Allied forces deployed in the Middle East were inadequate to offer the Turks any aid. Even if the Turks did hold up a Soviet advance, the build-up of Allied reinforcements would not be sufficient to hold the Tripoli–Homs area. Therefore, their choice of the Ramallah line as the main defensive position would not be affected by

[35] Ibid.

any Turkish military action, and it remained 'the best alternative main defensive position in the light of the forces available'.[36]

The Pentagon conference approved a new contingency plan for global war, codenamed *Doublequick*. This was a master plan for Allied operations in Europe, the Middle East and the Far East. It was to form the basis upon which detailed campaigns for each theatre were to be planned. The codename *Doublequick* was apparently soon compromised. The British side renamed theirs *Speedway*, while the Americans called theirs *Fleetwood*.[37]

The new plan, essentially the same as the old, made a fresh, more sober assessment of the balance of forces that the Allies would be able to deploy against the Soviets, in defence of the United Kingdom, and for the campaign in the Middle East.[38]

Speedway reduced the number of British aircraft available for the defence of the British isles from a previous maximum of 520, to 200–300 fighter aircraft, and 80 bomber aircraft. On the ground, the British would have some six to seven territorial divisions, 90% of whom were World War Two reservists, all poorly-equipped. *Speedway* also considered action to be taken in the event that the strategic air offensive did not have the desired effect, and that the United Kingdom itself was lost as a strategic base.[39]

The strength of the American Task Force in the Mediterranean was now reduced from prior estimates, to 300 aircraft by the end of the first month of war, and 600 by the end of the second (as will be seen below, most of these carrier-based aircraft were in fact earmarked for the campaign in southern Europe). On the other hand, *Speedway* did provide for an American Marine battalion to be flown from the US carrier Force in the Mediterranean to secure the Bahrain–Dhahran oil area on the outbreak of war.[40]

The Pentagon conference of October 1948, revealed a widening chasm between British and American strategic conceptions in regard to the Middle East theatre. The American army planned on concentrating its divisions against the Soviets in Europe. It was reluctant to disperse its forces to other theatres, and feared the vulnerability of forces convoyed through the Mediterranean. The US Army's view was complemented by that of USAF, which had great confidence in its own strategic air offensive, and preferred to hold a strategic reserve of ground forces uncommitted, ready to be exploited in Europe.

36   Ibid.
37   JP (49) 19, 22 Feb. 1949, Defe 6/8. PRO.
38   Report by Directors of Plans, JP (48) 130, 4 Nov. 1948, Defe 6/7. PRO.
39   Annex to COS (48) 210, 16 Dec. 1948, Defe 5/9. PRO.
40   JP (48) 131, 18 Nov. 1948, Defe 6/7. PRO.

Only the U.S. Navy was in favour of a Middle East campaign, perhaps because operations against the Soviets in the Mediterranean would give the Navy a major role to play, and because the Navy had a deep interest in Middle East oil (despite the fact that until late 1950, a post-war glut of oil on the world market reduced the strategic importance of Middle Eastern oil). As noted cynically by the British side, the Middle East's role in American global strategy, at least in the short term, was reduced almost entirely to its function as a launching-platform for the strategic air offensive.[41]

However, in contrast to the views of their superiors in Washington, the strategic assessments of American planners charged with the Middle East theatre in fact coincided more or less with those of their British counterparts. Major-General Ray T. Maddocks, US Director of Plans and Operations, Egyptian theatre, agreed with the British that the Soviet Middle East task force would be vulnerable, and its logistic support meagre. However, he reconciled himself to the fact that the Allies would be unable or unwilling to devote sufficient forces to interdict the initial Soviet advance. His forecast of the outcome differed only slightly from that of the British. General Maddocks believed that the Soviets would reach the Acre – Sea of Galilee line with five divisions by D + three months, and have a nine-division force deployed against Egypt by D + five months (this approximated the *Sandown* estimates).[42]

Speedway retained *Sandown's* assumption of American help in the Middle East, as noted above: by D + 6 months, the Allies hoped to have in this theatre, 4⅔ British, and 3½ American divisions, with 250 British, 150 Commonwealth and 350 American aircraft.[43]

The Allied build-up in the Middle East was dependent on the Mediterranean sea-lanes remaining open. But, by December 1948, not only were the Americans retreating from their commitment to the Middle East but British planners now estimated that Allied forces might face up to a maximum of 11 Soviet divisions (*Sandown* had estimated nine), supported by 400 aircraft, with an additional 700 aircraft operating from airfields conquered in Turkey.[44]

On the other hand, the British side were apparently encouraged by American reassurances on the effects of the planned air offensive. The COS adjusted the premises of *Sandown* in order to take the air factor more fully into account. The Soviet threat would be reduced con-

---

[41] JP (48) 130, supra.

[42] Memorandum by Major General Ray T. Maddocks, Director of Plans and Operations, 15 Feb. 1949, RG 319 (Army Staff) P and O, 49-50, TR TS, Case 8/2, NA.

[43] Ibid.

[44] Annex to plan *Speedway*, COS (48) 210, 16 Dec. 1948, in Defe 5/9, and Prem 8/745. PRO.

siderably, if they assumed the attrition of Soviet communications and logistic systems by Allied air and ground forces. Therefore, the planners concluded:

Owing to the length and vulnerability of his communications the enemy's build up is likely to be appreciably less. The Allies should thus have a reasonable chance of at least defending Egypt.[45]

The COS posited that the Soviets would have to advance on Egypt 'by restricted, lengthy and vulnerable approaches, through territories with few natural resources.' But even so, in 1949, the planners warned that it would take the Soviets up to four-and-a-half months to concentrate the forces necessary to threaten the Suez Canal (in contrast with the six months predicted by plan *Sandown*).[46]

Like their American counterparts, British strategists now believed that there was only one way to block the Soviets 'to a degree sufficiently great to enable our small Army to hold them before reaching areas vital to us' – and that was to exploit the same logistic weakness that the Americans had already pinpointed in 1945 – the Soviets' vulnerable lines of communication along the coastal plain of Palestine.[47]

British strategy was imploding into a minimal goal of defending the Egyptian strategic base at the Ramallah line in Palestine. Due to lack of resources, *Speedway* had recognised the need to withdraw from most of Britain's positions in the Middle East upon the outbreak of war. Should a serious Soviet threat develop, the British would 'neutralise' (i.e. sabotage) the oil fields of Persia, Iraq and Kuwait, in order to deny them to the Soviets. The British assumed that the Americans would do likewise in Saudi Arabia. The British would also attempt to demolish rail and road communications in Persia.[48]

At this point, an analogy might be ventured between Allied strategy in the Middle East during World War Two, and their strategic planning for the same theatre after that war. In retrospect, it is fairly clear that Rommel's great offensives across the Western desert, in 1941 and 1942, came within a hair's breadth of ejecting the British from Egypt. In effect, during World War Two, the British had been too weak to defend their Middle Eastern Empire against the Germans. It was only because Hitler had been concerned more with his offensive against the Soviet Union, that he had not given Rommel the logistic and matériel support he had needed to complete his conquests.

After World War Two the German threat to the Middle East was

[45] Ibid.
[46] COS (49) 232, 12 July 1949, Defe 5/15. PRO.
[47] Staff Study *Intermezzo*, COS (48) 111, supra.
[48] JP (48) 131, supra.

replaced by the Soviet. The postwar analogy lay in the fact that during the early years of the Cold War, the Americans, as the Germans in 1941, felt unable to disperse their limited forces over too many theatres of war. And like the Germans in 1941, they determined that the campaign against the Soviets in Europe must assume a higher priority in their planning than the Middle East.

After World War Two, the Allies anticipated that a Soviet offensive against the Middle East, with the Suez Canal as its goal, would need to be supplied by extended, vulnerable lines of communication, just as Rommel's forces had been. Rommel's Panzers had found their graveyard in the Western desert. In the late 1940s, Allied planners hoped that Stalin's armoured forces, if they attacked, would find theirs on the exposed coastal plain of Palestine.

As noted already, at the Pentagon conference in October 1948, the Americans had backed their refusal to commit more troops to the Middle East with reassurances that the strategic air offensive would decimate Soviet conventional forces, thus reducing the gravity of the Soviet threat to the Middle East. However, in 1949, this central premise of American global strategy – the ability of American strategic air power to counterbalance Soviet conventional superiority – was itself called into question by more sober strategic appreciations prepared by American experts.

In May of that year, the Harmon report, a study commissioned by USAF of the effect of the use of atomic weapons in war, concluded that the Soviets' ability 'to advance rapidly into selected areas of Western Europe, the Middle and Far East, would not be seriously impaired' by the Allied atomic air offensive. That offensive would affect, not the Soviet attacking forces, but their logistic infrastructure, petroleum supplies and other stocks. Therefore, the report concluded that the Soviet attack itself would not be halted or blocked by attacks from the air, but would grind slowly to a standstill, as supplies dwindled and ran out. The Soviets' offensive capability would thereafter diminish progressively (the Harmon report was in fact suppressed by USAF, which at the time was trying to expand and secure a budget increase).[49]

In August 1949, after further bickering with the British over the Middle East, the JCS yielded somewhat and agreed that, in the event of war, American forces allocated to the western Mediterranean might be transferred to the Middle East to help out the British.[50] But this was little more than a goodwill gesture, intended to pacify the British. And even this symbolic move was withdrawn shortly after.

[49] The Harmon Report, 11 May 1949, reprinted in Melvyn Leffler, *A Preponderance of Power: National Security, the Truman Administration and the Cold War*, Stanford: Stanford University Press, 1992, pp.360–64.   [50] Leffler, ibid., pp.286–87.

During the summer of 1949, the British learned of the American planners' intention to reassign the force that they had pledged to the Middle East (some 3⅓ divisions and 350 tactical aircraft) to West Africa. From the base that they would build up there, they would try to retain a foothold on the Iberian peninsula, if possible up to the Pyrenees – in an attempt to avert the need for amphibious landings to reconquer the Continent.[51] (On the American decision, see above, Chapter 2.)

The COS prepared their counter-arguments for the upcoming ABC conference to be held in Washington in October They referred to the American intention to use the Iberian bridgehead as the springboard for a vast land offensive against Soviet-occupied Europe (following the precedent of the Allied offensive against German-occupied Europe in World War Two). However, the COS pointed out, the Pyrenees and southern Spain were unsuitable for the Americans' strategic objective. This was because there were only two exits out of Spain, on either side of the Pyrenees, and the element of strategic surprise would therefore be forfeited. The COS also believed that it would be most difficult to supply the air support (necessary to retain air superiority) for a campaign in Spain. And finally, the COS believed that it would have a disastrous effect on French morale if the latter learned that American divisions were being sent to North Africa 'at a time when French forces were being withdrawn from there to fight on the Continent.'[52]

But the COS did not believe that they could move the JCS from their current idea of retaining some bridgehead in Europe. Therefore, they decided to try to interest the JCS in the Brittany–Brest area as an alternative to Spain.[53]

The Directors of Plans asked whether the COS still intended to hold the Middle East at all costs, as they had previously maintained at all previous meetings with the Americans? Should they tell the US planners at their forthcoming meeting that the UK was determined to hold this theatre, even if that meant relying almost solely on British Commonwealth forces? The COS confirmed that this was the case, and that they must not relent on securing American aid for the Middle East. The COS suggested that the British team in Washington press the Americans to promise 'maximum assistance' from their naval and air forces in the Mediterranean, and try to secure their agreement to send 'at least one Regimental Combat Team to Israel', in order to secure (or ensure) the latter's military collaboration.[54]

---

[51] Report on ABC conference, 26 Sept.–14 Oct. 1949, in JP (49) 133, 14 Oct. 1949, Defe 6/11; annex I to JP (49) 126 (Final), 3 Nov. 1949, Defe 4/26; and plan *Cinderella*, annex to COS (51) 686, 28 Nov. 1951, in Defe 5/35. PRO.

[52] COS (49) 131st, 8 Sept. 1949, Defe 4/24. PRO.

[53] Ibid.   [54] Ibid.

The ABC conference of 1949 marked a bitter turning-point in Anglo–American military relations. The British were taken by surprise, and disillusioned with the Americans' withdrawal from the Middle East. The JCS adhered rigidly to their new scheme for an Iberian lodgement. They refused to commit any of their own forces to the Middle East and, likewise, turned down the British plea to send a 'token force' to Israel (see below, Chapter 7.)

Not only did they withdraw their own contingent, but Gen J. Lawton Collins, Chief of Staff, US Army, even objected to the British plan to send at least one division of reinforcements to the Middle East in the event of war. Gen Collins suggested that the British reinforcements would be needed more urgently in France. Air Marshal Tedder was shocked by this suggestion, and queried whether the Americans fully appreciated the full importance of the Middle East. He warned that if the Arabs received any hint that the West was going to abandon that theatre, 'then the Cold War would be as good as lost'.[55]

The British team reported back on the Washington talks:

> The Americans are determined not to become embroiled in a Middle East campaign which they fear will draw their forces into a 'side-show' theatre instead of allowing them to build up for the re-conquest of Europe.[56]

The British JPS commented wryly that had it not been for the Americans' sensitivity to the United Kingdom's 'national policy', their list of priorities might well not have included the Middle East at all.[57]

However, as noted already, the Middle East, and the Abu Sueir air base in particular, continued to retain a significant role in American plans for the strategic air offensive. Consequently, American planners did agree to make a limited contribution to the Middle East in the air. While refusing to station any American air forces in the Middle East, they did concede that American strategic bombers 'might require to stage through Abu Sueir on the return leg of their missions'. The Americans also agreed that their air forces would take part in the interdiction of any Soviet advance against the Middle East. However, they doubted whether there would be any tactical targets in this theatre for SAC. But the Americans refused bluntly to allocate any naval forces specifically for control of sea lanes through the Mediterranean.[58]

Naturally, the British did not reconcile themselves as readily as the

[55] Meeting between JCS and Air Marshal Tedder, 5 Oct. 1949, CCS 337, (7-22-48) S.1, RG 218, 1948–50, NA.

[56] Annex I to JP (49) 126 (Final), 3 Nov. 1949, Defe 4/26. PRO.

[57] JP (49) 133, 14 Oct. 1949, Defe 6/11. PRO.

[58] Annex 1 to JP (49) 126, supra.

Americans to the loss of the Middle East. But all their attempts to draw the Americans into a Middle Eastern commitment were in vain.

A further round of Anglo–American political talks in Washington in November 1949, produced a very tepid joint statement. Somewhat incongruously, it reaffirmed that the United States had 'no desire to compete with or hinder the UK government in its activities in the Middle East'. To the contrary, each country had an interest and desire in buoying up the position of the other. The most that the British could extract from the Americans was their agreement to a statement of British sentiment that: 'Should the United States government choose to assume a greater responsibility in this area, such a decision would be welcomed by the United Kingdom as being to a common advantage.' The State Department, which did not see eye-to-eye with the Pentagon's abdication of any American military role in the Middle East, agreed to consider how the United States might take more constructive action in the area.[59]

But even this statement earned George McGhee (Assistant Secretary of State at NEA), a reprimand from the JCS. The latter insisted that American strategic interests in the Middle East, compared to those in other areas, were 'almost negligible'. The JCS did, however, make it clear that this did not indicate any change to the high priority which they allotted to the Middle East. Only that even higher priorities in other regions made it impossible to devote any significant part of their very limited military resources to this particular area.[60]

D. THE BANKRUPTCY OF THE RAMALLAH LINE STRATEGY

British prognoses on the outcome of a Middle East campaign fluctuated wildly (as did American), both because of American vacillations, and perhaps even more so, because of economic exigencies.

As noted above, the conference of the ABC planners at the Pentagon, in October 1949, revised *Speedway*. The new plan, *Galloper*, was for a possible war between March 1950 and July 1951. *Galloper* forced British strategists to readjust their plans for the Middle East, to take into account new intelligence assessments of the Soviet threat to this theatre; the 'secession' of the American contingent from the Middle

---

[59] Statement by American and British working groups (headed by George McGhee of the State Department, and Sir Michael Wright of the British Foreign Office), in Washington, following talks from 14 to 17 Nov. 1949, *FRUS*, 1949, Vol. VI, p.64.

[60] Note by Mr Bray, chief of programme staff, Mutual Defense Assistance Program, 21 May 1950, ibid. pp.122–123; and memorandum of 6 Feb. 1950, by Mr Ohly, deputy director of Mutual Defense Assistance program, on talk with General L.L. Lemnitzer, special assistant to the Secretary of Defense on Foreign Military Assistance, *FRUS*, 1950, Vol. V, p.123, n. 6.

East; and 'the increased importance of Turkey as an element in the defence of the Middle East.'[61]

The British Defence Co-Ordination Committee (BDCC), Middle East was commissioned to re-examine and to revise *Sandown*. In the Spring of 1950 *Celery* would replace *Sandown*.[62]

Fortunately, from the British point of view, the loss of the American contingent was now offset partially by 'the increased importance of Turkey as an element in the defence of the Middle East'.[63] Indeed, the gravitation of Turkey into the Western orbit now developed into a primary factor influencing Middle East planning.

Even if British plans still centred on the Ramallah line, they could now plan on the Soviet advance into the Middle East being slowed up considerably. This was due to new assessments regarding Turkish resistance which, it was now believed, would be much stiffer than hitherto estimated.[64]

At the beginning of 1950, British military intelligence estimated that if the Turks resisted a Soviet attack, and the Allies aided them with aerial and engineering support, the Soviets would be unable to develop any offensive against the Suez Canal until the second year of war. However, the contradiction inherent in the plan lay in its own estimate that Allied support for the Turks was unlikely to be forthcoming until at least July 1951.

Galloper's prognosis divided up the Middle East campaign into three phases.[65]

The first phase:

Assuming little indigenous resistance to the Soviets, apart from that of the Turks (fighting with their own resources alone), the following situation was now expected to develop by D + 3 months:

a. The Soviets were expected to deploy nine divisions against Persia and Iraq, and to have completed their occupation within this first phase. It was feared that smaller Soviet units might simultaneously attempt to outflank Turkish resistance with advances through the eastern desert regions. Forward Soviet reconnaissance elements might have made contact with Allied forces in the desert east of the Aleppo–Amman line.

b. Soviet forces would be advancing through Turkey, but they were not

---

[61] Annex to JP (50) 94, (Final), supra.

[62] Annex to JP (50) 94 (Final), 22 Sept. 1950, Defe 4/36. PRO.

[63] Plan *Galloper* and enclosures, JP (49) 134, 1 March 1950, Defe 6/11. PRO.

[64] Ibid.

[65] For following, see ibid., and JIC (U.K.) (49) 80 (Final), 28 April 1950, in COS (50) 141, Defe 5/20. PRO.

expected to have reached the Mediterranean coast at Alexandretta before D + 4 months.

The Soviets were expected to employ massive air power. Their campaign through Persia and Iraq would be supported by about ten air regiments (a total of 450 aircraft); and the campaign against Turkey by about 40 air regiments (a total of 1800 aircraft); of the latter, only twenty could be maintained in Turkey (and only half of these could be maintained south of Alexandretta.) Apart from this, the Soviets were expected to hold in the southern area of the Soviet Union a reserve of about 26 air regiments for operations in the Middle East and in Greece.

British planners all but dismissed the threat that the Soviets might divert aircraft from their Long Range Strategic Air Force for missions in the Middle East – unless they felt it necessary to counter Allied strategic air missions launched from that region (a curious statement, since in 1950 the Abu Sueir base was still being developed for use by the American B-29s).

The second phase:

The Soviets would probably be concentrating their forces in Iraq, in order to secure the Mosul–Aleppo railway, while at the same time consolidating their lines of communication through Turkey. If the Turkish railways and rolling stock were captured intact, this phase might be completed by D + 5 months. But the Joint Intelligence Committee (JIC) believed that a more realistic estimate was D + 7 months.

The third phase:

The JIC did not believe that the Soviet forces in Iraq would be strong enough by themselves to threaten Allied positions in the Levant. They would need to wait for those forces coming from Turkey, and the determining factor would be the rate at which they managed to establish a rail line of communication through Turkey.

The main Soviet threat against Syria was not now expected to materialise before D + six months, instead of the D + three months estimated hitherto. The JIC believed that once the Soviet occupation of Turkey had been completed they would launch their final offensive against Egypt, through Palestine. The forces coming through Turkey would bring the size of the Soviet assault on Palestine up to something in the order of five divisions within D + five months, eight to ten divisions by D + seven months, and a maximum of ten divisions by the end of the first year. The JIC estimated that at that stage, at D + 12 months, the Soviets would launch their main assault against Syria and Palestine.[66]

[66] Ibid.

The gravest danger now, one that *Galloper* made glaringly obvious, was the Soviets' overwhelming superiority in the air. The challenge of securing superiority in the air, on which *Sandown* had laid such emphasis, now appeared to be beyond Allied resources. The Americans had withdrawn their Middle East complement of 350 aircraft, which had appeared in the *Sandown* force levels. *Galloper* underlined the serious weakness of British air defences, and shortage of fighter aircraft in the Middle East. This would leave Allied forces dangerously vulnerable to attack by Soviet long-range aircraft, and by their tactical air forces, once they had conquered airfields in Iraq, Persia and Syria.[67]

In April 1950, British Intelligence estimated that by D + six to eight months, the Soviets would deploy substantial air forces in the skies of the Middle East – some 900 tactical aircraft, with substantial reserves. The British now feared early Soviet air attacks against the Egyptian base, delivered by 'powerful tactical air forces, operating from airfields in southern Turkey and Southern Europe' (the Soviets were now expected to have simultaneously overrun and occupied Italy, Sicily and Greece within the first three months of war).[68]

Against this aerial armada, and against the Soviet ground forces, British planners expected to be able to put into the skies no more than 152 fighter aircraft (including fighter ground/attack aircraft), 80 medium bombers and 24 light and tactical bombers. (This number included British reinforcements to be brought from the Far East, about which there was considerable doubt.)[69] But even *Galloper*'s minimal deployment of aircraft in the Middle East provoked the opposition of the RAF, since even this meagre allotment of aircraft was achieved by the JPS by the transfer of British aircraft from Europe and the Far East to the Middle East.

Whereas the COS still retained the Middle East as second priority only to Europe, the RAF objected that the transfer of over 100 aircraft from Europe and the Far East to the Middle East was unsound strategy. They argued that the country's small bomber force should not be split up between Europe and the Middle East – Western Europe should have first priority. *Galloper* had reallocated 80 medium-range Lincoln bombers (to be taken from Europe) and 32 ground attack aircraft (to be taken from Hong Kong) to the Middle East.[70]

At the RAF's request, the COS asked the JPS to re-consider the strategic implications of this redeployment of air forces. But the latter

[67] JP (49) 134, supra.

[68] JIC (U.K.) (49) 80 (Final), 28 April 1950, in COS (50) 141, Defe 5/20. PRO.

[69] DCC (5) 41, Final, 21 April 1950, in ibid.

[70] JP (50) 40 (S), 25 March 1950, *Strategic Implications of a Reduction of Air Forces Available in the Middle East*, in Defe 6/12. PRO.

re-affirmed their earlier decision. They argued that 'on consideration of global strategy: any substantial reduction in the meagre air forces allotted in Plan *Galloper* to the Middle East would prejudice its defence.'[71]

By the Spring of 1950, the COS were in fact moving into line with their American counterparts, in favouring some kind of a continental commitment, even if they disagreed vigorously about their Allies' new 'West African' strategy. The COS, who naturally had always regarded the survival of the United Kingdom as their first priority, came to see that a Soviet conquest of Europe would threaten that very eventuality.[72]

It was appreciated that a major offensive by Soviet forces against the Middle East would leave them over-extended and vulnerable. However, the Soviets might well be willing to take such grave risks in order to exploit initial British weakness, and to secure 'the prizes at stake'.[73]

If the prognosis forecast by *Galloper* materialised, the last hurdle facing the Soviets before the final assault on Egypt and the Suez Canal, would be Palestine. Thus British strategists were still confronted with the vital question of where to build their 'last-ditch' defence line before the Canal.

The British Middle East Command was inevitably much less sanguine about the situation in their theatre than the planners in London. In May 1950, they questioned whether the Soviets would in fact wait to reinforce themselves with those forces engaged in the conquest of Turkey, before pushing on with their offensive against Egypt. They estimated that if the Allies had not deployed enough forces to the north and east of Israel within the first two months of the war, the Soviet commander in Iraq would exploit Allied weakness and launch his assault on Palestine without even waiting for the Soviet forces in Turkey to join him. This made it all the more imperative and urgent to secure Israeli military co-operation. The C. in C. Middle East concluded:

> The importance of Israel's co-operation in preventing this earlier Russian threat in the Levant cannot be over-emphasized.[74]

In the spring of 1950, in response to these forebodings, and due to the new situation created by *Galloper*, the COS asked the C. in C.s Middle East to revise *Sandown*, and prepare a new plan for their

[71] JP (50) 40 (Final), 20 April 1950, Defe 6/12. PRO.

[72] Richard Aldrich, John Zametica, 'The Rise and Decline of a Strategic Concept: the Middle East, 1945-1951', in Richard Aldrich, ed., *British Intelligence, Strategy and the Cold War, 1945-51*, London/New York: Routledge, 1992, p.264.

[73] DCC (5) 41, Final, supra.

[74] Review by C in C Middle East, *Middle East Strategy and Israel*, in JP (50) 48, 19 May 1950, Defe 6/13. PRO.

theatre, based on the Lebanon–Jordan line, instead of the Ramallah line.

On instructions from the Foreign Office, the COS now placed more emphasis on Israel's key strategic position, and Britain's need to secure military and strategic rights on her territory. This new emphasis was due also both to Israel's realignment with the West, as given expression during the Korean War; and to the growing sense of despair of ever reaching a new base agreement with the Egyptians.

The COS appreciated that Israel would be most unlikely to co-operate with the Allies on the basis of *Sandown*, a plan that took as its premise the abandonment in advance and probable occupation by the Soviets of the northern half of her territory. In that event, rather than reconcile herself to that fate, Israel might well seek terms with the Soviets. If that happened, the Allies would have to occupy Israel by force.[75]

British concern to secure a military understanding with the Israelis or, at the very least, to guarantee in advance and secure transit rights through Israeli territory, prompted the British Government to send General Sir Brian Robertson, C. in. C. British Forces, Middle East, to Israel in February 1951. (On these talks see below, Chapter 7.)

During the summer of 1950, international attention focused on Korea, where the first 'hot war' involving Western and Communist forces since World War Two erupted. On 25 June 1950, North Korean forces invaded South Korea. On 8 July, in the absence of the Soviet Union, the United Nations voted to intervene on behalf of South Korea, and appointed an American General, Douglas MacArthur, as commander of UN forces in Korea.

In June 1950, under the shadow of the developing Korean crisis, the BDCC Middle East reviewed the Middle East theatre plan. Plan *Sandown* was revised and replaced by *Celery*. With the American and British chiefs of staff preoccupied with the Far East, and the prospect of any American or Commonwealth commitment to the Middle East yet more remote, the BDCC found itself unable to agree to the COS request to move the fortified defence line to the north of Israel.

The Ramallah line remained the 'last-ditch' defence position, due to the even more limited forces now expected to be available. In the Fall of 1950, British planners still had no idea of how many land forces the Americans were currently willing to commit to the Middle East, nor how many American aircraft would be available. The BDCC was acutely aware of *Celery*'s weaknesses, but insisted that it

---

[75] JP (50) 106, 1 Aug. 1950, annex to COS (50) 135th meeting, 22 Aug. 1950, in Air 20/8113. PRO. The original copies of this document were retained by the Defense Department.

remained the only realistic plan in view of the limited forces at its disposal.[76]

The gap between strategic *desiderata* and shortfalls in manpower and equipment was indeed acute. But the JPS castigated *Celery*, and insisted on a revision that would move the final defence line to the Lebanon–Jordan line. They impressed upon the Middle East commanders the importance of putting up a fight to the north of Israel. Initial attempts should be made to harass and hold up a Soviet advance in Syria and Lebanon. If Allied reinforcements were not forthcoming, British forces might indeed be forced, in the last resort, to withdraw to the Ramallah line. But by that time, they might have achieved two of their main objectives: 'to secure the co-operation of Israel and to delay the Russian attack'. The more northern line had the additional advantage that it included within its perimeter all the principal airfields in the Levant. The JPS concluded that the Ramallah line could not be considered at all suitable 'as a line on which the main defence of the Middle East should be planned.'[77]

The dangers of an Israeli refusal to co-operate were again underlined, since by now, British planners were not confident that they would dispose of sufficient forces even to fight their way into southern Israel, if the Israeli army resisted. The JPS pointed out that the BDCC offered no solution, and no alternative course of action to this problem.

The initial phase of the war would be critical, and the British would be unable to dissipate effort and forces fighting the Israelis. The planners warned:

> unless sufficient forces are deployed forward to deter a direct Russian advance from Iraq, we might be brought to battle at about D + 3 months on ground not of our own choosing and before our build-up had been completed.[78]

The JPS conceded that prior studies had established the fact that the Ramallah line was the last possible point at which to hold up the Soviets, in order to provide sufficient depth for the defence of Egypt, and 'to prevent attack by short-range tactical aircraft'. But they protested that the Ramallah line left Israel 'wide open to Russian penetration', and again warned that 'if the Russians were on the point of entering Israel and the Allies were patently incapable of preventing them, Israel would be likely to come to an arrangement with Russia.'[79]

[76] JP (50) 106, supra, and COS to Commanders-in-Chief, Middle East, 22 Sept. 1950, annex to JP (50) 94, Defe 6/14, and Defe 4/36. PRO.

[77] JP (50) 94, ibid.

[78] Annex to ibid.

[79] Ibid.

Therefore, repeated the JPS, their main hope of securing the vital co-operation of Israel would be to establish their initial defence position further to the north and east, and to deploy enough forces on that line to contain the Russian threat (or at least to convince the Israelis that they could!).

One of the reasons the BDCC had argued for adherence to the Ramallah line, was their argument that the logistics of maintaining a main base to the north of Israel would be above the administrative capacity of the supply route from Aqaba. The JPS suggested this problem might be solved by securing rights to use the port of Beirut and, once Israeli co-operation was secured, by using Haifa port as well.

Finally, the JPS reminded their superiors that unless they deployed sufficient forces in northern Jordan and western Syria, there would be little to deter the Soviet commander in Iraq from advancing to the Mediterranean coast at D + 80 days, with the four divisions which he would then have at his disposal. This nightmare contingency would almost certainly materialise should the Russian commander learn of the British weakness in this theatre.[80]

In addition, political pressure was exerted on the Middle East Command by the Ministry of Defence. The Ministry reiterated the arguments of the JPS about the advantages of the Lebanon–Jordan Line, and the 'overriding disadvantages' of the Ramallah line, because of the probable Israeli defection to the Soviets. Such doubts were still fed by severe misgivings about Israel's communist leanings, doubts that did not dissipate entirely, even after Israel's UN vote for the West during the Korean crisis.[81]

Nonetheless, whatever the dictates of sound military doctrine, the final decision as to the Middle East defence line would depend upon what forces could be allocated initially to this theatre, how soon reinforcements could be rushed in, and upon how extensive and effective Turkish opposition would prove to be.[82]

In all Allied defence plans for the Middle East, the minimum force levels required exceeded by far those that Britain and the Commonwealth were likely to have available for the foreseeable future (in September 1950, as a result of the Korean war, the British extended military conscription to two years). Everything still hinged on the American contribution, on land, sea and air. But the COS doubted

---

[80] Ibid.

[81] Ministry of Defence to GHQ, Middle East Land Forces, 28 Sept. 1950, E1193/18/G, FO 371/81963. PRO. On Israel's 'neutrality', cf., Uri Bialer, *Between East and West: Israel's Foreign Policy Orientation 1948-1956*, Cambridge: Cambridge University Press, 1990.

[82] JP (50) 106, supra.

whether they could count on any Commonwealth or American reinforcements within the critical first six months of the war.[83]

Thus, notwithstanding its glaring deficiencies, the Ramallah line was retained as the basis of Britain's Middle East defence plan. The JPS objections may have been based upon cogent and irrefutable military logic. But with the limited forces at their disposal, the COS were obliged to accept the risks, and to bow to the ruling of the Middle East commanders.[84]

This was tantamount to admitting that they could not in fact defend the Middle East – although at this stage, no one was yet willing to admit this.

The British appealed to the Americans at the highest levels in Washington. They still persevered, desperately, in their campaign to secure an American commitment to the Middle East. At political-military talks held between the two countries in July 1950, the British side tried to divest itself of 'primary responsibility' for the Middle East. But finally, after some 'frank discussion' over 'semantic difficulties', the British conceded that this was an area in which the United States should look to them to take the initiative. At the same time the British side reiterated the hope that the Americans would reconsider the question of giving it more support.[85]

In September 1950, at further informal talks held between Geoffrey Furlonge, head of the Eastern Department at the Foreign Office, and George McGhee of NEA, Furlonge outlined the main points of a new British defence paper, which again stressed the indispensability of the Egyptian base. He suggested that within the context of the redeployment of military forces throughout the region, 'even a small US ground force at Dhahran would have a good psychological effect'. Michael Wright, the other Foreign Office representative, suggested stationing American ground troops in Tripolitania. Furlonge pleaded that 'a comparatively small outlay of military equipment in the Arab states would have a disproportionately greater return by enhancing the security of those states'. George McGhee responded that this was 'largely the

---

[83] Ibid. In Nov. 1950, the British still anticipated the following Commonwealth forces for the Middle East:

Australia: one–two divisions; one armoured brigade; three fighter squadrons.

New Zealand: one division; one armoured brigade.

South Africa: one armoured division, possibly one further division, and nine fighter squadrons.

cf. annex to JP (50) 167, 22 Nov. 1950, Defe 6/15. PRO.

[84] Ibid.

[85] Philip Jessup (ambassador-at-large) to Secretary of State Acheson, 25 July 1950, on Political/Military talks held in Washington from 20 to 24 July 1950, *FRUS*, 1950, Vol.V, p.189.

UK's responsibility', although the United States 'might be able to help to a limited extent'.[86]

The State Department feared that the Arab Middle East, as well as Turkey, perceiving British weakness, would indeed begin to question whether the West could defend them against Soviet aggression. Differences arose within the US administration, between the State Department and the JCS. General Collins refused to budge, insisting that the Middle East must remain exclusively a British responsibility. McGhee pleaded that he was not asking the army to take on military responsibilities in case of war, but to support new initiatives in peacetime, which would have more of a symbolic, than a substantial nature. In addition to the grant of military aid, Mcghee also stressed the importance of securing Turkish entry into NATO.[87]

With the progressive decline in British military power available for the Middle East, there came a corresponding increase in Allied concern about the alignments and potential military contribution of the indigenous states of the region. The Allies felt that those régimes were likely to throw in their lot with whichever side they became convinced was going to win the war. With the initiation of hostilities by the Soviet Union, they would demand immediate Allied action, to convince them that the West intended, and was able, to defend them.

Not only did the securing of base rights in Israel become a top priority, but urgent consideration was now given to the strengthening of regional forces, especially those of Turkey, Egypt and Israel, and to the expansion of the as yet British-officered Arab Legion.

The US State Department shared British concern about the political leanings of the various states in the region. A departmental paper written in October 1950, which assessed the reactions of Israel and the Arab states to a Soviet invasion of the Middle East, estimated that if the Western Allies did not move immediately against the Soviets in force, and defend set positions in the region:

> the Arab States and Israel would be unable or unwilling to resist and would be obliged to submit to the U.S.S.R. Most of the Government leaders and some members of the upper classes would attempt to flee their countries and form governments in exile.[88]

The department concluded that the régimes of the region, regardless of their feelings towards the West, would, in the event of inaction or timidity on the part of the West, 'feel helpless and seek means of

---

[86] Note of talks held on 18 Sept. 1950, ibid., pp.194–6.

[87] Leffler, *A Preponderance of . . .* pp.421, 424.

[88] Memorandum by Wells Stabler, Officer in Charge of Egypt and Anglo-Egyptian Sudan Affairs, 24 Oct. 1950, *FRUS*, 1950, Vol.V, p.224.

survival'. In any state that felt it could no longer count on the West for protection, there would come forward leaders who would either attempt to maintain neutrality, or try to make a deal with the Soviets. The Americans did not believe that indigenous resistance would constitute a significant problem for Soviet forces.[89]

However, there was never any real prospect of genuine military co-operation or joint contingency planning between Britain and the indigenous states of the Middle East. British strategists themselves imposed severe restrictions on their military talks with these states. The COS categorically vetoed any frank discussion with either the Arabs or the Israelis of Allied plans for the defence of the Middle East. This was due not only to fears of breaches of security but also to the fact that, by this stage, any disclosure of the weakness of the British position in the Middle East would be more likely to lower, than to raise local morale, and encourage defection, rather than adherence to the Allied cause. The COS continued to insist that the position might be improved if the Americans could be induced to make a concrete military commitment to the defence of the region.[90]

British planners believed that the most effective move to convince the Middle Eastern states of the dangers of the Soviet threat, and of Britain's determination to defend their region, would be the deployment in that theatre of 'a highly mobile unit with armoured and air support'. But there was no prospect of raising such a unit for the present. Due to other military commitments overseas, Britain's strategic reserve had to be located in the United Kingdom itself. No units from it could be spared for the Middle East, and there could be no guarantee that any part of the reserve would be available in war for service in that theatre.[91]

E. TURKEY BEGINS TO ASSUME PRECEDENCE OVER EGYPT

In October 1950, a further round of political-military talks took place in Washington. The central goal of the British side was to persuade the Americans to give the Middle East theatre a higher priority, especially in the Cold War; and to persuade them that Egypt was a more important strategic asset than Turkey.[92]

---

[89] Ibid.

[90] Ibid.

[91] JP (50) 106, supra.

[92] The talks took place between 23–26 Oct. 1950. For discussions on the importance of the Middle East, see minutes in E1195/10, FO 371/81967; on the effect of the Turks' inclusion in Allied war plans, cf. COS (48) 123, 16 Oct. 1948, Defe 5/8. PRO.

But the Washington talks were overshadowed by the Korean conflict, and the American JCS remained adamantly opposed to extending their military commitment beyond Europe and the Far East.

On 24 October, at a 'political' meeting with State Department officials, Mr B.A.B. Burrows, (counsellor at the British Embassy, Washington), tried to persuade the Americans that the Egyptian base remained essential to Allied Middle Eastern strategy. The British were about to move a brigade into Iran, which they considered would make a significant contribution to Allied objectives in the Middle East. The Egyptian base was essential for the trans-shipment of this brigade.[93]

Burrows also told his audience that Egypt would be 'essential in the event of a localised Korean type of conflict in the Middle East'. The Egyptians would not be able to defend the Cairo-Suez area without British troops. He suggested that due to the current state of Anglo–Israeli relations, the Americans were better positioned than the British to secure the use of military facilities in Israel, in particular, 'the strategic port of Haifa'. In reply, McGhee stated that he understood that 'the possibility of sending US forces to the Middle East was remote', since US planning 'had concentrated more heavily upon the strengthening of Turkey. . .'[94]

McGhee's point was made more forcefully, and authoritatively two days later, by General Collins. At a meeting of the Chiefs of Staffs of both countries, together with Foreign Office and State Department officials, Gen Collins emphasised that the Americans were playing a very active role in the Middle East in the Cold War, especially in providing training missions to Greece, Turkey and Iran. However, notwithstanding the importance the JCS allotted to the Middle East, the British side must appreciate that:

> the United States could make no land or air contribution to the defence of this area for at least the first two years of a conflict.[95]

Gen Collins intimated that in the event of a hot war, even their tactical naval aircraft (operating from US carriers in the Mediterranean), would be needed in Italy. The American record of the meeting states that US Admiral Sherman then intervened, to state that if the Soviets

[93] Record of meetings in *FRUS*, 1950, Vol. V, pp.230–38.

[94] Meeting of 24 Oct. 1950, ibid., p.231. Present were Burrows, and Messrs McGhee, Fraser Wilkins, Rountree, Ferguson, Lewis Jones, Charles Yost and John Howard, all of the State Department.

[95] Meeting between JCS and COS, with Messrs Jessup and Yost of the State Department, and Ambassador Franks and Mr Burrows of the British Embassy, Washington, 26 Oct. 1950, ibid., p.236. The quote is taken from the British record of the meeting, in E1195/10, FO 371/81967. PRO.

did not try to 'break into Italy', the US might be able 'to provide some tactical naval assistance' to the British, either in the Aegean, or in the Middle East. The British side recorded that Sherman had stated that operations in Italy would be a first call on US Naval forces in the Mediterranean, but had added 'that it was also important to keep the Russians out of the Eastern Mediterranean and to maintain a through line of communication to the Middle East'.[96]

The Americans adhered to two basic positions at the discussions; first, they ruled out the deployment of any American forces to the Middle East during the first two years of a global conflict against the Soviets; and second, they assigned higher strategic importance to Turkey than to Egypt.[97]

Some Foreign Office officials in Whitehall tended to agree with the Americans, rather than with their own negotiators. Commenting on the American rejection of the COS *idée fixe* about the Egyptian base, one official commented:

> The Americans in fact regard the defence of Turkey as more important than that of Egypt, and that if Turkey were held the Canal Zone could not be successfully attacked by the enemy. In the face of all our military thinking to the contrary, one hesitates to offer an opinion. But my own view is that the Americans are right, in theory. Whether we have the men is another matter.[98]

Another official suggested that they check out the possibility of transferring their base facilities in Egypt to Turkey! He appreciated that there was an obvious objection to this – that any facilities in Turkey would be closer to, and therefore more vulnerable to, Soviet air bases. But the Foreign Office was of course preoccupied with the intractability of the negotiations with Egypt, and understood that they had failed to persuade the Americans about the essentiality of Egypt to Allied strategic planning, notwithstanding the still current strategic role of Abu Sueir. The Foreign Office noted also that Turkey did have one overriding advantage over all other countries in the region – that of being probably 'the only country in the Middle East which would receive us gladly'.[99]

These comments might perhaps be dismissed as the digressions of weary, disillusioned officials. However, there could be no gainsaying the glaring differences over the Middle East which now divided the Allies. At Washington, the JCS not only turned down British pleas for direct aid in the Middle East, but they rejected the British defence con-

---

[96] *FRUS*, 1950, Vol. V, p.236; *FRUS*, 1950, Vol. III, p.1093; and Ell95/10, supra.

[97] *FRUS*, 1950, Vol. V, pp.230–38.

[98] Minute by L.A.C. Fry, 23 Oct. 1950, E1193/28, FO 371/81963. PRO.

[99] Minute by D.N. Brinson, 23 Oct. 1950, ibid.

ceptions for that theatre. They insisted that a line further to the north of the Ramallah line be established.

The JCS accused the British of being over-cautious, and claimed that their fears of Soviet penetration were exaggerated. The JCS accused their British counterparts of having underestimated the difficulties of terrain facing the Soviets, and the logistic problems they would need to solve due to their extended lines of communications. The British were accused also of having underestimated the degree to which Allied bombing of Soviet forces and bases, and demolition of their approach routes, would interdict the Soviet advance. The JCS insisted that the only realistic defence of the Middle East was at the 'Outer Ring', and that the British had inflated the size of the forces that would be required to hold this line.[100]

The JCS now took a more forceful stand on the need to defend the 'Outer Ring', the line running from the Taurus Mountains through Lake Van, the Zagros mountains of Iran, down to Bander Abbas. The COS believed that this was due to a new American awareness of the need for Middle Eastern oil, in the event of a prolonged war. In that event, there would be insufficient reserves in the Western Hemisphere to meet Allied military requirements. The COS assessment was based apparently on a statement made at the conference by US Air Force Chief of Staff, General Hoyt S. Vandenberg, that whereas there was much disagreement between the experts about the importance of Middle Eastern oil, he believed that it *would* be needed, especially after the second year of a war.[101]

The ABC planners' conference at Washington in October 1950, had devoted some time to the question of Middle Eastern oil, not only to Allied needs, but also to Allied plans for sabotaging the oil fields and refineries, to prevent the Soviets exploiting them. The general consensus had been that they should reconsider existing demolition plans. This was because, firstly, it was now doubted whether the Soviets would be able to exploit Middle Eastern oil in war. And secondly, it was feared that if Allied demolition plans became known in the Middle East, the morale of the indigenous states would drop.[102] The latter would realise that the West had few hopes of defending them, and would inevitably consider 'hedging their bets'.

The ABC planners resolved to conduct a combined Anglo–American staff study of the minimum forces that would be needed to hold the

---

[100] COS report on talks with JCS, in annex III to JP (50) 162, 10 Nov. 1950, Brief for C in Cs, Middle East, 21 Nov. 1950, Defe 6/15. PRO.

[101] British Military Mission, Washington to Ministry of Defence, 26 Oct. 1950, E1195/4, FO 371/81967. PRO; and *FRUS*, 1950, Vol. V. p.237.

[102] Ibid., pp.236–37.

Outer Ring in war. The study was to assess the aid they might obtain from indigenous regional forces – those from TransJordan, Iraq and Iran, and especially Turkey.[103] The study was to be conducted by the British C. in C.s Middle East, in conjunction with US Admiral Carney, CINCELM, and the American Military Missions in Turkey and Iran. The conference decided also that the State Department and Foreign Office would consider the possibility of presenting a united diplomatic front to Egypt, in order to secure vital base facilities in that country.[104]

The Washington Conference of 1950 marked the watershed of Britain's traditional Middle East strategy, which now began a painful process of realignment to that of the Americans. Given the adamant attitude of the JCS, the British were obliged to reconsider their exclusive focus on Egypt, and to devote serious consideration to the Americans' Northern Tier strategy. As noted by the State Department, the British themselves had now conceded that on current estimates, they would be unable to defend even the Suez area, even if aid from the Commonwealth was forthcoming. The shortfalls in British forces, especially in the air, could be made up only by the Americans.[105]

---

[103] British Military Mission, Washington – Ministry of Defence, 26 Oct. 1950, supra; and R.J. Bowker – Sir E. Dening, 18 Jan. 1951, E1192/5G, FO 371/91219. PRO; and undated (sometime in Nov. 1950) State Department paper, annex I to McGhee – Acheson, 27 Dec. 1950, *FRUS*, 1950, V, pp.7–8.

[104] Annex III to JP (50) 162, 10 Nov. 1950, Defe 6/15, PRO; and Summary of conclusions and agreements of Washington conference, 23–26 Oct. 1950, *FRUS*, 1950, Vol. III, pp.1687, 1691.

[105] Undated State Department paper, *FRUS*, 1950, V, p.8.

7 Israel's place in Allied Middle East plans

A. ISRAEL'S MILITARY AND LOGISTICAL IMPORTANCE

From the spring of 1949, with the signature of the first armistice agreements between Israel and the Arab states, Allied planners began to take stock of the new geo-strategic reality in the Middle East.

Western strategists were agreed that Israel's military performance against the Arab states had radically altered the power balance in the Near and Middle East. In contrast to the earlier 'experts'' forecasts of Israel's military defeat, or attrition at the hands of the Arabs,[1] in March 1949, American planners concluded that:

> Israel . . . has demonstrated by force of arms its right to be considered the military power next after Turkey in the Near and Middle East.[2]

In July 1950, Air Marshal Lord Tedder, Chief of the British Air Staff, and General Omar Bradley, chairman of the JCS, concurred that apart from Turkey, the Israeli armed forces now constituted the most effective force in the Middle East for a possible delaying action against a Soviet offensive.[3]

Compared to the Arab states, Israel had a higher proportion of trained manpower of military age, much of which had been trained in the British, or in Central European armies. Although fewer in absolute numbers than the manpower available in the Arab states, Israel's population could be mobilised more rapidly for military purposes (Israel had one of the highest mobilisation ratios in the world). It was believed that Israel was able to call up somewhere in the region of 200–250,000 males for military service.[4]

[1] Cf., Michael J. Cohen, Colonel William Eddy, 'The Oil Lobby and the Palestine Problem', *Middle Eastern Studies*, Vol. 30/1, Jan. 1994, pp.166–80.

[2] Memo on US Strategic Interests in Israel, March 1949, Israel, 1949–50, box 160, RG 319 (Army Staff), National Archives. (NA)

[3] Report by Philip Jessup to Secretary of State, 25 July 1950, on meeting of Allied political and military officials in Washington *FRUS*, Vol. V, 1950, p.189.

[4] Cf., Memorandum drafted by Sam Kopper, 27 Dec. 1950, *FRUS*, Vol. V, 1951,

By 1951, the British estimated that Israel had about two combat-ready divisions, and some 70 military aircraft (In 1951, the IAF in fact had a total of 87 combat aircraft, fighters and bombers).[5] Given the decline of the British military presence in the Middle East, and the Americans' refusal to commit any forces to this theatre, the Israeli armed forces were valuable assets, if deployed on the side of the Allies.

However, the enduring Arab–Israel conflict precluded the Allies from reaping any regional benefit from Israel's newly-demonstrated military prowess. Any thought of regional military planning, combining Israeli and Arab forces, had to be ruled out. Israel and the Arab states would not co-operate under the same command, nor would the Arabs agree to the deployment of Israeli forces on their territory.[6]

But of far more importance to the Allies than Israel's military potential, was her geo-strategic location in the Middle East. The JPS on both sides of the Atlantic believed that in the event of war with the Soviets, Palestine (now partitioned between Israel, Transjordan and Egypt), would become either a key battleground or at the very least, an area through which their vital communications would have to pass. In an emergency, Britain would need to deploy its (and later, Commonwealth) troops, with all their logistic support systems, through and on Israeli territory, without any hindrance from the local armed forces or population.[7]

In the event of war, the British would require unhindered use of the Baghdad–Haifa arterial road for the transport of troops and supplies to their initial forward positions. They might also want to develop an additional east–west road across Palestine, further to the south of the Baghdad–Haifa route.[8]

American planners expanded on the wider, strategic importance of regional communications running through or close to Israel. They pointed out that Israel now lay astride all the strategic land approaches to the Cairo–Suez area; the main land routes from the Caspian Sea area of the Soviet Union, through Iran, Iraq, and Saudi Arabia to Egypt and the Levant – all passed through or close to Israeli territory. The

pp.11–13; and Moshe Sharett (Israeli Foreign Secretary) to Secretary of Defense Marshall, 23 Dec. 1950, *FRUS*, Vol. V, 1950, pp.1079–81.

[5] David R. Devereux gives a figure of 150 aircraft for the IDF. This was in fact the number that the British suggested helping build up the IAF to; cf. *The Formulation of British Defence Towards the Middle East, 1948–56*, London: Macmillan, 1990, p.151. On the IAF, cf. Major Isaac Steigman, *Operation 'Kadesh': The IAF from 1950-1956 – Buildup and Operations*, Tel Aviv: Israeli Ministry of Defence, 1986, p.22 (in Hebrew).

[6] George McGhee to Philip Jessup, 19 Oct. 1950, *FRUS*, Vol. V, 1950, pp.217–20.

[7] JP (49) 11, 11 Feb. 1949, in Defe 4/20, and Defe 6/8. PRO.

[8] Michael Wright (Foreign Office) to Ministry of Defence, 25 March 1949, COS (49) 107, Defe 5/13. PRO.

Egyptian–Israeli border now lay 150 miles to the east of the Suez Canal. Likewise, all the oil pipelines that carried Middle Eastern oil to the Mediterranean either traversed Israeli territory, or passed nearby.[9]

With their special interest in Turkey, the Americans also stressed the fact that the direct land routes from the Cairo–Suez area to Turkey, both rail and road, now passed through Israeli territory. In particular, the Allies would need to use the Cairo–Alexandretta railway for the transport of supplies to Turkey. The Americans were concerned also that the Haifa oil refineries, the terminus of one of the main oil pipelines in the Middle East, should supply Allied, rather than Soviet war needs.[10]

British planners estimated that in the event of war, they might initially manage to maintain their advanced forces via supply lines through Aqaba and Beirut, but only for up to two months. After that, they would be unable to continue operations without logistic facilities in Israel. After D + two months, the increasing load on their lines of communication, and the time needed to develop airfields and installations and to set up headquarters, would make it imperative for the British to gain access to Israeli communications.[11]

The Allies would also need complete freedom of access to Israel's ports, communications, and telegraph systems. In peacetime, the well-developed (by the British) network of Israeli airfields would have to be kept at the highest operational level, so that with the outbreak of war, Allied air forces would be able to use them immediately. The JCS agreed that Israel's 'system of well-developed airfields and bases' would be important for the operation of 'medium and short-range' aircraft, to interdict Soviet forces advancing against the Middle East. Conversely, if the Red Air Force secured access to Israeli airfields, Soviet aircraft would be able to interfere seriously with Allied operations in that theatre, and to pose a major threat to the Suez Canal base.[12]

During the first Arab–Israeli war, the British had done everything in their power to ensure that as many of Palestine's military and strategic facilities remained in 'reliable' Arab hands. They had employed every diplomatic stratagem, and even teetered to the brink of war with Israel, in their efforts to reduce to a minimum the latter's control over the Negev desert. In the West Bank, there had been no need for British

---

[9] JCS 1684/28, 1 April 1949, CCS 092 Pal (5-3-46), sect. 7; and CD 6-2-47, 16 May 1949, RG 330 (Secretary of Defense), box 22. NA.

[10] Ibid.

[11] Major-General Redman (Director of Military Operations) to M.R. Wright (Foreign Office), 7 Nov. 1950, ER1022/31, FO 371/82515. PRO.

[12] JP (49) 29, 30 March 1949, Defe 6/8; and JP (49) 59, 11 July 1949, Defe 4/23, PRO; and JCS 1684/28, 1 April 1949, CCS 092 Pal (5-3-46) sect. 7; and CD 6-2-47, 16 May 1949, RG 330 (Secretary of Defense), box 22. NA.

intervention, as Israel and Jordan (and Egypt) had *de facto* partitioned mandatory Palestine between them (above, Chapter four).

The British had preferred that the region's limited strategic road system remain in Arab hands and they had reasoned that the more limited the territory to which Israel could be confined, the easier it would be for British forces, if necessary, to overcome any Israeli resistance to Allied use of her facilities and communications!

On the other hand, if the Allies did manage to secure Israeli co-operation, this would remove the inherent threat that the Israeli army constituted for Jordan. In that case, Jordan might release the Arab Legion from its stations guarding the Israeli–Jordanian frontier, for employment elsewhere, in support of the Allies.[13]

At the end of October 1948, Egypt and Israel were still fighting in the Negev, but Palestine's West Bank was already effectively partitioned between Israel and Jordan. The British JPS considered the logistical advantages of gaining access to the West Bank, via their Jordanian ally/proxy. They pointed out that if British troops were already stationed in the Jordanian-occupied West Bank, they 'would be well placed to force their way through' Israel, in the event of any resistance by the latter. With Jordan's Arab Legion, and Egypt's army in effective occupation of sections of what had been mandatory Palestine, the JPS considered, somewhat prematurely, the possibility of stationing a British division in the Gaza–Beersheba–Hebron area.[14]

At the end of the Arab–Israeli war, the COS elaborated on the strategic benefits that they could now hope to reap from Greater Transjordan (i.e. from Transjordan's acquisition of Palestine's West Bank):

(1) It lies astride one of the main lines of approach from the Caucasus and the Caspian to the Suez Canal and the Delta.
(2) It covers the direct route from the head of the Persian Gulf to Aqaba and thence to the Suez Canal and the Delta.
(3) It flanks our possible defensive position across Palestine.
(4) It is potentially an area in which forward air bases could be established.
(5) The Arab Legion is the only properly organised, trained and equipped force in the Middle East.[15]

The Americans agreed that the development of some limited base facilities in Palestine would undoubtedly be of value. However, as was

[13] Major Gen. H Redman (Director of Military Operations) to M. R. Wright (Foreign Office), 7 Nov. 1950, ER1022/31, FO 371/82515. PRO.

[14] JP (48) 108, 26 Oct. 1948, Defe 6/7. PRO.

[15] COS draft memo of 18 April 1948, cited in Avi Shlaim, 'Britain and the Arab–Israeli War of 1948', in Michael Dockrill, John Young, eds, *British Foreign Policy, 1945–56*, New York: St Martin's Press, 1989, p.82.

the case with Egypt, they themselves refused to become involved in any way in Israel. In August 1948, the JCS had ruled out any American military involvement in a UN peacekeeping force in Palestine, on the grounds that a considerable number of American troops might become bogged down in Palestine.[16]

In October 1949, the JCS rejected a British request that they station a Brigade Group in Israel, to guarantee that 'Israel was for us and not against us'. The JCS argued that Israel would eventually demand more than a Brigade Group, to indicate that the West was determined to defend her territorial integrity. They added that American domestic political pressure would insist on reinforcing the exposed Brigade with up to two or three divisions. The result would be that substantial American forces would become bogged down in Israel, which would result in the loss of flexibility in other theatres, and prejudice to global strategic planning.[17]

As noted already, Israel also figured prominently in British plans for the defence of the Middle East against a Soviet land offensive. Plans *Sandown* and *Celery* had both forecast that the key battle against the Soviets in the Middle East would be fought on Israel's coastal plain. The BDCC had insisted that with the limited forces currently available to them, the Ramallah line was the only option available to them (as opposed to the Outer Ring line, which the Americans were pressing on the British). It was appreciated that any forward campaign in the Middle East would be militarily unsound unless the Allies could rely upon a lines of communication through Israel.[18]

As noted already, the JPS could not emphasise enough the importance of securing Israel's military co-operation, in helping the Allies to pre-empt the threat of an early Soviet advance into the Levant.[19]

The British drew up two contingency plans for the defence of the Middle East; one on the assumption that Israel would co-operate from the start; and the other, on the assumption that she would initially remain neutral. But both depended on Israel's eventual co-operation, and both strategies would be jeopardised seriously if that co-operation was not forthcoming within $D + 3$ months, at the latest.[20]

In September 1950, Lt Gen Brownjohn, the Vice CIGS, pointed out the contradiction inherent in plan *Celery*, in respect to the Ramallah

[16] JCS 1684/29, 19 April 1949, 091. Israel, box 160, RG 319 (army staff): and NSC 27, 23 Aug. 1948, PPS records, 1947–53, box 30, RG 59. NA.

[17] Annex to JP (49) 126 (Final), 3 Nov. 1949, Defe 4/26. PRO; and minutes of JCS meeting with Air Marshal Tedder, 5 Oct. 1949, CCS 337, (7-22-48) S.1, RG 218, 1948–50. NA.

[18] JP (49) 59, 11 July 1949, Defe 4/23; JP (50) 48, 19 May 1950, Defe 6/13; and Combined CINCME–CINCELM study, annex G, COS (51) 189, 4 April 1951, Defe 5/30. PRO.

[19] JP (50) 48, 19 May 1950, Defe 6/13. PRO.

[20] CINCME–CINCELM study, supra.

line. Brownjohn, who was supported by Air Marshal Sir John Slessor, reminded the C. in C.s Middle East that their plan to make a stand on the Ramallah line in effect abandoned the northern half of Israel's territory, where a large part of her population and industry were situated. Obviously, Brownjohn pointed out, Israel would not consider co-operation on these terms, and might even be provoked to seek terms with the Soviets. Therefore, they simply had to take up initial positions on the Lebanon–Jordan line, even if they were eventually forced to fall back on to the Ramallah line.[21]

But what were the British to do if the Israelis refused to grant them access to their military and strategic facilities?

In 1949, the CIGS, Field Marshal Slim, conceded that the co-operation of the Israelis was most important. But what price would the Israelis exact in return for their services? Slim adhered to the traditional British position that the friendship of the Israelis must come second to that of the Arabs. Therefore, he warned, in the event of war, if the Israelis refused to co-operate, they might have to take what they wanted in Palestine by armed force![22] The question remained whether the British would have sufficient forces to do so?

The COS replied in the negative. In April 1950, they estimated that it would require something in the order of 'two divisions with tactical air support', in order to undertake successfully a forcible entry into Israel. This force would have to be available prior to any global emergency, so that it could manage to fight its way through Israel, and establish itself well to the north and east of Palestine, before the Soviet threat to that country developed.[23]

By 1950, the British simply did not dispose of a force on that scale in the entire Middle East, let alone one that could be devoted solely to the mission of subduing Israel.[24] Not only that, but if Israel sought terms with Russia, and resisted a British entry into Palestine, the Jordanians would probably insist on retaining the Arab Legion on the Israeli–Jordanian frontier. And finally, as the JPS reminded the COS, unless they deployed sufficient forces, early enough, to the north and east of Palestine, in order to deter the Russian force advancing through Iraq, they might be brought to battle on a battlefield not of their own choosing, before they had the chance to bring in sufficient reinforcements.[25]

[21] Draft telegram to C in Cs, Middle East, in appendix to JP (50) 94, 22 Sept. 1950, Defe 6/14; and COS (50) 157th., 27 Sept. 1950, Defe 4/36. PRO.

[22] Annex to COS meeting, 16 Feb. 1949, COS(49), 26th, Defe 4/20. PRO.

[23] DCC (5) 41, Final, 21 April 1950, in COS (50) 141, 28 April 1950, Defe 5/20. PRO.

[24] Major Gen H Redman (Director of Military Operations) to M.R. Wright, 7 Nov. 1950, ER1022/31, FO 371/82515. PRO.

[25] Draft telegram to C in Cs, Middle East, appendix to JP (50) 94, 22 Sept. 1950, Defe 6/14. PRO.

The COS concluded that an agreement with Israel, brokered through American influence, was 'perhaps the only solution'.[26]

There was some debate, on both sides of the Atlantic, about Israel's 'neutrality', or 'non-alignment' policy. Israel was torn between its economic dependence on the West, and its need to maintain cordial relations with the Soviets, so as to facilitate permission for the emigration of Jews from the Soviet bloc to Israel. The turning point came in June 1950 when, forced to take sides, Israel supported the American-sponsored UN intervention in Korea.[27]

The old 'communist bogey' calumny (above, Chapter 4) was finally laid to rest. By mid-1950, London and Washington were agreed that Israel was ideologically oriented to the western democracies, and economically dependent for its survival upon American Jewry. Both were also agreed that the key factor that would determine Israel's orientation in the event of a war with the Soviets, would be the West's ability to convince her that the Allies were determined and able to defend her territorial integrity. The Israelis would want to receive arms and training staffs for the IDF, and to know if the West's contingency plans included 'the all-out defence of the Middle East against the Russians'.[28]

A JIC report, circulated during the month before the North Koreans invaded the South, warned that the threat, or the use of force against Israel was likely to make the Israelis even less willing to co-operate with the West. It stated that political pressure from American Jewry, or the threat or use of economic pressure by the West would be more productive. However, agreeing with American estimates, the report concluded that if Soviet forces were about to enter Israel, and the Allies were patently unable to prevent them, the Israelis would be likely to try to make a deal with the invader. In order to avert this scenario, and to guarantee Israeli co-operation:

> . . . the Allies must provide firm evidence of their intention to engage the Russian armies north and east of Israel, which could only be done by deploying forces in that area.[29]

---

[26] DCC (5) 41, Final, 21 April 1950, in COS (50) 141, 28 April 1950, Defe 5/20. PRO.

[27] Cf., Uri Bialer, *Between East and West: Israel's Foreign Policy Orientation, 1948–1956*, Cambridge: Cambridge University Press, 1990.

[28] Memo by Richard Ford (US Chargé at Tel Aviv), 12 Oct. 1950, TA Embassy, 1950–52. 321.9. box 5, RG 84, Foreign Service Posts, NA; and JIC (770) 50, in JP (50) 48, 19 May 1950, Defe 6/13. PRO.

[29] JIC (770) 50, ibid.

B. ISRAEL AS AN INTERIM REPLACEMENT BASE FOR EGYPT

As early as in July 1945, Palestine had been considered by the JPS as a suitable location for the Imperial Strategic Reserve. At that time, Palestine's main 'asset' had been the freedom of action that Britain still enjoyed under the League of Nations Mandate. With characteristic lack of foresight, the JPS had concluded that Palestine was:

> the only territory between Malta and Aden in which we can confidently expect to have facilities for the stationing of troops or the establishment of installations.[30]

In March 1946, as the British took stock of Egyptian nationalist intransigence, the COS appointed a sub-committee (of the Principal Administrative Officers) to recommend alternative sites to the Egyptian Base in which to store those stocks that would need to be evacuated from Egypt. As noted above, one of the proposals debated was Mombasa, in Kenya. However, even if Kenya was developed, Britain would still require accommodation in the Africa–Aden–Port Sudan area, in order to 'bridge the gap between the main support area and the forward area'. In 1946, Palestine and Cyrenaica were the principal candidates.[31]

However, in May 1946, the C. in C.s Middle East ruled out Palestine as an alternative location for the stores and personnel that might have to be withdrawn from Egypt. But the COS were still sanguine about Britain retaining the Mandate for Palestine. And in that case, the COS estimated that they would need to garrison at least two divisions in Palestine, for several years to come. They therefore asked the government for permission to begin planning the permanent accommodation for a garrison in Palestine.[32]

Foreign Secretary Bevin was somewhat ambivalent. On the one hand, he objected vigorously to any suggestion of moving the Middle East headquarters to Palestine:

> Palestine is in an uncertain political position, and if we spend millions of pounds there we might in ten years have to move, or our presence there might become a source of international dispute.[33]

However, at the tactical level, he adopted the same attitude to the

---

[30] JP (45) 167, 10 July 1945, E5141, FO 371/45378. PRO.

[31] COS Principal Administrative Officers' report, CSA (46) 91, 9 Sept. 1946, in Air 20/2461. PRO. Cited in Michael J. Cohen, *Palestine and the Great Powers, 1945–1948*, Princeton: Princeton University Press, 1982, p.38.

[32] Ibid.

Jews in Palestine as he did to the Egyptians. Bevin believed that once the Jews appreciated that the British were no longer so dependent upon Palestine for their strategic purposes, they (the British) might find it easier to settle the inter-racial conflict in Palestine. Once that conflict was settled, they might well consider the establishment of bases and the obtaining of facilities in that country.[34]

But Prime Minister Attlee, who was in any case in favour of moving British forces out of the Middle East, pointed out that the internal unrest in Palestine (in 1946) merely underlined 'the insecurity of developing that country as a main base'. Attlee also questioned, on purely military grounds, the advisability of placing a base as far forward as Palestine.[35]

At a meeting of the Defence Committee, convened on 19 September 1946, the COS sub-committee considered a plan for constructing a base in Palestine that would take from 10 to 14 years to complete. The Foreign Office ridiculed the plan given that, at the time, they were not certain of retaining tenure of Palestine for even a single year longer! Bevin also intimated that any conspicuous construction of British military installations in Palestine at that juncture might undermine concurrent negotiations with the Arabs and Jews. The COS switched tactics. Complaining of the deplorable living conditions endured by the troops in Palestine, they asked for planning permission for a 'very modest garrison'. Attlee acquiesced, on condition that no publicity be attached, nor any contracts tendered.[36]

But four months later, the British Cabinet had decided to hand the Palestine imbroglio over to the United Nations, with no recommendations. The road to Britain's own evacuation, and the forceful partition of Palestine was embarked upon. Israel's military success, in establishing itself well beyond the borders proposed by the UN Partition Resolution (29 November 1947), had presented new challenges for British diplomacy.

Once Israel had become a militarily-established fact, the British military had in 1949 debated at some length the need for reaching an agreement, or even a defence treaty with the Israelis, in order to guarantee the use of her facilities in wartime. In March 1949, the JPS urged that either the UK or the US should conclude a military treaty with Israel – one that would guarantee the Allies full use of her military facilities and, if possible, the aid of her army.[37]

[33] Bevin memo of 13 March 1946, DO (46) 40, Cab 131/21. PRO.
[34] Ibid.
[35] DO (46) 17th. 27 May 1946, Cab 131/1. PRO.
[36] Minute by Robert Howe, 19 Sept. 1946, and DO (46) 25th, same date, in E9755, FO 371/52559. PRO.
[37] JP (49), 30 March 1949, Defe 6/8, and JP (49) 59, 11 July 1949, Defe 4/23. PRO.

It was almost self-evident that it would be inappropriate for the British themselves to approach the Israelis. During the latter stages of the Palestine mandate, and even more so during the latter stages of the first Arab–Israeli war, Anglo–Israeli relations had deteriorated to their nadir. The Israeli leadership, and Ben-Gurion in particular, had developed an anathema for the British which, focusing on the alleged anti-semitism of Foreign Secretary Bevin, bordered on the neurotic.[38]

In August 1949, Bevin informed the Cabinet that Britain would not seek strategic facilities in Israel in peacetime, largely because of 'the political pressure' to which this might expose them. He believed that the Americans would find it easier to secure the required agreement with Israel.[39]

In May 1950, the C. in C.s Middle East, in their review of strategy in their theatre, entreated the government to take urgent steps, in conjunction with the Americans, to improve relations with Israel, so as to ensure her friendly co-operation 'in war and during the period when war is imminent'.[40]

But the Foreign Office regarded any *démarche* towards Israel as premature. At the same time, referring to persisting Israeli animosity toward the UK, the Foreign Office stressed the importance of doing: 'everything possible to counter any tendency to Maginot-mindedness on the part of the Israelis'.[41]

American planners agreed that Britain and the United States had almost identical strategic interests in the Middle East. However, in evident reference to President Truman's diplomatic support for Israel, over the opposition of his State Department, the JCS noted that:

> the international reactions to the Palestine question have produced a complex, entangled political and psychological situation . . .[42]

At the end of April 1949, the American CINCELM pressed the JCS to allot the highest priority to ensuring Israel's friendship. He warned of the possibility of Israeli resistance to the entry of Allied troops, 'particularly British', into Palestine. During at least the early stages of any emergency, only British troops would be available, and they were likely

---

[38] On Zionist (and Ben-Gurion's in particular) attitudes to Bevin, cf. Cohen, *Palestine and . . .*, pp.66–67, 76, 226–7; and Avi Shlaim, *Collusion Across the Jordan: King Abdullah, the Zionist Movement and the Partition of Palestine*, Oxford: Oxford University Press, 1988, pp.84–5.

[39] CP (49) 183, 25 Aug. 1949, Cab 129/36. PRO.

[40] Review of Middle East Strategy by C.in Cs, Middle East, JP (50) 48, 19 May 1950, Defe 6/13. PRO.

[41] Minute by John C. Wardrop, 22 Nov. 1950, ER1022, FO 371/82515. PRO.

[42] JCS 1684/28, 1 April 1949, CCS 092 Pal (5-3-46) sect. 7; and RG 330 (Secretary of Defense) box 22, CD 6-2-47, 16 May 1949. NA.

to encounter serious interference with their operations. A hostile Israel would also hinder seriously hinder the construction of forward airfields on her territory, and the free movement of forces and equipment along their planned lines of communication.[43]

In fact, the British representatives in Cairo (not known previously for their benign disposition towards Israel) had for some time been pondering whether they should not spurn the Arabs and throw in their lot with the Israelis. It will be recalled that in early 1949, these same officials had pressed London to take military measures against Israel in the Negev, to ensure that the strategic arteries of the Middle East remained in 'reliable' Arab hands (above, Chapter 4).

Their second thoughts were not generated by any sudden infatuation with the Israelis. By early 1950, the British establishment in Cairo had become exasperated with Egyptian 'intransigence'. John Troutbeck, head of the British Middle East Office in Cairo, mused on the idea of teaching the 'ungrateful' Egyptians a 'lesson':

> It sometimes seems to me that the Egyptians are a little too confident in their belief that we cannot do without them, and are singularly blind to their dependence on us. A visit to Tel Aviv might help to show them that for better or worse there are other people in the Middle East to-day whose affairs concern us, and that they may have rivals for our support.[44]

But the Foreign Office reined in the officials in Cairo. It would be imprudent to base British interests in the region entirely on Israel. The latter's economic importance to Britain was never likely to match that of the Arab states – Israel could never replace the oil and cotton Britain imported from the Middle East. And the Arab states would always have 'far greater strategic importance geographically'. Britain's main Middle East base, for geographical reasons, had to be in Egypt; the airfields she required for offensive purposes were primarily in Egypt, with Iraq, Jordan, and Syria 'playing an appreciable role'. Air bases in Israel would indeed be useful, but could never substitute adequately for those on Arab soil.[45]

Nonetheless, in the summer of 1950, following yet another 'unsatisfactory turn in the talks with Egypt', the Foreign Office asked the COS to look into the possibility of either Israel or Cyprus taking Egypt's place as Britain's main base in the Middle East. Their headquarters and installations might be located in one of these countries, with the striking-force being stationed in the Gaza Strip (on which, see above,

---

[43] C in C, Atlantic and Middle East (Navy) to JCS, 29 Sept. 1949, appendix to JCS 2034/1, 381 NE TS., P and O, 49–50, RG 318 army staff. NA.

[44] John Troutbeck to Michael Wright, 6 Feb. 1950, ER1054, FO 371/82528. PRO.

[45] Minute by Michael Wright, 20 April 1950, E1055, FO 371/81928. PRO.

Chapter, 5). And all this, if only to demonstrate to the Egyptians that their facilities were not so essential to Britain as they apparently believed. The Foreign Office appreciated that the implications of such a move, if militarily and strategically feasible, would be very far-reaching; any agreement with Israel would mean the end of any British military presence in Egypt. But they would first need to check if there was any chance that the Israelis would grant them facilities, and if so, at what price?[46]

Shortly after, in late September 1950, Sir Knox Helm, the British *chargé* at Tel Aviv, reported on a meeting with the Israeli Chief of Staff, General Yigal Yadin. The latter had made it quite clear that, for the present, there could be no question whatever of Israel permitting the establishment of British military bases on her territory in peacetime. However, at the same time, Yadin stated that he and his government appreciated that in the event of war, their country would be on the side of the West, and that the Allies would need to use Israeli airfields. Yadin agreed that it would be best to make preparations for the latter contingency straight away.[47]

In October 1950, the British Secretary of State for Air, Viscount Stansgate, on a visit to Israel, also enquired about the acquisition of base rights in Israel. It was explained to Stansgate that, for the present, this would be unacceptable to the Israeli public. However, the Minister received assurances that, in the event of a Soviet attack, the West would enjoy Israel's full support.[48]

Apparently carried away by these Israeli expressions of support for the West, Knox Helm went so far as to propose that, for political reasons, Britain should try to secure Israeli agreement to the establishment of her Middle East HQ, and/or a base for the Striking Force, on Israeli soil proper. Helm suggested Haifa as a suitable location, rather than the Gaza area, which was currently under discussion. Helm reasoned that the Gaza project, which in effect would require 'active Israeli strategic collaboration . . . would involve the Israelis in all of the liabilities whilst conferring on them few of the advantages' that would accrue from using their territory. On the other hand, a main British base in Israel proper would bring her both economic benefits, and provide a 'comprehensive guarantee' against Arab aggression.[49]

But the COS ruled out the idea of transferring their main base instal-

---

[46] Geoffrey Furlonge to Lt Col Henenge (Secretary to COS), 31 Aug. 1950, FO 371/81962. PRO.

[47] Sir Knox Helm to Wright, 29 Sept. 1950, ER 1223/33, FO 371/82578. PRO.

[48] Devereux, *The Formulation . . .*, p.151.

[49] COS (51) 28, 18 Jan. 1951, enclosing FO to Secretary, COS, 12 Jan. 1951, Defe 5/27. PRO.

lations to Israel on military grounds. It would be militarily imprudent to locate such large quantities of stocks and stores so far forward; and, in the event of war, they would have neither the time nor the resources in which to re-establish the main base back in Egypt.[50]

However, if Egypt was irreplaceable as Britain's main Middle Eastern base, what were the British to do if in the final account, they were nonetheless forced, for political reasons, to evacuate their base there?

At the beginning of October 1950, the JPS advised that in the event of their withdrawal from Egypt, their regional HQ would have to be located wherever Army HQ (MELF) and Air HQ (MEAF) were situated. These installations should all be located close enough to Egypt to enable them to return there upon the outbreak of war 'as rapidly as possible and with the minimum dislocation of command and control'. On these counts, Israel in fact appeared to be the most suitable location. Upon the outbreak of war, the MELF and MEAF HQs, and the nucleus of the Regional HQ, would be able to return rapidly to Egypt, leaving in Israel 'the commanders and staffs responsible for the conduct of operations'.[51]

The JPS next made a detailed study of the advantages, and problems involved in establishing an interim base in Israel. The functions of such a base were elaborated as follows: to accommodate those stores which could not be left in Egypt; and to provide services and maintenance for their Middle East garrison during the early stages of a war, until they were able to re-establish themselves in Egypt.[52]

Israel was well situated from the logistical point of view, and any installations constructed there might continue to assist Allied operations even after the Egyptian base had been reactivated. The port of Haifa could be expanded to meet British requirements. Finally, Israel would be able to supply all the labour Britain might require, both skilled and unskilled.

However, several hurdles would first have to be overcome. First and foremost were Israel's own political objections to the return of the British, in any form and for whatever reason. The Allies would require guarantees of immediate access to Israel's facilities upon the outbreak of war, and full transit rights to all adjacent countries, both in peace and in war. There were also doubts as to whether Israel would agree to the stationing of the British Striking Force in the Gaza Strip.

The JPS in effect ruled out the establishment of a British base, even interim, in Israel. They doubted very much whether Israel would allow the stationing of British troops on her soil in peacetime – both the right

---

[50] JP (50) 124, 11 Sept. 1950, Defe 6/14, PRO.
[51] JP (50) 124, final, 4 Oct. 1950, Defe 6/14. PRO.
[52] For this and following, see appendix D to JP (50) 141, 16 Oct. 1950, Defe 6/14. PRO.

and left wings in Israel would undoubtedly oppose it, and if the government of the time chose to ignore this opposition there might even occur 'some recrudescence of terrorism'.

And in any case, the Arabs would certainly react unfavorably to the establishment of any British military facilities, and to the stationing of British troops, in Israel. Most of all, the JPS feared that the Iraqi government might use an Anglo–Israeli military agreement as a pretext upon which to abrogate the Anglo–Iraqi treaty.[53]

This left the British with the option of trying to secure transit rights through Israel in peacetime, and access to her military facilities in an emergency. It was in order to sound out the Israelis on these questions, that the COS began to consider sending General Sir Brian Robertson, C. in C., MELF, to Israel.

The British had received several indications since the summer of 1950 of Israel's pro-Western disposition. In July 1950, Admiral J.H. Edelsten, C. in C. British Naval Forces in the Mediterranean, had paid a short courtesy visit to Haifa. Edelsten had been impressed with the Israelis' 'siege mentality', the fear that they were about to be attacked by the Arab states. In his view, Israel's sense of isolation, and her grave economic problems (caused mainly by expenditures on new immigrants, and arms) made her the more amenable to defence talks with the West.[54]

By early December 1950, both the War Office and the Admiralty favoured a direct approach to Israel. At the very lowest estimate, they would need advance guarantees of transit rights through Israel in an emergency.[55]

The Foreign Office still demurred. The latest reports from Knox Helm in Tel Aviv indicated that the rapprochement with Israel should not be 'hurried', since the Israelis, perceiving British difficulties with the Egyptians, might chose to extort a high price for their services. Furthermore, the Foreign Office thought that American intercession on their behalf, or at the least, support for their own *démarche* toward Israel, was a *sine qua non*. They felt that the State Department had yet to be convinced of Israel's strategic importance to the West. Furthermore, the Americans assumed that in order to secure Israel's military facilities during a war, it would suffice to promise to keep her supplied with the necessities of life.[56]

[53] Ibid.

[54] Admiral Edelsten to Admiralty, 17 July 1950, FO 371/82576; COS (50) 459, 7 Nov. 1950, Defe 5/25; and ibid.

[55] R. J. Bowker to Sir Esler Dening, 18 Jan. 1951, E1192, FO 371/91219. PRO.

[56] Minute by John Wardrop, 22 Nov. 1950, ER1022, FO 371/82515; and Furlonge – Knox Helm, 7 Dec. 1950, ER1022/33G, FO 371/82515. PRO.

But in late December 1950, the Israelis themselves approached the Americans for military aid. They suggested that the US establish in Israel strategic stockpiles of essential materials, including preserved foods, grain, oil seeds, petroleum and basic raw materials. Israel suggested that the US issue contracts to Israeli arms factories, and help develop Israel's port facilities.[57] At the end of the month, Theodore (Teddy) Kollek, Minister at the Israeli embassy in Washington, told Mr Stuart Rockwell, head of the Israel desk at the State Department, that Israel's policy of non-identification had been a failure; and that Israel was willing to place its army of 30–40,000, plus reserves, at the disposal of the West, and would allow Western armies to use its military facilities. Rockwell made it clear to Kollek that:

> ... the UK had a primary role to play in the defense of the Near East, and that any plans which the US might have for this defense would certainly involve cooperation with the UK.[58]

Kollek explained that there still existed a 'psychological barrier' between the Israelis and the British, even if he conceded that this was decreasing rapidly. The Israelis were given to understand, quite clearly, that they would have to deal with the British in regard to their security needs. The Americans reported to the British on the Israeli initiative, and advised them to 'act quickly', to take advantage of Israel's current mood.[59]

In September 1950, the COS had sent Gen Robertson on a round of visits to Arab capitals, (and 'possibly Tel Aviv'), for discussions with their defence Ministers on the defence of the region against a possible Soviet attack. During the winter, Robertson had visited Baghdad, Amman, Beirut, Damascus and Riyadh.

At the beginning of 1951, in consultation with Bevin, the decision was taken to despatch Gen Robertson to Israel. One last, decisive factor tipped the scales. In mid-December 1950, a further round of talks between Bevin and the Egyptian Foreign Minister had broken down. At the same time, the latter, while insisting that his country would not

---

[57] Moshe Sharett (Israeli Foreign Minister) to Gen Marshall (Secretary of Defense), 23 Dec. 1950, *FRUS*, 1950, Vol. V, pp.1079–81.

[58] Record of conversation between Teddy Kollek and Stuart W. Rockwell (Officer in charge of Palestine, Israel and Jordan Affairs), 28 Dec. 1950, *FRUS*, 1950, Vol. V, p.1083, and also conversation, at lunch, together with Col. Vivian (Chaim) Herzog (Military Attaché, Israeli Embassy), and Major General James Burns (Department of Defense), idem, pp.1084–85.

[59] Washington Embassy to Foreign Office, telegrams of 5 Jan. 1951, E1073/2, E1073/3, FO 371/91206. PRO; and Ben-Gurion diary entry, 27 Jan. 1951, Ben-Gurion Archives (BGA).

co-operate in any way with Israel, had quietly let it be known that he would have no objections to an Anglo–Israeli agreement.[60]

C. GENERAL ROBERTSON'S VISIT TO ISRAEL, FEBRUARY 1951

In mid-January 1951, Sir William Strang (Permanent Under-Secretary at the Foreign Office), invited Eliahu Elath, the Israeli envoy in London, for a 'private talk' at the Travellers Club. Strang informed Elath that Gen Robertson wished to visit Israel on 19 February, for strictly military talks. Perhaps because this was a 'private talk', Strang went beyond the existing consensus, that Israel would not contemplate a British return to Palestine. He told Elath that Britain was seeking defence treaties in the Middle East, either regional or bilateral. He doubted if either Jordan or Egypt would join them. So what the British had in mind was either to set up bases in Israel; or to build a British base in the Gaza area, with a corridor [through Israel] to Jordan.[61]

Taking Strang literally at his word, Elath flew to Tel Aviv to deliver the message in person to Prime Minister Ben-Gurion. The latter was furious with Elath for giving the matter such publicity. Ben-Gurion dismissed Britain's 'insulting proposal' out of hand. The Israeli Prime Minister was willing to sign a tripartite treaty with both Britain and the United States, but not with the British alone. He felt that the US had never harmed Israel, in contrast to the UK, and he wanted the former, not the British, to defend the Middle East, including Israel.[62]

Ben-Gurion feared that giving bases to the British would not only arouse the ire of the Soviets (and thereby sabotage any chance of further Jewish emigration from Eastern Europe) but would also place Israel at the Arabs' mercy. The presence of British bases in Israel would curtail Israel's freedom 'to deal with' the Arabs if they infringed the armistice agreements.[63]

But Ben-Gurion was looking for concrete evidence of the West's commitment, in the currency of military and economic aid. So he did not veto Robertson's visit.

At the beginning of February, Elath returned to London with the official reply that Israel would never side against the West in a conflict. However, any discussion of bases was still 'premature'. Israel wanted to

---

[60] Furlonge minute, 12 Dec. 1950, ER1022/35, FO 371/8215, and L. C. Fry brief for Bevin, 15 Feb. 1951, E1201/50, FO 371/91240. PRO.

[61] Cf. Bialer, *Between East . . .*, pp.235–36; and Ben-Gurion diary entry, 27 Jan. 1951, BGA.

[62] Ben-Gurion diary, ibid.

[63] Ibid.

know how she was to fit into a region where she was still unrecognised by the Arab states, with some of whom Britain had special treaty or contractual relations?[64]

Strang's initiative had apparently been only a 'trial balloon'. Ben-Gurion's reply did not surprise or deter the British who, in any case had determined already that Gen Robertson should not raise the base issue.[65]

Robertson was briefed to be extremely cautious in his approach, and to bear in mind persisting Israeli memories of the British occupation, and their reluctance to make an open commitment to the West, for fear of alienating the Soviets. Ben-Gurion was expected to want to 'talk business'. But Robertson was instructed not to commit Britain in any way, for fear of possible repercussions on the Arab world. He was to outline the strategic importance of the Middle East for the West, in view of the Soviet threat.[66]

Robertson's primary task was to try to secure the Israelis' agreement to the use of their facilities in the event of war, and to ascertain what the Israeli 'price' would be. In war, Britain would require the unrestricted use of Israel's roads, railways, ports, and other communications, and unrestricted overflying rights. Robertson was to enquire about the capacity of Israeli facilities to handle military traffic, and to find out how the British might help to expand that capacity. It was made clear to Robertson that the Israelis would not hand over control of their facilities to the British, either in peace or in war. Finally, he was instructed to adopt a gradual approach, and warned 'to beware of their trying to cause you to show your hand without a corresponding frankness on their part'. He was also given a list of arms that Britain was *not* willing to supply to the Israelis (in particular, modern tanks and radar, and jet aircraft).[67]

Gen Robertson was advised also that the Israelis would 'fanatically oppose' any violation of their territorial integrity, by either the Soviets or the British themselves, and 'would naturally prefer a Russian southward drive to be met not in but rather to the north of Israel'.[68]

Thus Gen Robertson was sent on a virtually impossible mission. He was to try to convince the Israelis that the West was determined and able to repel a Soviet offensive against the Middle East. Yet at the

---

[64] Knox Helm to Foreign Office, 4 Feb. 1951, E1201/37/G. FO 371/91240. PRO; and Bialer, *Between East. . .*, p.237.

[65] J. Wardrop minute, 5 Feb. 1951, E120/37, FO 371/91240. PRO.

[66] Political briefs for Gen Robertson, annex to JP (51) 21, 9 Feb. 1951, Defe 6/16; and DO (51) 8, 13 Feb. 1951, Cab 131/11. PRO.

[67] Ibid.

[68] Foreign Office to Secretary, COS, 12 Jan. 1951, in COS (51) 28, 18 Jan. 1951, Defe 5/27. PRO.

same time, he was barred from revealing to the Israelis what they most wanted to know – the true nature of Britain's defence plans for the Middle East. This was because their current plan, *Celery*, still rested on the Ramallah line, which cut right through the centre of Israel.

In addition, as pointed out in the Defence Committee by Emmanuel Shinwell, the Israelis were unlikely to be drawn into the Western camp if Britain was unwilling to supply them with what they most required, and without which they were unlikely to be militarily effective – modern radar, jet aircraft and tanks. But Shinwell was in a minority. It was pointed out that they were only seeking transit facilities in peacetime. Furthermore, Chancellor of the Exchequer Hugh Gaitskell took care to stress that 'if the Israelis wanted arms from us they would have to pay for them'.[69]

Gen Robertson arrived in Tel Aviv on 19 February 1951. He opened his visit with a short courtesy call on Foreign Minister Sharett. Their talk ranged across foreign policy issues, such as Jewish immigration from Eastern Europe, reparations from Germany, and the situation in central Europe. Only at the close of their meeting did Robertson revert to the military situation in the Middle East. He reassured Sharett that the Americans were changing their attitude to the region, and preparing with the British for the danger of a Soviet attack on the Middle East![70]

Gen Robertson held his first meeting with Ben-Gurion at 4.45 p.m. that same afternoon. It lasted for just under one-and-a-half hours.[71] He opened the meeting by elaborating on Britain's strategic interests in the Middle East. To their traditional interests, had now been added the goal of 'preventing the spread of Communism into Africa'. He tried to reassure Ben-Gurion that the Middle East would be easier to defend than Europe, since the Soviets would be unable to deploy their 'massive force' easily across the region's desert wastes.

This did not convince Ben-Gurion. He asked whether the British were really prepared to defend the Middle East. Which forces would they have at their disposal, which resources would they mobilise, and what would be Israel's role?

As Robertson reported back to London, the question as to what role Israel was to play was raised by Ben-Gurion very 'forcibly'. But the

[69] Defence Committee meeting, 16 Feb. 1951, DO (51) 2d., Cab 131/10. PRO.

[70] Editorial note, *I.D.* 1951, Vol. 6, p.116.

[71] The following account of their meeting is based on both the British and the Israeli records. Gen. Robertson's own reports on the meetings are to be found in his despatch to the Foreign Office, 22 Feb. 1951, E1201/58, FO 371/91240; also in COS (51) 153, 21 March 1951, Defe 5/29. The Israeli account was written by Michael Comay (Head of the Israeli Foreign Ministry's British Commonwealth division), who was present; it is to be found in file 2457, Central Zionist Archives (CZA), and in *I.D.*, 1951, vol. 6, no. 68, pp.116–24; see also Ben-Gurion diary entry, 19 Feb. 1951, BGA; and Bialer, *Between East. . .*, pp.238–9.

latter had displayed no interest in playing a passive role. He was concerned for Israel's very survival. Ben-Gurion persisted – how seriously did Britain intend to defend the Middle East, and did Robertson believe that they had a reasonable chance of doing so?

But this was the very question most difficult for the British to answer. The British were precluded by the Arabs from deploying the Israeli army on Arab territories; and precluded for obvious reasons from revealing their real contingency plans. Robertson's answer was a blend of obfuscation and disingenuity.

He replied that British troop dispositions in the Middle East (in Egypt, Cyrenaica, Tripoli and Cyprus) were no secret. In time of war, they would bring in reinforcements. As for the defence of Israel itself, he explained to Ben-Gurion that 'the proper place to defend the Middle East as a whole is in the mountains of Turkey and the mountains of Iran and Iraq'.

He tried to persuade Ben-Gurion that Britain's 'relatively weak' ground forces, with the aid of the Air force, would be able to hold up the Soviets in the mountain passes. In this connection, Robertson laid great stress on the importance of the Turkish contribution, in holding the north and north-eastern approaches to the Middle East. Naturally, Robertson did not mention to his interlocutor that Britain would not for the foreseeable future have sufficient forces to hold the mountain line (the Outer Ring). And that so far, the Americans had proved impervious to British pleas for reinforcements in the Middle East theatre.

In response to Ben-Gurion's question about Israel's role, Robertson stated that the best airfields north of Egypt were in Israel. Israel in fact controlled 'most of the communications to the north and east', the areas in which they hoped to engage the Soviets. As Robertson conceded, it was Israel's communications that interested him most:

> We would want to come through Israel as soon as there was a definite threat of aggression, or at least as soon as the first Russian entered Persia or Turkey . . . The question for me is, whether British troops would be allowed to go through your country and whether our planes could use your airfields when aggression against the Middle East became imminent?

Ben-Gurion asked whether the British were interested only in Israel's communications and airfields, or did they want her also to take an active part in the fighting? He wanted Israel to be privy to Western planning and to play an active role in the West's common war effort. He tried to impress Robertson with Israel's military potential (they had mobilised 16–20% of the population in 1948, and could do even better now) which, if mobilised for the West, would be the equivalent of Britain bringing in reinforcements.

Ben-Gurion next named the 'price' for Israeli co-operation in war. Israel, he claimed, was the only modern European state in the region, and it would be in the West's strategic interest to build up her industry and agriculture, as well as her military potential, in peace time. Israel would then be able to serve as a workshop and supply centre for the Allies in time of need.

Robertson stalled again. He would like to see Israeli forces deployed to the maximum advantage, but he could not now tell what role would be 'politically practicable'. Ben-Gurion asked Robertson, almost rhetorically, whether the British did not want to supply them with arms for fear of possible Arab objections. Robertson responded, again disingenuously, that his government was now ready to supply arms, subject only to availability.

Ben-Gurion spoke at length of Israel's ideological disposition towards the Western democracies. He told Robertson that 'a small proportion' of Israel's population, perhaps 10–12%, were oriented towards the Soviet Union. But 85% would fight for the two goals to which he had referred – Israel's independence, and its democratic way of life. He continued that experience had shown that their Jewish way of life could not survive under dictatorship. Therefore, Israel now saw its future as lying with the West. However, that allegiance would depend upon the West first taking practical steps to help Israel consolidate herself along the lines he'd already noted.

Robertson agreed that Israel might become an important workshop in wartime, and hinted that certain things might be begun with now. However, when he again asked Ben-Gurion for an assurance that British troops would be welcomed through Israel in war, it was Ben-Gurion's turn to prevaricate. The latter tabled another proposal – that the British should help mediate a peace agreement between Israel and Egypt. This too 'would be worth a number of divisions' to them.

The meeting ended with Robertson pleading for a little more trust between their countries, and a confidential exchange of military information. With not a little naïveté, he tried to assure Ben-Gurion that Israel's military secrets would be safe with the British – that he would 'sack' any of his officers who passed them on to the Arabs.

Gen Robertson next held two meetings with Gen Yigal Yadin, the Israeli Chief of Staff.

At 8.45 a.m. on 20 February, the two generals met for a little over half an hour, accompanied only by military personnel. Robertson did most of the talking. He tried to persuade Yadin that the Soviets would have great difficulty traversing the natural barriers of the Middle East. However, he was less than candid when he stated that *the Anglo–American defence line would run through the mountains of Turkey, Iraq and*

Iran (my emphasis) He tried again to convince his interlocutors that Israel could now trust the British, that their military secrets would be safe with them. And as 'proof', he pointed to the undeniable fact that he was not telling the Israelis the Arabs' secrets! And finally, Robertson again stressed that Israel's major contribution to the Allied war effort would lie in the fact that her territory lay across the main lines of communication between Egypt and the front lines. With regard to arms supplies, Robertson made it clear that supplies from the West would depend upon the role allotted to Israel. As an example, he stated that it would be easier for him now to order AA guns for Haifa harbour, than to secure anything else.[72]

At 11.45 p.m. the next day, 21 February, the two generals again met, this time for a little over an hour. Major Coverdale, Robertson's *aide de camp*, was the only other person present. This time Gen Yadin elaborated on the structure and problems of the IDF. He explained the Israelis' sensitivity to divulging military details to the British. It was due in part to the fact that the Arab Legion was still commanded by British officers. Some of these had served in Palestine, and some might still serve as a channel for passing on Israel's secrets to the Arabs; he also noted the joint Anglo–Egyptian military manoeuvres, as an example of the close military collaboration that existed between the British and the Arabs. Yadin advised the general not to believe that there were any secrets in this part of the world, and revealed that Israel had received all kinds of rumours leaked from Robertson's talks with the Arabs. Yadin concluded that the IDF could not make do with Robertson's general ruminations about the defence of the Middle East. They would need to know the role envisaged for Israel in the defence of the Middle East. Robertson retorted that he had been misunderstood. He believed that Israel should play an active role in time of war – but he wasn't yet sure what that role should be.[73]

It was from this point, Israel's role in the event of war, that Robertson resumed, when he met Ben-Gurion for the second and last time that same evening at 6.00 p.m. Their talk lasted just over an hour.[74]

Robertson tried to humour Ben-Gurion. He explained that he had perhaps given the wrong impression at their first meeting. When he had stated that a 'primary' role for Israel would be as a base and communications centre, he had used 'primary' in the sense of important. He

---

[72] Cf. Israeli note of the meeting, in *I.D.*, 1951, Vol. 6, No. 69, pp.124–5.

[73] Israeli note of Yadin – Robertson meeting, 21 Feb. 1951, ibid., No. 71, pp.128–9.

[74] What follows is based on Comay's summary, ibid., No. 72, pp.129–35; and Gen Robertson's report of 22 Feb. 1951, in E1201/58, FO 371/91240, and COS (51) 153, Defe 5/29. PRO.

hadn't come to elicit an official decision on base facilities from the Israeli government, but only to collect data, on which Britain could base her theatre plans for the Middle East. He had not received a clear reply on this at their previous meeting and was hoping for one before he left.

Robertson was unclear which role Israel could actively play, but was ready to discuss this with the Israelis. He stressed that Britain would like to see Israel 'as an active partner', but due to 'political considerations', this would require further study.

At this point, Ben-Gurion dropped a political 'bombshell' – one that came to overshadow the whole visit, and one that has become the focus of most subsequent historical accounts. Noting first that he was talking about the very survival of Israel, which could not be guaranteed without allies, and that this was his own private opinion, he stated: 'Israel should act in an emergency as if she were a member of the British Commonwealth . . . *He did not mean that Israel should become a member of the Commonwealth but that she should behave and be treated as if she were'.*[75]

Ben-Gurion wanted Britain's full recognition of Israel's superior military and strategic assets. If the British continued to treat Israel as she did her Arab Allies, she would 'miss the main point'. Israel would fight for its freedom, come what may. But in the event of war, would Britain treat her like it treated New Zealand, as if she were a member of the Commonwealth? Ben-Gurion stated that this was his reply to Robertson's persistent queries about Israel's military facilities.

Gen Robertson was quite evidently taken aback, and somewhat confused. After some hesitation to collect his thoughts, he expressed his admiration for Ben-Gurion, as being a 'big man'.[76] Of course, this was a political issue, and Ben-Gurion would not expect a reply from him, a general. He undertook personally to do everything he could to foster this type of a relationship.

Robertson then reverted eagerly to military details, and expressed willingness to help Israel develop and extend its logistical infrastructure. He was especially interested in communications, land and air, between Israel and Jordan, where the British held garrisons at Amman and at Aqaba. He informed the Israelis that the British also had treaty rights to station the RAF in Jordan, rights that they had not yet taken up. They might extend the runways at Mafraq, in order to accommodate RAF aircraft. If they did, they might request air transit rights across Israel, in order to maintain this force. Robertson also asked for flying rights across Israel in peacetime, for both civilian and military aircraft.

---

[75] Robertson report, 22 Feb. 1951, ibid. My emphasis.
[76] Comay account, *I.D.*, 1951, Vol. 6, No. 72, pp.129–35.

There was some discussion also about the vital Suez–Aqaba overland route. When Ben-Gurion spoke of Israeli plans to develop a new port at Elath, across the bay from Aqaba, Robertson expressed great interest, and readiness to furnish British aid.

Robertson suggested that talks between the two countries be continued at the military staff level; on the Israelis' role in war, and the standardisation of weapons, and training. But Ben-Gurion made it clear that he first wanted London's reply to his initiative – he was interested in what was going to happen now! Robertson tried again to allay the Israeli Prime Minister's fears – the British government 'intended to defend the Middle East with all available resources' and, if Ben-Gurion wanted him to do so, he would despatch British troops to Israel in the event of war.

This second and last meeting ended with what Robertson later termed 'a rather verbose statement' by Foreign Minister Sharett. The latter tried to impress Gen Robertson with what a difficult decision the government had taken in receiving him at all, in the face of widespread and vigorous domestic opposition. Robertson was not impressed, and in his report to London, dismissed the 'few demonstrations' that had taken place as 'domestic squibs'.[77]

At their first meeting, Gen Robertson had suggested sending to Israel some of his officers, either in uniform, or in civilian clothes, in order to check out the state of their communications systems. The Israeli record, which notes Robertson's suggestion, does not record any Israeli reply. But Robertson reported back that the Israelis had agreed to a visit by British officers in civilian clothes.[78] It would take a further 20 months before that visit took place.

D. ASSESSMENT OF AND REACTION TO
GEN. ROBERTSON'S VISIT

Ben-Gurion himself never apparently explained the motive behind his Commonwealth proposal. A recent interpretation by an Israeli historian has suggested that he did not seek a definite treaty (as suggested early by Bar-Zohar, his first biographer), but wanted merely to 'outline the sort of preconditions which had to exist before such a relationship could become possible'.[79] This explanation is incomplete.

Ben-Gurion had a habit of floating 'grand', even 'grandiose' ideas. It

[77] Robertson report, 22 Feb. 1951, supra.
[78] Comay record, *I.D.*, 1951, Vol. 6, p.122; and COS (51) 282, 7 May 1951, Defe 5/31. PRO.
[79] Cf., Bialer, *Between East . . .*, pp.238–9.

would appear to this author that there exists a quite simple explanation for this particular one.

Ben-Gurion had been convinced by the Americans that, in the event of a global war, the British would be responsible for the defence of the Middle East. However, he was still incensed at Britain's traditionally pro-Arab policies, which had brought Israel and Britain to the brink of war just two years earlier. He had yet to be convinced that Bevin's attitude had changed. He respected the ideals and valour of the British people, but Labour's policies in the Middle East, as orchestrated by Bevin from the Foreign Office, were anathema to him.

Gen Robertson had in fact done little to allay Ben-Gurion's suspicions. Both sides had held their cards very close to their chest, and neither side to the dialogue had deluded himself otherwise. Robertson's hands were in any case firmly tied behind his back. Ben-Gurion now wanted the British to make a symbolic gesture that would indicate beyond any doubt that their policy in the Middle East had undergone a revolution.

He therefore aimed for nothing less than British recognition of a privileged position for Israel in the Middle East. He was no longer prepared to play 'second fiddle' to the Arabs. If Israel was really so militarily and strategically important to the Allies, as Robertson insisted, Ben-Gurion wanted material, manifest proof.

Thus, having elicited very little from the general at their first meeting, he had asked at their second meeting for a public guarantee of Britain's commitment to Israel's survival in the event of war. This was his reasoning in asking that Israel, in an emergency, be treated like New Zealand.

In addition, and of perhaps no less consequence, such a public guarantee would have enabled Ben-Gurion to justify to the Israeli public, and to his coalition colleagues, such a radical switch in Israel's established foreign policy, from non-alignment, to open military alliance with the West.

In effect, the British had been upstaged by Ben-Gurion. As they realised now, the Israeli 'price' for the use of their facilities and communications would be nothing less than a defence commitment similar to that which they had given to their Commonwealth Allies. They concluded this from Ben-Gurion's statement to Gen Robertson: 'In saying this to you I have answered all your questions'. Gen Robertson and Knox Helm reported back to London that Ben-Gurion had been sincere. His proposal had not simply been a 'smokescreen', to avoid giving a straight reply.

In fact, the British should not have been entirely taken aback by Ben-Gurion's proposal. He had told Knox Helm the previous June that many in Israel thought it too late already for Israel to become a part of the British Commonwealth. But he, Ben-Gurion, did not think so.[80] Many British colonies that had been granted independence, had subsequently been co-opted into the Commonwealth.

But the Foreign Office had no intention of granting Ben-Gurion's request. However, given that the military were not yet ready to relinquish Israel's facilities, their reply would have to be drafted with the utmost care, to avoid the impression of a snub.[81] They still deluded themselves that they would able to secure what they required in Israel through diplomatic *legerdemain*.

The Foreign Office understood very well that what Ben-Gurion wanted was that if the tide of war turned against the Allies in the Middle East, they would concentrate everything on defending Israel, 'regardless of wider strategic considerations'. Therefore, in order to impress Ben-Gurion, it was decided that their reply should be sent over the signature of the new Foreign Secretary, Herbert Morrison.[82]

But before drafting its reply, the government commissioned an updated COS analysis of the feasibility of constructing an interim base in Israel. The COS had not only derived encouragement from Ben-Gurion's proposal, but were ever more concerned at the persisting crisis with Egypt, and the certain prospect of having to evacuate that country by 1956 at the latest. On 7 March 1951, the COS reported back to the Defence Committee:

> From a military point of view the only practicable location for an interim base to support the forces in peace and in the opening stages of a war would be in Israel . . .
> Unless the military requirements for an interim base in Israel can be met or unless some means can be found to ensure the full functioning of the Middle East Base in Egypt in peace after December 1956, *we must accept the fact that from 1957 onwards the chances of losing the Middle East altogether in the early stages of a war are very real.*[83]

But at the same time, the COS appreciated that what they were proposing – the stationing of large numbers of troops in Israel, and the construction there of a number of air bases – would in fact be tantamount to a renewed British occupation. An interim base in Israel would take some eight years to build, although it might be partially operational by 1956 (the expiry-date of the Anglo–Egyptian treaty); and, last but

---

[80] Knox Helm to Foreign Office, 1 July 1950, ER1054/37, FO 371/82529. PRO.

[81] John Wardrop minute, 3 March 1951, E1201/61, FO 371/91240. PRO.

[82] John Wardrop minute, 16 March 1951, E1201/64, Ibid. Morrison replaced Bevin, who retired due to ill-health, on 9 March 1951.

[83] DO (51) 26, 7 March 1951, Cab 131/11. PRO, my emphasis.

not least, the cost of building the projected base in Israel, now estimated at some £50 million, was prohibitive.[84]

Thus the COS were forced to conclude that the construction
of a military base in Israel in peacetime was both politically and economically unfeasible. The Defence Committee confirmed the conclusions of the JPS:

> On the grounds of expense and because it would be unrealistic to count on
> Israeli help to the extent required, *there can be no question of establishing an interim
> base in Israel, the only location suitable for it.*[85]

In the meantime, Ben-Gurion turned down the British request for
permission for the RAF to fly through an air corridor over Lydda
(Israel) to Mafraq (Jordan). Ben-Gurion pleaded that he had to postpone his answer until after the elections in Israel (held on 30 July 1951).
He feared that the sight of RAF aircraft flying across Israel would be
used by the Opposition against him. This would serve neither Israeli
nor British interests. Eventually, in response to repeated British
requests, in December 1951, Ben-Gurion agreed to four flights of
unarmed British transport planes across Israeli territory per week.[86]

But the COS still attached the highest priority to securing Israel's
agreement to the use of her military facilities in war, and to transit rights
in peacetime. They advised against jeopardising this prospect by linking
it to the far more dubious question of Israel readmitting large numbers
of British troops to her country in time of peace.[87]

In the light of these assessments, the Foreign Office drew up a draft
reply to Ben-Gurion, which was amended and approved by the Defence
Committee on 9 April 1951. Morrison made it clear that while not
wishing to 'rebuff' Ben-Gurion, the government could hardly accept his
proposal, especially in view of Britain's relations with the Arab world.
Any public display of British solidarity with Israel might jeopardise the
current willingness of some of the Arab states (especially Jordan and
Iraq) to collaborate with them militarily. Finally, they would not know
exactly which facilities they would require from Israel until they had
concluded the talks with Egypt.[88]

The Defence Committee confirmed the general sense of the reply,
and decided also that Britain could not offer Israel any heavy military

---

[84] Ibid; and annex to JP (50), 141, 17 Jan. 1951, Defe 6/14. PRO.

[85] JP (51) 49, 29 March 1951, annex to COS (51) 58th, Defe 4/41. PRO. My emphasis.

[86] Knox Helm to Foreign Office, ER1224/2, ER1224/3, 7 March, and 2 April 1951, FO
371/91735. PRO; and Michael Comay – John Chadwick, 5 Dec. 1951, 130-02/2457/1, Israel
State archives (ISA).

[87] DO (51) 26, supra.

[88] Morrison draft letter, and cover note, 5 April 1951, DO (51) 44, Cab 131/11. PRO.

equipment. However, at the suggestion of the pro-Israeli Aneurin Bevan (Minister of Labour and National Insurance), the committee did delete a long passage from Morrison's letter which it was feared might offend the Israelis. The passage referred to Britain's long association with other Commonwealth countries ('ties of blood'), that could not be extended to countries outside the Commonwealth.[89]

Morrison's final reply, sent on 23 April, expressed British appreciation of Ben-Gurion's 'spirit of friendliness', and stated that the development of relations between the two countries 'must be a gradual process.' He concluded that the best way to begin would be 'to establish practical co-operation in the military field'.[90]

Following his meeting with Ben-Gurion, Gen Robertson had conjectured on possible ways to meet the Israeli demand for an active fighting role in the Middle East. He noted that some American circles held the idea that if they had to choose between the Arabs and the Jews, they should throw in their lot with the latter. Robertson rejected this idea, even if, as he agreed: '. . . this conclusion appears at first sight to be justified because undoubtedly the Jews are a much more promising military proposition than all the Arab States put together'.

Robertson believed that Britain should try to secure the support of both the Jews and the Arabs, and 'should not drop either in favour of the other'. He conceded that they had to rule out the use of Israeli troops in Arab territories. Given this, he suggested that Israel might either supply a ground contingent to Turkey, or perhaps a garrison for Cyprus. However, Robertson believed that the Israelis' main contribution to the Allied war effort should be in the air. The difficulty with this idea was that Britain would be required to supply Israel with modern aircraft, which were 'not readily available'.[91]

During the spring, the COS studied Gen Robertson's report, and his proposals for using Israeli forces in the Middle East. The COS agreed that Israel could make a significant contribution to the Middle East theatre, and that they were unlikely to grant any military facilities in peacetime, unless they first received the type of commitment asked for by Ben-Gurion.[92]

The Israelis kept the strength of their armed forces strictly secret. But, in July 1951, the JPS estimated that with Allied aid, the Israeli armed forces could be built up to the following strengths; two army

[89] DO (51) 8th., 9 April 1951, Cab 131/10. PRO.

[90] Morrison–Ben-Gurion, 23 April 1951, *I.D.* 1951, Vol. 6, No. 138, p.262.

[91] Robertson report, 22 Feb. 1951, in Tel Aviv to Foreign Office, E1201/58, FO 371/91240, and COS (51) 153, 21 March 1951, Defe 5/29. PRO.

[92] For this and following see JPS memorandum, *The Role of Israeli Forces in War*, annex to JP (51) 56, 9 July 1951, Defe 6/16. PRO.

divisions, backed by reserves; a Navy of seven escort vessels and about 16 motor torpedo boats; and an Air Force of up to 150 aircraft – of which the Israelis themselves could provide about 70.[93]

The Israeli forces might be especially valuable during the early stages of a war, when British forces on the spot would be understrength, particularly on the land and in the air. But the JPS appreciated that the Israelis would fight best if they were convinced that they were thereby contributing directly to the defence of their own territory.

Unlike Gen Robertson the JPS did not rule out the deployment of the IDF on Arab territory. They suggested two possible deployments, that would involve Israel defending her own territory, from a forward position:

(a) To the east of Israel. To meet one of the main threats to the Inner Ring, which would follow the Baghdad–Rutba–Mafraq route through Iraq and Jordan, and then develop against the whole of Israel.

(b) To the north of Israel: (i) In Syria, to meet possible threats along the caravan routes from the east, which would terminate at Aleppo and Homs and subsequently turn south towards Israel. (ii) In Southern Turkey. To meet the main threat to the Inner Ring from the north, which – if not held – would subsequently threaten Israel.[94]

However, the JPS believed that the IDF was currently organised only for limited operations, along short lines of communication, and that it was in urgent need of modern equipment (which could be supplied only by the Americans). They recognised also that the Arabs would object to Britain building up the Israeli army. However, the JPS concluded that the IDF already constituted a threat to the Arabs, and Israel would improve her military potential anyway, whether the British helped them or not.

Therefore, the JPS concluded that they should plan to include an Israeli contingent in an Allied theatre force, under British Command. This would be deployed on whichever front the greater Soviet threat developed; either to the East, in Jordan; or to the north of Israel, to block a Soviet advance through southern Turkey along the Levant coast. The Israeli Navy might help with the defence of coastal convoys, and minesweeping operations. Finally, in addition to its combat role, the IDF could undertake the maintenance of the lines of communication through Israel and her logistic infrastructure in general.[95]

---

[93] An official history of the IAF estimates that in mid-1951, the Israelis had 137 fighter and bomber aircraft, of which just 85 were operational: 17 Spitfires, 9 Mustangs, 26 Mosquitos, 2 B-17s, and 31 Harvards. Steigman, *Operation 'Kadesh'. . .*, p.22.   [94] JP (51) 56, supra.
[95] Ibid.

But the JPS agreed with Robertson that Israel's main contribution should be in the air. They proposed helping to build up a modern IAF of 150 aircraft. This conclusion was strongly sponsored by Air Marshal Sir John Slessor, (and backed up by the CIGS, Gen Sir William Slim) when the COS discussed the JPS paper. Slessor stated that:

> Israel was the only Middle East country which could provide the manpower suitable for an effective air force . . . the Israelis, if trained, made excellent mechanics, whereas, no matter what training was given to Arab personnel, they fell far short of what was required for a modern Air Force.[96]

The IAF's main role would be the defence of Israeli skies, and to provide air reconnaissance for, and ferry supplies to the Allied force in Jordan. If the IAF could build up a fighter/ground attack force in time, it might also provide air cover for the Allied force on the ground. Given the grave deficiencies in Allied Air forces in this theatre, the IAF might provide invaluable aid. At the same time, the JPS believed that Israel would insist on large land forces, and resist any plan to enlarge her Air forces at the expense of her army.[97]

The Foreign Office had already vetoed the supply of modern aircraft to Israel, on political grounds, for fear of losing Arab friendship. It feared that the Israelis would use the new aircraft against their Arab neighbours – they had already bombed a Syrian village, and the conflict between the two countries was far from settled.[98] During further consultations, it was decided, in October 1951, that Britain would not release any jet aircraft to Israel.[99]

At the COS meeting which discussed the JPS paper on Israel, John Wardrop of the Foreign Office, gave notice that any deployment of Israeli troops on Arab soil might cause the Arabs to withdraw all co-operation and facilities from the Allies.[100]

For their part, the Israelis were disillusioned with, and felt slighted by Morrison's letter. It had 'merely reiterated previously expressed generalities', and did not appear to address Ben-Gurion's proposal with the earnestness that they had expected. In Israel, Gen Makleff, the Israeli Deputy Chief of Staff, warned the British Service Attaché, Lt.

---

[96] COS (51) 114th., 11 July 1951, Defe 4/45. PRO.

[97] JP (51) 56, supra.

[98] Geoffrey Furlonge, at COS (51) 101st, 22 June 1951, Defe 4/44. PRO.

The Israeli–Syrian dispute centred on Israel's cultivation of fields in the demilitarised zone that had been delimited between the two states in 1949.

[99] John Wardrop to Minister of Defence, 1 Jan. 1952, ER1193/30G, FO 371/91730. PRO.

Rolls Royce and Glosters had informed Israeli Ambassador Elath that they could supply Israel with two squadrons of jet fighters (Meteors), once governmental approval was obtained.

[100] COS (51) 114th supra.

Col. Pender-Cudlip, that it was useless to ask the Israelis about their arms requirements, 'and then doing virtually nothing about it.' Makleff repeated Ben-Gurion's request, that Israel be made privy, 'at least to some extent', to Britain's plans for the defence of the Middle East.[101]

E. ISRAEL AND THE MIDDLE EAST COMMAND (MEC)

Ben-Gurion did not reply to Morrison's letter until the end of November 1951. There were other reasons for the delay, apart from the disillusion with Morrison's reply.

Perhaps the most significant factor in the delay was the rumours which reached Israel during the spring of 1951 about the establishment of an Anglo–American sponsored MEC, on which Egypt was to be given a senior position (on which, see the next Chapter). It will suffice to note here that the MEC, a desperate, British-inspired plan to salvage her tenure of the Canal base, now dominated, and took first priority in Allied strategic considerations in the Middle East during the summer and winter of 1951.

The MEC was an Allied project, and the decision to give preference to Egypt was a joint Anglo–American one. As early as in February 1951, a meeting of US Chiefs of Mission in the Middle East advised that the Arab states would acquiesce in a regional defence programme that included Israel, provided it was sponsored by both the UK and the US, and provided also that they, the Arabs, 'were not required to deal directly with Israel'.[102]

Still mindful of Truman's sentiments on Zionism and Israel, the State Department had taken good care to secure the President's advance approval of the MEC proposal. It was explained to him that the project was vital to Western security interests in the Middle East, and that the best way turn the Arabs against it would be to associate Israel publicly with their offer. Protests were to be expected from the Israelis, especially when the West began to favour Egypt with military aid. They would have to ask the Israelis to exercise 'considerable forbearance'. The sponsors of MEC would remind Israel that her security interests were still covered by the Tripartite Declaration of May 1950. With some disingenuity, Secretary Acheson reassured Truman that SACME 'would work closely but quietly' with Israel from the inception of the MEC. And finally, Truman was told that the MEC, far from

---

[101] Conversation between the Israeli Deputy Chief of Staff, Mordechai Makleff, and the British Service Attaché, Lt. Col Pender-Cudlip, 1 Sept. 1951, Defe 7/203. PRO.

[102] Conclusions of conference of Middle East Chiefs of Mission, Istanbul, 14–21 Feb. 1951, *FRUS*, Vol. V, p.53.

endangering Israel's security, was likely to provide a channel for securing a peace settlement between Israel and the Arab world. Truman approved the new initiative, and licensed Acheson to take whatever steps he thought necessary to carry it through.[103]

The Israelis were indeed extremely anxious about the MEC which, for Ben-Gurion at least, seemed to presage a return to Britain's traditional appeasement of the Arabs. He refused absolutely to consider any collaboration with the British, so long as there was any chance that Israel's military secrets might be passed on by them to the Arabs, to Egypt in particular.[104]

The Israelis let the British know that if they were about to create any defence organisation for the entire region, Israel would first want to know the broad outlines of the organisation's defence plans for the Middle East, and the role envisaged in it for Israel – before they gave any reply on their own readiness to co-operate.[105]

The British reiterated, bluntly, that they could not at present divulge anything about Allied defence plans for the Middle East. At the same time, the Foreign Office asked the COS, rhetorically, if they had faced up to the fact that securing a base for the MEC in Egypt might '*ipso facto* deny them the co-operation of Israel', which appeared to be almost as vital as Egypt to Britain's strategic plans for the region.[106]

The COS stated that there were now 'overwhelming arguments in favour of locating the headquarters and base of the Allied Command [MEC] in Egypt'. As a final, desperate effort to win over the Egyptians, the British decided to offer them preferential treatment over Israel and the rest of the Arab world. Egypt would be invited to become a 'founder member of the club'. Israel and the other Arab states would be offered 'associate membership'.[107]

In making this decision, the COS took fully into account the risk not only that Israel might deny her co-operation to the West, but also that some of the other Arab states were expected not to take too kindly to Egypt being given so privileged a position. The COS were willing to take this risk, on the assumption that if the Soviets attacked the Middle East, Israel would 'sooner or later' have to join the Allies. This of course would not make up for the loss of all the 'preliminary joint planning'

---

[103] NEA – Secretary of State, 12 Sept. 1951, PPS 47–53, box 30, RG 59. NA; Acheson forwarded the memo to Truman on the same date, and Truman signed his approval on 24 Sept.; cf., *FRUS*, 1951, Vol. V, pp.186–87, and note 3, p.187.

[104] Cf., Furlonge memorandum, 14 Sept. 1951, E1191/137, FO 371/91223. PRO.

[105] Foreign Office to Secretary, COS, 4 Sept. 1951, reporting on Chadwick meeting with Comay on 20 Aug., in COS (51) 515, 7 Sept. 1951, Defe 5/33. PRO.

[106] Furlonge memo, 14 Sept. 1951, supra.

[107] John Wardrop to Charles B. Duke, British Middle East Office, Cairo (BMEO), 5 Oct. 1951, E1192/140G, FO 371/91223. PRO.

in peacetime that would be required if Israel was to become an effective ally. However, the COS preferred to put off the crossing of that particular bridge for the present – knowing only too well that the chances of Egypt accepting the MEC offer were rather low.[108]

But even this proved too much for the British Defence Co-ordinating Committee, Middle East (BDCC, ME) at Cairo. They insisted that it would be 'impossible' even to grant Israel associate membership on the MEC. Any association whatever of Israel with the new project would lead to its proscription by Egypt, and the other Arab states.[109] But this was to be Britain's last concession to Egypt.

Charles Duke of the BMEO reported the general feeling of exasperation with Egypt that pervaded British officialdom in Cairo. The BDCC, supported by Gen Robertson, had expressed the following view:

> . . . if the Egyptians turned nasty over our new command proposals [MEC] (perhaps I should say continue nasty), *we should switch over entirely to Israel and establish ourselves really strongly there and leave the Arabs to the peace of their deserts.* The most valuable thing . . . they have to offer is oil and they would probably have to go on letting us have that as they would be unable, or could be prevented from selling it anywhere else.[110]

True to form, the Foreign Office was more circumspect. They preferred to await the outcome of the new MEC initiative, before adopting doomsday solutions. Only if both Israel and the Arabs refused to become associated with the new body, would the British have to consider other ways of associating Israel with the West.[111]

In October 1951, the ground literally burned under Britain's foothold in the Middle East. At the end of September, Dr Mussadiq of Iran had ordered the British to leave Abadan. They did so, in humiliating fashion, on 4 October. The British and the Americans advanced their timetable on MEC, and rushed to present the new proposals to the Egyptians, in an attempt to pre-empt a unilateral abrogation. But four days later, and evidently deriving inspiration from the Iranians, the Egyptian Parliament formally and unilaterally abrogated the 1936 treaty with Britain. On 13 October, the ambassadors of the MEC sponsoring powers – the US, UK, France and Turkey – presented the Egyptians with the draft proposal of the MEC project (see next Chapter).

On the same day (a Saturday morning), in Tel Aviv, Knox Helm advised the Israel Foreign Office of the new *démarche*. Helm explained

---

[108] Ibid.
[109] Charles B. Duke to G. Furlonge, 8 Oct. 1951, E1192/169G, FO 371/91224. PRO.
[110] Ibid, my emphasis.
[111] Furlonge to Duke, 26 Oct. 1951, E1192/169G, FO 371/91224. PRO.

that due to the paramount importance of the Egyptian base, Egypt was to be offered a position as a founder member of MEC. He told the Israelis that the new move had been decided upon just hours before, due to the Egyptian actions. Later on, the American ambassador, Monnett B. Davis, also called, to plead with the Israelis not to go public with accusations that Britain was appeasing the Egyptians.[112]

Ben-Gurion's initial reaction was one of pure shock and alarm. He confided to his diary that the new project was one of the gravest events to have occurred in the recent past, perhaps graver even than the assassination of King Abdullah (on 20 July 1951).[113]

On 15 October, Ben-Gurion received ambassador Davis at his home in Tel Aviv. The Israeli Prime Minister treated the ambassador to a tirade. Referring to a Reuter's report that the Egyptians had already rejected the MEC offer, Ben-Gurion stated that if this was true, it 'would save the Western Powers from a fatal mistake'. While he appreciated fully the positive aspects of the new Command, Ben-Gurion stated that it would be:

> futile to build such defence on the co-operation of a country which had never fought for freedom and democracy and would not now risk anything for it . . . Egypt simply did not belong to the 'free world' . . . They did not care a hoot about the West, but would exploit Western overtures in order to blackmail . . . The military training and arms Egypt stood to gain . . . would never be used against Russia, but would certainly be used against Israel when circumstances permitted.[114]

The ambassador was not surprised by Ben-Gurion's outburst, and refuted his assertion that the Allies 'were being unrealistic in their approach to Egypt', and neglecting Israel's interests. The Allies had no illusions about the Egyptian Army, but it was 'a plain fact of geography . . . that the Suez Canal and the main Middle East base were situated on Egyptian territory.' The MEC was the only way the Allies might yet secure rights to use that base, which all the military experts agreed was essential for the defence of the Middle East against a Soviet attack. When Ben-Gurion asked what would happen if the Egyptians did in

[112] W. Eytan to Israeli Missions abroad, 13 Oct. 1951, *I.D.*, 1951, Vol. 6, pp.694–96. The last time the British had 'disturbed' the Israelis on a Saturday morning, had been at 4.45 a.m. on 29 June 1946, when they had arrested 2,700 Jews, including leaders of the Jewish Agency, and a significant part of the *Hagana* officer corps. (In Zionist history, this day became known as 'Black Saturday'.) cf Cohen, *Palestine and . . .*, p.85.

[113] Ben-Gurion diary entry, 14 Oct. 1951. BGA.

[114] Comay note of Ben-Gurion – Davis meeting, 15 Oct. 1951, *I.D.*, 1951, Vol. 6, pp.708–11.

fact reject the scheme, Davis replied that the Allies had not accepted Egypt's unilateral abrogation of the 1936 treaty.[115]

Ben-Gurion interjected. While recognising the Allies' good intentions, he insisted that they were unrealistic. He drew comparisons with the position in 1939 when, on the eve of the war, 'Zionist interests in Palestine had been sacrificed on the plea that it was essential for strategic reasons to secure the goodwill and co-operation of the Arabs.' He had claimed then that no concessions would bring the Arabs to fight on the Allied side – and events had proved him right. He suggested that history was repeating itself, and the Americans were now making the same mistake that the British had made in 1939. The real forces in the Middle East, Ben-Gurion claimed, were the Western Allies, Turkey and Israel. Western defence schemes should be based on them. When Ben-Gurion expressed his fear that Israel would now be excluded from Western plans, Davis replied, somewhat disingenuously, that the Allies would not allow the Egyptians to impose a veto on anyone. However, Davis all but contradicted himself immediately, when he added that Israel's participation should not be given too much publicity at this stage, 'since it would make it more difficult to secure the co-operation of the Arab States'.[116]

On top of this shock, Ben-Gurion received a very crude warning from the Soviets against joining any Western-sponsored defence schemes for the Middle East. The Soviets claimed that this would mean that Israel was joining NATO's aggressive plans against the Soviet Union and the Peoples' Democracies.[117]

However, once it became clear that the Egyptians were not, at least for the present, joining the MEC, Ben-Gurion decided to reply to Foreign Secretary Morrison's letter of the previous April. He hastened to try to obtain some concrete security agreements with the West, before the Egyptians changed their minds!

F. THE BRITISH MILITARY MISSION TO ISRAEL, NOVEMBER 1952

Ben-Gurion had undoubtedly been encouraged, not to mention relieved, by the Egyptians' rejection of MEC. This presented Israel with its chance to ingratiate itself with the West. By this time Ben-Gurion had second thoughts about MEC. On 11 November, at a meeting with US ambassador Davis, he first expressed his appreciation of the West's

---

[115] Ibid.
[116] Ibid.
[117] Israel Legation in Moscow to Foreign Ministry, 22 Nov. 1951, *I.D.*, Vol. 6, pp.821–23.

decision to defend the Middle East, via MEC. But he now agreed that it would indeed be best if Israel were to become associated informally, not openly, with the new organisation, so as not to alienate the Arabs. He also admitted to two Israeli apprehensions about becoming associated publicly with MEC; first, following the Soviet warning, he feared that Jewish immigration from Iron Curtain countries might be stopped in reprisal; and second, he feared Arab aggression, should they discover the size of Israel's standing army.[118]

By this point in time, general elections had taken place in both Israel (30 July) and in Britain (25 October). Ben-Gurion had retained power. But in Britain, the Labour party had been defeated by the Conservatives. Ben-Gurion's reply was addressed therefore to Antony Eden, once more Winston Churchill's Foreign Secretary. Ben-Gurion was presumably also encouraged by Churchill's return to power (*after* the failure of the MEC initiative with Egypt), still wishfully believing that the latter was a friend of Zionism.[119]

On 23 November, Moshe Sharett met Antony Eden in Paris. As the first ever meeting between British and Israeli Foreign Secretaries, the meeting was pregnant with symbolism, and a mutual desire for rapprochement. Sharett saw a new 'parallelism of interest' between their two countries in the region, caused by Egypt's 'tearing up' of the 1936 treaty with Britain, and by her embargo on the transit of Israeli shipping through the Suez Canal. Israel was now ready for practical military talks, whereby the UK could 'help strengthen Israel, and Israel could place her strength behind the UK'. Sharett also expressed Israel's agreement to her exclusion from MEC, and stated that Israel would in fact prefer direct defence arrangements with the British and the Americans. Sharett referred to a list of Israeli requirements of aid and technical advice; in communications, training facilities, the modernisation of the Haifa oil refinery, and the laying of an oil pipeline from Eilat to the Mediterranean coast, for the transmission of Persian Gulf oil. Eden was particularly attracted by this last idea.[120]

Following these contacts, on 28 November, Ben-Gurion sent his official reply to the British government, proposing 'direct conversations on concrete plans', along the lines he had proposed to Gen Robertson the previous February.[121]

Eden discussed with Prime Minister Churchill the reply to be sent to Ben-Gurion. Although the British were still hoping to set up

---

[118] Davis to State Department, 11 Nov. 1951, *FRUS*, 1951, V, p.247.
[119] On the reasons for Churchill's abandonment of Zionism, in 1944, Cf., Michael J. Cohen, *Churchill and the Jews*, London: Frank Cass, 1985.
[120] Sharett–Eden talk, 23 Nov. 1951, FO 371/91716. PRO.
[121] Ben-Gurion to Eden, 28 Nov. 1951, *I.D.*, 1951, Vol. 6, p.835.

MEC, with Egypt, Eden stated that they would need Israel's military co-operation whatever the case, and it would be best to gain time by starting discussions with her as soon as possible. Churchill concurred.[122]

On 30 January 1952, Eden's positive reply was delivered personally by the British ambassador in Tel Aviv. He proposed that a small military mission visit Israel, in plain clothes, for exploratory discussions on the general issues of Middle East defence. The mission would be empowered to discuss only purely military issues.[123]

It was left to the JPS and the COS to work out the terms of reference for the military mission to Israel. The COS decided that the mission's main aim would be to ascertain what Israel could contribute to the defence of the Middle East, and what her essential requirements would be in the event of war. If the Israelis pressed the issue, which they almost certainly would, the mission was also authorised to discuss Israel's active role in war, and training assistance for her armed forces.[124]

The JPS again stressed that the mission must not disclose British plans for the defence of the Middle East theatre. However, they were empowered to make it clear that those plans would depend on the use of Israel's 'ports and communications'. Bearing in mind Israeli concerns over the sincerity of British intentions, the JPS urged the mission to try to persuade the Israelis that Britain did not intend merely to fight a delaying action on her territory, but was determined to defend the Middle East as a whole:

> *without disclosing our plans for the defence of the Middle East* we must emphasise that those plans include the defence of Israel, and that we consider her integrity essential to our strategic plans.[125] (my emphasis)

The mission was to try to elicit assessments from the Israelis on how much development work would be required on their roads, railways and ports, in order to meet British requirements in war. Finally, they would require Israeli assurances that they would be ready to secure and guard the British lines of communication through their country.[126]

The JPS adopted Robertson's conclusions of the previous February, to the effect that, due to inevitable Arab objections to the deployment of Israeli forces on their soil, Israel's main contribution should be in the

[122] Minutes of Eden and Churchill meeting, 22 Dec. 1951, Prem 11/489. PRO.
[123] F. Evans to Ben-Gurion, 30 Jan. 1952, No. 38, p.66, and M. Comay to E. Elath (London), 31 Jan. 1952, No. 39, p.67, in *ID* 1952, Vol. 7; and Aide memoire by British Minister, Tel Aviv to Israeli Foreign Ministry, 20 May 1952, No. 159, p.235, idem.
[124] COS (52) 3d, 7 Jan. 1952, Defe 4/51. PRO.
[125] Annex to JP (52) 3, 20 March 1952, Defe 6/20. PRO.
[126] Ibid.

air. The mission should ascertain if Israel agreed to this definition of their role. It was hoped that the Arabs 'might not object so intensely to overflying'.

British military requirements in Israel were now defined as: the use of Haifa port as an emergency repair base, and perhaps as a major supply depot; accommodation at Haifa for some 200 Navy personnel, and three major air defence units, up to 3000 men; storage accommodation elsewhere for tented camps, and eight major units of the RAF, again, up to 3000 men; and finally, the use of four airfields for light bombers, and general access to Israel's communications system.[127]

On the Israeli side, Ben-Gurion instructed the head of his delegation, Gen Mordechai Makleff, the deputy COS, that the talks were to be conducted on the basis of two friendly states with equal rights. His principal concern remained to find out what were Britain's plans for the defence of the Middle East. Where were the lines she intended to defend? To what extent would the Americans, and other Allies, take an active part in defending them? Makleff was also to ask for aid and equipment, for a potential force of 250,000 men. However, he was forbidden to go into any details on the IDF's structure and makeup. And finally, Makleff was to find out how much aid the West would give Israel to improve her ports and communications.[128]

The Anglo–Israeli military talks were thus clearly doomed to failure from the outset. Each side was determined to withhold the information most sought after by the other. Britain wanted unhindered access to Israeli military installations, and to discover the extent of the military aid that Israel could offer her in the event of war. The Israelis would not provide such information until they could be certain that Britain had given up for good her pro-Arab alignment. But Britain had not yet relinquished all hope of remaining in the Egyptian base, and of securing the co-operation of other Arab states in the Middle East. So she would not agree to the type of bilateral defence treaty the Israelis were looking for. And finally, there was the ever-present, insurmountable problem that Britain could not comply with Israel's demand to disclose her plans for the defence of the Middle East, for these would have revealed, as the British appreciated only too well, their inability to guarantee Israel's own territorial integrity – i.e. the fact that the Ramallah line cut through the very midriff of Israel! (On the revision of Britain's Middle Eastern strategy during the Fall of 1952, see Chapter 10.)

The military mission did not in fact arrive in Israel until October 1952. Firstly, there was some bickering over the mission's terms of

---

[127] COS (52) 170, 18 March 1952, Defe 5/38. PRO.
[128] Ben-Gurion to Gen Makleff, 1 Oct. 1952, BGA; also *I.D.*, 1952, 7, pp.549–51.

reference. The Israelis feared becoming 'bracketed with the Arab States as a British sphere of influence', and balked at British references to plans for the defence of the Middle East as a whole. They insisted on a specific commitment to the defence of Israel. Next, the British wanted to send a delegation of eight men, and the Israelis insisted on just three. A 'compromise' of five was agreed upon. And finally, by the time agreement was reached, in July 1952, Gen Makleff went off to the IDF summer manoeuvres for two months.[129]

The Israeli and the British military teams held three meetings in Tel Aviv, on 7 and 8 October 1952. The British team was headed, significantly, by an Air Vice Marshal, D. MacFadyen, and included other army and RAF personnel. The Israeli team (of six men), was headed by Gen Makleff, and included Col Dan Tolkowsky, Chief of Staff of the IAF, and Lt Col Yehoshofat Harkabi, of Israeli Intelligence. The following is based on the Israeli record of the talks – the British record being still closed.[130]

At their first meeting the Israelis tried to impress the British team with Israel's strategic importance, and suggested that the Eilat–Haifa route might provide an alternative to the Suez Canal. Air Vice Marshal MacFadyen, following his brief, concentrated on trying to convince the Israelis of the NATO Allies' determination to defend the Middle East. He stated that Israel's territorial integrity was 'absolutely essential' to their plans: 'We do intend to defend the Middle East as a whole; there is no question of any individual country going by the board as far as we are concerned.'

Then Gen Makleff, also acting on orders, made it quite clear that Israel's willingness to take part in the West's plans for the defence of the region would depend on a specific commitment by the Great Powers to defend Israel. Once convinced of that, Israel would be ready to grant to the West the use of all her military facilities and communications systems in time of war. Israel's own military contribution would be contingent upon the extent of the threat posed to her own security at that time by her Arab neighbours. Makleff then pressed MacFadyen to reveal British defence plans for the region. He reiterated Ben-Gurion's point that Israel would insist on taking an active part in the war. The offensive was the best means of defence, and they had no intention of just sitting back to wait for the aggressor.

Air Vice Marshal MacFadyen made it clear that while the Middle

---

[129] Israeli reply to British aide memoire, Eytan to Evans, 6 June 1952, *I.D.*, 1952, 7, No. 183, pp.285–89; and M. Comay to E. Elath, 14 Sept. 1952, Ibid, pp.516–17; also Bialer, *Between East and . . .* p.258; and Davis (Tel Aviv) to Secretary of State, 17 July 1952, 784A.5/7-1752. NA.

[130] File 532/73/174, IDF Archive.

East would become a theatre of 'great importance' in war, the primary front would have to be Western Europe. When asked by Makleff if the Middle East had any offensive potential, MacFadyen replied: 'Very much so'. Perhaps revealing more than he should have done, Mac-Fadyen then noted that it was an excellent base for strategic bombing, being close to targets that could not be reached from western Europe.

At that point, Lt Col Harkabi interjected, bluntly: 'With your permission, I would like to ask where do you intend to establish the lines of defense, primary and secondary lines?'

Back in February 1951, Gen Robertson had not faced such direct questioning. The military mission that visited in October 1952 was unprepared for this eventuality. They were taken aback by Harkabi's directness, and a cloud of tension descended on the meeting.

MacFadyen fumbled: 'You are asking me a difficult one now'; and he went on to repeat Gen Robertson's generalities about the real defensive line of the Middle East lying in the Turkish mountains, on the passes. Then, again going precariously beyond his brief, MacFadyen stated that once they lost these mountains, there were no defensive lines before the Lebanon mountains and the Jebel Druze.

The Israelis pursued their quarry, and MacFadyen gave ground, (and too much information), even if he did manage to paint the scenario much brighter than it actually was. Harkabi asked how long did they think they would be able to stop the Soviets in the mountains of Iraq? MacFadyen replied: 'the delay might be up to say, four months.' Makleff believed that everything should be done to stop the Soviets in Iraq, but he was concerned that it would take months to transport the necessary forces to that front. MacFadyen replied that this was the reason they would rely on the air offensive – but for that, they would need air bases.

Harkabi pressed again: '. . . you are going to lose your two main air bases there [in Iraq], Habbaniya and Shaiba?' MacFadyen replied that this was so. The Iraqi air bases were good for tactical missions, but were too far forward for bomber airfields. And it would take many years for Iraq to develop a proper control and radar (C. & R.) air defence system. (There exists also a technical problem of operating fully-loaded bombers in extremely high temperatures, such as pertain in Iraq. In this respect too, Israel with its milder climate, was more suitable than Iraq.) When Harkabi asked which airfields the British intended using instead of those in Iraq, MacFadyen replied: 'Well, that's what we were going to ask you!'

Then Harkabi returned to the Israelis' main concern:

We are very interested in understanding your system of defense closer to our

front lines, that is, the second circle or second line of defense which you have
shown more or less on the map.

Again, the British tried to prevaricate with generalisations. Lt. Col.
Heathcote replied that the details in each theatre would be decided by
the force commanders, air and land. But he then dropped yet another
indiscreet hint:

> The Jebel Druze and the Lebanon ranges are the main defense areas, but at
> same point, depending on how many forces you've got, you must draw back
> your flank.

The British side tried to maintain that the Turks had only recently
entered NATO, and that as yet there were no definite plans. At a later
point, when Harkabi asked what was to be the role of each country in
the region, MacFadyen replied that they had not yet gone that far in
their planning.

The tension and the Israelis' frustration rose, as they failed to elicit
any details, or frank responses from the British officers.

At their third and final meeting, on 8 October, and presumably after
consultations with his superiors, MacFadyen tried to retrieve the
Israelis' confidence:

> I was a little horrified to hear we left a false impression in one respect and that is
> we have given the impression that we have no plan. That is not correct . . . What
> I mean is that we have no Allied plan under NATO as Turkey has now joined us.
> The NATO people have not got down to it. We have our old plan which in
> emergency would be put into effect but that is not up-to-date. I wouldn't want
> you to think we have no plans.

Then came the moment of truth. Makleff asked whether they weren't
going to discuss the British plan? MacFadyen finally admitted the bare
truth: 'I'm afraid we're absolutely debarred . . . from giving any details.'
The basic duplicity of the British position had got the military mission
into a tangle from which, try as they might, the British officers were
unable to extricate themselves.

There ensued some discussion on whether MEC (by now, re-named
MEDO) should be a part of NATO or not. Lt Col Heathcote said that
the Allies would have to determine Turkey's role: Turkey had just been
inducted into NATO, but of necessity, MEC would have to include
Turkey. To this, Makleff retorted that in *his* talks with the Turks, they
had stated that they were not committed at all to the Middle East, but
regarded themselves as European, and they looked westwards.
Heathcote expostulated that it was 'ridiculous for them to face one
way'.

Harkabi pressed home unrelenting on the still-unanswered question of British plans to defend the Middle East, the Israelis' main concern:

> What we are trying to find out is, what are the actual military plans, which have nothing to do with the Allies. As a matter of fact the Allies have yet to come into the picture, the command has not yet been formed . . . what we would like to know are the outlines of this emergency plan. What we ask for is the very broad lines of such a plan?

Makleff added: 'Now I am fogged . . . We expected these talks to be between you and us, and not between the Allies and us . . . we expected to discuss your plans. You have made up your minds to take part in the defence of this area. You probably remember the exchange of letters.'

MacFadyen tried to maintain that there had been no prior agreement to discuss their plans in detail. He asked to make it clear that there was now no up-to-date plan, in view of recent developments with Turkey – but there was 'the old plan of the British'. He pleaded that he was not trying to hide anything, and had in fact already gone way beyond his briefing (which was true enough)!

Naturally, this failed to mollify the Israeli side. Makleff stated that what might be 'details' for the British, might be a plan for Israel. Israel still did not understand how their region was going to be defended, and what forces would be allotted to do the job.

MacFadyen finally confessed that he saw the Israelis' point, and apologised that he was not empowered to go further. He concluded lamely with the hope that the talks would continue, and that the British side would be authorised to go into details.

There was some further discussion – on British use of routes from Egypt and Sinai northwards through Israel; on Britain's desire to stockpile arms and stores in Israel; and on Britain's need for access to three airfields in Israel (Tolkowsky replied that Israel had inherited five airfields from the British, four of which were operational, and that they were in mid-construction of a new one).

In effect, the talks ended in stalemate. The British sent a disingenuous report to the Americans: 'Despite an inauspicious beginning, meetings adjourned in most cordial atmosphere, to reconvene early date.')[131]

Israel had made it crystal clear that the West should not expect her military co-operation, in either peace or war, unless they took her in as a full and equal partner. By definition, this was patently impossible under Britain's current overall strategy for the Middle East. First, since the British feared that, if the Israelis did learn of their plans for the defence

---

[131] Report of 13 Oct. 1952, 784A. 5/10-1352. NA.

of the Middle East, it would reveal their impotence in the region and
might even induce them to make a deal with the Soviets.

And second, military co-operation with Israel remained, as ever, subordinated to Britain's relations with the Arabs. The Israelis had made it
clear that they wanted to develop balanced military forces, and would
aid the Allies in the Middle East – provided they received military aid,
and that they were convinced that there was no danger of attack by the
Arabs. But due to anticipated Arab opposition, the JPS again concluded
that Israel's main military contribution should be in the air. This was
due to the following factors: the British could not ever be certain of
being allowed to deploy Israeli land forces on Arab territory, though
they did hope that the Arabs might ultimately agree to Israeli aircraft
overflying their countries; the Israelis had better technical support for
their Air force than any other country in the region; and the Allies'
greatest deficiency in theatre forces was in the air.[132]

But the Foreign Office determined that full co-operation with Israel
might become a practicable proposition only if Britain abandoned all
hope of military co-operation with the Arabs.[133] And, as put indelicately
by the BDCC (ME) in March 1953: 'We must not seriously prejudice
our position with the Arab States for the sake of a relatively small
accretion of strength from an Israeli Air Force'.[134]

True to form, Churchill did enter a characteristically blustery
demurral:

> I do not mind it being known here or in Cairo that I am on the side of Israel and
> against her ill-treatment by the Egyptians. The idea of selling Israel down the
> drain in order to persuade the Egyptians to kick us out of the Canal Zone more
> gently is not one which attracts me.[135]

But the main conclusion drawn by the British was that in order to
progress any further with Israel, they would need to make a joint
approach to Israel with the Americans. It was quite clear that the
Israelis would not co-operate with the West unless they received substantial quantities of military equipment. And this could be supplied
only by the Americans. Therefore, the COS proposed that due to
Israel's dependence upon the Americans for both economic and military aid, the government should work to secure American support
for their policy in regard to Israel: the provision of strategic facilities,
making her major military contribution in the air, and 'making available

---

132 COS memorandum, D (53) 21, 26 March 1953, Cab 131/3, and Prem 11/489. PRO.
133 Minute by P. S. Falla, 19 Feb. 1954, VR1195/1G, FO 371/111118. PRO.
134 DCC (53) 46, 23 March 1953, Defe 11/87. PRO.
135 Churchill minute to Sir William Strang, April 1953, Prem 11/465. PRO.

Army formations for employment outside Israel according to theatre defence plans, and in the light of political conditions existing at the time.'[136]

In May 1953, the Defence Committee authorised the COS to conduct secret talks with the Americans about military co-operation with Israel. However, with great prescience, the Foreign Office feared that the new Eisenhower–Dulles administration (since January 1953) would 'be reluctant to see the West identified more closely with Israel'.[137]

However, in August, the Cabinet decided to postpone any approach to the Americans, in the lingering hope of yet reaching a defence agreement with the Egyptians. Whatever the case, the British would be unable to decide finally which facilities they wanted from Israel, before they knew finally what the Egyptians would give them.[138] It would appear that this factor, the renewed hope of reaching an agreement with the Egyptians, effectively stifled any move by Churchill's administration to resume talks with Israel.

Once the talks with Egypt took on a more promising look, it only remained for the British to take the formal decision to abandon any military alignment with Israel. This was done in January 1954.

By the beginning of that year, Britain was about to adopt a more 'forward' strategy in the Middle East, one that would involve the deployment of British forces in Iraq and Jordan (see Chapter 10). Even when evacuating the Suez Base, the British hoped to secure re-entry rights in time of war. However, if they failed to reach an agreement with Egypt, the British position in the Middle East would deteriorate greatly. Therefore, as Foreign Secretary Eden told the Cabinet in January 1954:

> It is for consideration, therefore, whether we should not reverse or modify our policy of basing our defence plans on Arab alliances and instead seek to develop co-operation with Israel and Turkey. Both are more stable, militarily more efficient, and have expressed readiness to co-operate in the defence of the area . . .[139]

But Eden drew the categorical conclusion that Britain had to abandon any idea of basing her policy in the Middle East either 'wholly or mainly on co-operation with Israel'. This was due to the perennial argument that any such co-operation would alienate the Arabs, 'from whom we shall continue to want facilities and co-operation', and oil;

[136] D (53) 21, supra.

[137] Defence Committee meeting on 6 May 1953, Cab 131/13, and note by Secretary to COS, same date, Defe 11/60; and C (53) 228, 7 Aug. 1953, in Cab 129/62, and Prem 11/489. PRO.

[138] Ibid., and unidentified minute of 12 Sept. 1953, E11910/1, FO 371/104242. PRO.

[139] Eden memorandum, 7 Jan. 1954, C (54) 6, Cab 129/65. PRO.

because the deployment of British forces in Israel would not meet the strategic requirement of holding the north-eastern frontier of Iraq; and finally, because they would in any case be unable to utilise Israeli forces on Arab territory. The COS concurred with these conclusions, although they suggested that they might still try to secure from Israel 'facilities for oil storage and the repair of heavy equipment'.[140]

[140] C.(54) 9, 9 Jan. 1954, Cab 129/65. PRO. The British noted that even in the unlikely event that the Israelis did allow them to station troops in their country, they would have to station at least a brigade so that the force would not become 'hostages in Israeli hands'. Minute by J. E. Powell-Jones, 24 Sept. 1954, VR1195/4G, FO 371/111118. PRO.

8   Regional defence schemes

During 1951–52, two projects for the defence of the Middle East were ventilated – the still-born Middle East Command (MEC) and its equally abortive successor, the Middle East Defense Organisation (MEDO). Given Britain's ever-apparent inability to defend the Middle East on her own, and the Pentagon's unwillingness to help her, the MEC project appeared as a *panacea* to Britain's problems with Egypt, and in the region in general.

MEC and MEDO were to have served two equally important purposes. First, to finesse the Egyptians into a new base agreement with the Western Allies. This would have superseded the Anglo–Egyptian agreement of 1936, while leaving the British base installations essentially intact. And equally important for the British, the MEC might serve as a channel for an American military involvement in this theatre.

From December 1950, and until the summer of 1951, a protracted debate took place between the civilian and military branches of the American administration. The State Department, fearful for the Allies' interests in the Middle East, pressed the Military for gestures, even if more symbolic than substantial, to support the British in the Middle East. Ultimately, the Military agreed to join MEC, but for its own ulterior motives. Their agreement was a tactical move, offered as a *quid pro quo* for British agreement to Turkish entry into NATO.

A. THE ORIGINS OF MEC

In 1945, the new Labour Foreign Secretary, Ernest Bevin, had tried to bring a novel, 'socialist' approach to British policy in the Middle East. He believed that Arab nationalist animosity towards Britain derived from the fact that successive Conservative governments had aligned themselves too closely with the Arab feudal landed classes, the *pashas*, to the detriment of the common people, the *fellahin*. In consequence, the benefits brought by Britain to the Middle East had been confined to 'a narrow circle of unrepresentative leaders, leaving the masses with no material interest in prolonging British tutelage.'[1]

At a conference of Middle East ambassadors convened by Bevin in London in September 1945, he outlined a new regional concept for strengthening Britain's relations with the Middle Eastern states 'on the basis of mutual cooperation and the promotion of their social and economic well-being'. In a memorandum for the Cabinet, Bevin proposed the establishment of a 'Middle East Development Board or Council', to be composed of members from the British and Middle East governments. The Board's function would be 'to direct economic and social development along the lines of a coherent, co-ordinated, regional plan.'[2]

It was Bevin's hope that *'regional economic development plans might lead eventually to regional defence plans'*, naturally, all under British aegis.[3] (My emphasis.)

But Bevin's initial hopes for regional co-operation were dashed by his failure to reach agreement with the Egyptians and the Iraquis on the revision of the existing treaties with those two countries, and by the intractability of the Palestine problem, which in 1948 erupted into the first Arab–Israeli war.

British strategic planners also perceived clearly the virtues of uniting the Middle East under British military leadership into a united regional command to resist Soviet encroachment. In 1947, the JPS stated that Britain's first priority in the Middle East must be to secure greater American military involvement in the region, preferably in the form of a Middle East Pact. They believed that Britain's ultimate goal in the region was 'to combine all the Middle East countries into one comprehensive security arrangement'. In 1949, they repeated their recommendation, reiterating that, like NATO, any security pact in the Middle East would have to be supported by both Great Britain and the United States. Until such a pact was devised, they would have to continue trying to secure their fundamental military requirements either by bilateral treaties with the individual states of the region, or via joint agreements that included the United States.[4]

Initially, the American Military would have nothing to do with British

---

[1] Cf., Wm. Roger Louis, *The British Empire in the Middle East, 1945–1951*, Oxford: Clarendon Press, 1984, pp.16–18; and Michael J. Cohen, *Palestine and the Great Powers, 1945–1948*, Princeton: Princeton University Press, 1982, p.32.

[2] CP (45) 174, 17 Sept. 1945, in Cab 129/2, PRO; reproduced in Ronald Hyam, editor, *British Documents on the End of Empire: The Labour Government and the End of Empire, 1945–1951*, Series A, Vol. 2, London: Her Majesty's Stationery Office, 1992, part III, p.213; see also Howard Sachar, *Europe Leaves the Middle East*, London: Allen Lane, 1974, pp.408–9.

[3] Cohen, supra, p.33.

[4] Annex to JP (49) 29, 30 March 1949, Air 20/2463. PRO.

notions of a Middle Eastern pact. First thoughts on such a pact assumed the extension of NATO's responsibilities to the Middle East. In the autumn of 1949, evidently inspired by the recently-concluded North Atlantic Treaty (April 1949) Bevin suggested to the Cabinet that they initiate a Middle Eastern pact, modelled on the Atlantic one, 'supplemented by additional bilateral, or multilateral defence arrangements.'[5]

This was, and would remain, anathema to the American military. In mid-1949, Gordon Merriam of the PPS also dismissed the idea out of hand (using arguments not dissimilar to those raised by the British themselves in 1944, when dismissing the idea of Arab federation):[6]

> The creation of a regional pact . . . of the Middle Eastern countries offers no solution, not only because of the discord among them which has been created by the Palestine problem, but also because of deep-rooted suspicions which antedate that question and have been intensified by it. Moreover, and this is a fundamental difficulty, the area lacks a power centre on the basis of which a pact could be built.[7]

It has been suggested that in 1949 the British might have been weighing up the opportunity offered by an Egyptian proposal to set up an Arab League collective security pact directed against Israel. But Bevin's proposal of October 1949, would have excluded Israel and the Arab states. Initially, his plan was to include only the Northern Tier countries – Greece, Turkey and Persia. This would have circumvented the problems of inducting the reluctant Americans, and of securing Arab agreement to a pact which included Israel.[8]

Bevin was conscious of the criticism that the conclusion of any Middle East pact might raise false hopes that Britain would be able to defend the region in the event of a Soviet attack. Bevin knew that current defence planning for the Middle East ruled out all hope of holding any line to the north or east of Palestine within the coming year or two. However, he noted also that long-term strategy contemplated holding 'a more advanced line as far north as the Taurus' (i.e. the Northern Ring),[9] a line which predicated Turkish co-operation.

But Bevin was not deterred by the creation of false pretenses. He

[5] Bevin cabinet memorandum, CP (49) 209, 19 Oct. 1949, in Cab 129/37. PRO.

[6] On British doubts about the Arabs' ability to unite, cf., Michael J. Cohen, *Palestine: Retreat from the Mandate, 1936–1945*, London/New York: Elek/Holmes and Meir, 1978, Ch. 8.

[7] PPS Memorandum by Gordon P. Merriam, 13 June 1949, *FRUS*, 1949, Vol. VI, 1979, p.35.

[8] Bevin memorandum, CP (49) 209, supra; and David R. Devereux, *The Formulation of British Defence Policy Towards the Middle East, 1948–56*, London: Macmillan, 1990, p.45.

[9] Ibid.

recalled that similar false hopes had just been raised with the continental members of NATO none of whose territories (under current Allied planning), could yet be defended against Soviet attack. In the Middle East, Allied planners would have to select the optimal defence line irrespective of the conclusion or non-conclusion of a Middle Eastern pact. In Bevin's view, the principal function of such a pact would be to increase the goodwill and confidence of its member countries towards the Allies, and to increase their determination to align themselves with the Allies in the event of war.[10] (These were the very same ideas that the State Department would press upon the JCS in 1951.)

The British raised the idea of a Middle East Pact at the annual Pentagon talks, in November 1949. They regarded American participation in a MEC as a *sine qua non*. But, as already noted, the Americans quashed any idea of an American commitment in the Middle East.

In a joint statement issued after the conference (evidently dictated by the Americans), the Allies declared that it would be premature for them to pass judgement on the Egyptian proposal for an Arab collective security pact, and their position on that project would remain non-committal. The statement went on to assert that the current policy of the American administration excluded its adherence to any Middle Eastern pact on the Atlantic model, and that in any case, such a pact would not of itself meet Britain's strategic requirements. The statement concluded that such needs would have to be met by the conclusion of bilateral treaties between Britain and the Arab states.[11]

American strategists were preoccupied with, and still digesting the full consequences of, the NATO pact. For them NATO represented a revolutionary, first ever peacetime continental commitment.

In late November 1949, a conference of chiefs of American Middle East missions, convening in Istanbul, concluded that: 'it would be premature for the United States to consider associating itself with any possible regional grouping in this area.' A confidential brief issued after the conference stated:

> . . . American adherence to the Atlantic Pact constituted a radical departure in the foreign policy of the United States and . . . any additional American commitment of like nature should not be undertaken without the most careful examination of all the factors involved.[12]

[10] Ibid.

[11] Note of Washington talks, 14, 17 and 22 November 1949, *FRUS*, 1949, Vol. VI, p.70.

[12] Conclusions of Near East chiefs of mission, Istanbul, 26–29 November 1949, ibid., pp.168–75; the brief, on p.176, 'Recapitulation of Conclusions for Confidential Guidance of Chiefs of Mission in Oral Presentation to Governments' is unsigned and undated; see also, Devereux, *The Formulation* . . ., p.45; and Hahn, *Containment and* . . ., p.26.

In March 1950, a further meeting of US Chiefs of mission, convened this time in Cairo, reached similar conclusions. But this time, the confidential briefing that emerged came out in clear opposition to the Egyptian-sponsored Arab security pact:

> The United States . . . should not encourage any regional grouping directed against any other state in the area but should give its support to such regional arrangements as promised to bring about political stability, peace, and improvement of economic conditions.[13]

Notwithstanding the apparent impracticability of a MEC, the British began in 1950 to look to the project as an instrument which might resolve their differences with the Egyptians while at the same time enabling them to retain their Suez base.

Initially, in April 1950, the British conceived of a trilateral agreement between themselves, Egypt and Turkey, linked perhaps to NATO. The inclusion of the Turks, the British hoped, might overcome Egyptian apprehensions about being dominated in a bilateral treaty with a stronger partner. Predictably, the Americans reacted unenthusiastically, considering the new scheme to be 'unworkable and untimely'. Above all, the Americans wanted first to see NATO established more firmly in Europe, before they would consider extending its commitments to the Near East.[14]

However, during a conference of English, French and American Foreign Ministers in London, in May 1950, (one of whose results was the so-called 'Tripartite Declaration'), the British revealed to the Americans the latest idea of the COS, 'for a form of Anglo–Egyptian military partnership to assist the defence of the Near East in case of Soviet aggression.' One of the side-benefits of such an arrangement, the British hoped, would be that the Egyptians would become more dependent upon them for military supplies.[15] The Americans refrained from passing any opinion.

One historian has claimed that the tripartite declaration constituted 'the first overt American commitment to Middle East security'. Indeed, the State Department initiated the declaration, and pushed it through

---

[13] Report on Near East regional conference, Cairo, 16 March 1950, *FRUS*, 1950, Vol. V, p.3.

[14] Philip Jessup (London) – State Department (Washington), 27 April 1950, *FRUS*, 1950, Vol. III, p.884; also Hahn, *Containment and . . .* p.26.

[15] NSC 65/2, 10 May 1950. NA. The Tripartite Declaration, signed by the United States, Britain and France on 25 May 1950, was an attempt to control the Middle East arms race, and to guarantee the existing borders between Israel and the Arab states. cf., Wm Roger Louis, *The British Empire . . .*, pp.583–90; Devereux, *The Formulation of . . .*, p.46; and Peter L. Hahn, *The United States . . .*, pp.97–102.

over Pentagon objections.[16] Perhaps the British themselves believed initially that the declaration re-committed the Americans to the Middle East. In effect, the declaration reflected only the Allies' aspiration to preserve the status quo in the Middle East. It was in fact issued some eight months after American planners had 'withdrawn' their military contingent from the Middle East.

The COS hoped that the rest of the Arab world and Israel would also eventually join the new Middle East 'defence arrangement'. In a background paper written in May 1950, they defined their 'Ultimate Aim' for the Middle East:

> The ideal military arrangement in the Middle East would be a regional pact consisting of the United Kingdom, the Arab League States, Israel, Turkey, Persia and possibly Greece, in which Egypt, as a willing partner, would provide the base facilities required.[17]

While conceding that the antecedents of the MEC proposal may be traced to earlier events, Professor Louis suggests that this memorandum constituted a 'significant beginning' for the project.[18]

Shortly after the issue of the tripartite declaration, early in June 1950, the CIGS, Field Marshal Slim, visited Cairo in the hope of jump-starting the stalled bilateral talks between Britain and Egypt. Slim was the first to raise the MEC idea officially with the Egyptians. His records indicate that he met only with King Farouk.

King Farouk asked about the Western Union, and stated that Egypt needed to join some sort of a similar military arrangement. Farouk agreed with General Slim's assertion that no country could now defend itself on its own. Slim then gave three reasons why British troops had to remain in Egypt; first, so as to guarantee the defence of Great Britain herself; second, since if Britain withdrew from Egypt, then her Allies in the region and the Dominions would conclude that Britain 'was withdrawing from the cold war and would lose heart'; and third, because without the British military presence, Egypt was indefensible. According to Slim, Farouk concurred in every word that he uttered, and agreed that Great Britain was Egypt's only ally. The king believed that the United States relied upon the British in the Middle East.[19]

In a follow-on letter to their meeting, Slim wrote to King Farouk that the British wanted to 'break with the past', and place Anglo–Egyptian

---

[16] Hahn, *The United States . . .*, p.101.

[17] DO (50) 40, 19 May 1950, Prem 8/1359, PRO, quoted in Louis, *The British Empire . . .* p.583.

[18] Ibid.

[19] Field Marshal's Slim's note of his meeting with King Farouk, 4 June 1950, Prem 8/1359. PRO.

relations upon a new footing. Referring to the MEC project, Slim asserted that Britain would abandon any idea of the 'occupation' of Egypt, and that Anglo–Egyptian relations should henceforth be those of equals, along lines similar to those of the member nations of NATO.[20]

It is unclear why Gen Slim apparently met only with King Farouk.[21] Egypt was not exactly a 'constitutional monarchy' on the English model. But neither was Farouk a free agent. He did not speak for the members of his government or Parliament, who were apparently more attuned than him to the nationalist sentiments of the masses.

Furthermore, it soon became apparent that Egypt would not enter any new Middle East pact (if at all) with the British alone, but only if the United States adhered as well. It was to this object, that of securing American adherence to a Middle East pact, as well as to a renewed American military commitment to the Middle East, that the British next applied themselves, at the annual Pentagon conference, held in October 1950.

B. THE STATE–PENTAGON DEBATE ON MEC

But, as noted already, the JCS had refused adamantly to reverse their decision of just the previous year, to send to West Africa the contingent that had been earmarked for the Middle East.

On the eve of the 1950 Pentagon conference, the JCS came out strongly against the MEC project. They argued that in the absence of any superior authority to co-ordinate or execute military planning, any new Middle East security arrangement would be militarily unsound. In addition, echoing Bevin's earlier argument, they asserted that joint defence plans for the area would add little to the security of the indigenous states, all of which, 'with the exception of Turkey', were militarily weak.[22]

After the Allied conference in Washington, the British position in Egypt deteriorated still further. On 16 November 1950, in his 'speech from the throne' opening the new session of the Egyptian Parliament, in the presence of King Farouk, Egyptian Prime Minister Nahas Pasha demanded 'the total and immediate evacuation of Egypt by British forces and the unity of Egypt and the Sudan under the Egyptian crown.' Nahas stated that the 1936 treaty was no longer valid, and

---

[20] Gen Slim to King Farouk, 13 July 1950, ibid; and Louis, *The British Empire . . .*, p.589.

[21] Prof Louis, ibid, p.715, writes that Slim met with 'Farouk and other Egyptian leaders'; however, he relies on Slim's own report of 4 June, as did this author, which reports on only one meeting, that with Farouk.

[22] State Department paper, cleared by the Department of Defense, 'Security of Greece and Turkey', 11 Sept. 1950, *FRUS*, 1950, Vol. III, p.280.

warned that his government 'would not hesitate to declare it void'. As Nahas delivered his speech, widespread rioting against the British engulfed Cairo.[23]

The State Department embarked on a campaign to persuade the Pentagon to reverse its veto on any military commitment to the Middle East. The initiator, and principal intellectual inspiration of the State Department case was George C. McGhee, assistant Secretary of State for Near Eastern and African Affairs.[24]

McGhee could not have failed to be influenced by a series of reports that came in at the end of November 1950, from Jefferson Caffery, the influential American ambassador in Cairo.[25] On 22 November, Caffery reported that, assuming that the United States did have important strategic interests in the Near East, they had to devise ways to help the British remain on in Egypt. If British evacuation was to be averted, they must consider only those alternatives that would permit the British, and *perhaps the Americans*, to have bases in Egypt. Given the 'overly publicised xenophobic stand' of the Wafd government, Caffery believed that the only deal that the Wafd would be able to sell to their public would be 'a three-party pact with Egypt as full sovereign participating member'. The 'price' that Britain and the United States would have to pay would be high, and would include arms supplies and 'at least a facade of military consultation which would give outside appearance of a full exchange of views on a sovereign basis.'[26]

Caffery believed that American intervention in Egypt was essential, since British influence in that country was at an all-time low. In contrast, American prestige was higher than it had been for years.[27] The deterioration in the situation in Egypt would provide the cornerstone of the State Department case for the need for a revision of the administration's Middle Eastern policy.

In Washington, McGhee's first task was to persuade his own Secretary of State, Dean G. Acheson. In an internal memorandum addressed to Acheson at the end of 1950, McGhee referred to the potential dangers inherent in the American neglect of the Middle East; to the fact that they had entrusted their vital strategic interests in the

[23] Editorial note, *FRUS*, 1950, Vol.V., p.324.

[24] Both Acheson and McGhee claimed in their memoirs that the State Department's sponsorship of MEC dates from Acheson's letter to Secretary of Defense Marshall, on 27 Jan. 1951. However, the documents reveal clearly that following the Pentagon conference of October 1950, McGhee was the prime mover in this debate. cf. Hahn, *'Containment and . . .'*, p.28, note 13.

[25] Prof Louis refers to Caffery as 'one of the most distinguished, and also most formidable members of the United States Foreign Service.' Louis, *The British Empire . . .*, p.716.

[26] Caffery – Secretary of State, 22 Nov. 1950, *FRUS*, 1950, Vol. V, pp.322–23.

[27] Caffery – Secretary of State, 25 Nov. 1950, ibid., p.323.

region to the British, whose position was most evidently, and rapidly, deteriorating. Following Caffery's lead, McGhee's major innovation was to propose a joint Anglo–American command structure in the Middle East, i.e., a MEC. He made the following points:

1. American actions in the Middle East so far had not reflected the NSC assessment that the defence of the region was 'vital' to the defence of the United States itself.
2. The British, who had been given primary responsibility for the defence of the region, lacked 'both manpower and resources' with which to do so, and had excluded from their plans the defence of the Saudi Arabian oil fields and the American air base at Dhahran.
3. If the Middle East was lost to the Soviets, it would have great psychological impact upon the free world as a whole, upon Western Europe in particular, as well as upon the British Commonwealth countries, for whom the routes and communications running through the region were of especial strategic significance.
4. Middle Eastern oil was vitally important. It was essential to European economic recovery in the short term, and would be essential in the long term also to the United States. Neither would the Soviets be able to consolidate their conquest of Europe without the oil of the Middle East.

And finally, in reply to a central argument of the JCS (that the Middle East could be reconquered after the main battle had been decided in Europe), McGhee argued that if the West did not actively defend the states of the Middle East, it was doubtful if the latter would ever support the West again, after the war's conclusion. If the United States remained aloof from Middle East defence, American prestige in the region would decline, and American companies might be denied access to and concessions in the region following its 'liberation'.[28]

McGhee distinguished between American involvement in, and a full military commitment to the Middle East. He proposed that the administration make an early public announcement, declaring its 'vital security interest in the defence of the Middle East as a whole', and its readiness to help the countries of the Middle East resist aggression. The United States should, together with the British, embark on a programme of strengthening the indigenous military forces of those Middle East states that would participate in the region's defence. McGhee urged that if it should prove necessary, in order to mobilise the co-operation of the Arabs, the United States should:

[28] For this and following, see McGhee – Acheson, 27 Dec. 1950, *FRUS*, 1951, Vol. V, 1982, pp.4–6.

. . . urge the UK to offer to renounce its existing treaty rights in Egypt, Jordan and Iraq, *if and when alternative and adequate security arrangements can be made.*[29] (my emphasis)

They should, at an early date, station a Marine battalion at the Dhahran air base, in order to reassure Ibn Saud personally, as well as to boost morale in the Near East in general. The defence of the 'Outer Ring' should become an Allied target, for which the Allies should allocate forces, once more urgent needs elsewhere had been met. And finally, McGhee urged, they should:

. . . establish (for political as well as military reasons) a combined US–UK command structure in the Middle East which would stimulate basic cooperation among the states of the area not now possible through indigenous organizations or groupings such as the Arab League.[30]

McGhee was quick to reassure Acheson that the new structure 'would not alter the fact that the UK and the Commonwealth have primary responsibility for the defence of the area'. However, in evident reference to the pervading nationalist anathema to Britain's continuing colonial hold over the Middle East, McGhee asserted that the new structure would make it easier for the Arab states and Israel to co-ordinate plans directly with the Allied command.

A few days later, McGhee made a specific plea, both in writing to Acheson and verbally before the NSC, that the administration work for a reversal of the JCS veto on any American military commitment to the Middle East. He argued that given British weakness in that area, the JCS veto, for at least the first two years of any war, amounted in effect to 'the abandonment, without even a token defence effort, of most if not all of the Middle East in time of global war'.[31]

McGhee claimed that major changes had occurred on the world scene since the previous October. The rate of US military build-up had increased, and NATO was more firmly established. But there was an increasing danger that the states of the Middle East would not remain within the Western orbit, unless the Allies gave them some 'practical evidence' of their interest.

McGhee challenged the 'defeatist' attitude of the JCS. They could

---

[29] Ibid, p.5.

[30] Ibid, p.6.

[31] For this and following, see memorandum, 'Re-Evaluation of US Plans for the Middle East', *FRUS*, 1951, V, pp.6–11. The editors of the *FRUS* volume found no date or signature on the document they selected. Peter Hahn claims that the date was 29 December 1950, and that the author was again McGhee. Hahn also claims that McGhee put these same arguments to a meeting of the NSC on 29 Dec. 1950. Cf., Hahn, *The United States . . .* p.28.

not justify the abandonment of the Middle East in time of war on the grounds that the Soviets and their satellites had the ability to occupy the region. Given that the United States and the UK had similar security interests in the region, it was only the more striking that there was no similarity in their defence plans. Not only were the British too weak to defend the region on their own, but their weakness was well known throughout the area. To continue in the traditional belief that the US could rely upon the British to defend their interests in the region was 'to indulge in wishful thinking.' Finally, he pressed for an urgent re-evaluation of American plans for the defence of the Middle East 'away from the concept of primary British responsibility and toward the concept of combined US–UK responsibility and active US–UK cooperation in the development and implementation of plans'.[32]

McGhee summarised his views for Acheson's approval, prior to a meeting between top officials of the State Department and the JCS, scheduled for 31 January 1951. He pressed home the point that only the direct participation of the United States in the defence of the Middle East could reverse the political disaffection of the peoples of the region with the West. This was due to their growing suspicion that the US had left the defence of their region to the British, and would not intervene in the event of war.[33]

McGhee's initial paper, proposing a joint Anglo–American command structure in the Middle East, was apparently modified within the department, to soften the anticipated impact upon the JCS. His original idea was toned down to a proposal for: 'the stimulation and coordination of local area defence efforts through combined US – UK leadership'. Two projects mentioned specifically were the need for a radical strengthening of Turkey's armed forces, and 'the development of stability-in-depth in the Arab States and Israel.' Once more, it was stressed that the initiatives proposed would not alter the fact that the British and the Commonwealth had primary responsibility for Middle East defence.[34]

On 27 January 1951, Acheson wrote to Secretary of Defense Marshall, describing the political deterioration that had occurred in the Middle East since the last Pentagon conference. He claimed that without more affirmative moves on the part of the United States, it was doubtful whether they could continue to count on the support of many of the Middle East states.[35]

[32] *FRUS*, 1951, Vol. V, pp.9–10.

[33] McGhee – Acheson, 15 Jan. 1951, (based on initial draft prepared by John B. Howard, regional planning adviser of NEA, 12 Jan.), ibid., pp.24–27.

[34] Ibid, p.25.

[35] Acheson – Marshall, 27 Jan. 1951, ibid., pp.21–23.

On 31 January, State Department senior staff met with the JCS. Although the meeting had been scheduled in order to discuss the Far East, it was agreed to discuss the Middle East briefly, in view of McGhee's impending departure for a tour of the region.

McGhee opened the discussion. The State Department's concern was to ensure that the United States' 'major investments' in the Middle East, in Greece, Turkey and Iran, were well protected. They believed that 'a regional approach to the problem of Middle Eastern defences was called for'. The British had 'grudgingly accepted' responsibility for the region, but they planned to defend only the Suez Canal, to which purpose they had at their disposal only 11,000 combat troops. The department's proposals involved only limited amounts of material aid, to only a few countries – to Syria, the Lebanon, and Israel. Other countries of the Middle East were already being taken care of by other American aid programmes, or by the British. In summary, McGhee warned that unless the United States became involved in the defence of that region now, they would not be welcomed back after another war.[36]

The JCS rejected McGhee's proposals out of hand. General Omar N. Bradley, chairman of the JCS, indicated that he 'did not differ' with much of what McGhee had said. (This comment referred apparently to the current arrangement whereby the British held prime responsibility for the Middle East.) What concerned Bradley most was the Turks' refusal to co-ordinate planning with the British alone. This was confirmed by McGhee, who suggested, however, that the Turks might agree to talk with a joint Anglo–American team.

US Admiral Forrest P. Sherman, Chief of Naval Operations, opened the JCS broadside. Arguing from what he apparently deemed to be orthodox military imperatives, Sherman insisted that they must first build up the Allied military position in Western Europe, and only after that, in the Middle East. Sherman asserted that they could not commit troops to the Middle East, when they were so short of troops elsewhere. In fact, Sherman claimed, 'the proportion of troops available to the need' was better in the Middle East than in any other theatre. For the time being, they would have to content themselves with naval and air support for the area.

General J. Lawton Collins, US Army Chief of Staff, dismissed McGhee's proposal vehemently. He asserted that the US was 'on the outside periphery of the Middle East', not in the centre, in the Cairo–Suez area. Collins was sceptical about the advisability of a military mission even in Saudi Arabia, much less in Syria, the Lebanon and

---

[36] For this and following, cf., the State Department record of the meeting, ibid., pp.27–40; also Devereux, *The Formulation* . . ., p.49, and Hahn, *The United States* . . ., p.111.

Israel. He inferred with some disdain that the reasons why the peoples of the Middle East wanted American leadership were:

> (1) we will furnish equipment and pay the bills; and (2) in the event of war, they think, we will send troops and aircraft to the Middle East.
>
> We are kidding ourselves and kidding them if we do anything which indicates that we are going to put forces in that area. The forces to do that are just not in sight.[37]

Gen Collins accused the British of wanting them to pull their Middle East chestnuts out of the fire, and insisted that they must 'stick to the periphery' (i.e. the Northern Tier). If that periphery broke, then of course the war would have to be run from Cairo–Suez. However, to assume now any responsibility for the Middle East would be to take on obligations that they would be unable to meet in time of war.

At this point, Admiral Sherman intervened, to express some sympathy for the State Department's point of view. The more he considered the problem, the more he appreciated that passing responsibility for the Middle East to the UK, while lifting responsibility from American shoulders, in fact solved nothing, since the UK was unable to defend the area. Gen Collins agreed with Sherman's low estimate of British capabilities, but insisted that those of the US in that theatre were yet lower.

Paul Nitze, director of the PPS, now intervened. Western Europe was now protected by NATO. Therefore, it appeared to his staff that the area now most seriously threatened by future Soviet action was the Middle East. The only deterrent to a Soviet advance in that theatre might be the fear that such action would provoke an American reaction.

McGhee stressed again that State's proposals would not involve the commitment of any American troops to the area, either in peace or in war. Their proposals should be regarded as an insurance policy, to protect their investments along the Northern Tier, in Greece, Turkey and Iran. They were proposing aid in the amount of between $5–10 millions. Neither were they suggesting that the US assume military leadership in the area. They were proposing that the US assume a role subordinate to the UK, and that 'the U.S. and U.K. should form an interlocking base for a regional defense effort'.[38]

Gen Bradley asserted that the basic problem was 'the lack of organisation in the Mediterranean area'. It was for Gen Eisenhower, SACEUR, to determine what would be the relations between the Mediterranean and European theatres. Until Eisenhower settled that problem, it mattered little what either they or the British said about the

---

[37] *FRUS*, 1951, Vol.V., p.33.   [38] Ibid, p.36.

defence of the area, since neither country was able to commit any troops.

McGhee insisted that they must have 'some kind of a theatre command', and that Turkey had to be included in the Middle East theatre. Admiral Sherman disagreed. He thought they must hold Turkey in abeyance for the present, since it bordered both on Europe and on the Middle East. But Gen Collins concurred with McGhee – from the point of view of the Turkish army, Turkey was a part of the Middle East. However, Gen Collins was concerned less with the size of any American military commitment to the Middle East than with the psychological problem. They could not allow the countries of the Middle East to delude themselves that the US would come to their aid. They would be 'kidding them and kidding ourselves' if they took on such responsibilities.

McGhee insisted that they were already running that same risk, with their programmes in the Northern Tier countries. It would require but a small additional effort in the Middle East, 'as a form of insurance and as evidence of our faith'. He added that he would rather give the peoples of the Middle East some illusions now, than leave them in their current state of mind. Dean Rusk, Assistant Secretary of State for Far Eastern Affairs, intimated that for some time to come, they would be 'kidding' in Western Europe also.

But Gen Collins was adamant. It would be an act of bad, not good faith. The 'big job' was 'first, last, and always' to win the battle in Europe. He repeated the Pentagon view that even if they lost the Middle East temporarily, but held on to Western Europe, they would be in a satisfactory position. After they had won the main battle in Western Europe, they could 'go down to the Middle East and clean up whatever problems' they found there.

There was little if any meeting of minds. The Military remained unpersuaded. The only concrete result was the State Department's agreement to Gen Bradley's request that they draft an NSC paper on the division of the Balkans, Near East and Middle East into separate commands. This would become a critical question during the course of 1951, as Turkey assumed an ever more prominent role in American strategic planning. The State Department did manage to secure the acquiescence of the JCS to State discussions with the British on the issue of responsibility in the Middle East.

Within less than two weeks, the NSC had drafted a paper on American policy towards Israel and the Arabs. The draft repeated the department's central thesis that it would take a relatively small American investment to ensure that the Arab states and Israel remained oriented to the West. If they did not make this investment, it was doubtful if their support could be mobilised during a global war, or regained after one. American policy should be directed toward securing base rights in the region; as a concrete step to achieving such rights, they should despatch limited arms shipments to Israel and the Arab states, at an early date. They should also develop 'fighting groups and techniques' suited to the conditions of the area and, upon request, send small American missions of technical advisers, and accept local military personnel for training in American and British staff colleges.[39]

C. TURKEY'S ROLE IN NATO AND IN THE MIDDLE EAST

The JCS were not convinced by State arguments for increased (even nominal) American military involvement in the Middle East. However, they had been impressed by reports on British weakness and decline in the region. In view of the British demise, the JCS looked increasingly to Turkey as the single regional power upon which to base American strategic planning in that theatre. However, as noted already (Chapter one), the Turks would not permit significant strategic developments on their territory until they were allowed into the NATO alliance. By 1951, the JCS feared that unless Turkey was offered a NATO commitment, the United States would lose her base rights in that territory.

However, Anglo–Turkish friction, and British objections, prevented Allied induction of the Turks into NATO. The British regarded Turkey as a Middle Eastern power, to be incorporated in British contingency plans for the Middle East, and subordinated to British military headquarters in Cairo. In contrast, the Turks regarded themselves as a European power, and refused to place their forces under British command in the Middle East.[40]

Herein lay the basic parameters for an Anglo–American 'deal' that would be hammered out during the summer of 1951. In order to meet the strategic goals of both the Americans and the British, the latter would waive their opposition to Turkish entry into NATO; and the Americans would agree to join MEC, and persuade the Turks to do so as well.

Further to the conclusions of the Pentagon conference of October 1950, two rounds of talks were conducted between the British and American Middle East commanders, on the British-held island of Malta; the first round from 23–24 January, the second from 10–13 March 1951. The British team was led by General Sir Brian Robertson,

---

[39] Draft NSC paper, 10 Feb. 1951, ibid, pp.46–47.
[40] Cf., Devereux, *The Formulation of . . .*, p.49.

C. in C., MELF; the American side was led by Admiral Robert Carney, CINCELM.

At the first round of talks, discussion centred on the question of whether, for planning purposes, Turkey should be included in Europe, or in the Middle East. Gen Robertson stressed the British view that Turkey was essentially part of the Middle East, and that Allied strategy should plan to help the Turks win their battle, not to salvage the situation that would arise in the event of their defeat. Robertson argued that even if the JCS had insisted on leaving the British Commonwealth responsible for the Middle East, the British Middle East HQ in Cairo should still be considered an Allied HQ, carrying out an Allied mission. The Turks, with whom the British had a long association, and to whom they were treaty bound, should be told to co-ordinate their plans with the British HQ, Cairo.[41]

Air Chief Marshal Sir John Baker, C. in C., MEAF, added that their planning for an air defence system along the Outer Ring was dependent on full co-ordination with the Turkish air force, and free access to the Turks' air defence system.[42]

There could be little doubt that from the purely military and strategic point of view, Turkey constituted an integral part of the Middle East theatre, one of the key components of the Outer Ring defence system. This evident fact was conceded by Admiral Carney. However, noted Carney, the Turks themselves preferred to look for aid to the United States, who was currently providing all the money and equipment for her armed forces. Carney stated that the Turks had even forbade him from divulging their strategic plans to the British. He could reveal only that the Turks' strategic conception for the Middle East was basically the same as that of the Allies.

Carney agreed essentially with Robertson's position that the British and American effort in Turkey should be co-ordinated. He deprecated the Turks' secrecy. But on the other hand, in view of the Allies' own weakness in this theatre, he did not feel that the time was yet ripe for frank talks with the Turks.

In between the two rounds of Anglo–American staff talks at Malta, McGhee toured the Middle East, from February to March 1951. He opened his tour in mid-February with a week-long conference in Istanbul with the US Chiefs of Mission, Middle East. The major item on the agenda was again the strategic importance and role of Turkey in the event of a war against the Soviets. The discussion, which touched also on the British position in Egypt, illustrated well the primacy already given by the Americans to the North Tier strategic conception.

[41] Devereux, ibid, p.49; and report on talks in C. in C., Mediterranean to Admiralty, Jan. 1951, in FO 371/91219. PRO.   [42] Ibid.

The conference concluded that it was vital and urgent to initiate moves to include Turkey in NATO. There was strong popular Turkish feeling in favour of the West, but if no offer was forthcoming shortly, the Turks might well switch to a policy of neutrality. Until the United States made a commitment to her, they could not be certain that Turkey would declare war, unless attacked directly. Only a direct commitment by the United States could ensure Turkey's immediate co-belligerency, and Turkish permission for Allied use of the strategic infrastructure which they were in the process of building up in that country.[43]

In focusing on Turkey, the conference recognised the importance of her role in the Middle East campaign. In his report on 'the strategic implications' of the conference, Admiral Carney stressed the military significance of Turkey, Greece and Yugoslavia to SACEUR, in tying down substantial Soviet forces in the event of a conflict. However, Carney continued, Turkey had a dual role to play, not only in Europe, but in the Middle East also. He concluded that military aid to Turkey should be 'the most extensive', in the hope of promoting not only 'the Turkish capacity for great resistance', but also 'some limited Turkish offensive'.[44]

The conference also dealt at some length with various options for setting up a regional defence system. The US chiefs of mission believed that the Arab states would join such a system, provided that it was sponsored and supported by both the UK *and* the US; and provided that they would not be required to deal directly with Israel. It was still generally assumed that any Middle East defence grouping would be set up as an appendage of NATO. In marked contrast to their pressure for the acceptance of Turkey (and Greece) into NATO, the mission chiefs were against associating the Middle Eastern states in any way with NATO. McGhee reassured the conference that beyond working for the inclusion of Greece and Turkey in NATO, the administration had no plans for making defence commitments to any other state in the Middle East.

At the second round of the Malta talks, Turkey again provided the main focus of discussion. The British side could not remain indifferent to the Turks' military potential, especially in view of American military investment in that country. Naturally, they wished to mobilise that potential for the Middle East campaign. In his report back to the COS,

---

[43] For this and following, cf., Conclusions and Recommendations of Chiefs of Middle Eastern Missions conference, Istanbul, 14–21 Feb. 1951, *FRUS*, 1951, Vol. V, pp.50–7.

[44] Admiral Robert B. Carney, Strategic implications of Istanbul conference, Tab B, Berry (Deputy Assistant Secretary of State for NE, South Asian and African affairs) to Secretary Acheson, 15 March 1951, ibid, p.103.

Gen Robertson now referred to Turkey as the most militarily powerful of all the indigenous states of the region. British planning should therefore consider the battle in Turkey 'as an integral part of the campaign in the Middle East'. They would have to do everything to ensure that it was won. Robertson criticised British planners for having given the wrong impression that they were apathetic to the battle in Turkey, until the Turks were pushed back to the Taurus mountains. Even if at present they knew nothing of Turkish war plans, they should, if they had the resources, go to the aid of the Turks from the outset of war, and not wait until the Turks were pushed back.[45]

Air Marshal Baker urged the commitment of more Allied Air forces to the defence of Turkey, which was in danger of being overwhelmed by the Soviet air effort. Given that the Allies would be fighting in the Outer Ring at the end of 'a long and vulnerable L of C.', they would need at least air parity. Their two 'saving factors' were the existence of two good operational air bases in Iraq and Jordan, to which the Allies might deploy their air forces forward. Their only problem would be 'to find the air forces' to operate from them![46]

The US chiefs of mission conference at Istanbul (held in February 1951), had also held a short, but most significant discussion on Egypt. The British proposal to set up a MEC based in Egypt, as a way of getting round the Anglo–Egyptian impasse, was again rejected. While recognising the strategic importance of Egypt, the conference recommended that it be brought into some 'general scheme of defense planning by other means than through a possible association with the NATO.'[47]

Thus while there was something of a meeting of American and British minds at Malta on the strategic and military potential of Turkey, there was no consensus on the question of Egypt. Whereas the British military remained committed to Egypt, the Americans were coming rapidly to the conclusion that the British base in Egypt was provoking more political trouble than its strategic worth. This was perhaps the major conclusion that McGhee drew from his visit to the Middle East in general, and to Egypt in particular.

On his way back to the United States, McGhee stopped over in London for a week, for consultations with his Foreign Office counterparts. Referring to the global situation, he stated that the next 18 months, while the West was still re-arming, would be critical. But he alarmed his interlocutors when, referring to the continuing deadlock

[45] Gen Robertson report on Malta Talks, March 1951, COS (51) 166, 30 March 1951, in Defe 5/29. PRO.

[46] Ibid.

[47] Istanbul conference, 14–21 February 1951, *FRUS*, 1951, Vol. V, pp.50–57.

over Egypt, he stated that: '*the political advantages of an acceptable settlement seemed to outweigh the strategic advantages of what might be ideal arrangements from a military standpoint.*'[48] (my emphasis)

The Foreign Office forwarded to the State Department an official demurral, expressing concern at the impression McGhee had left, that 'the United States valued Egyptian co-operation more highly than it did the retention of strategic facilities for defence of Middle East'. Wells Stabler, the NEA official who dealt with the message, rejoined that the British impression was not correct. Stabler admitted, however, that the United States was 'considerably concerned' about the impasse in the Anglo–Egyptian negotiations.[49]

McGhee also reported to the British on his talks in Cairo with Mohamed Salaheddin Bey, the Egyptian Foreign Minister. The latter had convinced McGhee that the Egyptians would not budge from their demand that the British evacuate their forces, before anything else. The withdrawal would have to be completed within 12 months, although the Egyptians might agree to 18. Notwithstanding the conclusions of the Istanbul conference, McGhee had tested Salaheddin on the possibility of replacing the British garrison with a multinational, or UN force. He had even suggested that the United States might appoint a deputy commander under General Robertson (!). The Egyptian Foreign Minister remained non-committal (which McGhee took as a positive sign).[50]

McGhee's argumentation was somewhat anomalous. On the one hand, he alarmed the British by stating that a political agreement with Egypt was of paramount importance, at whatever strategic cost. On the other, he still toyed with variations on the MEC theme, notwithstanding the opposition of US diplomats in the field.

Even the Foreign Office now agreed with their ambassador in Cairo, Sir Ralph Stevenson, that there was little or no chance of the Egyptians agreeing to the stationing of foreign troops on Egyptian soil. What McGhee perhaps feared most was that the British might resort to subduing the Egyptians by force. He thought that such a step would be extremely unwise, and urged them not to resort to such a radical course.[51]

The Istanbul conference convinced the administration in Washington of the urgency of aligning Turkey with the West, in NATO if

[48] Note of McGhee informal discussions with Foreign Office officials, 2 April 1951, ibid, p.106.

[49] Note of conversation between Denis A. Greenhill, first secretary at the British embassy, Washington, and Lewis Jones and Wells Stabler of NEA, 27 April 1951, ibid, p.109, note 6.

[50] Note of McGhee's discussion with Foreign Office officials, and Sir Ralph Stevenson, British ambassador, Cairo, on 10 April 1951, ibid, p.359.

[51] Ibid.

possible. This urgency was pressed home in late April 1951, in a forceful telegram written by George Wadsworth, the US ambassador to Turkey. Wadsworth reported that the Turks claimed, 'with considerable justification', that their application for NATO membership came from a position of 'strength rather than from weakness'. They failed to comprehend how certain NATO powers were reluctant to accept the aid of 'the strongest army in Europe, and the only nation in the Middle East capable of withstanding aggression. Together with the Greeks, the Turks would constitute "Eisenhower's strong right flank" '.[52]

These themes were developed in a major policy paper presented to the President in May 1951 (NSC 109). Turkey was described as:

> . . . the strongest anti-Communist country on the periphery of the USSR and the only one in the Eastern Mediterranean and Middle East area capable of offering substantial resistance to Soviet aggression . . . Turkey's alignment with the free world furnishes a protective screen behind which the defensive strength of the countries in the Eastern Mediterranean and Middle East can be developed . . .[53]

If the West did not support Turkey, Soviet domination of that country would give the latter the strategic advantages of control of the Straits, and also lead them to conclude that the United States would not resist Soviet or satellite aggression against other countries in the Near or Middle East.

NSC 109 concluded that apart from maintaining its military and economic aid programmes to Turkey, the United States should press forthwith for the inclusion of Turkey as a full member of NATO – in order to guarantee Turkish co-belligerency, the full use of Turkish military facilities, and the closure of the Straits to the Soviets. If this step was delayed for an unacceptable duration, they should conclude alternative security arrangements with the Turks, that would not prejudice Turkish entry into NATO 'at the earliest practicable date'. The administration's determination to work for the early admission of Turkey into NATO was among the key factors in transforming its (particularly the Pentagon's) attitude to MEC.

By the Spring of 1951, Allied strategic planning for the Middle East appeared to pivot along two separate, albeit interfaced axes; the first, the need to incorporate the Turks in NATO, and to include them in Allied planning for the Middle East; and second, the need to retrieve the British, or at least the Allies', position in Egypt (a new round of Anglo–Egyptian negotiations in April 1951 again ended in deadlock).

The State Department needed both to convince the Pentagon about

[52]　Wadsworth – Secretary of State, 24 April 1951, *FRUS*, 1951, Vol. III, p.516.

[53]　For this and following, cf., NSC 109, 11 May 1951, PSF, HST.

some measure of American involvement in the Middle East; and to secure British agreement to Turkish entry into NATO. The British needed American involvement in the Middle East: in order to extricate themselves from their bilateral dispute with the Egyptians and, by now no less important, so that the Americans would agree to work for a Turkish military commitment to the Middle East. During the summer, the US and the UK each appeared to accommodate their ally's strategic goal.[54]

It will be recalled that when in Cairo, McGhee had raised the possibility of stationing in Egypt some multinational, or UN force to replace the British garrison. McGhee evidently had the MEC in mind. Even if the Egyptian Foreign Minister had not exactly responded enthusiastically, McGhee now looked to the MEC as the last chance of saving the Allied position in Egypt. Again, he succeeded in persuading Secretary Acheson, who became convinced that MEC was an ingenious scheme to assuage Egyptian nationalist sensibilities, while permitting continued Allied use of the Suez base in wartime. MEC was in fact a transparent stratagem to disguise a continued British presence along the Canal. But Acheson was prepared to throw in special inducements for Egypt, including military and economic aid, and technical assistance.[55]

McGhee hoped also to get the military to agree to a nominal American military presence in Egypt, to sweeten the bitter pill of continued British presence for the Egyptians. In preparation for Anglo–American staff talks that were to take place in Washington in May 1951, a State–Defense working group met on 26 April, to determine the lines upon which the US and the UK should co-ordinate their efforts in the Middle East. Measures suggested included: the development of 'fighting groups and techniques suitable to local capabilities and terrain'; the placing of orders for raw materials and equipment; the expansion of psychological warfare in the region; and 'show-the-flag' visits.[56]

On 2 May 1951, McGhee met with the JCS to report on his Middle East tour. His ambiguity about the British position in the Middle East did little to persuade the JCS to reverse their policy of non-involvement in that theatre. McGhee stated quite bluntly that the British were increasingly unpopular in the region, and that antagonism to them extended to the West as a whole. At present, the British constituted a

---

[54] Cf., Devereux, *The Formulation* . . . pp.51–2; and Hahn, *The United States* . . ., pp.112–13.

[55] Cf., Melvyn P. Leffler, *A Preponderance of Power: National Security, the Truman Administration and the Cold War*, Stanford: Stanford University Press, 1992, p.425.

[56] Acheson – Defense Secretary Marshall, 26 April 1951, RG 330, Sec Defense, CD 092, box 230, NA; and note of State – Defense Working group, 26 April 1951, in *FRUS*, 1951, Vol. V. p.124.

liability to the United States and, McGhee reiterated: 'This liability is such that it may exceed the military value of cooperating with them in the area'.[57]

However, McGhee was convinced that they must co-ordinate their efforts with the British, in a 'regional approach to the problem of defense'. He believed that only American intervention could prevent the defection of the Arab states from the Western orbit. McGhee had also raised the MEC project with the Turks. But the latter, like the Greeks and the Iranians, refused to accept a British command. McGhee reiterated that they would have to reach agreement with the British over the division of commands and responsibility in the region.

The JCS presumably arrived at the meeting enlightened by an intelligence report distributed just the week before. The report (of which McGhee had probably been one of the authors) now lent added weight to McGhee's prior warnings about British decline in the Middle East. It warned that Britain would welcome an American contribution to the defence of the area, but 'would expect to remain the senior partner'. The report noted also the danger of 'neutralism' in the region, and the desire of indigenous states for 'a unilateral US and UK guarantee of protection *without any commitment on their part*'.[58] (My emphasis.)

Admiral Sherman quoted from the report at the meeting on 2 May. He suggested that the problem was both the growth of nationalist agitation, and 'a shrewd estimate by these countries that the U.K. is no longer a great Power.' Sherman was supported by General Hoyt S. Vandenberg, USAF Chief of Staff, who agreed that the countries of the Middle East were turning to the Americans as the dominant world power. Since the peoples of the Middle East understood power better than they in the West did, Gen Vandenberg stated that they (the Americans) might further their aims more by the use of old-fashioned power politics:'By sending our fleet and by flying our bombers around, we would get more cooperation at less cost'.

Gen Collins, in characteristically brusque fashion, expostulated:

All that you [McGhee] have said this morning indicates to me that you have concluded that we should take over in the Middle East.[59]

Not taken aback, McGhee retorted that if they had sufficient forces, which he understand they did not, that might indeed be the best course to adopt.

In conclusion, McGhee referred to Turkey as their 'greatest asset in

[57] For this and following, see memo on State – JCS meeting, 2 May 1951, ibid., pp.114–17.
[58] NIE-26, 25 April 1951, PSF, box 253, HST.
[59] *FRUS*, 1951, Vol. V., p.116.

the Middle East', and warned of the very real danger that she might turn neutral, unless given a security commitment by NATO. McGhee noted that the Turks were ready to build up 25 extra divisions if the Americans helped them. But Gen Collins was equally negative about finding the equipment to fit out the Turks. McGhee retorted that at least they should bring them into NATO.

It would appear that this meeting marked a watershed in American military thinking. McGhee's message, even if ambiguous, had its own iron logic. The British were a declining power, perhaps already a spent power. The Turks were now the strongest regional power, but could not fulfil their military potential without American aid. And without the protection of NATO's security umbrella, the Turks would not co-operate with the Allies. In time of war, they might even deny their strategic and military assets to the West. The JCS no longer vetoed any military involvement in the Middle East. McGhee had opened the door to a limited American involvement in this theatre.

D. MEC AND THE SACLANT – MEDITERRANEAN COMMANDS DISPUTE

Final JCS acquiescence in MEC came almost as an incidental by-product of a major political–military dispute over supreme Allied command in the Atlantic. The crisis had erupted in February 1951, with the announcement of the appointment of an American admiral, William M. Fechteler, as Supreme Allied Commander, North Atlantic (SACLANT).

Winston Churchill, head of the Opposition, had criticised the appointment vigorously in Parliament. Seizing a convenient oppor-tunity for attacking the Labour Government, Churchill succeeded in arousing the patriotic passions of a nation that had yet to reconcile itself to the end of Empire, and to American pre-eminence.

The British reaction to Admiral Fechteler's appointment is reflected authentically in a private letter written by Air Marshal Sir John Slessor (Chief of the Air Staff), to his close friend and wartime comrade, Gen Eisenhower, head of SHAPE. In March 1951, Slessor wrote that the Atlantic command announcement had been 'badly handled politically'. The British reaction had been: 'an inevitable psychological reaction of a maritime people, all of whom have a percentage of salt water in their veins'. Slessor, not immune himself to imperialist nostalgia, added: 'Britannia did rule the waves 3 to 4 hundred years before 1942 – and did so, incidentally, to the great benefit of the United States'.[60]

[60] Slessor to Eisenhower, 9 March 1951, cited in Louis Galambos, ed., *The Papers of Dwight*

In response, the British insisted on the appointment of a British officer to head a separate Mediterranean command, independent of SACEUR. When the Americans began to press the British to concede the induction of Greece and Turkey into NATO, the British demanded command both of a NATO Eastern (Aegean) Command, and of MEC. The Americans opposed this, and proposed the appointment of a British commander as CINCEAST (Eastern Mediterranean), subordinate to SACEUR. To complicate the issue further, Greece and Turkey themselves refused to serve under a British officer, and insisted on serving under Admiral Carney, now CINCSOUTH (Southern Europe).[61]

British pressure to compensate them with a supreme command in the Mediterranean, prompted the JCS, in early March, to postpone Fechteler's appointment, until differences with the British had been settled.[62] (The SACLANT appointment was in fact held in abeyance until the spring of 1952. In the meantime, in August 1951, Admiral Fechteler was appointed CNO.)

Allied discussions over the Atlantic and Mediterranean commands just happened to coincide, and now merged with the other issues already on the Allied agenda for the Middle East – Turkish entry into NATO, and MEC.

The Labour government, embarrassed by the domestic storm over the perceived injury to 'national prestige and glory', soon pressed for 'compensation', in the form of the appointment of a British admiral as Supreme Commander in the Mediterranean. Eisenhower himself favoured this idea, provided that the US Sixth Fleet, present in the Mediterranean for the protection of SACEUR's right flank, remained under his own direct command.[63]

On 3 March 1951, Eisenhower discussed the issue with Admirals Sherman, and Carney. Eisenhower's chief concern was to build up European morale and support for NATO. He feared that the SACLANT crisis might lead to a loss of British support for NATO. He felt that it was now 'absolutely necessary' that a British officer be given 'an important position in the Mediterranean command structure', in order to offset the loss in prestige the British felt over the SACLANT appointment. The admirals retorted that the United States would be providing the majority of the naval forces in the Mediterranean. Carney

David Eisenhower, Vol. XII, Baltimore/London: Johns Hopkins University Press, 1989, p.97, note 4.

[61] Walter S. Poole, *The History of the Joint Chiefs of Staff: The Joint Chiefs of Staff and National Policy*, Vol. IV, 1950–1952, Wilmington: Michael Glazier, 1980, p.310.

[62] Ibid., note 3.

[63] Eisenhower diary entry, 2 March 1951, in Galambos, *The papers . . .*, Vol. XII, p.83.

complained that the British wanted to seize 'strategic control of the entire war effort from the North Cape to the Indian Ocean'. But Eisenhower insisted that they should 'be generous in the matter of titles and could afford to call the British "Supreme" even though our contribution was greater'.[64]

During the month of April, the crisis deepened, as the Labour government responded to adverse public reactions. The new Foreign Secretary, Herbert Morrison, warned that continuing crisis threatened to poison Anglo–United States relations.[65] Though in a speech before the Commons on 19 April, he played down the appointment of an American SACLANT, stating that in any case, British naval forces predominated in the North Eastern Atlantic, and that the British admiral in that sector would in fact have *de facto* absolute powers.

In private, the British let it be known that they would now welcome the early appointment of Admiral Fechteler, in order to pave the way for the subsequent designation of a British admiral as Supreme commander in the Mediterranean. But the Americans insisted on retaining direct control of their own ships in that theatre. However, they were also sensitive to the political ramifications of the crisis, and the potentially unfavorable effects of their actions upon 'the already insecure' Labour administration. Thus the State Department, in consultation with the JCS, offered to re-open the entire issue of the naval commands with the British.[66]

Anglo–American consultations on the naval commands were held in Washington, on 16 and 24 May 1951. The British side was led by the British ambassador, Sir Oliver Franks, and Air Chief Marshal William Elliot, head of the British Joint Staff Mission in Washington. The American delegation included Paul Nitze, George McGhee and Elbert Mathews of the State Department, and the JCS.[67]

Initially, the American side tried to restrict the discussion to the issue of naval command in the Mediterranean, without entering into the question of command arrangements in the Middle East. But the British raised the MEC project at the very first meeting, on 16 May 1951.

Ambassador Franks demanded the appointment of a British supreme

---

[64] Ibid., note 3, pp.90–1. A report by Capt. George W. Anderson, Gen Greunther's naval assistant for plans, policies and operations, written on 25 Feb. 1952, estimated that of the conventional forces that would be available in the Mediterranean in wartime, 40 per cent would be provided by the Americans, 20 per cent by the British, 15 per cent by the French, 12 per cent by the Italians, and less than 10 per cent each by the Greeks and the Turks. cf., Galambos, Vol. XIII, 1989, p.1022, note 1.

[65] Hahn, *The United States . . .*, p.112.

Ernest Bevin had relinquished the post of Foreign Secretary in March, due to ill-health.

[66] Acheson – US embassy, UK, 28 April 1951, in *FRUS*, 1951, Vol. III, pp.517–519.

[67] Editorial note, ibid, pp.522–4.

commander for the Mediterranean. He explained that the British regarded that sea as a single 'distinct strategic entity – a "unitary sea" – washing the shores of both Europe and the Middle East'. The British wanted a 'degree of equivalence' between their respective positions in the Atlantic and in the Mediterranean. In return for their agreeing to an American SACLANT, to whom British naval commanders would be subordinate, the British wanted a British SACME, under whom would serve an American commander responsible for all naval forces in the Mediterranean.[68]

At first, the JCS rejected the analogy drawn by Franks, and countered that General Eisenhower envisaged a NATO front extending no further east than Yugoslavia and Greece – therefore, the Middle East should be a separate theatre, under British command. The American Service chiefs regarded British ambitions as anachronistic, and inconsistent with 'U.S. political influence, relative military strengths, and over-all responsibilities.'[69]

But General Collins and Admiral Sherman did not reject the MEC project out of hand. Being immovably against a British supreme command in the Mediterranean, the JCS perhaps now saw the MEC as suitable compensation, to assuage British pride, at an affordable price. It was the first time that the JCS gave serious consideration to the establishment of a separate Middle East Command. This presented an opening for the British to initiate a discussion on the MEC. They wanted the new command to include, at a minimum, British and Turkish troops under a British Supreme Commander Middle East (SACME).

The JCS did stress their problems with the MEC, primarily the paucity of their own resources. But they now conceded that American interest in the Middle East had grown, given the existence of US military missions in Turkey and Iran, and with Turkey about to be brought into NATO.[70]

At the second meeting, the JCS rejected out of hand the British demand for a separate, British-led Mediterranean command between SHAPE and the Middle East. (The British demand for a supreme command in the Mediterranean was in fact never satisfied; it fell foul of American insistence that its own naval vessels in the Mediterranean come directly under SACEUR; and to universal opposition to a British commander – both from the member nations of NATO, and from Greece and Turkey.) Ambassador Franks conceded that those Ameri-

[68] Ibid., p.523; also Poole, *History of the JCS* . . ., Vol. IV, 1950–1952, p.336.

[69] Cf., Admiral Robert B. Carney to Gen Dwight Eisenhower, 1 June 1951, Papers of Robert B. Carney, (2) (July 1949 – December 1951), box 21, The Eisenhower Library (EL).

[70] Cf., *FRUS*, 1951, Vol. III, pp.522–23; *FRUS*, 1951, Vol. V, p.144, note 1; and Devereux, *The Formulation* . . ., p.52.

can forces (naval and air) imported into the Mediterranean that were American, should come under American command.[71]

The 'package deal' evolving between the Allies – the admission of Turkey into NATO and American and Turkish adherence to MEC (now made the more urgent by the need to assuage hurt British pride), was next taken up at the highest levels on both sides of the Atlantic.

The British Cabinet, meeting the week after the Washington talks, agreed that Britain would have to concede the American proposal for the inclusion of Turkey in NATO. Minister of Defence Shinwell pointed out that their opposition to Turkish entry into NATO would only alienate the Turks, whom they needed for any effective defence of the Middle East. But if they persisted in refusing the Turks entry into NATO, and left the Americans to make them a unilateral guarantee, the Turks would then be drawn exclusively into the sphere of SACEUR in Europe. On the other hand, if they agreed to Turkish entry into NATO, they would: 'be in a better position to press for a Supreme Allied Command, Middle East, with a British Commander, in which Turkey would play a vital part'.[72]

CIGS Slim underlined Shinwell's point that they could not effectively defend the Middle East without the Turks. He claimed that the admission of the latter into NATO would not draw Turkish military forces to the defence of the West, since they would be required urgently in the defence of the Middle East. (Slim did not explain why the Americans, or for that matter, the Turks, would necessarily regard a Soviet threat to the Middle East as more urgent or important than a Soviet threat to Western Europe.)

The Cabinet noted also that only the involvement of the Americans (whose protection the Turks sought) in MEC might hasten Turkish involvement in Allied plans for the defence of the Middle East. Even if the Americans currently refused to commit their own forces to this theatre, the British direly needed their Allies to become more involved in 'the building up of Middle East defences under British auspices'.

Attlee made it clear that British agreement to Turkish entry into NATO was to be held as a bargaining chip against American adherence to MEC. The government would do no more than express its agreement in principle to include the Turks and the Greeks in NATO, contingent on a prior examination of the military implications involved. Simultaneously, they should seek a clarification of American views on

---

[71] Cf., Galambos, *The Papers* . . ., Vol. XIII, pp.1022–23, notes 1, 7; and *FRUS*, 1951, Vol. III, p.524.

[72] For this and following, see Cabinet minutes, 22 May 1951, CM (51), Cab 128/19. PRO.

the organisation of MEC, in order to secure effective Middle East defence planning with other Middle Eastern countries.[73]

One day later, on 23 May 1951, the PPS circulated a paper in Washington that elaborated on the implications for the United States of the new Middle East Command. The Americans recognised that the British needed MEC in order to meet their own pressing needs for American involvement in the Middle East, and for the integration of the Turks in the land defence of the Middle East. The PPS recommended that the US make an early announcement of their joint sponsorship of MEC, due to British domestic pressures for participation in command arrangements in Europe and in the Middle East. The Turks, once in NATO, would be committed to both the European and the Middle Eastern theatres. In the latter, the Turks would be asked to accept the command of a British SACME, although they would have their own deputy to SACME. The Turkish commitment to the Middle East was vital, concluded the paper, since Turkey was 'the anchor of the outer defence ring of the Middle East'.[74]

The details of the MEC were settled at a series of high level Anglo–American staff meetings during June and July 1951.

On 7 June, the Defence Committee approved the COS terms of reference for further negotiations on the MEC. The British intended to demand a high price for their agreement to Turkish entry into NATO – American agreement to a British SACME, and the inclusion of Greece and Turkey in MEC.[75]

They set their opening position naively high, in an attempt to retain in their own hands as large a share of the Mediterranean and Middle East commands as possible. The SACME should be British, working in close association with NATO. Greece and Turkey should be associated with MEC, not with Eisenhower's European flank. The British Naval C. in C. Mediterranean and the US Sixth Fleet would come under SACME's command. The British would press for the establishment of a Middle East Defense Board under SACME's chairmanship, to include representatives of Britain, the United States, Turkey, and Greece. France, which would in fact contribute nothing to the Middle East, should also be included, for political reasons.

However, the Cabinet formula on the naval commands was toned down by the COS, who met with Gen Bradley the next day, 8 May. The COS compromise proposal for the Mediterranean commands

---

[73] Ibid.

[74] PPS Working Paper, 'Command Structure in the Middle East', 23 May 1951, *FRUS*, 1951, pp.144–48.

[75] Conclusions of Defence Committee meeting of 7 June 1951, in annex to JP (51) 106, 18 June 1951, Defe 6/17. PRO; and Devereux, *The Formulation . . .*, p.53.

effectively settled this aspect of the Anglo–American dispute. Lord Fraser, the British First Sea Lord, proposed a 'functional division' of the naval commands in the Mediterranean; a British SACME, who would 'command and operate all the British naval forces and bases throughout the Mediterranean'. In addition, Admiral Carney (CINCELM), would be C. in C. of SACEUR's southern flank. As such, Carney would command all American naval vessels in the Mediterranean, and be responsible for the protection of Mediterranean communications to Eisenhower's southern flank in Europe. This proved to be 'very much in line with' Gen Bradley's own way of thinking. (On 18 June, SHAPE announced Carney's appointment as C. in C. Allied Forces, Southern Europe – CINCSOUTH.)[76]

In return, Bradley affirmed American agreement to the establishment of a MEC, to be 'effective both in peace and war'. But he warned that the State Department would probably not agree to the association of the new command with NATO, as the time was not yet ripe for the latter body to become a worldwide organisation. CIGS Slim admonished that the MEC would have to be 'very much more definite' than what the US had so far proposed.[77]

The Anglo–American talks were resumed in Washington on 19 June. The American side included the JCS, Mathews of NEA, and John Ferguson, deputy director of the PPS. The British team was headed by ambassador Franks, and Air Chief Marshal Elliot. The meetings produce a 'tentative agreement' on the establishment of MEC.[78]

The British compromise proposal regarding the Mediterranean commands was approved. The British now compromised on Greece and Turkey too. They proposed that Turkish forces should come under SACME, whereas Greek forces would come under Eisenhower's southern command. General Collins proposed that Turkey join NATO and MEC simultaneously. The State Department preferred to appoint a separate NATO Supreme Allied Eastern commander, and a British SACME. It was agreed that a Turkish officer would be appointed as deputy SACME, given that Turkey would be providing the major part of the land forces. But only admission into NATO could possibly persuade the Turks to serve under a British command in the Middle East. However, as Bradley had warned, the State Department still opposed extending NATO's commitment to the Middle East, an extension that would raise domestic problems for the Americans. The Middle East was not to be linked directly to the NATO area, and

---

[76] Record of meeting between Gen Bradley and the COS in London, 8 June 1951, *FRUS*, 1951, Vol. III, pp.528–30; and Galambos, *The Papers . . .*, Vol. XII, p.377, note 1.

[77] Ibid, and Poole, *History of the JCS . . .*, Vol. IV, 1950–1952, p.336.

[78] Poole, ibid.

except for Britain and Turkey, no NATO members would be involved in the fighting there.[79]

The State Department believed that it would 'mislead and dishearten' the indigenous peoples of the Middle East if they were given the impression that the West was interested in their defence only because their region protected NATO's southern flank. State proposed that Turkish forces be deployed in two separate commands, in the east and west of Turkey; in the west, those forces deployed at the Straits would be part of Eisenhower's southern flank; while those in the east would form a separate command along the Outer Ring mountain line, 'blocking Russian entry into the Middle East through the Caucasus'.[80]

The British also proposed the establishment of a Middle East Defence Board to serve under SACME, to be composed of a British chairman, and members from the United States, France, Greece, Turkey, and Italy. The Board's function would be to obtain the 'voluntary co-operation' of the Arab states and Israel in defending the Middle East. However, the British proposal denied any seats on the Board to the latter. The Americans disagreed. They wanted the indigenous states of the Middle East to become involved in Middle East defence arrangements, via positions on the Defense Board.[81]

By mid-July 1951, the MEC project had been all but finalised, and agreed upon by the Allies. The final proposals conformed largely to the Americans' *desiderata*. The MEC, headed by a British SACME, would *not* be a NATO command. Its headquarters staff would include representatives from the US, the UK and the British Commonwealth, France and Turkey. But no American forces would be available for service in the Middle East. The Allies agreed that, if possible, the MEC headquarters would be located in Egypt. However, with an eye to the ever-deteriorating British position in that country, they stipulated that if this proved impossible, Cyprus might provide an alternative.[82]

Greece and Turkey would be admitted as full members of NATO. As soon as this was accomplished, the United States would urge Turkey to join MEC and to 'play a full part in the defence of the Middle East'. In a compromise between the British and American views, it was agreed that the Middle East Defense Board would be 'open to voluntary participation of the Arab States and Israel, irrespective of their present defensive capabilities'.[83]

[79] Cf., Note of State – JCS – UK meeting on 19 June 1951, in *FRUS*, 1951, Vol. III, pp.535–45; memo by John Ferguson on same, 6 July 1951, in idem, p.551; and Devereux, *The Formulation* . . ., pp.53–5.

[80] Unsigned memorandum, 9 July 1951, RG 59, PPS 47–53, box 30. NA.

[81] Ferguson memo, 6 July 1951, supra; Devereux, *The Formulation* . . ., p.53;

[82] For this and following, cf., unsigned memorandum of 16 July 1951, RG 59, PPS 47–53, box 30. NA.   [83] Ibid.

Britain's initial resistance to the co-option of the Arabs into MEC institutions soon softened. By the end of July, in view of the Egyptians' unyielding stand on the question of British evacuation, the latter went further still than the American proposals, and decided to invite Egypt to become a founding member of MEC. The British hoped this would provide sufficient inducement to get Egypt to agree to MEC. However, the decision was taken as a dire last resort, with little or no conviction. The British doubted if they could even find a suitable Egyptian officer to sit on MEC headquarters staff, and equally, they doubted if any Allied country, 'certainly not the UK', would agree to commit its forces to an Egyptian command. The COS proposed therefore that the Egyptian officers on the MEC should command only their own forces, unless the other Arab states were willing to serve under them.[84]

But the British still wanted the alignment of MEC with NATO. They conceded that no American forces would be assigned to MEC, but insisted that American officers be appointed to SACME's head-quarter's staff. They believed that nothing less than the appointment of a high-ranking American officer to SACME's HQ would convince the Middle Eastern states that the Americans were committed to their defence. The British also entertained hopes that the appointment of an American officer to a high position on MEC would improve their chances of securing aid (naval and air) from the US 6th Fleet carrier force for the Middle East campaign. It was still assumed that American heavy bombers would be delivering the strategic air offensive from Abu Sueir.[85]

During the autumn, the situation in Egypt deteriorated further, and fears arose that the Egyptians were about to abrogate the 1936 treaty unilaterally. The complex machinery of Allied Middle Eastern diplomacy – working for the admission of Turkey and Greece into NATO, and the subsequent establishment of MEC (with Turkey and Egypt as founding members) – moved into high and urgent gear. Some American officials still deluded themselves that a quick *démarche* toward Egypt, accompanied by promises of US military and economic assistance, might dissuade the Egyptians from cancelling British base rights along the Suez Canal.[86]

---

[84] Foreign Office to COS, 31 July 1951, in COS (51) 449, 2 Aug. 1951, Defe 5/32; and annex to JP (51) 131, 23 July 1951, Defe 6/18. PRO.

[85] Annex to JP (51) 131, ibid.

[86] Cf., Leffler, *A Preponderance . . .*, pp.425–6.

E. THE TURKISH ENTRY INTO NATO, AND THE PROMOTION OF MEC

The British wanted to make Turkish entry into NATO conditional upon the latter's prior agreement to join MEC. But the Americans vetoed this proposal. The latter now regarded Turkish admission into NATO as 'an emotional-psychological' issue, one on which they could not afford to deny the Turks. The State Department determined to de-couple the two issues. Turkey's admission into NATO would not be made conditional on its prior agreement to fulfil the role assigned its forces in the proposed MEC. The Americans chose to rely on the Turks' assurances that they regarded the defence of the Middle East as indispensable to the defence of Europe, and that once inside NATO, they would co-ordinate with the appropriate parties in regard to assuming their proper role in the defence of the Middle East.[87]

At a State – JCS meeting on 20 August 1951, it was agreed to instruct the US representative to the NATO Standing Group, Admiral Wright, to insist that 'command arrangements for the Middle East could not be considered a precondition to the admission of Turkey to NATO'. In effect, the *Turks*, rather than the *British*, now held the upper hand in the Anglo–American–Turkish triangle. The Americans conceded the Turks' condition (the reverse of what the British wanted) that before they participated in the MEC, they should first be admitted unconditionally into NATO.[88]

At the close of its seventh session, held in Ottawa from September 15–20th, the North Atlantic Council agreed on the admission of Greece and Turkey into NATO. It now remained for Turkey to make good on its commitment to join MEC, and for the Allies to 'sell' the idea to the Egyptians.

Even as the induction of Turkey into NATO was proceeding, Anglo–American attentions were drawn to Egypt. The continuing, inexorable deterioration in Anglo–Egyptian relations, and the spectre of a unilateral Egyptian abrogation of the 1936 treaty, led to an intensive series of meetings between English and American civilian and military leaders during the first week of September. The purpose of these meetings was to enhance still further the inducements to be offered to Egypt in return for her joining MEC.

[87] Cf., memorandum on conversation between B.A.B. Burrows (Counsellor, British Embassy), and G. Lewis Jones Jr, director, NEA, 6 July 1951, *FRUS*, 1951, Vol. III, p.565; State Department working paper for Foreign Ministers meeting, (10–14 Sept. 1951), 28 Aug. 1951, p.570, ibid.; and memorandum by Edmund J. Dorsz (director of Office of Greek, Turkish and Iranian affairs), 10 Aug. 1951, *FRUS*, 1951, Vol. V., p.162.

[88] Note of State – JCS meeting on 20 Aug. 1951, in *FRUS*, 1951, Vol.V, p.172, note 2; and State Department working paper, 28 Aug. 1951, ibid.

Indeed, one of the reasons the Americans had vetoed any early announcement at Ottawa on the MEC command arrangements, had been the fear that such a step might prejudice the manoeuvres to bring the Egyptians into MEC. As the Americans saw it, hopes of averting an Anglo–Egyptian crisis now hinged on setting up the MEC in such a way as to satisfy both 'British strategic needs and Egyptian pride'.[89]

During further meetings in Washington, a new package of inducements for the Egyptians was hammered out. Egypt was to be given 'a position of high authority and responsibility within the ME Command Structure'. The Allies would offer her a place on the MEC Chiefs of Staff, and representatives Committees; Egyptian officers would be appointed to the integrated staff of the Supreme Allied Command, Middle East; in return, it was hoped that Egypt could be persuaded to allow the MEC HQ to be located on her territory.[90]

The question of British evacuation, which lay at the heart of the problem, was to be handled as follows; the British base installations would be handed over 'formally' to the Egyptians, on the understanding (i.e. condition) that they would be transformed simultaneously into an Allied base under the British SACME. All British forces not allocated to SACME were to be withdrawn immediately from Egypt. In order to appease the Egyptians on this point, it was proposed that when SACME came to determine the size of the Allied contingents to be stationed in Egypt, he would 'consult' with the Egyptian authorities.[91]

It is difficult to ascertain whether the authors of this latest 'sweetener' really believed the Egyptians would swallow the bait. This latest gambit remained a poorly-disguised scheme for a continued British presence in Egypt. What possible significance could the 'formal' British handing over of their base have had for the Egyptian nationalists – if they had to hand it over forthwith to a British officer, albeit with the impressive new title of SACME? What significance could there be in the evacuation from Egypt of those British troops not required by SACME, if the latter, and not the Egyptians, would in fact retain the prerogative in this decision?

This final package was indeed a measure of desperation, *faute de mieux*. It would prove to be the last chance of persuading the Egyptians to agree to continued British control (albeit in the name of the Allies) of the vital strategic installations along the Suez Canal.

[89] Cf., note of State – JCS meeting on 29 August 1951, ibid, p.173, note 2.

[90] Summary of Anglo–American talks, reported in Acting Secretary of State – Egyptian Embassy, 8 Sept. 1951, ibid., p.181; and minutes of Meeting of British Ministers, 4 Oct. 1951, CAB 130/71. PRO.

The British side was headed by Under Secretary of State, Sir Reginald Bowker, and by Air Chief Marshal Elliot; the American side was represented primarily by senior officials of NEA.

[91] Summary of Anglo–American talks, ibid.

On 12 September, the new proposal was submitted to and approved by President Truman. The State Department was still apprehensive about the President's reaction, given his history of support for Israel. They therefore forewarned him of possible negative reactions from the Zionist lobby. They warned him, somewhat disingenuously, that the preferential treatment that was to be offered to Egypt, was part of a programme to prepare that country 'to play a major role in the defence of the Middle East'. As such, it would require considerable forbearance on the part of Israel. However, as Secretary Acheson himself conceded, the new proposals were in fact being offered to Egypt, not in order to transform that country into a militarily significant regional power, but:

> In order to assure the continued availability to the West of the vital British base in the Suez Canal area and, at the same time, to meet the strongly-voiced demands of Egyptian nationalists for 'evacuation'and 'unity of the Nile Valley' (the Sudan problem) . . .[92]

Truman was reassured that SACME would work closely, albeit quietly with Israel from the start. But they could not offer to Israel the same status on MEC as Turkey and Egypt. Should the Israel lobby object to the deterioration in Israel's position in the Middle East power balance, the administration might reply that on the contrary, the MEC would increase hopes for a general peace settlement in the region, both with Egypt, and other Arab states. Truman was informed also that even if Egypt refused to co-operate, the Allies would go ahead with the establishment of MEC, and set up its headquarters elsewhere than in Egypt (i.e. in Cyprus).[93]

This appendage may have appeared somewhat illogical, given the whole *raison d'être* of MEC, to secure continued use of the British Base in Egypt. However, the inclusion of Turkey had transformed the whole dynamics of Allied strategy in the Middle East. MEC, with American participation, would now be needed in any case, in order to ensure Anglo–Turkish collaboration in the Middle East.

---

[92] Acheson – Truman, 12 Sept. 1951, *FRUS*, 1951, Vol. V, pp.185–6.
[93] Ibid.

9   The demise of the Egypt-centred strategy

A. THE ANGLO–AMERICAN DEBATE ON MIDDLE EASTERN STRATEGY

As noted already, there was a long-standing difference between British and American strategists over the best line on which to defend the Middle East against a Soviet offensive. It will be recalled that the British COS had chosen the Inner Ring as the most practicable line at which to engage the brunt of a Soviet advance; and the Ramallah line as the last defence position, from which there would be no retreat.

The American JCS favoured the Outer Ring, the line running from Turkey east to Iran and the Persian Gulf, through the Taurus and Zagros mountains. The JCS accused the British of exaggerating the Soviet threat to the Middle East, and since 1949 had refused to commit any American forces to this theatre. They accused the British of not having taken into account the attrition and damage that would be wreaked by the strategic bombing and demolition of the few passes that the Soviet forces would have to funnel through. Thus, the JCS complained, the British had overestimated the size of the forces needed to defend the Outer Ring.[1]

The JCS argued even that the Allies should, with Turkish collaboration, hold the Erzerum position in Turkey, and fall back on the Outer Ring only as a last-ditch position (see map no. 4). By the end of 1950, with the Americans still refusing to commit any land or air forces to the Middle East, the COS feared that their Allies placed a higher strategic priority upon the defence of Turkey than on the Egyptian base. The JCS reasoned that if they built up Turkey as a military bastion, and Turkey was able to hold out against a Soviet offensive: '. . . it would be virtually impossible for Russia to attack successfully the Cairo–Suez–Levant area.'[2]

---

[1] C. in C., ME to COS, 2 Nov. 1950, E1193/18, FO 371/81963. Public Record Office (PRO).

[2] Annex to JP (50) 146, 19 Oct. 1950, Defe 6/14. PRO.

In January 1951, the British and American theatre commanders met at Malta, to discuss and compare their strategic concepts for the defence of the Middle East. The two sides agreed essentially on the major points. The British side agreed (and always had) that the optimal line of defence for the Middle East was the Outer Ring. For their part, the American team conceded that for the present, the forces available in the area were inadequate for this task. It was agreed to carry out a joint study to determine which parts of the Middle East were essential to the Allies; and, having done that, to indicate what forces would be necessary for their defence, or to indicate the risks involved in leaving them vulnerable.[3]

The result of the joint study, completed in April 1951, was a compromise – 'to make full use of the natural defensive features formed by the LEBANON and ANTI-LEBANON MOUNTAINS'. This in effect was the so-called Lebanon–Jordan line – from the Lebanese coast, through Jebel Druze and down to Aqaba (see map no. 4). The Allies would try to fight delaying actions as far forward of this line as possible, in the Syrian desert, in an effort to cover the Turkish southern flank and the main approaches to the Levant. However, the Ramallah line was still determined as the last defence position before the Suez Canal. The joint report concluded that the areas of key strategic importance in the Middle East were Turkey, Egypt, and 'the oil fields of IRAQ, PERSIA, and the PERSIAN GULF area' (in that order). However, since the forces to defend all these areas were not available, the Allies were still forced to settle for a plan that involved the abandonment of Iraq, Persia, large areas of Syria and Jordan, and the oil fields of the Middle East.[4]

However, the JCS remained unmoved by this report. In August 1951, Gen Bradley explained to the COS why the Americans placed such a high priority on the building up of Turkey. He argued that the Soviets would be reluctant to bypass Turkey on their way to the Canal, leaving strong forces on their right flank. The COS retorted that if the Allies concentrated exclusively on Turkey, the Soviets would be able to conquer the Suez Canal from the East with relatively light forces; and once they had taken Iraq and Syria, the Turks' own southern flank would be dangerously exposed. The British side took some small comfort in the knowledge that the Pentagon and the State Department had yet to settle their differences on the Middle East theatre.[5]

---

[3] Report on Malta conference, 23–24 Jan. 1951, GHQ, MELF to Ministry of Defence, 26 Jan. 1951, E1192/10, FO 371/91219. PRO.

[4] Annex G to combined CINCME – CINCELM study of British short-term plan for the defence of the Middle East, COS (51) 189, 4 April 1951, Defe 5/30. PRO.

[5] COS (51) 133d meeting, 20 Aug. 1951, Defe 4/46. PRO.

As noted in the previous chapter, the JCS had been finally enticed into token involvement in the Middle East during the summer of 1951, only as a result of the 'package deal' sold to them by the British. In return for British agreement to Turkish membership of NATO, the Americans had agreed to take a leading role in MEC, to be located, if possible, in Cairo.

But before either part of the deal had been consummated, the Foreign Office noted 'depressing indications' from Washington that the Americans were ready 'to sell us down the river in Egypt'; that they were not really interested in a MEC based on the Canal Zone, but were 'merely paying lip service' to the British strategic conception, in order to get the Turks into NATO. This prompted the Foreign Office to commission from the COS a professional assessment of the American strategic concept. If they disagreed with it, the COS were to draw up a paper explaining why the American plan was incapable of application.[6]

The COS had in fact already prepared a reply to JCS accusations that the British were exaggerating the force levels needed to hold the Outer Ring. Their first comment was that the effects of demolition and interdiction from the air on the Soviet advance could not be estimated accurately, even if they did reduce the enemy threat substantially. Not only would the British have insufficient forces to defend the Middle East but they also had to take into account the fact that for at least the next two years, their rearmament programme (accelerated with the outbreak of the Korean War) would not yield sufficient equipment for those army formations allocated to the Middle East.[7]

In June 1951, the COS estimated that the defence of the Outer Ring (provided the Soviets had not already taken Iran), would require more than double the ground forces that would be needed for the defence of the Inner Ring: the Outer Ring would require eight divisions and 900 aircraft by D + 30 and 15 divisions and 1350 aircraft by D + six months; in contrast, the Inner Ring would require one division and 482 aircraft by D + 30; and seven divisions and 1,062 aircraft by D + 6 months (these last figures included two divisions and 250 aircraft allocated for the defence of the Turkish front).[8]

But even so, in mid-1951, the COS estimated that by D + 4 months, there would be a deficiency of two divisions and 500 aircraft, and by D + 9, *after* the still-anticipated arrival of Commonwealth reinforcements (one infantry division each from Australia and New Zealand, and one armoured division from South Africa), that deficiency would *rise* to five divisions and 750 aircraft(at a meeting of the COS, CIGS Slim

[6] Minute by Sir Pierson Dixon, 21 Aug. 1951, E1192/138, FO 371/91223. PRO.
[7] MDM (51) 2, 6 June 1951, Cab 21/1787. PRO.
[8] Ibid.

pointed out that the best they might hope for would be that at D + 9
months, there would be equipment for just three of the 7 Infantry
divisions supposed to be available).[9]

By the end of 1951, the COS had finally abandoned the Ramallah
line. However, while agreeing with the Americans that it would be best
to meet a Soviet advance on the Outer Ring, the COS again concluded,
due to the paucity of resources, that Allied strategy in the Middle East
had to be based upon the defence of the Inner Ring. This, together with
the defence of parts of the oil fields in isolation, would meet the Allies'
minimum requirements.[10]

One of the key advantages now seen by the British in the Inner Ring
position, was that, in the long run, its defence would require fewer
British forces than the Lebanon–Jordan line, since the main burden
would now be carried by Turkish forces. The Inner Ring was also 'the
only effective means of securing the Southern flank of Turkey and the
Turkey–Levant communications.' In effect, in placing ever more
reliance on the Turks, the COS were moving closer to the position of
the American planners. They now noted:

> For as long a period as Turkey is able to contain the Russian offensive, the
> requirement in the Levant sector is only for relatively small forces to ensure that
> the enemy is deterred from the limited offensive from the East.[11]

On 26 October 1951, Winston Churchill had replaced Clement
Attlee as Britain's Prime Minister. One of his first initiatives was to visit
Washington for talks with President Truman. Among Churchill's
primary objectives was to try to secure an American military commitment to the defence of the British base in Egypt. Churchill's visit would
bring to a head the differences between the Allies regarding their
Middle East strategy.

There is no reason to believe that Churchill's views on the Middle
East in 1951 had changed much since his last tenure at No. 10 Down-
ing Street, which had ended in July 1945. A confidential minute written
in January 1945 to his Chief of Staff, General Lord Ismay, provides a
representative reflection of Churchill's beliefs about this region:

> We really cannot undertake to stop all these bloodthirsty people slaying each
> other if that is their idea of democracy and the New World. The great thing is to

[9] COS (51) 93d, 6 June 1951, Defe 4/43, and E1192/130/G, FO 371/91223. PRO.

[10] MDM (51) 2, 6 June 1951, Cab 21/1787. PRO. The COS estimated that it would
require one division, anti-aircraft and artillery units, and a small fighting force, to defend the
oil fields of Ras Tanura, Bahrain and Qatar in isolation.

[11] Annex to COS (51) 755, 18 Dec. 1951, Defe 5/35, which confirmed JP (51) 82, 16 Oct.
1951, Defe 6/17. PRO.

hold on to the important strategic places and utter wise words in sonorous tones ... We are getting uncommonly little out of our Middle East encumbrances and paying an unduly high price for that little.[12]

In 1945, Churchill was already convinced that the UK could not maintain her position in the Middle East, especially not in Palestine, without active, and 'constructive' American involvement. In July 1945, he addressed the following minute of despair on the Palestine question to his Chiefs of Staff and to the Colonial Secretary:

> ... I do not think we should take the responsibility upon ourselves of managing this very difficult place while the Americans sit back and criticise ... I am not aware of the slightest advantage which has ever accrued to Great Britain from this painful and thankless task. Somebody else should have their turn now.[13]

Shortly after taking office in October 1951, Churchill received a private note from his old wartime scientist friend and mentor, Lord Cherwell (Professor F. E. Lindemann), now serving in the Cabinet (as he had in Churchill's wartime Cabinet) as Postmaster General. Cherwell applied Churchill's 1945 views on Palestine to the entire Middle East. He undoubtedly knew that he was on firm territory, when he advised Churchill that responsibility for the Middle East should be handed over to the Americans:

> Now that we have lost India and Burma the freedom of the Suez Canal is an international rather than a specifically British interest ... Middle East oil is an immensely valuable asset. But we have already abandoned our Persian oil and the remainder is largely in American hands. *Is it* not for America rather than for Britain to defend it?
> The other reason for holding the Middle East is to prevent another large accession of territory and manpower to the Communists. This falls under the Truman Doctrine and as such is more an American than a British responsibility. For these reasons it would seem that *the U.S. should undertake the defence of the Middle East.*[14] (My emphasis)

Churchill replied that he would hold on to Cherwell's paper, which contained 'many unpleasant truths'. He concurred that it was now of the utmost importance to get the Americans involved in the Middle East.[15]

In preparation for his visit to Washington, Churchill was briefed by

---

[12] Churchill to Ismay, 28 Jan. 1945, Prem 3/296/9. PRO.
[13] Churchill to COS and Colonial Secretary, 1 July 1945, E4849, FO 371/45377. PRO.
[14] Cherwell to Churchill, 8 Nov. 1951, Prem 11/208. PRO.
[15] Churchill to Cherwell, 10 Nov. 1951, ibid.

the COS on Britain's strategic requirements in the Middle East. He learned for the first time that until 1949, the Americans had planned to allocate some three divisions and 350 tactical aircraft to the defence of the Middle East. And that in 1949, they had switched to a 'centre strategy', and transferred to North-West Africa those forces previously earmarked for the Middle East. According to the COS, until early in 1950, the Americans had still planned to deploy a brigade group and 75 fighter aircraft at Dhahran.[16]

At present, the Americans insisted that they would be unable to commit either land or air forces to the defence of the Middle East for at least the first two years of a war – although they might despatch some US naval aviation, from carriers of the US Mediterranean Fleet.

Churchill's mission in Washington would be to seek a reversal of this position. This would involve reaching agreement on a 'combined politico-military policy for the Middle East', including co-ordination of air operations; the deployment of an American contingent to Dhahran; and the appointment of American officers to high positions on MEC.[17]

On the other side of the Atlantic the Pentagon had little respect for, and less patience with, Churchill's military acumen. Their attitude was shared, indeed nurtured by certain quarters from within the British military itself. In October 1951, two weeks before the general election in England, General Lord Ismay wrote a personal letter to Gen Eisenhower, commander of SHAPE, on the persisting Anglo–American feud over the SACLANT command (see previous chapter). Ismay stated that 'on the main issue', Churchill 'was, and still is, as obstinate as a mule'. He next went on to analyse Churchill's gifts and deficiencies as a military leader, as revealed during World War Two:

> Like you, I always felt that he had an unrivalled knowledge of the broad strategy of war, and that in the political–military field he was the outstanding expert of our day – indeed of any day. At the same time, he was, and still is, completely ignorant of the mechanics of modern war and logistics . . . Taken by and large you managed to wean him away from most of his plans for picking up small and superficially attractive prizes which had no real bearing on the conduct of the war as a whole.[18] (My emphasis.)

Gen Ismay's assessment may well have been applied by General Eisenhower and his colleagues to the major bone of contention between the Allies in the Middle East – the persisting crisis over the British base in Egypt.

[16] COS (51) 759, 18 Dec. 1951, Defe 5/35. PRO.
[17] Ibid.
[18] Ismay to Eisenhower, 11 October 1951, Hastings Ismay collection, box 60, Eisenhower Library (EL).

The Americans' opinions of Churchill were more than reciprocated by the new Prime Minister. When Eisenhower won the presidential election in November 1952, Churchill would find it expedient to delete several passages from the drafts of his memoirs of World War Two those telling 'how the United States gave way, to please Russia, vast tracts of Europe they had occupied. . .' As for Truman, Churchill regarded him as 'a novice, bewildered by the march of events and by responsibilities which he had never expected'. As for the Republicans, who had been 20 years out of office, Churchill was in general unfavourably impressed with their 'brashness and impatience'. According to his private secretary, 'Jock' Colville, during a further visit to Washington, in January 1953, Churchill made 'unjust and dangerous' comments about them. After meeting John Foster Dulles, Eisenhower's Secretary of State-elect, Churchill fumed that he would have no more to do with the man, 'whose "great slab of a face" he disliked and distrusted'.[19]

In preparation for Churchill's visit, in January 1952, Gen Omar Bradley, chairman of the JCS, briefed Secretary of Defense Lovett on the Middle East. The JCS still insisted that overall responsibility for this theatre should remain with the British. However, in the event of war, American political and military interests would not be 'restricted to the security of the Suez Canal and its adjacent bases.' The JCS believed that the Allies' interests would be served best by holding substantial areas in Turkey, and a portion of the Persian Gulf oil fields. The best way to defend the entire region, including the Suez area, would be to take up positions 'as near to the borders of the USSR as feasible'. Secretary Lovett was instructed to find out from Churchill what were 'the intentions and capabilities' of the British with regards the Middle East as a whole, as distinct from the local defence of the Suez Canal; and whether the British expected significant reinforcements from the Commonwealth.[20]

Prime Minister Churchill and President Truman met on 5 and 9 January 1952. Churchill was asked to elaborate on his views on the Middle East. Leaning heavily on Cherwell's brief, he argued that Britain's position had changed significantly since the evacuation of India, and since Britain no longer enjoyed the services of the Indian army. He endeavoured to persuade the Americans, repeatedly, that the British were fulfilling an 'international duty' in Egypt:

---

[19] Extracts from the diary of Churchill's private secretary, Sir John Colville (*The Fringes of Power*), and of Sir John Shuckburgh (*Descent to Suez*) as quoted by Martin Gilbert, *Winston S. Churchill: Vol. VIII, Never Despair, 1945–1965*, Boston: Houghton Mifflin, 1988, pp.788, 791–2.

[20] Gen Bradley to Secretary Lovett, 28 Dec.1951, CCS 381 EMMEA (11-19-47) S.6. NA.

. . . one cannot consider the Middle East as a British area of imperialism or national satisfaction, nor one the responsibility for which should be left only to the United Kingdom.[21]

Churchill pressed the Americans to despatch a 'token brigade' of American, French and Turkish forces to Suez. He claimed that such a show of Allied solidarity would bring the crisis in Egypt 'very quickly to an end'. Furthemore, Churchill continued, the British forces now in Egypt had to be redeployed to Europe, and to the UK itself, which was 'completely unprotected'.

Each side's report on the American response differs. The history of the JCS states that it was agreed that Foreign Secretary Eden and Secretary Acheson would pursue the idea. Eden wrote in his memoirs that Churchill had stated that the British were not asking for any American military help in Egypt, since they had ample forces of their own.[22]

But Secretary of Defense Lovett wrote in a private letter at the time to Gen Eisenhower, that Churchill's plea for an American 'token force' to help out 'in the Suez Canal mess' had been 'promptly refused'.[23] As we now know, nothing in fact did ever come of Churchill's request.

In effect, the British now pinned all their hopes for Middle East defence on procuring American pressure on Turkey to make a major contribution to the Middle East, within the frame of the MEC. Notwithstanding events in Egypt, some of the British military yet nurtured delusions that the defence of the Middle East would focus on and radiate outwards from the Suez axis, with the Turks fulfilling the major military role in this theatre, albeit subordinate to a British SACME.

Churchill conceded that the Turks should come under Eisenhower's command (SHAPE) – a better arrangement than their sending a token brigade to the Canal; he urged that the sooner the 'four-power pact for the area' (MEC) came into effect, the better. Once that happened, MEC should provide forces for the Canal zone, to bolster the British troops already there. Foreign Secretary Eden stated that the setting up of MEC was the main issue now before them; who would command it? What troops would be provided? And what would be Turkey's role under MEC?

[21] For this and following, cf record of meeting on 8 Jan. 1952, in PSF General File, box 116, Truman Library (HST); also *FRUS*, 1952–54, Vol. IX, part 1, pp.171–6.

[22] Walter S. Poole, *The History of the Joint Chiefs of Staff: The Joint Chiefs of Staff and National Policy, Vol. IV, 1950–1952*, Wilmington: Michael Glazier, Inc., 1980, pp.343.; and Sir Anthony Eden, *Full Circle: The Memoirs of Sir Anthony Eden*, London: Cassell, 1960, p.248.

[23] Secretary Lovett to Gen Eisenhower, 24 Jan. 1952, Eisenhower pre-Presidential papers, 1916–52, Lovett file (1), (Oct. 1951–May 1952), box 72. EL.

Acheson tried to assuage the British, stating that 'both sides were close to agreement'. Once Turkey and Greece were finally in NATO, 'by March or April at the latest', they would get down to planning the MEC, as a command quite distinct from NATO.

The Chiefs of Staff of both countries, Generals Bradley and Slim, were present at the meeting. They agreed that due to the Turks' refusal to operate under a British SACME, they should come under US Admiral Carney (CINCELM), in a separate Balkan command. But Silm's main concern was precisely that the Turks should *not* devote all their effort to the European and Balkan theatre:

> . . . the Turks insist that they are not a Middle Eastern power, but the good God has put them spang in the middle of the Middle East. Turkey is the only country in the area that can make a real contribution to the military defence of the area.[24]

In effect, the 'Turkish problem' remained unresolved. Bradley did not agree with Slim's proposal that 'the Commander of the Turkish front should be a deputy in the Middle East Command'. He insisted that they could not subordinate a NATO commander to SACME.

The Allied politico–military talks in Washington left a sour taste in the mouths of all concerned. Secretary Lovett reported that Churchill had tried to have them release him from the previous government's agreement to the SACLANT command, as 'unworkable and unnecessary down-grading of the British'. Churchill had also visited Ottawa, and tried to mobilise the Canadians to his side. But the latter had informed the Americans that they were 'standing firm', as

> they knew he would return to battle and employ 'every guile, every trick of debate and every emotional plea with his vast repertory'.[25]

The American side had pointed out, somewhat disingenuously, that since SACLANT was a NATO command, only NATO could reverse it. But Churchill's position had also been undermined by the opposition of his own military staff, including 'Pug' Ismay. Lovett noted, cynically, that this '. . . must have been an infuriating, but not altogether new, experience for him.'[26]

At their final meeting, Churchill had relented on the SACLANT command. Lovett's general appraisal of the new British Prime Minister, shared by not a few on both sides of the Atlantic, was little short of patronising:

[24] Record of meeting on 8 Jan. 1952, in PSF General File, box 116, Truman Library (HST); also FRUS, 1952–54, Vol. IX, part 1, pp.171–76.

[25] Secretary Lovett to Gen Eisenhower, 24 Jan. 1952, Eisenhower pre-Presidential papers, 1916–52, Lovett file (1), (Oct. 1951–May 1952), box 72. EL.

[26] Ibid.

> . . . a considerable amount of education is going to have to be done to overcome
> his [Churchill's] tendency to live completely in the past and to forget or under-
> estimate the enormous changes which have occurred since the war in the rest of
> the world.[27]

Churchill was finding it difficult to live down his imperialist reputa-
tion. He had stressed the change in Britain's position in Egypt consequent on the British evacuation of India. But his obstinacy over the
SACLANT command, against the opinion of his own military advisers,
confirmed the Americans in their belief that the elder statesman was in
fact incapable of change. They derided his fixation with the mighty
Suez base (and his readiness to continue to command in the Middle
East, 'if the Americans wished it'), notwithstanding the virtual collapse
of the British position in Egypt.

And without any firm decision in regard to MEC (by now MEDO),
the British position in the Middle East continued to deteriorate. Back in
London, Eden's Foreign Office conceded that the Americans now
held the keys to the Middle East. The Americans would either have to
publicly commit forces to the region, and 'to parade their ships and air
fleets regularly.' Or they would have to subsidise the British costs in
keeping their forces there. Putting a literary flourish on the inevitable, a
senior Foreign Office official concluded:

> . . . we shall have to draw the inevitable and regrettable conclusion that the
> United States will now become the prime mover in the Middle East. If we yield
> our primacy gracefully, we may be able to see the new ship launched gracefully.[28]

In the meantime, following Churchill's visit to Washington, and the
Allied commanders' conference at Malta, the JCS had instructed the
Strategic Plans Group (SPG) to make a study of the force levels needed
to defend the Inner and Outer Rings. Their estimates proved to be yet
higher than those of the British. And to make matters worse, the
American planners did not perceive any great advantage in defending
the Inner, rather than the Outer Ring. For they disagreed with their
British counterparts that the defence of the shorter line would require
substantially fewer forces than the longer one.

The defence of the Outer Ring mountain line would be aided by the
demolition and blocking of the six strategic passes that afforded access
through it. But American planners still estimated that the Outer Ring
would require 17 infantry and two armoured divisions, and 1200 aircraft; on the other hand, they estimated that the defence of the Inner
Ring would require 14 divisions, (including one armoured), and the

[27] Ibid.
[28] Minute by Chris Gandy, 21 July 1952, E1056/98, FO 371/98259. PRO.

same number of aircraft as the Outer Ring. The Americans did agree with the British on one point – that the forces currently available in the Middle East were way below those needed even for the defence of the Inner Ring.

Although American planners hoped that the Turks would provide 10 of the 14 divisions needed, that still remained a hope for the future (the Turks had offered to provide six additional divisions for use in the Middle East, if the Americans equipped them). The British were unable to muster anything approaching the remaining four divisions required, and the British Commonwealth had yet to make any definite commitment. The most serious deficiency, as ever, was in the air. According to American estimates, of the 1200 aircraft needed for the defence of either line, there were currently but 375 stationed in the Middle East![29]

Paul Nitze, chairman of the PPS, commented wryly that British plans were totally unrealistic, due to the great disparity between the forces needed, especially in the air, and those they could currently plan upon. He suggested that the American planners devote some thought to this problem, so as to transform their strategy in the Middle East into 'something more than wishful thinking'.[30]

A conference of military representatives of France, the UK and the US in Washington, from 19 to 25 May 1952, brought only further disillusion to the British side. The COS reported back that the Americans had made it clear that 'they had two main interests in the Mediterranean area and were not thinking of any overall Mediterranean or Middle East strategy':

> Their [the Americans'] first interest was in the European theatre, and all the U.S. Naval and Naval Air requirements were in support of the Southern flank of SACEUR. The interest of the American Air Force was on behalf of the Strategic Air Command.[31]

It is, however, worth noting, that the Americans still planned on using Abu Sueir as a post-strike staging base for their B-36 heavy bombers (up to 30 sorties a day), and as a pre- and post-strike staging base for the B-47 and B-50 medium-range bombers (up to 90 sorties a day).[32]

---

[29] Discussion between the Strategic Plans Group (Grantham, Goodney, Garland), and State Department representatives (Paul Nitze of the PPS, Wells Stabler and Lewis Jones of NEA) 8 May 1952, PPS 47-53, box 30, RG 59. NA.

[30] Ibid.

[31] COS (52) 312, May 1952. PRO.

[32] Ibid.

B. MEC AND THE EGYPTIAN CRISIS

In the meantime, during the winter of 1951–52, the MEC project had proceeded to its rapid _dénouement_. The crisis in Egypt had simmered through the summer and fall of 1951. On 1 September, the UN Security Council had passed a resolution calling on Egypt to lift its prohibition on the passage of Israeli oil tankers through the Suez Canal. It has been claimed that the UN decision was a major reason for the Egyptians' unilateral abrogation of the 1936 treaty in October 1951; that the Egyptians regarded the UN decision as outside interference, which 'wounded Egyptian pride without achieving the desired result'; and that the decision exacerbated Egyptian nationalist feeling about the presence of 38,000 British troops in the Canal Zone.[33]

However, the Egyptian action was precipitated at least as much, if not more, by another Middle Eastern drama, just about to reach its climax – the Anglo–Persian crisis. There can be little doubt that from October 1951, both the British and the Egyptians had this crisis in mind, which had come to a head at the end of September 1951. On the 25th of that month, Dr Mohammed Mussadiq, the Persian Premier, gave the British staff at Abadan (the largest oil refinery in the world, run by British engineers) seven days notice to leave the island.

At a meeting of the British Cabinet two days later, the military pressed for implementation of contingency plans to seize the island by force. But the Cabinet, led by Attlee, decided overwhelmingly against. Attlee anticipated a negative American reaction, and feared that any military operation at Abadan would exacerbate yet further Iranian nationalist anti-British fervour. The British evacuated Abadan on 4 October. At the time, it was regarded universally, not least by the Egyptians, 'as an indication of British weakness and decline'.[34]

By the end of September, clear indications had also been received that the Egyptian government and Parliament would, by 10 October, enact into law the unilateral abrogation of the 1936 treaty. The British and the Americans agreed to despatch to Turkey, post-haste, a mission of three generals (CIGS Slim, Chairman of the JCS Bradley, and a French general, Lecheres). The generals were to discuss the MEC organisation with the Turks, and thence to travel to Cairo to present the scheme, embellished with substantial inducements, to the Egyptians.[35]

[33] The Security Council vote was 8–0. Both the United States and Britain voted against the Egyptian action. The Soviet Union, China and India abstained. Cf., Hahn, _Containment and . . ._, pp.32–4.

[34] Cf., Eden, Sir Anthony, Full Circle: _The Memoirs of Sir Anthony Eden_, London: Cassell, 1960, pp.225–6, and Louis, _The British Empire. . ._, pp.686–9.

[35] Cf., McGhee conversation with the Turkish ambassador, Washington, 28 Sept. 1951,

On the day that Abadan was evacuated (4 October), British Ministers and military leaders convened in London to discuss the crisis in Egypt. One cannot underestimate the anticipated influence of the ongoing election campaign on the government's foreign policy at this critical juxtaposition of the Iranian and Egyptian crises. The humiliating *dénouement* of the Iranian crisis could not have been far from the minds of any of the Ministers. On the eve of a general election, the Labour government could not afford to suffer a second humiliating eviction from Egypt, following that from Abadan. (As noted already, Labour would in fact lose the elections.)

The desperation of the British position may be gauged by the fact that the Cabinet chose to ignore the prescient warning of the Cairo embassy, that it would be futile for Gens Bradley and Slim to visit Cairo, as the Egyptians would not join MEC before the 1936 treaty was abrogated, and all British forces evacuated from Egyptian soil. But in the Cabinet, Foreign Secretary Morrison appeared to believe that only the MEC proposal might still avert a unilateral abrogation of the 1936 treaty by the Egyptians. He warned that the effect of an Egyptian abrogation upon public opinion at home would be 'calamitous'.[36]

However, the British also had a tactical motive in persisting with the MEC project. If the Egyptians did abrogate the 1936 treaty, notwithstanding Anglo–American efforts to appease them, the British would feel more confident of having the Americans behind any course they subsequently chose to adopt. They would be able publicly to denounce the Egyptians' unlawful action, and thereafter hold the Canal base by force of arms, under the 1936 treaty. (Ministers were, however, informed that the British garrison in Egypt would be unable to protect all British nationals in that country).[37]

On 6 October 1951, Foreign Secretary Morrison sent a telegram to the Egyptian government, advising them in confidence that he hoped to forward to them definite defence proposals by 10 October. However, on the very next day, 7 October, the Nahas government pre-empted the British and submitted to King Farouk bills of abrogation, both of the

FRUS, 1951, Vol. V, p.194. The Turks initially objected to Gens Slim and Lecheres accompanying Bradley, but were prevailed upon by the State Department to receive them, in order to reflect the solidarity of the powers, and the multilateral nature of the MEC project. Cf., Wadsworth (US ambassador to Turkey) to Secretary Acheson, 25 Sept., and Acheson to Wadsworth, 26 Sept. 1951, in *FRUS*, 1951, Vol. III, pp.580–3. General Charles Lecheres was Chief of Staff of the French Air Force, chairman of the French JCS, and French representative on the Military Committee of the North Atlantic Council.

[36] Minutes of Ministers' meeting, 4 Oct. 1951, Cab 130/71. PRO; and David R. Devereux, *The Formulation of British Defence Policy Towards the Middle East, 1948–1956*, London: Macmillan, 1990, pp.58–9.

[37] Ministers' meeting, 4 Oct., ibid.

Anglo–Egyptian Treaty of 1936, and of the Sudan Condominium agreement of 1899. On the next day, Prime Minister Nahas proclaimed Egypt's official, unilateral abrogation of the 1936 treaty. The bills were tabled before the Egyptian Parliament on 8 October and voted into law on 15 October.[38]

On 9 October, the British government announced that it did not recognise the Egyptian actions, and would maintain its full rights in Egypt under the agreements of 1899 and 1936. The next day, 10 October, Secretary Acheson released a press statement, pointing out that the agreements between England and Egypt had no provisions for unilateral abrogation by either of the parties. Acheson added that he hoped a resolution to the crisis might be found in the new proposals (i.e. MEC) that were to be presented to the Egyptians within a few days.[39]

In a long letter to Secretary Acheson, sent on 12 October, Morrison outlined also the 'passive security measures' that Britain was taking in Egypt, and contingency plans (*Rodeo*) for the eventuality that the Egyptians attempted to cut off the British base from its supplies. The Foreign Secretary also urged his American colleague not to allow the Egyptian action to deflect the Allies from presenting the MEC proposals. He wrote that if the Egyptians agreed now to join MEC, then the Canal base might yet become an Allied base. Morrison insisted that the British were holding the Egyptian base 'on behalf of the free world', and as such, if the Egyptians refused to join MEC, the British 'intended to stay in Egypt at whatever cost'.[40]

Both the British and American ambassadors in Cairo advised against putting the MEC proposal to the Egyptian government at the present juncture. Caffery feared that if the Allied proposals were now aired in public, they would be rejected by the Egyptian government 'with great popular applause' and 'pulled to pieces in the press and Parliament'.[41]

However, both Morrison and Acheson, and some of their senior officials, overrode their ambassadors' warnings. Acheson and McGhee thought that Nahas might be bluffing, that the MEC proposal might in fact provide him with an honorable retreat from the abrogation crisis. On 13 October, the four ambassadors of the proposed MEC (American, British, French, and Turkish) presented the plan to Egyptian Foreign Minister Salaheddin. The latter insisted on seeing the ambassadors individually. He rebuffed all appeals for some positive

[38] Cf. editorial note, *FRUS*, 1951, Vol. V, pp.205–6, and Foreign Secretary Morrison to Secretary Acheson, 12 Oct. 1951, idem, pp.398–401.

[39] Editorial note, ibid., pp.397–8.

[40] Morrison – Acheson, 12 October 1951, ibid, pp.398–401.

[41] Editorial note, p.206, ibid.

comment. Two days later, on 15 October, Salaheddin informed the Egyptian Parliament that the government found the MEC plan 'wholly unacceptable and would reject it'. On the same day, the Egyptians formally notified the American government of its rejection.[42]

On the day the Egyptian communication was received in Washington, State Department officials held a brief conference with the JCS, to discuss the implications of the Egyptian rejection, and the American position with regard to the anticipated British determination to maintain its position in Egypt by force. Paul Nitze, director of the PPS, stated that supporting the British in Egypt might not be the best course of action, 'but in the absence of anyone else willing to expend their resources and assume responsibility there', he felt that this was their only course.[43]

On 17 October, Acheson cabled Morrison, to assure him of the United States' 'full political and diplomatic support' for any measures the British might deem necessary to secure their base and to keep the Suez Canal open. Acheson supported Britain's contention that Egypt's unilateral abrogation was illegal, and her determination to retain her forces in the Canal Zone under the 1936 treaty, 'until some alternative arrangement was found'.[44]

But were there any realistic alternatives still open to the Allies? The British and the Americans now disagreed over whether they should approach other Arab states with the MEC project. The British side did not wish to appear to be 'chasing after' the Arabs; whereas on the American side, there were fears that if they delayed, the other Arab states might close ranks with the Egyptians at the next meeting of the Arab League.[45]

Not only had the British suffered a severe setback in Egypt, but in the meantime, the generals' mission to Turkey furnished them with another 'severe disappointment'.

Generals Bradley, Slim and Lecheres had arrived in Ankara on 12 October, in the middle of the abrogation crisis. Adnan Menderes, the Turkish Prime Minister, reaffirmed the Turks' 'keen desire' to make a substantial contribution to NATO and to the defence of the Middle East. Menderes agreed also that if the Egyptian government invited the generals to Cairo, he would appoint a Turkish general (and staff) to join the three Western generals.[46]

---

[42] Cf., ibid., p.226, note 3, and Hahn, *Containment and . . .*, pp.35–6.

[43] State–JCS meeting, 15 October 1951, Lot File no. 61 D 417, Box 50, NA; *FRUS*, 1951, Vol. V, editorial note, p.402.

[44] Acheson – Morrison, 17 October 1951, ibid., pp.404–5.

[45] Walter S. Gifford (US ambassador, London) – State Department, 17 Oct. 1951, ibid., pp.229–30.

However, at the same time, the Turks also insisted that they be treated 'as an inseparable part of the Europe which is facing Russia', and not as an indigenous Middle Eastern state, on a par with the Arabs. They refused adamantly to serve under a British SACME, and demanded to come under the command of SACEUR, General Eisenhower. Turkish national pride was clearly on display.[47]

The Turks' reservations about British command in the Middle East, combined with the crisis in Egypt, gave the British grounds for pause. Sir Reginald Bowker, Under Secretary of State at the Eastern Department of the Foreign Office, told the Americans that the Ankara talks had left them with the impression that the Turks were interested more in NATO than in MEC. Bowker believed that before approaching any of the other Arab states on the MEC project, they would first have to conduct further talks with the Turks over their role in the Middle East, and the whole question of the command structure.[48]

By now, both the American and the British administrations were divided internally over whether to proceed with the MEC initiative, notwithstanding the Egyptian rejection. The lower levels at the State Department were in favour of pushing ahead, while the higher echelons wanted to 'let the dust settle' before proceeding further.[49]

But at the end of October, the crisis in Egypt deteriorated yet further, into undeclared, open warfare between the British and the Egyptians. At the end of that month, five Egyptian troops were killed in a clash between British and Egyptian forces at Ismailia. The incident led to a wave of anti-British violence across Egypt, notwithstanding the fact that the Egyptian military had accepted responsibility for the Ismailia incident. The Egyptians waged guerilla attacks against British troops and communications in the Canal zone, and imposed a labour boycott on their base installations. The British rushed in paratroop reinforcements, seized Egyptian utilities and, at the onset of winter, curtailed the supply of fuel oil to Cairo. The Cairo mob was incensed, and took to the streets in wildly anti-British demonstrations.[50]

The Foreign Office feared giving the impression throughout the region that Egyptian actions had forced the Allies to reconsider, or even to cancel the MEC project. They believed that it would be fatal to leave the impression that the Egyptians held the key to the Allies' (i.e. Britain's) position in the Middle East. The Arab states must be left in

---

[47] Cf., Gen. Bradley – President Truman, two telegrams, both dated 18 Oct. 1951, in *FRUS*, 1951, Vol. V, pp.598–9; also Leffler, *A Preponderance. . .*, p.476, and Hahn, *The United States. . .*, p.127.

[48] Gifford – State Department, 17 Oct., supra.

[49] Minute by John Wardrop, 17 Oct. 1951, E1192/174, FO 371/91225. PRO.

[50] Hahn, *Containment and . . .*, p.37, and idem, *The United States. . .*, pp.137–8.

no doubt as to the Allies' determination to proceed with MEC, with or without the participation of any of the indigenous states of the region. The British also urged the Americans to declare that those states that did not co-operate with the West would not be eligible for appropriations under the Mutual Security Aid Program.[51]

At the beginning of November, the new Foreign Secretary, Anthony Eden, met in Paris with his American and French counterparts (Dean Acheson and Robert Schumann) to take stock of the MEC project. The British had little choice but to concur in the JCS' reduction of MEC's initial tasks to 'primarily one of planning and providing the Middle East states on their request with assistance in the form of advice and training.'[52]

By the end of the year, the British position in Egypt was tottering. Yet Churchill's government adopted an outwardly obdurate stance. The Americans criticised the British use of force, and indicated that it would hamper efforts to persuade the Egyptians to change their minds about MEC. In early December 1951, Burton Y. Berry, a senior official of the State Department, visited Egypt. He reported back to a joint meeting of the JCS and senior State Department officials, that the situation in Egypt was 'terrible'. There was universal hatred there for the British, with the result that:

> . . . the position we desire in Egypt, the area we want for our bases, and the influence of Egypt in the Arab world in support of our interests are denied to us.[53]

Berry thought that they would have to 'revamp' still further the MEC proposal, 'in order to give more flattery to Egyptian vanity'. No one in the Egyptian Cabinet, except for Foreign Minister Salaheddin had even taken the time to read the proposal. He believed that Egypt was 'rapidly going down the drain', and would be lost unless the trend was soon reversed.[54]

The problem of Turkey's incorporation into British planning for the Middle East was tackled at a series of meetings between the COS and General Bradley in London, and further staff meetings in Rome during December 1951. The outcome only partially satisfied British *desiderata*. Greece and Turkey would operate under a new Aegean Command,

[51] Foreign Office note, 17 Oct. 1951, Prem 8/1359; and COS (52) 34, 11 Jan. 1952, Defe 5/36. PRO.

[52] David Bruce (US ambassador, France) – Department of State, 6 Nov. 1951, *FRUS*, 1951, V, pp.243–45, and note 3. The Foreign Ministers were in Paris for the Sixth Regular session of the UN General Assembly.

[53] Minute of JCS – State meeting, 12 Dec. 1951, ibid., pp.434–7.

[54] Ibid.

under the command of Admiral Carney, CINCSOUTH. The new Aegean Command was to establish close links with the British SACME, to ensure that contingency planning in the Aegean fell in line with general plans for defending the Middle East. The COS were far from satisfied with this awkward compromise, but it was the best they could aspire to. They could only hope that the links between the two commands would be 'firm'.[55]

The Foreign Office, preoccupied still with controlling the damage caused by the abrogation crisis, and with Britain's waning prestige in the Middle East, pointed to the grave political shortcomings of the new Military Commands proposed by the Military. The removal of the Turks from direct subordination to SACME would weaken MEC; the removal of MEC headquarters from the Middle East would appear inevitably as a withdrawal from that region. And finally, the postponement of plans to establish MEC would confirm the very idea that the British had hoped to quash, that in rejecting MEC, Egypt had succeeded in upsetting their plans.[56]

In reality, the MEC proposal (and subsequently, its equally moribund successor, MEDO) was becoming largely an academic issue.

For the first time, perhaps, the British were compelled to begin to contemplate seriously how they were to defend the Middle East without their base in Egypt. They became preoccupied with saving 'face', and the tattered remnants of British prestige in the Middle East. In the new year, 1952, (by which point Britain's position in Egypt was perhaps irretrievably undermined), the COS complained bitterly that unless they did something very soon to implement the MEC proposals, they would 'become a joke', British interests and prestige in the Middle East would suffer, and the Americans and the Turks might lose interest.[57]

And the security situation in Egypt had yet to reach its nadir. On 19 January 1952, heavy clashes erupted between British troops and Egyptian police forces. The British force, deploying tanks and artillery, attacked an Egyptian auxiliary police base in Ismailia, suspected of harbouring terrorists. Forty Egyptian police officers were killed in the attack, for the loss of four British soldiers. The fighting lasted one week. The Egyptian police finally surrendered to British troops, but not before they had suffered heavy casualties – 64 killed.

The next day, January 26, extensive rioting swept Cairo. Twenty-six Western citizens were killed (including 17 Europeans; these included 12 British citizens burned alive); and 552 people were injured. Over 700 buildings, including nearly five hundred foreign-owned businesses,

[55] COS (52) 11, 3 Jan. 1952, Defe 5/36. PRO.
[56] Minute by John Wardrop, 23 Oct. 1951, E1192/306, 371/91228. PRO.
[57] COS (52) 34, 11 Jan. 1952, Defe 5/36. PRO.

were burned down. Among the principal targets of the Egyptian mob was the Turf Club, the epitomy of British colonialism in Egypt. It was razed to the ground. Some £23 million in damages were inflicted before the Egyptian army finally restored order. By this point, the damage to Egypt's internal political stability, and to its relations with Britain was irrevocable.[58]

The British command in Egypt expressed serious doubts whether the forces available at the Canal Zone would be sufficient to quell the disturbances, if the Egyptian government failed to. But in any case, the State Department turned down a British appeal for support for whatever military action the British might find it necessary to resort to; and warned them against any attempt at a military occupation.[59]

Sir Pierson Dixon, a senior Counsellor at the Foreign Office, writing in the middle of the sacking of Cairo, noted that power was a function of money, divisions, and prestige, which in effect meant 'what the rest of the world thinks of us'. Dixon appreciated that the British did not have enough of those assets to maintain their position in Egypt, on their own: '. . . the essential difficulty [in Egypt] arises from the very obvious fact that we lack power. The Egyptians know this, and that accounts for their intransigence.'

The only solution Dixon could think of was to seek the Americans' 'moral, financial and, if possible, military' support in carrying out a 'strong policy' in Egypt.[60]

However, it was gradually filtering through, even to the British establishment, that the deployment of troops to the Middle East, in support of the British position in Egypt, was just about the last thing that the Americans were willing to do for their Allies. Given that unpalatable fact, the British were forced to begin to consider the strategic and military ramifications of the loss of their base in Egypt. Short of a miracle, that base might now be erased from Allied Grand Strategy options.

In effect, there was already no realistic alternative to the Northern Tier strategy. Turkey was already the *de facto* inheritor of Britain's traditional position as the dominant power in the region.

[58] Report of 25 Jan. 1952, in *FRUS*, 1952–54, Vol. IX, part 2, pp.1752–5; and Poole, *History of the JCS . . .*, Vol. IV, 1950–53, pp.343–4; Howard Sachar, *Europe Leaves the Middle East, 1936–1954*, London: Allen Lane, 1974, pp.591–2; and Hahn, *Containment and. . .*, p.37.

[59] Report of 25 Jan. 1952, in *FRUS*, ibid., pp.1752–5; and George McGhee, *Envoy to the Middle World: Adventures in Diplomacy*, New York: Harper and Row, 1969, pp.231–2. In his memoirs, Eden makes no mention of the Americans turning down British appeals for support for British military action in Cairo.

[60] Minute by Sir P. Dixon, 23 Jan. 1952, FO 371/96920, PRO. quoted by John Kent, 'The Egyptian Base and the Defence of the Middle East, 1945–54', in *Emergencies and Disorder in the European Empires after 1945*, edited by Robert Holland, London: Frank Cass, 1994, p.51.

C. THE EXPIRATION OF MEDO

Significant changes were about to be introduced into British strategic thinking on the Middle East. But new strategies require negotiations (usually protracted) for new base rights and years for their construction. The COS felt unable as yet to dispense in wartime with the facilities offered by the Egyptian base.

The British feared that in the event of war, Admiral Carney, C. in C. of the new Aegean Command, would claim that the Turks had barely sufficient forces for the defence of Turkey itself; or that Carney would deploy the Turks in the battle for northern Italy and Yugoslavia, rather than in the Middle East. But Gen Bradley told the COS that the Turks insisted upon being integrated into the NATO Command first, and that it would be pointless to press them too hard, since they could not be coerced into assuming any role in MEC if they did not wish to do so. With the MEC project gathering dust on the shelf, the ground forces of Greece and Turkey were placed under the overall command of SACEUR, through CINCSOUTH; their air forces under the air commander, Southern Europe Command; while their modest navies were to remain under their own respective chiefs of staff.[61]

By 1952, the Americans had come to regard MEC more as a political, than a military project – as an instrument whereby the West might secure strategic and military facilities from the Arabs.[62]

The British had conceived of MEC on the assumption of Turkish subordination to British command in the Middle East. But Britain's traditional imperial hegemony in that region was by now an anachronism. The British were on the verge of losing the Egyptian base, their remaining major strategic asset in the region. And further, due to economic duress, they were about to redeploy the major part of what was left of their Middle East garrison out of that theatre.

Yet British planners still clung stubbornly to the hope that the MEC (soon to become MEDO) project would provide a solution to the impasse in their negotiations with the Egyptians. To some senior officials in the Foreign Office, MEC still appeared to be the sole means whereby Britain might yet secure an American commitment, both financial and military, to the Middle East. As late as in February 1953, (10 days after the Anglo–Egyptian agreement on the Sudan), the British C. in C.s Middle East pleaded for a 'new, more determined

---

[61] Cf., COS (52) 43, 16 Jan. 1952, Defe 5/36; and minute of COS – JCS meeting on 6 Jan. 1952, in COS (52) 11th, 22 Jan. 1952, Defe 4/51. PRO; and Acting Secretary of State to Turkish embassy, 13 Feb. 1952, *FRUS*, 1952–54, Vol. V, p.269.

[62] Brief (approved by State, Defense and JCS) for President Truman for meeting with Prime Minister Churchill, 4 Jan. 1952, *FRUS*, 1952–54, Vol. IX, part 1, pp.168–70.

attempt at the establishment of the Allied Middle East defence organisation.'[63]

The British felt that they had been duped by both the Americans and the Turks. The British Cabinet had agreed to the admission of Greece and Turkey into NATO, only on the understanding that the Americans would agree to the setting up of a MEC, to include the Turks, under a British SACME. The British now took a cynical view of American tactics. In their view, the latter's main concern all along had been to mobilise the Turks' military potential for the West, without caring too much, and certainly not as much as the British, whether that potential was deployed through MEC, or through Eisenhower's European Command. Retrospectively, George McGhee conceded that the need for MEC had been reduced considerably by the formal admission of Greece and Turkey into NATO.[64]

The Americans had by now despaired of the Egyptians ever allowing *Allied*, let alone British troops to remain on their soil. The British now realised that they would have to convince their Allies that MEC without the Turks would be 'military nonsense'.[65]

By 1952, few still believed that a 'revamping' of the MEC project could resuscitate it. In any case, the underlying British goals for MEC – to engage the Americans and the Turks in the defence of the Middle East, and to solve the Anglo–Egyptian dispute[66] – remained pathetically remote.

At the end of January 1952, Secretary of State Dean Acheson expressed the hope that the UK would exercise 'the utmost flexibility' in its discussions with the Egyptians, since the MEC proposal would possibly now have 'a particularly unpleasant ring' in Egyptian ears.[67]

In March 1952, one month after the official induction of Greece and Turkey into NATO, the CIA produced a special report on the prospects for the establishment of an 'Inclusive Middle East defence Organisation' (MEDO). The report all but buried the project. It concluded that Egypt would not join any MEC until she had settled her controversy with the British; and no outcome would be acceptable to Egypt which did not include the complete evacuation of British troops from Egyptian soil and British recognition of King Farouk as sovereign of the Sudan.[68]

---

[63] Sir Pierson Dixon (F) at COS (52) 77th, 5 June 1952, Defe 4/54; and BDCC (53) 16, 23 Feb. 1953, Defe 11/58. PRO.

[64] George McGhee, *Envoy to the Middle World: Adventures in Diplomacy*, New York: Harper and Row, 1969, p.25.

[65] CP 266 (51), 22 Oct. 1951, Cab 129/47. PRO.

[66] COS (52) 34, 11 Jan. 1952, Defe 5/36. PRO.

[67] Acheson to embassy in Cairo, 28 Jan. 1952, *FRUS*, 1952–54, Vol. IX, Part 2, p.1757.

[68] For this and following, cf., CIA Special Estimate, SE – 23, 17 March 1952, PSF, box 258, HST.

But even if the UK did meet Egyptian demands, the CIA did not believe that the latter would subsequently agree to the deployment of foreign forces on Egyptian soil in peacetime, or to anything more than a nominal Western command structure. Egypt might agree to a defence arrangement, if it was limited to the co-ordination of operational plans, to the provision of Western military aid, and to negotiations towards 'the development in peacetime, and the use in wartime of Middle East defense facilities.' On this basis, the Egyptians might agree to British or other Western technicians staying on to maintain the British bases. However, the Egyptians would insist that they themselves command all ground and air bases (a proposition that no Western planner was ready to contemplate).

The CIA believed that Syria, the Lebanon, Iraq and Jordan were more aware of the Soviet threat than the Egyptians. But no Arab state was likely to join a MEC without Egypt. However, the Arabs did have two strong motives for wanting defence links with the West. Their primary motive was to secure substantial Western military aid. And second, they would reason that the granting of such aid would strengthen the prospects that in the event of war the West would make a determined defence of their region against a Soviet invasion.

The CIA also noted the high level of Arab animosity to Anglo–French colonialism in the Middle East. Their report concluded that the Arabs would be the more attracted to a MEC if it led to a decrease in British and French, and an increase in American aid to the region. (However, the British had certainly not initiated the MEC project in order to facilitate their own replacement by the Americans in the Middle East!) And finally, for the long term, the MEC could not really succeed before the Arab–Israeli dispute was settled, and the peoples of the region began 'to give primary emphasis to the defence of the area against Soviet aggression'.[69]

This report was evidently studied thoroughly by Secretary Dulles in 1953, prior to his Middle East tour in May of that year (on which, see next chapter).

Following the bloody clashes in Egypt, the COS had also scaled down their ambitions for MEC, and again, had aligned them with the American view. At a meeting held on 22 January 1952, in the middle of the Cairo riots, CIGS Slim stated that in view of recent developments, MEC should be set up only in the event of war. Nothing was to be gained by setting it up in peacetime, since it would have no one to command except, possibly, British troops. The COS agreed that under present circumstances, MEC should be a planning organisation only, ready for immediate expansion in the event of war.[70]

[69] Ibid.   [70] COS (52) 11th, 22 Jan. 1952, Defe 5/36. PRO.

But the Americans rejected the British concept. They concluded that a MEC confined to 'planning, liaison and advisory functions' would be 'a military structure without a political foundation.' The Americans also baulked at the British proposal to set up a MEC Steering Group composed only of the US, the UK, Turkey and France. They predicted that the Arabs would refuse to take on any substantial obligations, but at the same time would resent being excluded. Gen Collins, who had long ago expressed his preference for the Turkish, as against the British option in the Middle East, commented wryly that they were pursuing conflicting objectives – attempting to preserve 'eroding British power and prestige', and trying to secure Arab co-operation.[71]

But Gen Collins, who still insisted that the United States could not contribute directly to the defence of the Middle East, had no practical advice as to how they were to preserve Western influence in that theatre. The State Department therefore persisted in its traditional policy; that the United States should 'take an increased share of responsibility' for the Middle East; and that they should shore up the British position in Egypt by continuing their efforts to establish a Middle East Command. This policy, embodied in NSC 129/1, was affirmed by the president on 24 April 1952. Truman agreed also to the paper's recommendation that the US should be prepared to:

> reinforce political and psychological pressures in the area by assigning US token forces in a Middle East defense arrangement if US willingness to take this action is seen as the key to the establishment of such an arrangement and to the settlement of the dispute between the UK and Egypt.[72]

The JCS appealed against this paper. As usual, they feared that a token force would require reinforcements to protect it, and thereby embroil the US in a larger military commitment than they could handle. They suggested that they encourage Turkey, 'with its stable pro-Western government', to assume 'primary leadership' in the Middle East. But the JCS views were rejected by the NSC.[73]

In June 1952, the British forwarded to Washington a new plan, along the lines of Gen Slim's January proposals. The Middle East Command (MEC) had been transformed into a Middle East Defense Organisation (MEDO). It was apparently hoped that the new nomenclature would be more palatable to the Arabs. MEDO was to be initially 'a planning, co-ordinating and liaison organisation', developing ultimately into a full-blown defence organisation.[74]

---

[71] Report of State–Defense Working Group 15 April 1952, Poole, *History of the JCS* . . ., Vol. IV, 1950–52, pp.347–8.
[72] NSC 129/1, 24 April 1952; and Enclosure B to JCS 1684/69, 3 May 1952, CCS 092 Palestine (5-3-46) sec. 14, quoted in ibid, p.345.   [73] Ibid., p.346.   [74] Ibid., p.348.

But the State Department still disagreed with London's attitude to the Arabs. They rejected the British suggestion that only those Arab states that could offer 'substantial assets' should be invited to join MEDO. And they disagreed also with the British proposal that MEDO be established even if the Arabs refused to join. But the American administration was still divided within itself over the Middle East. The JCS sided with the British view, urging that it was vital to proceed with defence arrangements for the Middle East without or without the Arabs' co-operation. Further meetings between British and American officials failed to produce agreement.[75]

But in July 1952, events overtook diplomacy yet again. The 'Young Officers'' revolution in Egypt overthrew the *ancien régime*, and expelled King Farouk. In September, an Egyptian officer, Lt. Col Amin, brought a message from Gen Neguib to US ambassador Caffery in Cairo that Egypt might join MEDO, and/or enter into partnership with the United States – in return for military and financial aid. Caffery made it clear that the Americans' ultimate goal was to set up MEDO, and that the British would have to play an integral role in that body. The Egyptian officer 'made noises about "evacuation" but', according to Caffery, he in essence concurred.[76]

In November, Caffery passed on his government's offer to supply 'police equipment', on a cash reimbursement basis. But Neguib, besieged by domestic political opposition, wanted much more. He told Caffery:

I may be dreaming but if you could find a way to let us have 100 tanks various doors would be opened including one leading to Middle East Defense.[77]

But the British vetoed any significant arms supplies to Egypt before a new agreement on the Canal Base was reached. The British also demanded that arms supplies to Egypt remain a British monopoly, since this remained Britain's sole bargaining counter. The Americans' (Caffery's?) initial euphoria soon evaporated, when Neguib later made it clear that before Egypt would join MEDO, the Sudan question must be solved satisfactorily, and the UK must set a definite date for the complete evacuation of her troops.[78]

Protracted Anglo–American negotiations on MEDO took place

[75] Ibid., pp.348–9; also COS (52) 89th, 23 June 1952, Defe 4/54, PRO; and David R. Devereux, *The Formulation of British Defence Policy Towards the Middle East, 1948–56*, London: Macmillan, 1990, p.68.

[76] Caffery to Department of State, 18 Sept. 1952, *FRUS*, IX, 1952–54, Vol. 2, pp.1860–1.

[77] Caffery – Department of State, 25 Nov. 1952, pp.1894–5, ibid.

[78] Caffery to Department of State, 28 Nov. and 3 Dec. 1952, ibid., pp.1900–1, 1903; and Poole, *History of the JCS . . .*, Vol. IV, 1950–52, pp.349–50.

during the winter of 1952–53. But the Egyptian refusal to negotiate on MEDO before a complete British withdrawal proved to be an insurmountable stumbling-block.[79]

The 'Young Officers'' revolution in Egypt had added a catalyst which finally led to a significant change in British strategy in the Middle East. For the first time, British contingency plans for the Middle East were drafted on the assumption that the base in Egypt could no longer be counted on.[80]

MEC had been part of the traditional, Egypt-centred British strategy in the Middle East. With Turkey in NATO, the way was open to an alternative, Northern Tier-based strategy.

[79] Devereux, *The Formulation of . . .*, pp.69–70.

[80] JP (52) 129, Final, 11 Nov. 1952, Defe 6/22. PRO; and US Army (London) to Department of the Army (Washington), 5 Nov. 1952, Lot file 57D 298, box 16, RG 59. NA.

10 The switch to the Northern Tier

A. THE CHANGE TO THE 'LEVANT–IRAQ' STRATEGY

During the summer and fall of 1952, a new 'forward strategy' was adopted in the Middle East. Underlying it was a novel 'mobile concept', which stipulated that a strategic reserve would be based in the UK, and have the ability to fly at short notice to any trouble spot across the globe.[1]

The British themselves had long appreciated that their plans for the defence of the Middle East were unrealistic. The Labour administration had hoped that it would succeed in persuading the Americans to renew their original commitment to this theatre. But Churchill's first post-war visit to Washington as Prime Minister, in January 1952, and the military talks in Washington in May of that year, finally dispelled any lingering illusions on this count. In addition, their Suez base notwithstanding, the British had been slowly digesting the evident fact (long appreciated by the Americans) that the Turks, and not they themselves, were now the major power in the Middle East.

However, Britain's new forward strategy did *not* originate from sound military orthodoxy. It was the inevitable consequence of economic stringency at home, which militated against the retention of large garrisons abroad. The Korean war had provoked roaring inflation and economic crisis in the UK, caused in part by the need to increase armaments, and to beef up forces in Europe. The COS themselves conceded this, when they tabled the new strategy, in October 1952:

> We made these recommendations, not because we believed that they were militarily sound, but because it was only in the Middle East that we could see any way of reducing, in the fairly near future, our overseas expenditure. The reductions could not be made without risk to our position in that most important area,

---

[1] *The Radical Review*: Mobility in the Middle East, JP (53) 24 (Final), 5 February 1953, Defe 6/23, and report by ad hoc committee on the Radical Review, RR (ad hoc) (53) 2, 9 Feb. 1953, Defe 11/87; and R. W. Ewbank, Secretary, COS Committee, to R. R. Powell, 23 Feb. 1953, Defe 11/87. PRO.

but we considered that the demands of N.A.T.O. and the Cold War in the Far East must take precedence if economic necessity forced a curtailment of our effort.[2]

The War Office even tried to mobilise the Foreign Office, in an attempt to stave off Treasury demands for a cut of £300 in the War Office budget. The Ministry found it impossible to achieve this, even though they were working out plans to cut down the size of the Army from 430,000 to 385,000 men – which would produce savings in the region of £100 million. In July 1953, General Macleod, Director of Military Operations (DMO) at the War Office, lobbied the Foreign Office, to enlist the latter's support for resisting those cuts that would bring their Middle East garrison below the level deemed necessary by the War Office.[3]

It will be recalled that it had been planned to leave a garrison of one mixed division and 160 aircraft in the Middle East. Originally, and conditional on an agreement with Egypt for the evacuation of the base in that country, it had been intended to split the division evacuated from Egypt as follows: one Infantry Brigade Group to Cyprus, one Infantry and one Armoured Brigade Group to Libya, and one Royal Marine Commando Brigade to Malta. With the consequent adoption of the mobile concept it was decided to station the two Brigade Groups originally intended for Libya in the UK. This would save the expenses involved in building the bases in Libya, and in transporting supplies and food to the Middle East garrison. Extra cost, however, would now be incurred, in increasing air transport resources, to ensure the full mobility of the forces on Cyprus and in the UK.[4]

The new mobile concept presented both military and political challenges. The two brigade groups stationed in the UK would not be trained in desert warfare, nor acclimatised to Middle East conditions; and they would need to be extremely mobile to reach their battle positions in time (this particular weakness was revealed painfully during the protracted and elaborate preparations required to mount the Suez Operation some 3½ years later). Finally, the evacuation of all British forces from Arab territory would undoubtedly lower the Arabs' faith and confidence in the West's ability to defend them. This might be partially offset, if Britain could secure Jordan's agreement to station troops and prestocking facilities on her territory.[5]

[2] COS (52) 514, 2 Oct. 1952, Defe 5/41. PRO; and Anthony Eden, *Full Circle: The Memoirs of Sir Anthony Eden*, London: Cassell, 1960, p.244.

[3] Minute by Roger Allen, 20 July 1953, JE1197/9, FO 371/102834. PRO.

[4] COS (52) 514, supra; and COS (52) 383, 18 July 1952. PRO.

[5] Ibid.

But the switch to the new strategy was not dictated by economic stringencies alone.

First and foremost, there was the painful weaning away from the long-entrenched Suez-centred strategy. By mid-1952, even the military appreciated the need to move out of Egypt, following the events of the previous months: Egypt's unilateral abrogation of the 1936 treaty, the bloody clashes at Ismailya, and the burning down of Cairo; and to crown it all, the officers' revolution of July 1952. At the beginning of 1953, Roger Allen (head of the African Department at the Foreign Office), noted the evident fact that the Suez Base was currently unable to fulfil any useful strategic function: 'The truth of the matter is that we are at present keeping 80,000 men in the Canal Zone for no purpose except to maintain themselves . . . It is useless to maintain troops simply to be shot at.'[6]

Second, there was the maturation of the Turks as a military factor. In March 1952, the Turks (with the Greeks) officially joined NATO, and thereby became part of the Allied bloc facing the Soviets. The COS believed that the re-organisation and re-equipment of the Turkish army by the Americans now meant that Turkey would either be able to hold out successfully against a Soviet attack or, at the worst, hold them up for longer than previously planned.[7]

In addition, and quite apart from the emergence of a strong Turkish front, it was now believed that nuclear interdiction would make large scale Soviet operations against the Levant unlikely, thereby reducing substantially the risk of a Soviet land conquest of the Suez base. In addition to 'the potential threat of an undefeated Turkey on one flank', the Soviets would now be faced with:

(i) an Allied strategic atomic offensive including attacks on the Caucasian oilfields;
(ii) atomic attacks against communications and airfields on her line of advance.[8]

The planners therefore no longer expected an initial Soviet air attack on the Suez base. The Allies would be afforded more time in which to deploy forces further to the north and east, to the passes that afforded entry into northern Persia and Iraq. The Soviets were now expected to concentrate on the conquest of Turkey, Iraq and Persia, combined possibly with raids across the Syrian desert.[9]

---

[6] Minute by Roger Allen, 14 Feb. 1953, JE 1192/18, FO 371/102796. PRO.

[7] Annex to JP (52) 69, 7 July 1952, Defe 4/55. PRO.

[8] Annex to JP (54) 101, 31 Dec. 1954, Defe 6/26. PRO.

[9] DCC, Middle East, review of Middle East Strategy, in COS (52) 519, 18 Sept. 1952, Defe 5/41. PRO.

But the nuclear threat worked both ways – not only to inhibit a Soviet advance, but in making large overseas bases hostage to a single enemy nuclear air strike. In August 1949, the Soviets had entered the nuclear club. This made UK bases, especially the sprawling Suez complex, increasingly vulnerable to, perhaps even defenceless, before a Soviet nuclear attack.

In the spring of 1952, the nuclear deterrent was for the first time incorporated as a central element in British global strategy. Nuclear weapons were seized upon as an 'economic' alternative to Britain's traditional reliance on conventional forces, the more so as until 1947, a large proportion of the latter had been provided by India. The Middle East was lowered in British priorities. It would be defended, on condition that it did not come at the expense of the defence of Great Britain herself, or Europe, and that it did not inhibit the strategic air offensive or the securing of major sea lanes.[10]

It has been suggested recently that the advent of the hydrogen bomb was but a convenient instrument, rather than the real cause, wherewith the Churchill administration justified its withdrawal from Egypt.[11]

This would not appear to be the case to this author. In effect, the Allies' position in the Middle East had become not unlike their strategic position in Europe, only more so. Against the Soviets' overwhelming conventional preponderance, the Allies had little choice but to rely on nuclear weapons. This trend became the more pronounced with the advent of thermonuclear technology. Both Churchill and Eden were preoccupied with the possibilities and consequences of the hydrogen bomb. In a private letter to President Eisenhower written on 21 June 1954, Churchill summarised the major factors leading to the revision of British Middle Eastern policy:

> As time has passed *the strategic aspect of the Canal Zone and Base has been continually and fundamentally altered by thermo-nuclear developments* and by a Tito–Greco–Turco front coming into being and giving its hand to Iraq and by America carrying NATO's finger-tips to Pakistan . . . These events greatly diminish the strategic importance of the Canal Zone and Base, and what is left of it no longer justifies the expense and diversion of our troops, discharging since the war, not British but international purposes . . .[12] (My emphasis.)

[10] David R. Devereux, *The Formulation of British Defence Policy Towards the Middle East, 1948–56*, London: Macmillan 1990, pp.114–15.

[11] John Kent, *The Egyptian Base and the Defence of the Middle East, 1945–54*, in Robert Holland, ed., *Emergencies and Disorder in the European Empires after 1945*, London: Frank Cass, 1994, p.62.

[12] Churchill to Eisenhower, 21 June 1954, Prem 11/702. PRO.

On the next day, Eden repeated the same views at a secret Cabinet meeting, stating that Britain's 'strategic needs in the Middle East had been changed radically by the development of thermo-nuclear weapons': 'Smaller bases, re-deployment and dispersal are a more efficient way of employing our strength.'[13]

The JPS feared from the outset that too much reliance would be placed on nuclear weapons. In a review of Middle East strategy, written in July 1952, they had warned:

> Should the atomic attack not prove fully effective, our small force [in the Middle East] would be unable to withstand the degree of penetration then to be expected, and might be cut off and annihilated.[14]

But for lack of alternatives, the planners believed that the risks had to be accepted.[15]

At the same time, the chances of obtaining Australasian reinforcements for the Middle East had receded almost to zero. The emergence of communist China as a first-class military power, combined with the communist insurgency in Malaya, meant that Australia and New Zealand would be fully preoccupied with events in the Far East.[16]

The new forward strategy was termed the 'Levant–Iraq' strategy. It was defined as the defence of the Zagros mountain passes (Ruwandiz, Penjwin and Paitak) connecting Persia and northern Iraq. It was hoped that Allied forces would have time to build up a main defensive position in the Levant, and to reach these passes before the Soviets did. The latter's advance into Iraq and Persia was to be delayed by RAF air attacks operating from forward bases, by commando raids, and by extensive demolition operations at the passes.[17]

By the Fall of 1952, British strategy in the Middle East was being reduced to holding the Soviet advance 'as far to the North and East as possible' in order to purchase the time during which 'the American strategic bombing offensive . . . the backbone of Allied Global Strategy' might take its toll. The JPS even amended the formulation of the original aims of the new strategy fearing that it 'may convey the impres-

---

[13] Cabinet meeting of 22 June 1954, Cab 128/27; Eden memorandum on Egypt, C.(54) 248, 23 July 1954, Prem 11/92, PRO. and Sir Anthony Eden, *Full Circle: The Memoirs of Sir Anthony Eden*, London, Cassell, 1960, p.260.

[14] Annex to JP (52) 69, 7 July 1952, Defe 4/55. PRO.

[15] JP (52) 129, Final, 11 Nov. 1952, Defe 6/22. PRO.

[16] Annex to JP (54) 101, 31 Dec. 1954, Defe 6/26. PRO; , and Jacob Abadi, *Britain's Withdrawal from the Middle East, 1947–1971: The Economic and Strategic Imperatives*, Princeton: Kingston Press, 1982, pp.81, 104, 180.

[17] COS (52) 519, 18 Sept. 1952, Defe 5/41; JP (52) 129, Final, 11 Nov. 1952; and annex to JP (52) 141, 23 Nov. 1952, Defe 6/22. PRO.

sion that our main purpose in defending the Middle East is to contribute to the security of American bomber bases.'[18]

The Iraqi passes would have to be defended by British, and indigenous forces – the Iraqi Army and the Arab Legion (though the Iraqis and Jordanians had yet to be informed of their new mission). The Iraqi forces were to be deployed primarily in the defence of the passes on their own northern border. But the new strategy depended upon moving up two British infantry brigades to this forward area by D + 10 days, and an armoured brigade by D + 15 days – the earliest time by which Soviet ground forces were now expected to arrive at the passes. This meant that the armoured brigade would have to be stationed in peacetime in the Levant. It was hoped that the forward forces could be supported from a new maintenance area sited in Jordan (instead of Egypt), working along two L of Cs to Iraq; one along the pipeline road to Mosul, and the second 'by road to Aleppo and thence by rail to Mosul.'

A study by British planners had concluded that Israel would have been by far the best site for a rear maintenance area. But they had ruled this out, on the usual grounds that it would alienate the Arabs.[19]

The advantage of the new Levant–Iraq strategy over the Inner Ring was that it required only limited forces initially, and that it would force the Soviets to fight their way 'into, and perhaps through Iraq.' At the very worst, the Soviet advance to the Inner Ring would be retarded.[20]

As ever, the critical deficiency remained the vast disparity between the force-levels expected to be available to the opposing sides. In addition to the UK's 'mobile' division earmarked for the Middle East, there was only Jordan's Arab Legion (⅔ of a division). No other forces were expected to be available until D + 6 months. And even at that juncture, only three more divisions were expected – two from England (territorial), and one (hopefully) from New Zealand. The DCC, Middle East, commented that these forces might be the minimum required for the Cold War, but they would not be sufficient even 'to repel Russian raids'.[21]

Notwithstanding the planners' future aspirations, under plans current at the end of 1952, to fly the 'mobile reserve' from the UK to any point in the Empire within 36 hours, reinforcements were not due to arrive in the Middle East until D + 4 months. But even worse, as pointed out by the Middle East commanders, further defence cuts

[18] Annex II to JP (52) 123, (Final), 13 Nov. 1952, Defe 6/22. PRO.
[19] JP (52) 129, 12 Nov. 1952, Defe 6/22. PRO.
[20] Ibid.
[21] Annex to JP (52) 69, 7 July 1952, Defe 4/55; JP (52) 159, Final, 11 Nov. 1952, Defe 6/22; and DCC (53) 16, 23 Feb. 1953, Defe 11/58, and Defe 11/87. PRO.

meant that by February 1953, the commitment to despatch the two British divisions to the Middle East was no longer 'firm'; and the 'projected mobile reserve of five RAF squadrons from the UK' was no longer available for the Middle East; and finally, military consultations with South Africa had revealed that it was now unlikely that that country would send any significant land forces to the Middle East during the first year of a war.[22]

The British Middle East commanders also castigated the tendency of both the COS and the JCS to rely more and more on the Turks for the defence of the Middle East. The DCC derided the 'exaggerated ideas . . . about the military power of Turkey', and intimated that the American military advisers in Turkey knew better. The stories of the 'valour of the Turkish soldier' were quite out of proportion. The COS and the JPS may have come round to the Americans' Turkey-oriented strategy, but the DCC most definitely had not: 'It is a misconception that the Middle East can be defended by holding Turkey: it is equally false to suppose that Turkey can hold out irrespective of what is happening in the Middle East.'[23]

Nor were the DCC, Middle East very sanguine about the fact that the Allies were to rely more on indigenous Arab forces, of Iraq and the Arab Legion of Jordan. The DCC conceded that the individual Arab could be 'brave and intelligent', and that several Arab countries had 'a fair supply of men with good technical aptitude'. However, the DCC ruled out the Arab states as a geo-political factor. In pressing home their argument, the DCC, (in what was, of course, a secret internal document), confirmed a common Israeli complaint (always denied by the British) about the dangers of arming the Arabs:

> To provide arms to the Middle East may be the easiest part of the business. The Arabs are very anxious to get arms, *really in order to attain superiority over the Israelis* and some of them are even willing to pay for them. It is far more difficult to get them to maintain their arms in peace, or to train them adequately for their use in war.
>
> . . . there is a great instability in their character both as individuals and nations. Their inability to combine, due to their mutual suspicions, is a great source of weakness which is demonstrated by the failure of the Arab Security Pact to result in any planning for action against the avowed common enemy, Israel.[24] (My emphasis.)

Nor could the British be sure any longer what base facilities would be available to them in the Middle East in the future. The Egyptian base

---

[22] JP (52) 129, Final, 11 Nov. 1952, Defe 6/22; and Memo by BDCC, ME, DCC (53) 16, 23 Feb. 1953, Defe 11/58. PRO.   [23] DCC (53) 16, ibid.
[24] Ibid.

was still regarded by planners as 'indispensable for the support of whatever strategy we adopt.' Since it was expected that the new forward strategy would take some years to implement, Egypt would have to remain the main Middle East base for the present. Only the Suez base had the necessary infrastructure to absorb the reinforcements anticipated, and hoped for. But planners could no longer rely upon the efficient running of that base, nor even on having access to it within the first six months of a war. The new strategy called also for the construction of extensive peacetime facilities in Iraq and Jordan (2 airfields in the Mosul area, a maintenance area in Jordan, as well as road and rail communications).[25]

But this construction work would take several years to complete, and would require the full co-operation of the Arab world. In the interim, Britain would be able to deploy only 'light mobile forces', and therefore in wartime, would remain totally dependent upon access to the Egyptian base (land and air) facilities; access for the Royal Navy to Alexandria, Port Said and Suez; and on the unrestricted use of the Suez Canal. In effect, this dictated the need to reach agreement with Egypt, almost at any price, in order 'to secure Egyptian co-operation in peace, and full partnership in war'.[26]

COS forecasts made in October 1952, were positively defeatist. Although the American strategic air offensive remained the only Allied counter-offensive option, it was not expected to 'cause an immediate retardation of the Soviet ability to deploy forces in the Middle East'. The COS complained that their new forward strategy, excluding the Turkish front, relied upon a 'small and inadequately equipped Iraqi Army' (comprising 'three weak divisions') which would receive only indirect support from the RAF. (According to American intelligence, at the end of 1952, the RAF had a mere 136 aircraft stationed in the Middle East.)[27]

The gravest risk in the new strategy was that Allied forces might be forced back to an unprepared position at the Inner Ring before the reinforcements from the UK (two divisions and 5 RAF squadrons?) had had time to take up their positions – at D + 4 months. This was in part due to the fact that the Aleppo – Mosul railway, upon which the logistic support of the British forces depended, was considered to be 'both tenuous and vulnerable'.[28]

---

[25] Ibid; annex to JP (52) 69, 7 July 1952, Defe 4/55; and JP (52) 159, Final, 11 Nov. 1952, Defe 6/22. PRO.

[26] Annex to JP (52) 141, 28 Nov. 1952, Defe 4/58. PRO.

[27] Annex to JP (52) 119, 3 Oct. 1952, Defe 4/57. PRO; and JCS briefing for State Department, 28 November 1952, *FRUS*, 1952–54, Vol. IX, part 1, pp.319–22.

[28] JP (52) 129, Final, 11 Nov. 1952, Defe 6/22. PRO.

What were the dimensions of those risks? American planners estimated that the Soviets would invest a total of over 20 divisions, and 1400 aircraft in the Middle East campaign (including Turkey). In addition, they estimated that the Soviets would have the ability to deploy three airborne brigades anywhere they chose behind enemy lines.[29]

Against Iraq itself, British planners expected the Soviets to launch an offensive of 10½ divisions; 1½ against the north-eastern passes, four against Baghdad, and five against Basra. In addition, they expected a Soviet airborne brigade to operate behind Allied lines from the outset.[30]

Britain's new strategy was based on the assumption that the Turks would hold up the Soviet advance at their eastern frontier, to avert a direct Soviet offensive down the coastal plain of Lebanon and Israel to Egypt. In addition, it was hoped that the Turks would prove able to defend successfully their eastern front, and the Straits, in order 'to prevent Soviet submarine and surface vessels debouching into the Mediterranean.' However, following the admonitions of the DCC, Middle East, the COS began to doubt whether the Turks' 'command structure and administration' were strong enough to mount and control such an operation.[31]

If the British were forced to withdraw from north-east Iraq (either to the Tripoli–Homs line, or to Mafraq in Jordan) there would remain only Israeli troops to prevent the Soviets from consolidating themselves in the Levant 'with its good network of communications and airfields'. A 'virtually unopposed' Soviet buildup in the Levant would expose the Turkish flank to grave danger. Furthermore, once the Soviets were in the Levant, the only forces between them and Suez would be Egyptian. Since the Mediterranean sea would probably be closed for the first six months of the war, the loss of Suez would mean 'the strangulation' of Turkish (and British) forces in the Near and Middle East.[32]

By the Fall of 1952, the COS prognosis for the Middle East campaign was disaster-laden. They had no illusions about being able to hold the entire Iraqi–Persian border with the forces available to them. They expected the Soviets to overrun Iraq quite easily, secure access to the Persian Gulf, and then turn the Turkish flank. They would then be well positioned to mount operations against the Levant and Egypt. In September 1952, the COS drew the following pessimistic conclusion:

[29] JCS briefing of State Department, 28 Nov. 1952, *FRUS*, supra.

[30] COS (52) 519, 18 Sept. 1952, Defe 5/41. PRO.

[31] Annex to JP (52) 69, 7 July 1952, Defe 4/55; JP (52) 159, Final, 11 Nov. 1952, Defe 6/22; and Middle East War Planning Directive, 13 Nov. 1952, annex to JP (52) 123, Defe 4/57. PRO.

[32] JP (52) 129, 12 Nov. 1952, Defe 6/22. PRO.

'. . . the Soviet forces will achieve a large proportion of their Middle East aims while we achieve none of ours.'[33]

The single point of comfort was that, even if the Soviets did overrun Allied forward elements in Iraq, they would be unlikely to 'reach Aleppo in the north before D + 6 months, and Israel in the south before D + 7 months'. By that time, the British hoped to have brought in two divisions from the UK, and 'some Commonwealth reinforcements'. With these forces, and the Arab Legion, they might yet make 'a worthwhile attempt' to hold the Levant position for, by now, the Lebanon–Jordan Line had replaced the Ramallah line as 'the ultimate rear defensive position.'[34]

The new forward strategy was approved by the new CIGS, Field Marshal Sir John Harding in November 1952. He noted that the new plan 'now made relations with Iraq and Jordan especially important'.[35]

B. THE 'MOBILE RESERVE' CONCEPT.

The major goal of the new concept, introduced in early 1953, was to reduce the Middle East garrison, while maintaining the capacity to reinforce it rapidly in the event of an emergency. 'Rapid, mobile forces' were to replace static and expensive defence lines.

By now, the JPS took it for granted that any settlement with Egypt would involve the evacuation of all British forces from her territory. Of the single division that had been allocated by the British for the defence of the Middle East, a single infantry brigade group, supported by eight regular RAF squadrons, would be left in the region itself, on the island of Cyprus. There were also some encouraging indications from Jordan that she might be ready to grant base facilities for the armoured brigade to be left in the Middle East.[36]

Henceforth, Britain's standing as a world power would depend upon her ability to fly out the strategic reserve from the UK to any part of the Empire within 36 hours.[37]

The 'mobile concept', which had been evolving since 1950, was elaborated upon in the 'Radical Review' of British strategy that was dis-

---

[33] COS (52) 519, 18 Sept. 1952, Defe 5/41. PRO.

[34] Ibid.

[35] Devereux, *The Formulation of . . .*, p.119.

[36] *The Radical Review*: Mobility in the Middle East, JP (53) 24 (Final), 5 Feb. 1953, Defe 6/23, and report by ad hoc committee on the Radical Review, RR (ad hoc) (53) 2, 9 Feb. 1953, Defe 11/87; and R. W. Ewbank, Secretary, COS Committee, to R. R. Powell, 23 Feb. 1953, Defe 11/87. PRO.

[37] Ibid., and COS (53) 559, 14 Nov. 1953, Prem 11/487, PRO; also Abadi, *Britain's Withdrawal. . .*, pp.129, 139, and *The Formulation of. . .*, p.118.

tributed by the JPS in February 1953. The Review defined Britain's goals in the Middle East as follows: in the 'Cold War', to reassure the Arabs that they would be defended against the Soviets in the event of war; and in a 'Hot War', to prevent the Soviets, as far as possible, from occupying the Middle East.[38]

To attain these objectives, Britain would need to maintain a 'reasonably strong' garrison in the Middle East, 'and have it there for everyone to see'. The JPS warned that even their original minimal estimates of a peace-time garrison of 'about one division and approximately 160 aircraft', would 'entail serious risks'. But since that estimate had been made, the situation in the Middle East had deteriorated yet further.

The main danger in the new concept was the risk that the Arabs would lose confidence in the West, particularly in the UK, although the JPS did not regard the UK as being significantly further (in flying time) than Libya, the Middle East alternative.[39]

The new concept was in fact but a thin veil, which barely covered Britain's military bankruptcy in the Middle East. As such, it came under scathing criticism by the DCC, Middle East. With not a little sarcasm, and rancour, the DCC commented that it was its responsibility to confine itself to: 'real solutions of the problem of defending this important area, and to exclude those which are only "make-believe".'[40]

However, if the UK could not afford 'a real solution' (whether due to political or economic reasons) but had to put forward 'a facade', the Committee felt itself bound by good conscience to put in the following *caveats*:

(a) Even if we feel that we must try to deceive others, we should not deceive ourselves or the Americans.

(b) Our bluff may be called one day and British soldiers and airmen may again find themselves committed to a hopeless venture. Therefore, we should not be content with our bluff, but should strive with might and main to convert it to the real thing.

(c) The facade must not be so transparent that it fails to deceive. There is already doubt in the Arab world about our ability to defend the Middle East: hence occasional talk of neutrality. If we reach an agreement with Egypt, involving the evacuation of the Canal Zone, our ability to defend the Middle East will be the public announcement of our intentions and our answer to such questionings; the effectiveness of that answer depends upon its size . . .[41]

---

[38] For this and following, cf annex to JP (53) 24, (Final), 5 Feb. 1953, Defe 6/23. PRO.
[39] Ibid.
[40] For this and following, see DCC (53) 16, 23 Feb. 1953, Defe 11/58. PRO.
[41] Ibid.

The DCC doubted that the force recommended by the COS, the single division and 160 aircraft, would meet their requirements. They recommended that, at the very least, an armoured force should be added, and that the MEAF should be reinforced with tactical bombers. Not only that but the MEAF should be relieved of all missions outside its own immediate theatre of operations.[42]

In effect, this was the nemesis of the British imperial dream in the Middle East. In the euphoric summer of 1945, the COS had 'cut down' the plan of the Cabinet Minister responsible for the region from seven, to five divisions. Less than five years later, the COS were reduced to barely one. Of this, just a single brigade (one-third of the division) was to be physically on hand in the Middle East.

C. AMERICAN INVOLVEMENT IN THE MIDDLE EAST

In May 1952, Paul Nitze, director of the PPS, asked the JCS to assess the position in the Middle East, and to recommend whether the US should employ part of her resources to shore up the British in that theatre. Nitze did not believe that British forces were sufficient to protect even 'the shortest line of defence east of the Suez Canal.' In their reply, the JCS predictably laid emphasis on building up Turkey as a 'first priority', and repeated their veto on the introduction of American troops into the Middle East. Instead, they urged exerting influence on British Commonwealth countries to commit forces, and recommended the grant of American aid to 'Pakistan, Israel and the Arab States', to enable them to enhance their own defence capabilities.[43]

During the summer of 1952, the State Department was advised of the changes taking place in Britain's Middle Eastern strategy. Initially, the Americans understood that the British were now thinking of defending the Lebanon–Jordan line: 'a portion of Turkey and of the Mediterranean sea coast from Lebanon south.' In mid-August, H. Freeman Mathews, Deputy Secretary of State, pleaded with the Department of Defence that the United States become more involved in the Middle East. The first step would be to make a new study of this theatre, to determine whether or not they should sponsor 'a forward defense of the Near East, designed to protect at least a portion of the oil and give greater protection to our strategic bases . . .'[44]

Mathews suggested that, by 1956 or 1957, the United States might

---

[42] Ibid.

[43] Poole, *The History of the JCS* . . ., Vol. IV, 1950–52, pp.371–2.

[44] H. Freeman Mathews (Deputy Under-Secretary of State) to Robert Lovett (Secretary for Defense), 15 Aug. 1952, *FRUS*, 1952–54, Vol. IX, part 1, p.266.

be able to furnish 'significant quantities' of military equipment to the Middle East. In preparation for future discussions on this issue between the State Department and the Department of Defense, he asked the JCS to make a study of the force levels that would be required for this mission, and the cost of equipping them.[45]

Predictably, the JCS were deeply divided among themselves. Gen Collins objected to diverting forces from 'regions of higher priority' to the Middle East. He maintained that in any event, neither side would be able to extract refined oil from the region for the first two years of the war. Admiral William M. Fechteler, now Chief of Naval Operations, insisted that they had sufficient means to defend the important areas of the Middle East 'under many, and possibly all, conceivable circumstances'. These conflicting views were referred to the JSPC, which was to take a full year, until October 1953, to deliver its report on the Middle East.[46]

In the meantime, even Defense Secretary Lovett was becoming frustrated with the failure of the JCS to address themselves seriously to the Middle East. In early November 1952, he confided to Secretary Acheson that he was making:

> an effort to compel the Joint Chiefs of Staff to take a realistic look at the Middle East now that the British position in Iran is altered . . . we are long overdue in getting the Middle East command and in getting a statement from the Joint Chiefs of Staff as to the meaning of the situation in the Middle East and to get a realistic proposal from the military on the Middle East.

Acheson was relieved to be able to agree 'with the Defense view that we had responsibility in the Middle East and had to do something about it.'[47]

On 18 November 1952, Deputy Secretary Mathews met with Gen Bradley, who gave him an oral reply to his queries of the previous August. Bradley quoted from the report presented by the SPG the previous May: a forward defence along the Outer Ring would require '19 divisions, 1,200 combat aircraft, and eight destroyers with supporting escort vessels and minesweepers'. But only 12 divisions were currently available – 10 Turkish, one British (still in Egypt), and the equivalent of a further division in Jordan and Iraq. As noted already, of the 1200 aircraft needed, a mere 136 RAF aircraft were currently available. It was hoped that these would rise to about 250 aircraft by

[45] Ibid; and Poole, *History of the JCS* . . ., Vol. IV, 1950–52, p.372.

[46] Poole, ibid., pp.372–3; and Robert J. Watson, *History of the JCS* . . ., Vol.V, 1953–54, p.325.

[47] Memo of telephone conversation between Robert Lovett and Dean Acheson, 6 Nov. 1952, Acheson conversations, box 80, HST.

D + four months, and that some carrier-based aircraft would be on hand. This would leave a deficit of some 950 aircraft! By the most optimistic estimates, they might hope, by 1955, to reduce the D-day deficit to 1 division and 580 aircraft.[48]

These statistics were repeated by the JCS at a meeting with State Department officials at the end of the month. Gen Bradley ended his presentation by pressing for the early establishment of a MEDO, to carry out the military planning required. Gen Collins stated that they might be able to defend Suez, but insisted that they had no chance of holding the Persian Gulf. The oilfields and the refineries had never been a high priority for Collins, given his belief, repeated here again at length, about the non-availability of Middle East oil in war.[49]

Egypt and MEDO were even now still regarded as the keys to the defence of the Middle East. (The JCS still expected that Allied bombers would launch attacks on Soviet targets from airfields in the Suez area, 'soon after D-Day'.)[50]

At the end of the year, British and American officials met in London, from 31 December 1952 to 7 January 1953. As noted already, soon after his rise to power in Egypt, Gen Neguib had hinted to the Americans that he might join MEDO in return for American economic and military aid. The State Department now seized on this final straw – a package deal whereby Egypt would settle its controversy with the British, join MEDO, and receive a generous aid package for its co-operation.

This was the central question on the agenda at the London meetings. The British welcomed American intervention, and willingness to join in a new MEDO initiative. But the British COS objected vigorously to the Defense Department's $10 million programme of military aid for Egypt. They feared that the new weapons might be used to kill British servicemen in Egypt. For their part, the Americans sensed that the British wanted to preserve all military aid to Egypt as a British prerogative, leaving the Americans to furnish only economic aid.[51]

At this meeting, the American side gave their formal approval to the new 'Levant–Iraq' strategy, which the JCS had already perused prior to the conference. The British tried to persuade their Allies that by D + 12 months, seven more divisions (British, New Zealand, Australian and

---

[48] Watson, *History of the JCS* . . ., Vol. V, 1953–1954, p.325.

[49] State Department – JCS meeting, 28 Nov. 1952, PPS 47–53, box 77, RG 59 NA; reprinted in *FRUS*, 1952–54, Vol. IX, part 1, pp.320–5.

[50] JSPG memo. to Gen Bradley, Harkins, and Admiral Burke, 26 March 1953, RG 218 1951–53. 381 (11-29-49) sectn 5. NA.

[51] Cf., Eden, *Full Circle* . . ., pp.253–4; Poole, *History of the JCS*. . ., Vol. IV, 1950–52, p.352; and Watson, *History of the JCS*. . ., Vol. V, 1953–54, p.327.

South African) would reinforce the initial force available, of one British and two Iraqi divisions, and two brigades of the Arab Legion.[52]

In Washington, following lengthy discussions with Acheson and Averell Harriman (director of the Mutual Security programme), on 7 January, President Truman vetoed any military aid, or sales of jet aircraft to Egypt. But he did agree to the sale of arms to Egypt, to the limits of the latter's financial capabilities.[53]

On the central question of Egypt, Churchill's position could hardly have been further removed from that of the Americans. On 30 December 1952, he advised his Cabinet that he was going to point out to President-elect Eisenhower that, whereas the British were not about to move out of Egypt under duress, he was going to press for American aid since it was beyond Britain's strength to maintain a permanent garrison of 70,000 in the Canal Zone.[54]

In early January 1953, following inconclusive meetings with outgoing President Truman, Churchill also met with President-elect Eisenhower, and with John Foster Dulles. His somewhat-patronising advice to both was 'to do nothing "for some four months". . . [but] let events in many places, Korea, Persia and Egypt for example, take their course, and then see where we found ourselves'.[55]

On 20 January 1953, Gen Dwight D. Eisenhower was inaugurated as President, in place of Truman. It would be left to the new administration and, in particular, to his dominant new Secretary of State, to check out the political proclivities of the new officers' regime in Cairo, and to pronounce the final demise of MEDO.

D. DULLES'S MIDDLE EAST REASSESSMENT: MAY 1953

In early March 1953, Foreign Secretary Eden visited Washington, where he met both with President Eisenhower and Secretary Dulles. According to Eden's record of the meeting, the President agreed with him that 'it was essential to maintain the base in Egypt and that if we were to evacuate the canal zone before making a Middle East defence arrangement we should be exposing ourselves to Egyptian blackmail.'[56]

Eden again stressed the importance of establishing MEDO. The President replied that, without a peace agreement between Israel and Egypt, 'MEDO would be rather meaningless'. Eden retorted that the

---

[52] Watson, ibid.

[53] Poole, *History of the JCS . . .*, Vol. IV, 1950–52, pp.352–3.

[54] Martin Gilbert, *Winston S. Churchill, Vol. VIII, Never Despair, 1945–1965*, Boston: Houghton Mifflin, 1988, p.786.

[55] Ibid., pp.790–1.

[56] Eden, *Full Circle. . .*, p.249.

new régime in Egypt would not make peace with Israel before first gaining the prestige of ousting the British from the Suez base. When asked by Eden to appoint a senior Military figure to join Allied negotiations with the Egyptians, Eisenhower named General John E. Hull (Vice COS of the US Army). According to Eden's record, terms of reference for such talks were agreed upon; they included peacetime maintenance of the Canal base and its immediate reactivation in the event of war; arrangements for the air defence of Egypt; a phased British evacuation; and Egyptian participation in MEDO.[57]

However, Eisenhower insisted that the Americans could not 'gate crash' the Anglo–Egyptian negotiations. They must first be invited by the Egyptians. But the latter declined to do this, and refused to discuss Middle East defence plans at all before the British agreed on the terms of their own troop withdrawals. In their turn, the British were not prepared to discuss their own withdrawal 'in isolation'. As Eden reported back to the British Cabinet, only the unlikely eventuality of the Americans agreeing to apply pressure on Egypt could possibly avert another deadlock.[58]

During 1953, Anglo–American relations over the Egyptian question reached their nadir. The British sensed that the Egyptians were exploiting to the full Allied differences over Egypt ('leaked' to them by ambassador Jefferson Caffery in Cairo). Sir Ralph Stevenson, the British ambassador in Cairo, sent a blistering report to the Foreign Office on American policy in Egypt. Even when giving due allowance for the ambassador's Cairo-centred 'provincialism', his telegram was framed in remarkably bitter terms. American policy in Egypt appeared to Stevenson:

> to be conditioned by a belief that Egypt was still the victim of British 'colonialism', and as such deserving of American sympathy. It also appeared to be influenced by a desire to reach a quick solution almost at any cost and by a pathetic belief that, once agreement was reached, all would be well. These considerations, combined with a horror of unpopularity and fear of losing their influence with the new regime, particularly on the part of the United States Embassy in Cairo, and also an apparent disinclination by the United States Government to take second place even in an area where primary responsibility was not theirs, resulted in the Americans, at least locally, withholding the wholehearted support which their partner in N.A.T.O. had the right to expect and which would have been of great, if not decisive influence on our negotiations.[59]

---

[57] Ibid., pp.251–3.
[58] *FRUS*, 1952–54, Vol. IX, part 1, pp.349–50; and CC (53) 20th., 17 March, 1953, Cab 128/26. PRO.
[59] Annex to CC (53) 20th, ibid.

In his report on his Middle East tour, Secretary Dulles confirmed Stevenson's accusations. He noted that the British interpreted American policy as one that 'hastens their loss of prestige' in the Middle East. Dulles conceded that, 'To some extent, regardless of efforts to the contrary on our part, this may be true.' He warned that they must search for solutions to their problems in the Middle East that would not harm relations with Britain, or 'unduly weaken or wreck the NATO alliance.'[60]

From 9 to 29 May 1953, Secretary Dulles made an extensive tour of the Near and Middle East, visiting Israel, Egypt, Iraq, Jordan, Syria, the Lebanon and Saudi Arabia. (He also visited India, Pakistan, Libya, Turkey and Greece). He was accompanied by Mutual Security Administrator Harold Stassen.[61] It was the first visit to the Middle East by a senior American statesman since 1944, when President Roosevelt had met with Ibn Saud.

Dulles' conclusions from his tour rang the death knell for the *ancien* colonialist *weltanschauung* in the Middle East. He was shocked by the anti-colonialist (i.e. anti-British) atmosphere pervading the region. In his report back to the NSC, he stated bluntly that the British position was 'rapidly deteriorating, probably to the point of non-repair.' Such British troops as still remained in the area were, according to Dulles, 'more a factor of instability rather than stability . . . The days when the Middle East used to relax under the presence of British protection are gone . . .'[62]

Dulles ruled out categorically any hope of basing Western defence plans for the Middle East on the Arab world:

> Political stability required for internal progress and building of defensive strength of area is lacking. Almost entire area is caught in fanatical revolutionary spirit that causes countries to magnify their immediate problems and deprecate the basic Soviet threat.[63]

Dulles counselled that the United States had to convince the Arabs that the United States pursued policies different from those of the old colonialist powers, of 'sympathy for the legitimate aspirations of the people in accordance with our own historical traditions'. They had to 'press the French and the British to move in this direction.' Dulles feared that the association in Arab minds of the United States with

[60] Dulles report, 29 May 1953, PPS 47-53, box 30, RG 59. NA; reprinted in *FRUS*, 1952–54, Vol. IX, part 1, pp.383–6.

[61] For the itinerary of the tour, and the American protocols of the meetings, cf., *FRUS*, 1952–54, Vol. IX, part 1, pp.1–167.

[62] Dulles report, 29 May 1953, supra.

[63] Ibid.

'French and British colonialist and imperialistic policies' constituted 'millstones around our neck'.[64]

He indicated also that they would have to distance themselves from the pro-Israeli position associated with the Truman administration. He concluded that the Arabs' loss of respect for the United States was in direct proportion to their [the Arabs'] proximity to Israel. The US would have to use every means to allay Arab fears of Israel, while bringing them to realise that that state was an irreversible fact of history.

In a priority telegram sent to Eisenhower from Baghdad, in mid-tour, Dulles warned the President that time was short, before the Middle East was irretrievably lost to the West. Any remaining hope for salvaging the situation would 'quickly dissolve', unless American policy was now able to 'show the capacity to influence British and Israeli policies, which now tend to converge in what is looked upon as new phase of aggression against Arabs.'[65]

Dulles had arrived in Egypt in the expectation that that country would provide the key to Western defence efforts in the Middle East. But he was soon disabused of any such hope, and came down decisively against continuing to rest Western strategic planning in the region on Egypt.

Upon his return from the Middle East Dulles made a public broadcast over the radio and TV networks, on 1 June 1953. For the public, Dulles adopted an optimistic tone about the situation in Egypt. He stated that both the British and the Egyptians were now agreed that British troops should be withdrawn completely. The key outstanding issue remained the retention of experienced administrative and technical personnel, to ensure the continued operational efficiency of the base. Dulles claimed that the retention of foreign technicians was not irreconcilable with Egyptian sovereignty, and that once agreement was reached, Egypt would be able 'to add a new bright chapter to a glorious past.'[66]

However, Dulles' opinion as recorded in his private notes, and in his report back to the NSC, was far less sanguine. In his own record of the trip, he noted the possibility of 'open hostilities between Egypt and U.K. troops'; that Naguib and his officers were 'almost pathological' on the British question, and that they would 'rather go down as martyrs, plunging Egypt into chaos, than agree to anything which public could call infringement of Egypt's sovereignty.' Dulles in fact doubted whether the Egyptians would agree to the use of the Suez base by the

[64] Ibid.
[65] Dulles to Eisenhower, 18 May 1953, Ann Whitman file, Dulles–Herter sub-series, Dulles, May 1953, box 1. EL.
[66] Transcript of speech, 1 June 1953, FR 299, Dulles Papers, Princeton University. (PUL)

West in the event of an emergency, and whether Egyptian technicians would prove able to maintain it in operational condition.[67]

In a mid-tour telegram to Eisenhower, Dulles warned that the UK–Egypt impasse was the most dangerous problem in the Middle East. If unresolved, it would lead the Arabs to 'open and united hostility to the West', and incline them perhaps to become receptive to Soviet aid. Loose talk on Israel and Egypt by Churchill at his January meeting with Truman still rankled with Dulles. In a diatribe reminiscent of his views back in 1921, Churchill had threatened to make common cause with Israel, and if necessary, maintain the British position in Egypt by force.[68] If that occurred, Dulles warned that:

> . . . any hope of extending United States influence over the Near East and building at least a minimum of strength here would have to be renounced unless we would publicly disagree with Britain and thus allow accomplishment of one of primary aims of Soviet Russia.[69]

Once in Egypt, Dulles had soon discovered that Gen Naguib was but a front man, and that the real power behind the Free Officers was Col Nasser (although Dulles' talks had perforce been conducted mainly with President Neguib). Dulles had failed to convince the Egyptians that the continued existence of the Suez base would not infringe Egyptian sovereignty. He had even drafted a formula with regards the maintenance of the base, that he believed might satisfy both British and Egyptian sensibilities. However, Gen Naguib had given him just a few weeks to 'moderate' the British stand, before the Egyptians took matters into their own hands. In his report back to the NSC, Dulles insisted that, quite apart from the ongoing conflict over the British base, Egypt would have to be left out of Western defence plans for the foreseeable future:

> the larger problem of political and economic stability in Egypt would be with us for years to come . . . *we must abandon our preconceived ideas of making Egypt the*

---

[67] Dulles post-tour notes, Dulles papers, PUL.

[68] Gilbert, *Winston S. Churchill, Vol. VIII*, pp.792–3. Churchill's secretary, 'Jock' Colville noted in his diary that it was regrettable that Churchill had made his comments in front of three officials, including JCS Chairman Gen Bradley, who would be staying on under the Eisenhower régime. Colville noted that most of the Americans present disagreed with Churchill, even if the large Jewish vote would prevent them making this known in public. On Churchill's 1921 proposal to arm the Zionists against the Arabs, so that British forces might be evacuated from Palestine, cf., Michael J. Cohen, *Churchill and the Jews*, London: Frank Cass, 1985, p.120.

[69] Dulles to Eisenhower, 18 May 1953, Ann Whitman file, supra.

key country in building the foundations for a military defense of the Middle East.[70] (My emphasis.)

Dulles' 'dismissal' of Egypt, as politically and economically unstable, signed the final death-knell for MEDO, and made the switch to a Northern Tier strategy inevitable. Dulles told the NSC that 'the old MEDO concept was certainly finished'. A new strategic conception was needed, and the only one that would now work would be one 'based on the contribution of the indigenous peoples.'[71]

The British were duly informed, that same month, that MEDO 'had been put on the shelf for the present'. Harold Beeley, counsellor at the British Embassy in Washington, intimated that the Foreign Office now had its own doubts about the soundness of the MEDO concept.[72]

In place of a MEDO based on Egypt, Dulles had found three candidates willing to form a new defence organisation: Turkey, Pakistan and Iraq. The NSC endorsed Dulles' conclusion that:

> . . . the present concept of a Middle East Organization with Egypt as the key, was not a realistic basis for present planning . . . the U.S. should concentrate now upon building a defense in the area based on the northern tier, including Pakistan, Iran, Iraq, Syria and Turkey . . . As for the countries further south, they were too lacking in realisation of the international situation to offer any prospect of becoming dependable Allies.[73]

Dulles now espoused a strategic axiom long since advocated forcefully by Gen Collins: '. . . there is today virtually no defense in the Middle East, except for the Turkish flank position.'[74]

Dulles had found Turkey to be 'a delightful contrast' to the rest of the Near East countries he had visited. The Turks were eager and willing to supply base rights to the Americans, and to collaborate militarily against the Soviets. The Turks felt that they alone stood in the way of a Soviet advance on the Middle East. The only problem was the danger of their over-reaching their economic capacity in their desire to rearm.[75]

Dulles found that Pakistan was, 'although Moslem, extremely friendly'. That country was also conscious of the Soviet threat, and will-

[70] Dulles report on Middle East tour to NSC, 1 June 1953, Ann Whitman file, NSC series, box 4. EL; reprinted in *FRUS*, 1952–54, vol IX, part 1, pp.379–86.

[71] Dulles report to NSC, 1 June 1953, Ann Whitman file, NSC series, box 4, EL; reprinted in *FRUS*, 1952–54, Vol. IX, part 1, pp.379–86; also NSC meeting on 9 July 1953, idem, pp.394–6.

[72] Meeting between Harold Beeley and John D. Jernegan (Deputy Assistant Secretary of State, NEA), 17 June 1953, *FRUS*, Vol. IX, part 1, pp.389–90.

[73] NSC meeting, 9 July 1953, supra.

[74] Dulles Report of 29 May 1953, PPS 47–53, box 30, RG 59. NA.

[75] Dulles post-tour notes, Dulles papers, PUL.

ing to receive American military aid without waiting on 'formal defence concepts'. Dulles believed that Pakistani troops were of a high standard, and would be most effective on the Allied side.[76]

The last link was Iraq. Dulles was favourably impressed by that country, which earned Dulles' accolade of having been more anxious about the Soviet threat, and more willing to enter into defence agreements, than any other Arab state. Dulles did not expect that the current Anglo–Iraqi treaty would be renewed. But relations with the British were relatively good. Nuri al-Said was believed to be largely responsible for this.[77]

E. THE IMPLEMENTATION OF THE NORTHERN TIER STRATEGY

Dulles' proposals dovetailed neatly with Britain's new Levant–Iraq strategy, which had already received the concurrence, in principle, of the JCS.

In the autumn of 1953, General Ayub Khan, C. in C. of the Pakistani army, indicated his desire to establish a defence line against the Soviets running from Pakistan, through Iran and Iraq, to Turkey. In September, Gen Khan visited Washington as guest of the Secretary of Defense. He indicated his readiness to afford the Americans base facilities in his country, and suggested bilateral military co-operation between their two countries. The JCS commissioned the JSPC to study the new situation in the Middle East, with respect to the demise of MEDO, and to Pakistan's potential role in the defence of the area.[78]

On 13 October 1953, the JCS finally received from the JSPC the study of the Middle East that it had commissioned a full year before (above). The report made the optimistic assumption that Turkey would succeed in blocking all Soviet advances along its eastern borders, and through eastern Turkey into Iraq and Syria. While the report concluded that the defence of Pakistan was not vital to the defence of the Middle East, it noted that it would be desirable, 'in order to pose a threat to the flank of Soviet forces attacking into Iran . . .' Assuming that the Turkish front held, the JSPC confirmed that the optimal defence line for the Middle East would be along the Zagros Mountains, 'from a point near the junction of Turkey, Iraq, and Iran to the head of the Persian Gulf'. This was the most southerly natural defence line that would protect all the Middle Eastern oil fields.[79]

---

[76] Ibid.

[77] Dulles post-tour notes, Dulles papers, PUL.

[78] Watson, *History of the JCS . . .*, Vol. V, 1953–54, p.336.   [79] Ibid., pp.336–37.

The forces that would be required to defend this line were estimated to be 'four divisions and 1,100 aircraft on D-day, rising to 10 divisions and 1,250 aircraft by D plus 60 days.' The committee had studied the chances of holding each of the four major oil-producing complexes in the Middle East: at Kirkuk (Iraq), Abadan (Iran), Kuwait, and Dhahran (Saudi Arabia)–Bahrain–Qatar. Any one of these complexes was capable of producing enough oil to reduce substantially the estimated oil deficit that the Allies would suffer during the first six months of war. The successful defence of these complexes would depend above all upon the availability of sufficient air power, as indeed, would the entire campaign in the Middle East.[80]

In a further report, dated 4 November 1953, the JSPC reported that initially at least, the defence of the Middle East would be dependent upon effective military collaboration between Turkey, Pakistan, Iran and Iraq. And, in view of the demise of MEDO, the committee urged the administration to encourage these countries to establish 'a planning association for co-ordinated defense of the Middle East'.[81]

The JCS approved this report on 13 November, and urged the Secretary of Defense to initiate action along its lines:

... from a military point of view, the time might be propitious for encouraging Turkey, Pakistan, Iran, and possibly Iraq or a combination thereof, to form a defense association ... of indigenous forces under an indigenous command. . . there would be no dependence upon a satisfactory resolution of the Anglo–Egyptian and Arab–Israel difficulties.[82]

The British were informed at the end of the year that the Americans would be linking their offer of military aid to Pakistan 'with the initiation of some military collaboration between Pakistan and Turkey'.[83]

The JCS, and Admiral Jerauld Wright, the new CINCELM, expressed their doubts as to whether the Zagros line could be defended before 1956 – owing to the time it would take to train indigenous forces. But on 6 April 1954, the JCS gave their final approval to a JSPC report on areas of vital importance in the Near and Middle East, all of which were to be defended by holding the Zagros Mountain line. These were listed as follows:

(1) the NATO right flank, (2) air base sites, (3) the Turkish Straits, (4) the Eastern Mediterranean, (5) the Cairo–Suez–Aden area, (6) the Persian Gulf and contiguous oil-producing areas.[84]

---

[80] Ibid., p.337.   [81] Ibid., p.338.
[82] JCS memorandum for Secretary of Defense, 14 November 1953, 780.5/11-1453, box 4041A, RG 59. NA.
[83] Cabinet meeting, CC 1 (54), 7 Jan. 1954, Cab 128/27 part 1. PRO.
[84] Watson, *History of the JCS . . . 1953–1954*, Vol. V, p.339.

But the JSPC also conceded that, for the foreseeable future, there was no prospect of holding the Zagros Mountain line, 'except perhaps through the exploitation of nuclear weapons'. Furthermore, there was little prospect of being able to export oil from the Middle East in any significant quantities, due to anticipated Soviet interdiction.[85]

In 1954, the JCS decided, for the first time, to take the initiative in the Middle East. (This may have had something to with the transfer to NATO in August 1953 of US Army Chief of Staff, Gen J. Lawton Collins, a long-time opponent of American military involvement in the region.) It was decided to initiate urgent consultations with the UK and Turkey on a co-ordinated defence defence of the region, and to begin planning for the provision of air and naval support ('including atomic operations') for British and Egyptian forces in the Cairo–Suez area for the defence of 'Turkey and other important base areas' and to seek base and transit rights in the Middle East. For the long term, the strategic goal was now defined as to 'encourage the development of a regional defense organization capable of conducting the ground defense of the line of the Zagros Mountains utilizing indigenous ground forces.'[86]

The development of a Northern Tier Pact was the mission of the State Department. The first stage was to induce Turkey to approach Pakistan. The Americans did this by linking arms supplies to both countries with their agreement to set up a mutual defence pact. It was also decided to demand guarantees from the recipients that the arms would not be used for aggressive purposes – a condition that would apply equally to aggression against Israel.[87]

In June 1954, the JCS approached the COS, asking them to join them in military planning for the defence of the Middle East. The first stage would be joint discussions with the Turks on the defence of the Zagros mountain line, and Turkey's southern and eastern flanks. The second stage would be Anglo–American staff discussions on a Middle East defence line, sufficiently to the north and east of Suez as to provide for the security of 'the Cairo–Suez–Aden areas, at least one major oil producing complex, preferably in the Persian Gulf area, and the Turkish south flank.'[88]

These were the strategic developments that lay behind the signing of the Pakistani–Turkish agreement of 1954, and of the Baghdad Pact in 1955.

With American covert sponsorship, Turkey and Pakistan duly signed an 'Agreement for Friendly Cooperation' on 2 April 1954. The agree-

---

[85] Ibid.   [86] Ibid., p.340.

[87] Dulles to embassy in Pakistan, 29 Dec. 1953, *FRUS*, 1952–54, Vol. IX part 1, p.441; and NSC 5428, 23 July 1954. NA; reprinted in idem, pp.530–31.

[88] Watson, *History of the JCS. . .*, Vol. V, 1953–1954, p.340.

ment dealt with cultural, economic and technical collaboration. It also included a clause providing for 'consultation and co-operation on certain defense matters'. The Agreement provided for the accession of other states considered by the contracting parties as able to further their purposes. In the same month, the United States and Iraq concluded an arms deal.[89]

The British were pleased by these developments, rightly seeing in them the basis of a defence pact based on the Northern Tier.[90]

The new military alliances being sponsored by the Americans along the northern tier undoubtedly eased the path to the Anglo–Egyptian agreements of 1954. They gave the Churchill administration a certain veil of legitimacy for giving up the Suez base. Since the closing stages of World War Two, Churchill had pressed for American involvement in the Middle East, in particular, in what had then been the British Mandate in Palestine. Now, having failed to transform the British struggle to retain the Egyptian base into an Allied mission, Churchill had lost heart and resolve.

In April 1953, Churchill penned for Eisenhower a 'heart-on-the-sleeve' personal reappraisal of the British position in Egypt. In somber tones, he referred to his parliamentary opposition, and to the economic burden of holding on to Egypt. He inferred that following the British evacuation of India and Burma, those Middle East interests that Britain still bore the sole burden of protecting were in fact 'international and NATO interests far more than British'. As for the Soviet threat, Churchill asserted that it had receded significantly, with the bolstering of the Northern Tier:

> The great improvement of the right flank of the Western Front achieved by the Yugo–Tito–Greek–Turko combination has made the danger of a physical attack upon Palestine and Egypt definitely more remote in distance and therefore in what is vital namely in TIME.[91]

In October 1954, the British signed an agreement with the Egyptians that provided for their evacuation of the Suez base within 20 months; British civilian technicians would be allowed to stay on, to keep the base in good operational order; and British troops were granted rights of immediate re-entry in the event of war.[92]

[89] Ibid., p.345; editorial note, *FRUS*, 1952–54, Vol. IX, part 1, p.491; also Geoffrey Aronson, *From Sideshow to Center Stage: U.S. Policy Toward Egypt, 1946–1956*, Boulder, CO: Lynne Rienner, 1986, p.84; and Michael B. Oren, *Origins of the Second Arab–Israeli War: Egypt, Israel and the Great Powers, 1952–56*, London: Frank Cass, 1992, p.66.

[90] Eden, *Full Circle . . .* , p.259.

[91] Churchill to Eisenhower, 5 April 1953, in Peter G. Boyle, *The Churchill–Eisenhower Correspondence, 1953–1955*, Chapel Hill: The University of North Carolina Press, 1990, p.35.

[92] Poole, *History of the JCS . . .*, Vol. IV, p.353.

The Northern Tier policy inaugurated by Dulles was a significant point of departure for American policy in the Middle East and Asia. As such, the administration had several reservations and anxieties.

The United States decided not to formally join the Northern Tier defence alliances. The decision to maintain a low-profile, behind-the-scenes role was motivated by the 'learning' of several 'lessons of history', primarily from recent experience with Egypt and Turkey.

First, the State Department concluded that MEDO had failed due to the overbearing Western role, in an area where anti-Western colonialism sentiment was rampant. This time, they wanted the indigenous states to start on their own, supplied with Western arms, but without an imperious, over-imposing Western pre-eminence. Second, drawing from their experience with Turkey, the Americans foresaw that Iran and Afghanistan would not risk joining any American-led Middle East defence pact directed against the Soviets, until that organisation had demonstrated its ability to provide them with a minimum degree of protection.[93]

The Americans also had good reason to fear that their direct association with Pakistan would provoke opposition from India (and perhaps Afghanistan). Indeed, Nehru did protest about the American agreement to sell arms to Pakistan. But Eisenhower accepted Dulles' argument that they should none the less go through with the deal. And this on the grounds that if they bowed to Nehru's objections, the latter would thereby be established as 'leader of all South and Southeast Asia', and no country in that area would dare to conclude defence agreements with the West without his assent.[94]

And finally, the Eisenhower administration appreciated that the new, American-sponsored 'defence' agreements would be likely to provoke 'strong Israeli opposition', and possibly exacerbate Arab–Israeli tensions, even to the extent of igniting another round of hostilities.[95]

The State Department had its answers ready. First, they replied that apart from Turkey, Israel currently had the strongest military forces in the Middle East, and was 'able to defend itself against any likely combination of Arab states'. No conceivable Western aid to the Arabs could change this power balance for a considerable period. Second, as noted already, the Administration presumed to protect Israel's interests by

[93] Jernegan – Beeley meeting, 6 Jan. 1954, *FRUS*, 1952–54, Vol. IX, part 1, pp.444–46; and memorandum prepared in the Office of Intelligence Research, 3 May 1954, idem, pp.503–504.

[94] Meeting between the President, Dulles, Admiral Davis, and Henry Byroade (Assistant Secretary of State, NEA), 14 Jan. 1954, ibid, pp.453–4.

[95] National Intelligence Estimate, 22 June 1954, ibid, pp.518–19; also, Gen. Radford to Secretary of Defense, 30 September 1955, 381 Emmea (9–19–47) Sectn 23, box 12, NA.

demanding guarantees from the Middle East recipients of aid that the arms would not be used for aggression against Israel.[96]

In July 1954, following an American–Iraqi arms sales agreement, the latter indicated their agreement to adhere to the Pakistani–Turkish agreement. At a meeting in Washington, the Iraqi Foreign Minister, Dr Fadhil Jamali, told Secretary Dulles that through their association with Pakistan, Turkey (and Iran), Iraq hoped to collaborate in the defence of the Middle East against the Soviet threat from the north.[97]

On 24 February 1955, Turkey and Iraq set up the Baghdad Pact alliance. Britain adhered on 4 April that same year. The Baghdad Pact completed the Northern Tier defence arrangements, which were to have replaced the traditional Egypt-centred strategy.

But the new alliance survived barely more than two years. In July 1958 a military *coup d'état* in Baghdad led to the fall of the pro-British régime, and the assassination of its leaders, King Hussein and Nuri al-Said. Four months later, in November, the last British troops left Jordan. The last pillars of British strategic planning in the Middle East had finally collapsed.

But these events are beyond the scope of this present work.

[96] Middle East Chiefs of Mission conference, 14 May 1954, ibid., p.506; and NSC 5428, 23 July 1954. NA; reprinted in idem, pp.530–31.

[97] Meeting between Secretary Dulles and Dr Fadhil Jamali, 12 July 1954, *FRUS*, 1952–54, Vol. IX, part 1, p.523. On Israel's efforts during this period to set up a 'peripheral alliance', to include Turkey, Iran and Ethiopia, cf., Isaac Alteras, *Eisenhower and Israel: U.S.-Israeli Relations, 1953–1960*, Gainesville: University Press of Florida, 1993.

Conclusion

There is always an easy solution to every human problem —
neat, plausible, and wrong!

H. L. Mencken

From 1946–47, a marathon debate took place inside the British
Cabinet on whether Britain should retain her bases in the Middle East.
Prime Minister Clement Attlee, and Chancellor Hugh Dalton, who
favoured evacuation of the entire region, were vanquished by Foreign
Secretary Bevin and the COS, headed by the CIGS, Field Marshal
Bernard Montgomery. Attlee's belief at the time in the possibility of
reaching amicable agreement with the Soviets, appears today (as it did
to the Military at the time) to have been naïve, at the least.

Yet in the long run, it was Chancellor Dalton's economic arguments
that determined grand strategy. Britain's sterling crisis of 1949,
followed the next year by the economic crisis brought on by the Korean
war, spelled the final death knell for Britain's overseas presence. From
1952, the Treasury (now headed by 'Rab' Butler) imposed arbitrary
financial ceilings on the Services budget. This forced the COS to make
harsh choices between overseas priorities. The demands of NATO in
Europe, and of the Cold War in the Far East, were given precedence
over those of the Middle East. The evacuation of Egypt became but a
matter of time. The 'mobile concept' and the 'Levant–Iraq' strategy
provided a veil to cover Britain's withdrawal from the Middle East.

It has been shown above that during the first decade after World War
Two, the Near and Middle East – Turkey and Egypt in particular –
played a central role in Allied contingency planning for the Middle East.

In the immediate post-war period, the blatant contrast between
Egypt and Turkey indicated a distinct strategic bias in favour of the
former. The Suez Canal base complex (which included ten air force
bases), inevitably assumed a central role in the Allies' strategic planning
for a war against the Soviet Union.

In contrast to the custom-made military facilities enjoyed by the
British under treaty (until 1956) in Egypt, the United States had to
invest huge sums in the development of a strategic infrastructure in
under-developed Turkey. (The funding had to be secured from the

Congress covertly under the aegis of the Truman Doctrine, issued ostensibly to protect Turkey and Greece from Soviet encroachment.)

But on the other hand, where the Turks welcomed the Americans with open arms in 1945, the Egyptians began an unrelenting campaign for British evacuation, and independence. British attempts to negotiate the retention of base, or at least re-entry rights in an emergency, all came to nothing.

For the Egyptians, the British, and *not* the Soviets, represented the real enemy. The British had conquered and 'temporarily' occupied Egypt in 1882, and now presented the major obstacle to Egyptian freedom and independence. The Egyptians regarded Israel (which had humiliated them on the battlefield in 1948) and not the Soviets as the more immediate military threat.

In contrast, the Turks needed no 'education' by the Allies about the dangers of Soviet encroachment. Turkish (and Ottoman) history had been plagued for centuries by the Russian Czars' advances to the warm waters of the Black Sea and the Mediterranean. During the nineteenth century, only the British Empire, pursuing its 'Eastern Policy', had preventing the Russians from achieving their goal. Soviet actions in 1945, when they demanded bases along the Straits, indicated that Josef Stalin was no different from his Czarist predecessors.

Once the Soviets demanded bases at the Straits after the War, the Turks welcomed American economic and military aid. (The Allies' need to oppose Soviet demands was one of the reasons why Bevin had initially offered to evacuate British forces from the Suez base). The Turks' single condition was that in return for permission to build bases on their territory, the Americans should provide a guarantee against Soviet encroachment or attack. This guarantee was not forthcoming until September 1951 when, once the Americans felt confident that NATO had been firmly established in Western Europe, Turkey and Greece were admitted as full members of that organization.

The MEC project, was a cynical, translucent subterfuge to prolong British military rights in Egypt under a pseudonym. It enjoyed but a brief, frenetic shelf-life. It has been shown that the fact that it was ever promoted by Britain and the United States was due to two reasons; first, to British desperation at the situation in Egypt; and second, to the Pentagon's conviction that without American support for MEC, their British ally would continue to block Turkish induction into NATO. Once the British were persuaded of the Turks' military pre-eminence in the Middle East, the MEC also provided the frame within which the Americans were to press the Turks to collaborate (under a British SACME) in the Middle East theatre.

But the Turks were not ready to play a subordinate role to Britain in the Middle East. And when, in any case, the British position in Egypt collapsed during the winter of 1951–52, the Turks (and the Americans) were provided with a convenient egress from the MEC. The British, having already conceded Turkish entry into NATO, felt that they had been duped by their Atlantic ally.

In late 1951, the Egyptian nationalists' campaign against the British came to a head, and deteriorated into open, if undeclared war. As had happened in Palestine between 1945–48, the British garrison in Egypt, originally there in order to maintain an Allied strategic base, became fully pre-occupied with defending itself against the indigenous population.

The events of that winter, as perceived clearly by the Americans, tolled the final collapse of British rule in Egypt, and with it, the end of all point in planning to use the Suez base for military operations. But Churchill's administration was preoccupied with national pride, status and prestige. As noted already by one scholar: 'By 1954 the British were fully aware that neither they nor their Western Allies could provide adequate reinforcements for the region, and they were prepared to use deceit to retain their prestige.'[1]

Israel too was allotted an important role in Allied contingency planning for the Middle East. British cynicism towards Israel matched that which she displayed toward Egypt. Britain tried to secure base rights from Israel, without taking that country into her confidence. Not only did Britain not trust any Middle East nation with its military secrets. But the British military knew only too well that the Israelis would never co-operate with the West on the basis of the Ramallah defence line, which cut Israel in half, from east to west!

Faced with obvious British subterfuge, and lack of candour, Ben-Gurion turned down her requests for base and transit rights. The British failed to persuade the Israelis that the Allies were determined, or even able, to defend their territorial integrity against a Soviet attack.

Britain also expected Israel to focus on the building up of its air forces, in order to serve better Allied strategic interests in the Middle East. It hardly seemed to occur to them that Israel's own primary concern was to build up its land forces, in order to repel the frequently-threatened Arab invasion, to reverse the results of the 1948 war!

Part of the explanation for British behaviour lies in the conviction of some officials that Israel was so desperately dependent upon the West (i.e. the United States) for both economic and military aid that she would tamely accept any terms on offer.

But, in the final account, neither the Egyptians nor the Israelis were

---

[1] David R. Devereux, *The Formulation of British Defence Policy Towards the Middle East, 1948–56*, London: Macmillan, 1990, p.120.

taken in by British subterfuge. Each was indeed preoccupied much more by their own regional conflict than with the Soviet menace.

British policy in the Middle East derived also from an overweening, paternalistic, imperialist attitude adopted towards the indigenous populations of her colonies.

She approached both Israel and Egypt in 1951, with ostensibly 'generous' offers of mutual defence treaties, in order to repel a Soviet offensive against the Middle East. But in reality, the British had no intentions whatever of making either country its true partners. And this, if only for the very good reason that Britain, denied American aid in the Middle East, could offer neither Israel nor Egypt any real hope of saving their countries from Soviet conquest. At the best, they might delay a Soviet conquest of Suez for between four to six months.

Political leaders in both London and Washington 'knew better' what was good for the Arabs and Israel, and berated them for being more concerned with their own immediate (petty?) problems, than with the more serious ones posed by the Soviet threat to Western strategic interests in that region.

The British never apparently comprehended that the states of the Middle East had priorities that could be legitimately different from those of the Allies.

To this paternalism was added a fundamental contempt for the Arabs' military prowess. A not atypical example may be quoted, from a letter written by Gen Sir Brian Robertson, C. in C., MELF, to the CIGS, Field Marshal Sir William Slim, at the end of 1950:

> These Egyptians are fundamentally cowards. They will march about the streets yelling slogans, insulting individuals and breaking up property; they will lie behind a hedge to commit murder if they think they are likely to get away with it. On the other hand, once they know that there is a serious chance that they may be beaten up themselves they will pack up at once . . . Another very effective way of frightening the Egyptians is to threaten them with ISRAEL . . .[2]

Up to the very end, not just until the Agreement of 1954 to evacuate Egypt, but also at the time of the Suez campaign in October 1956, Anthony Eden and his likes, in their myopic view of the world, apparently failed to appreciate fully the extent and depths of Egyptian nationalist antagonism towards the British, or the ability of Egyptian nationalist fervour to prevail over superior conventional military force.

The Americans were little better than their British ally. In Egypt, they tried to have their cake and eat it. American planners, even when favouring Turkey over Egypt, never relinquished the hope of using the

[2] Gen. Robertson to Field Marshal Sir William Slim, 29 Nov. 1950, WO 216/722. PRO.

Abu Sueir base for the strategic air offensive against the Soviets. Yet they refused to join the British openly in negotiations for the renewal of their base rights at Suez; nor to allow the British to inform the Egyptians of Allied plans to fly B-29s from Abu Sueir.

In 1951, when the JCS reluctantly joined the British in the still-born MEC project, it was primarily in order to win British acquiescence to Turkish entry into NATO. The Eisenhower administration pursued a policy of ingratiating itself with the Arabs. It was a policy that would lead to one of the more, if not the most serious, crises in Anglo–American relations after World War Two – in the wake of the ill-conceived, and even more badly executed, Suez Operation. Eisenhower and Dulles had deluded themselves that they could remain untarnished by British colonialism. But Nasser had not got rid of British paternalism only to exchange it for American paternalism!

It has been claimed that Secretary Dulles reoriented American policy in the Middle East to the Northern Tier. However, as shown above, this was not the case. British planners drew up the new 'Levant–Iraq' strategy, and obtained Pentagon approval – all before the inauguration of President Eisenhower. What Dulles did do, was to provide the political and ideological framework for the change to the Northern Tier strategy and the official burial of MEDO. The political expressions of the new strategy were the Pakistani–Turkish Pact in 1954, and the Baghdad Pact in 1955.

In retrospect, Allied contingency plans appear as little short of a farce! With the wisdom of hindsight, one might now ask what was the point of it all? Did the planners not realise how far their drawing-board schemes were removed from reality?

The Soviets could have conquered the Middle East with relative ease at any time during the first decade after the war, although they would have had to run the risk of nuclear retaliation. In 1949, Britain lost American military commitment to the Middle East. And the main strategic function of that theatre, to serve as a launching platform for the Allied strategic air offensive, was in fact never consummated. Even if the runways at Abu Sueir *were* readied for the B-29s, the special refuelling system they needed was *never* installed.

Both the Americans and the British knew that there was no question of manning the optimal defence line, the Outer Ring, in the forseeable future. Nor were there sufficient forces even to hold the Inner Ring.

But the historian is required also to ask what were the alternatives open to the Allies? Should they have simply abdicated power to the Soviets, and evacuated the Middle East? Had the Soviets established themselves consequently in the Near and Middle East, would Britain have felt safer? Would not NATO have been outflanked?

It has been suggested recently that the COS tended 'to plan on the basis of geostrategic concepts rather than economic or political reality'.[3] The inference appears to be that the COS should have taken into account factors other than military and strategic requirements.

However, it was the COS's duty to recommend to the government the best military measures to protect the nation's interests, and to warn of the risks if their recommendations were not adopted. Indeed, in respect of the need to hold Abu Sueir, the COS argued that nothing less than Britain's very survival as a state was dependent upon it. It was the government's, *not* the military's responsibility to define national priorities, to distribute the nation's resources as it saw fit – and to bear responsibility for the consequences.

And finally, Britain (*and* the United States after 1945) genuinely believed that the Near and Middle East were fated to live under the influence either of Western democracy or Soviet totalitarianism. And again, with the wisdom of hindsight, was it entirely hubris, or a *passé weltanschauung* that led the West to believe that their social and economic system (even in its diluted colonial version) was better than the Soviets'?

[3] Richard J. Aldrich, John Zametica, 'The Rise and Decline of a strategic concept: the Middle East, 1945–51', in Richard J. Aldrich, ed., *British Intelligence, Strategy and the Cold War, 1945–51*, London/New York: Routledge, 1992, p.236

Appendix

COSTS OF MAINTAINING BRITISH BASE IN EGYPT, 1937–1953*

(a)(i) Cost of maintaining the base in 1937, including £2.5m. for the maintenance of 10,200 British troops and 2,200 RAF personnel – £4m.

(ii) Cost of maintaining the base in 1951 immediately before abrogation of the Treaty, including £20m. for 25,000 British, 8,500 Colonial troops and 10,600 RAF personnel – £39m.

(iii) Cost of maintaining the base in 1953 including £35m. for 50,000 British and 17,000 Colonial troops and 14,400 RAF personnel – £56m.

(b) Cost of developing the base between 1946 and 1951, mostly on building or rehabilitation of temporary living quarters – £14m.

* Source: Ministry of Defence memorandum for the Prime Minister, Winston Churchill, 23 December 1953, in Prem 11/484. PRO.

Bibliography

A. UNPUBLISHED PRIMARY SOURCES

1. England

(i) Public Record Office, London (PRO)

Defe 4. Chiefs of Staff – meetings
Defe 5.—— – memoranda
Defe 6. Joint Planners – memoranda
Cab 127. Cabinet meetings
Cab 128. —— memoranda
Cab 131. —— Defence Committee
Prem 8,11. Prime Minister's Office
FO 371. Foreign Office – Political Correspondence
FO 800. Foreign Secretary's Private Files
FO 141. Embassy and Consular archives, Egypt

(ii) King's College, London.

The Liddell Hart Centre for Military Archives
The Alanbrooke papers

2. United States

(i) National Archives, Washington D.C. (NA)

RG 59. State Department General Records
RG 64. Foreign Service Posts
RG 165. Operations Division, Army Staff
RG 319. Plans & Operations, Army Staff
RG 218. Joint Chiefs of Staff
RG 273. National Security Council
RG 330. Secretary of Defense

(ii) Harry S. Truman Library, Independence, Missouri (HST)

Confidential File (CF)
Official File (OF)
Psychological Strategy Board Files (PSB)
National Security Council Records, 1947–53 (NSC)
President's Secretary's General File
Acheson papers
George McGhee Papers

(iii) Eisenhower Library, Abilene, Kansas (EL)

Pre-Presidential Papers, (Robert Lovett file)
White House Central Files
Ann Whitman File
National Security Council series
Eisenhower–Churchill correspondence
Dulles–Herter series
Robert B. Carney papers
Alfred Greunther papers
Lauris Norstad papers
Stuart A. Symington papers

(iv) Seeley G. Mudd Manuscript Library, Princeton University, New Jersey (PUL)

The John Foster Dulles papers
The Allen W. Dulles papers
The John V. MacMurray papers

3. Israel

Israel Defense Forces Archives, Givatayim (IDF)
Israel State Archives, Jerusalem (ISA)
Ben-Gurion Archives, Boker (BGA)

4. Unpublished Ph.D. Theses

Converse, Elliott Vanveltner III, *United States Plans for a Postwar Overseas Military Base System, 1942–1948*, Princeton University, 1984.

Lewis, Julian Murray, *British Military Planning for Post-War Strategic Defence, 1942–1947*, Oxford University, 1981.

Rosenberg, David Alan, *Toward Armageddon: The Foundations of United States Nuclear Strategy, 1945–1961*, University of Chicago: 1983.

Zametica, Omer, *British Strategic Planning for the Eastern Mediterranean and the Middle East, 1944–47*, Cambridge University: 1986.

B. PUBLISHED PRIMARY SOURCES

i. Foreign Relations of the United States (FRUS)
(all volumes prepared by the US State Department Historical Office, published in Washington, DC by the US Government Printing Office.)

1946: Vol. VII. 1969.
1948: Vol. IV. 1974.
1948: Vol. V. part 2. 1976.
1949: Vol. I. 1976.
1949: Vol. VI. 1977.
1950: Vol. I. 1977.
1950: Vol. III. 1977.
1950: Vol. V. 1978.
1951: Vol. III. part 1. 1981.
1951: Vol. V. 1982.
1952–54: Vol. V. 1983.
1952–54. Vol. IX parts 1 and 2. 1986.

ii. Galambos, Louis, editor, *The Papers of Dwight David Eisenhower*, Baltimore/London: The Johns Hopkins Press
vols. VI – VIII, 1978. vols. XII, XIII, 1989.

iii. Hyam, Ronald, editor, *British Documents on the End of Empire: The Labour Government and the End of Empire, 1945–1951*, series A, volume 2, London: Her Majesty's Stationery Office, 1992 (BD)

part I: High Policy and Administration
part II: Economics and International Relations
part III: Strategy, Politics and Constitutional Change

iv. Documents on the Foreign Policy of Israel: (ID)

vol. 1: May–September 1948: Yehoshua Freundlich, editor, Jerusalem: Hamakor Press, 1981.

vol. 2: October 1948–April 1949, Yehoshua Freundlich, editor, Jerusalem: Keterpress, 1984.

vol. 5: 1950, Yehoshua Freundlich, editor, Jerusalem: Keterpress, 1988.

vol. 6: 1951, Yemima Rosenthal, editor, Jerusalem: Graph Press, 1991.

vol. 7: 1952, Yehoshua Fruendlich, editor, Jerusalem: Keterpress, 1992.

C. PUBLISHED SECONDARY SOURCES: BOOKS

Aaronson, Geoffrey, *From Sideshow to Centrestage: US Policy Towards Egypt, 1946–1956*, Boulder, CO, 1986.

Abadi, Jacob, *Britain's Withdrawal from the Middle East, 1947–71: The Economic and Strategic Imperatives*, Princeton: Princeton University Press, 1982.

Aldrich, Richard J., ed., *British Intelligence, Strategy and the Cold War, 1945–51*, London/New York: Routledge, 1992.

Ambrose, Stephen E., *Eisenhower: The President*, New York: Simon & Schuster, 1983.

Asia, Ilan, *The Core of the Conflict: The Struggle for the Negev, 1947–1956*, Jerusalem: Yad Izhak Ben-Zvi Press, 1994 (Hebrew).

Barker, Elisabeth, *The British Between the Superpowers, 1945–1950*, Toronto: University of Toronto Press, 1983.

Bartlett, C.J., *The Long Retreat: A Short History of British Defence Policy, 1945–1970*, London: MacMillan, 1972.

Baylis, John, *Anglo-American Defence Relations, 1939–1984: The Special Relationship*, New York: St Martin's Press, 1984.

——, ed., *British Defence policy in a Changing World*, London, 1977.

Bell, Coral, *The Debateable Alliance; An Essay in Anglo–American Relations*, OUP, for RIIA, 1964.

Bialer, Uri, *Between East and West: Israel's Foreign Policy Orientation, 1948–56*, Cambridge: Cambridge University Press, 1990.

Botti, T.J., *The Long Wait: The Forging of the Anglo-American Nuclear Alliance, 1945–58*, New York: Greenwood Press, 1987.

Brown, Anthony C., *Dropshot: The American Plan for World War III with Russia in 1957*, New York: The Dial Press, 1957.

Campbell, John, *Defense of the Middle East: Problems of American Policy.* New York: Harper for the Council on Foreign Relations, 1960.

Carrington, C.E., *The Liquidation of the British Empire*, London: Harrap, 1961.

Chalfont, Alun, *Montgomery of Alamein*, New York: Atheneum, 1976.

Cohen, Michael J., *Palestine and the Great Powers, 1945–1948*, Princeton: Princeton University Press, 1982.

——, *Churchill and the Jews*, London: Frank Cass, 1985.

——, *Truman and Israel*, Berkeley: University of California Press, 1990.

Condit, Kenneth W., *The History of the Joint Chiefs of Staff*, vol II. *The Joint Chiefs of Staff and National Policy, 1947–1949*. Wilmington, DE: Michael Glazier, Inc., 1979.

Copeland, Miles, *The Game of Nations: The Amorality of Power Politics*, New York: Simon and Schuster, 1970.

Darby, Philip, *British Defence Policy East of Suez, 1947–1968*, London: Oxford University Press for RIIA, 1973.

Deighton, Anne, ed. *Britain and the First Cold War*, London: St Martin's Press, 1989.

Devereux, David R., *The Formulation of British Defence Policy Towards the Middle East, 1948–56*, London: Macmillan, 1990.

Dockrill, Michael, Young, John, eds., *British Foreign Policy, 1945–56*, New York: St Martin's Press, 1989.

Dow, J. C. R., *The Management of the British Economy, 1945–60*, Cambridge: Cambridge University Press, 1965.

Eden, Sir Anthony, *Full Circle: The Memoirs of Sir Anthony Eden*, London: Cassell, 1960.

Edmonds, Robin, *Setting the Mould: The United States and Britain, 1945–50*, Oxford, 1986.

Etzold, Thomas H., and Gaddis, John Lewis, eds., *Containment: Documents on American Policy and Strategy, 1945–1950*, New York: Columbia University Press, 1978.

Franks, Sir Oliver, *Britain and the Tide of World Affairs*, London: Oxford University Press, 1955.

Gaddis, John Lewis, *Strategies of Containment: A Critical Appraisal of Postwar American National Security Policy*, New York/Oxford: Oxford University Press, 1982.

——, *The Long Peace: Inquiries into the History of the Cold War*, New York/Oxford: Oxford University Press, 1987.

Gilbert, Martin, *Winston S. Churchill*: vol. VIII, *Never Despair, 1945–1965*, Boston: Houghton Mifflin, 1988.

Gowing, Margaret, *Independence and Deterrence: Britain and Atomic Energy, 1945–1982*, two vols, London: Macmillan, 1974.

Graham, Gerald S., *The Politics of Naval Supremacy*, Cambridge: Cambridge University Press, 1965.

Gretton, Peter, *Maritime Strategy*, London: Cassell, 1965.

Hahn Peter L., *The United States, Great Britain, and Egypt, 1945–1956*, Chapel Hill: University of North Carolina Press, 1991.

Hart, B.H. Liddell, *Defence of the West*, London: Cassell, 1950.

Hattendorf, John B., and Jordan, Robert S. eds., *Maritime Strategy and the Balance of Power: Britain and America in the Twentieth Century*, London: Macmillan, 1989.

Herken, Gregg, *The Winning Weapon: The Atomic Bomb in the Cold War, 1945–1950*, New York: Knopf, 1980.

Ismay, H.L., *NATO: The First Years, 1947–54*, London, 1955.

Jackson, William, *Withdrawal from Empire: A Military View*, New York: St Martin's, 1988.

Johnson, Franklin A., *Defence by Committee: The British Committee of Imperial Defence, 1885–1959*, Oxford: Oxford University Press, 1960.

Leffler, Melvyn P., *A Preponderance of Power: National Security, the Truman Administration and the Cold War*, Stanford: Stanford University Press, 1992.

Louis, Wm. Roger, *The British Empire in the Middle East, 1945–1951*, Oxford: Clarendon Press, 1984.

Louis, Wm. Roger, and Bull, Hedley, eds., *The Special Relationship: Anglo–American Relations since 1945*, Oxford: Clarendon Press, 1986.

Lyon, Peter, *Eisenhower: Portrait of a Hero*, Boston: Little Brown, 1974.

McGhee, George, *Envoy to the Middle World: Adventures in Diplomacy*, New York: Harper & Row, 1983.

Meyer, Gail E., *Egypt and the United States: The Formative Years*, Rutherford, N.J.: Farleigh Dickinson Press, 1980.

Monroe, E., *Britain's Moment in the Middle East*. London: Methuen, 1965.

Ovendale, Ritchie, *The English Speaking Alliance: Britain, the United States, the Dominions and the Cold War, 1945–1951*, London: Allen & Unwin, 1985.

——, ed. *The Foreign Policy of the British Labour Government, 1945–1951*, Leicester: Leicester University Press, 1984.

Pappé, Ilan, *Britain and the Arab–Israeli Conflict, 1948–51*, New York: St Martins's Press, 1988.

Piers, Brendon, *Ike: The Life and Times of David Dwight Eisenhower*, New York: Harper & Row, 1986.

Pimlott, Ben, *Hugh Dalton*, London: Jonathan Cape, 1985.

Pogue, Forrest C., *George C. Marshall: Statesman, 1945–1959*, New York: Viking Penguin, 1987.

Poole, Walter S., *The History of the Joint Chiefs of Staff*, vol. IV. *The Joint*

Chiefs of Staff and National Policy, 1950–52, Wilmington, DE: Michael Glazier Inc.,1980.

Rearden, Steven L., *History of the Office of the Secretary of Defense: The Formative Years, 1947–1950*, Washington: Historical Office of the Secretary of Defense, 1984.

Rosencrance, R.N., *Defence of the Realm: British Strategy in the Nuclear Age*, New York: Columbia University Press, 1968.

Ross, Steven T., *American War Plans, 1945–50*, London: Frank Cass, 1996.

Schnabel, James F., *The History of the Joint Chiefs of Staff: The Joint Chiefs of Staff and National Policy*: Vol. 1. 1945–1947. Wilmington, DE: Michael Glazier, Inc., 1979.

Seldon, Anthony, *Churchill's Indian Summer: The Conservative Government, 1951–55*, London: Hodder & Stoughton, 1981.

Sherry, Michael S., *Preparing for the Next War*, New Haven/London: Yale University Press, 1977.

Shlaim, Avi, *Collusion Across the Jordan: King Abdullah, the Zionist Movement and the Partition of Palestine*, Oxford: Clarendon Press, 1988.

Shteigman, Major Isaac, *Operation `Kadesh'*, Tel Aviv: Israeli Ministry of Defense, 1986 (in Hebrew).

Thetford, Owen, *Aircraft of the RAF Since 1918*, London: Putnam, 1968.

Watson, Robert J., *The History of the Joint Chiefs of Staff*, vol. V, *The Joint Chiefs of Staff and National Policy, 1953–54*, Washington DC: US Government Printing Office, 1986.

Watt, D.C., *Succeeding John Bull: America in Britain's Place, 1900–1975*, Cambridge: Cambridge University Press, 1984.

Williams, Francis, *A Prime Minister Remembers: the war and post-war memoirs of the Rt Hon. Earl Attlee*, London: Heinemann, 1961.

Young, John W., ed. *The Foreign Policy of Churchill's Peacetime Administration, 1951–55*, Leicester: Leicester University Press, 1988.

D. PUBLISHED SECONDARY SOURCES: ARTICLES

Aldrich, Richard J., Zametica, John, 'The Rise and Decline of a strategic concept: the Middle East, 1945–51', in Richard J. Aldrich, ed., *British Intelligence, Strategy and the Cold War, 1945–51*, London/New York: Routledge, 1992, pp. 236–74.

Boyle, Peter G., 'Britain, America and the transition from Economic to Military Assistance, 1940–51', *Journal of Contemporary History*, vol. 22, 1987, pp. 521–38.

Cohen, Michael J., 'Colonel William Eddy, the Oil Lobby and the Palestine Problem', *Middle Eastern Studies*, vol. 30/1, January 1994, pp. 166–80.

Darwin, John, 'British Decolonization since 1945: A Pattern or a Puzzle?' *Journal of Imperial and Commonwealth History*, vol. 12 (1983–84), pp. 187–209.

Gorst, A, Lucas S, 'Suez', *The Journal of Strategic Studies*, summer, 1989.

Hahn, Peter L., 'Containment and Egyptian Nationalism: The Unsuccessful Effort to Establish the Middle East Command, 1950–53', *Diplomatic History*, II/I, Winter, 1987, pp. 23–40.

Kent, John, 'The Egyptian Base and the Defence of the Middle East, 1945–54', in Holland, Robert, editor, *Emergencies and Disorder in the European Empires after 1945*, London: Frank Cass, 1994, pp. 45–65.

Leffler, Melvyn P., 'Strategy, Diplomacy, and the Cold War: The United States, Turkey, and NATO, 1945–1952', *The Journal of American History*, vol. 71/4, March, 1985. pp. 807–825.

Louis, Wm. Roger, 'American anti-Colonialism and the dissolution of the British Empire', *International Affairs*, 61/3, 1985, pp. 397–420.

——, 'Britain at the Crossroads in Palestine, 1952–1954', *Jerusalem Journal of International Relations*, vol. 12/3, September, 1990, pp.59–82.

Morsy, Laila Amin, 'The Role of the United States in the Anglo–Egyptian Agreement of 1954', *Middle Eastern Studies*, vol. 29/3, July 1993, pp. 526–58.

Rahman, Habibur, 'British Post-Second World War Military Planning for the Middle East', *The Journal of Strategic Studies*, 5/4, 1982, pp.511–30.

Rosenberg, David Alan, 'The Origins of Overkill: Nuclear Weapons and American Strategy, 1945–1960', *International Security*, vol. 7/4, 1983.

——, 'American Atomic Strategy and the Hydrogen Bomb Decision', *Journal of American History*, 66/1, June 1979.

——, 'The U.S. Navy and the Problem of Oil in a Future War: The Outline of a Strategic Dilemma, 1945–1950', *Naval War College Review*, vol. 29, summer, 1976,

Smith, Raymond, and Zametica, John, 'The Cold Warrior: Clement Attlee reconsidered, 1945–7', *International Affairs*, vol. 61/2, Spring, 1985.

Index